92   Lindsay, Jack   13,589
c/E   Cleopatra
             vh   298

CLEOPATRA

BY JACK LINDSAY

Leisure and Pleasure in Roman Egypt
Daily Life in Roman Egypt
Men and Gods on the Roman Nile
Last Days with Cleopatra
The Ancient World
Cleopatra

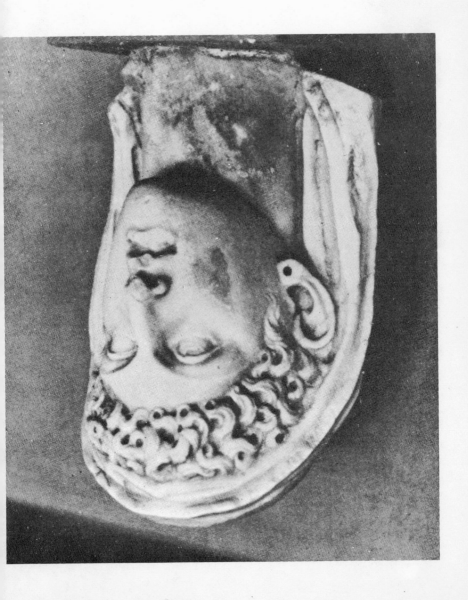

Cleopatra: head found on the site of her daughter's capital in Mauretania

CLEOPATRA

JACK LINDSAY

COWARD McCANN & GEOGHEGAN, INC.

NEW YORK

Contents

Introduction

Chapters

Introduction

Cleopatra is the most famous of all the women of antiquity, if we omit legendary figures like Helen of Troy. She owes her outstanding place to two main factors: she was one of the protagonists in the great period of change that was brought to a head by Julius Caesar, and she had the luck to have her story told at length in the biography of Marc Antony by Plutarch in his series of parallel lives of Greeks and Romans, written in the early second century A.D. Plutarch was a Greek and he used among his sources historians or memoir-writers more favourable to Cleopatra than were the Latin historians. His account has many qualities of genuine penetration and poetic insight; and though elements of the hostile tradition are mingled in it, it yet manages to convey a strong feeling of Cleopatra's charm and force, her distinct personality. Thus Shakespeare in turn was able to base his great tragedy on it.

Cleopatra certainly deserved her pre-eminent position. Ancient history did not lack women of character, who one way or another played a vigorous role in the course of events; but none of them can compare with Cleopatra for the importance of her activities. In none of them do we feel so powerfully a personality radiating over the centuries, which enables us to enter into the fullness of her aims, aspirations, sufferings, and achievements.

She was the last of the Ptolemies of Egypt. Her ancestor had been one of the marshals of Alexander the Great in his triumphant march out of Greece as far as North India. Alexander's tremendous exploit took only a little more than ten years; and he had no sooner created a vast Macedonian Empire over the extent of the old Persian Empire and much more, than he died suddenly in Babylon in June 323 B.C. His creation was too new; when his victorious presence was removed, it could not hold together in the form he had given it. What was permanent was the Greek imprint he left over much of the con-quered area; but he had built no effective system to govern the diverse regions with a unified control. A weak character, his half-brother, succeeded him as king; but the real wielders of power were the generals, dominated for a while by Perdiccas. Ptolemy son of Lagos was the shrewdest of them. Recognising that the system would break down, with the various satrapies or districts growing more and more independent, he bargained with Perdiccas for Egypt, the most self-contained region; and five months after Alexander's death he arrived there as the new governor. An added attraction was the decision made to send Alexander's body to Egypt, to the oasis of Siwa, where Alexander had gone across the desert to visit the oracle of Ammon and where the prophet had hailed him as son of Zeus, son of the supreme god. (The phrase was in fact of common use for a king of Egypt; all the pharaohs were sons of Amun-Re; but a special significance had been attributed to the salutation, raising Alexander to a semi-divine status in his conquering mission.) To hold the mummified body of the hero could not but help to give the ruler of Egypt a special position; and there was the further fact that Alexander had founded a great new port, Alexandria, on the Egyptian coast, some forty miles west of the old Greek trading-post of Naukratis. A small fishing village had stood on the site; but Alexander saw its possibilities. It lay on dry limestone above the level of the Delta with its swampy ground, within easy reach of drinkable and navigable water inland by a canal to be taken off the Nile. Out in the sea was a three-mile island which could be joined to the mainland by a mole and provide two harbours, one facing east, one west.

By 305 B.C. Ptolemy had made himself King of Egypt, with the priests and scribes giving him all the titles of the pharaohs. Fighting had gone on among the satraps, in which he had taken part, and the Empire had broken into separate regions. The main rival of Egypt was the kingdom of the Seleukids, centred on Syria; and for long there were bitter struggles between Seleukids and Ptolemies, which had the effect of exhausting both antagonists rather than stably extending their kingdoms. Internally there were violent dynastic quarrels; and a few words about these will illustrate the sort of tradition that Cleopatra inherited. Ptolemy II's daughter Berenice married the Seleukid, Antiochos II, who put away his wife Laodice for the purpose; later she was murdered with her baby son by Laodice—fighting, we are told, like a tigress. Ptolemy IV murdered his uncle, his brother, and his mother. Arsinoe, mother of Ptolemy V, was murdered by two ambitious courtiers when she became guardian of the infant king. The family relations of the period Ptolemy VI and VIII (covering from 181 to 116 B.C.) show an almost incredible mixture of savagery and power-lust. At one time, for some five years, the two brothers were ruling together, with their sister Cleopatra II married to one of them. When her husband died, she married her younger brother in turn and carried on as his wife after he had murdered her son. This second brother-husband of hers raped one of her daughters by the earlier marriage and later took her as his wife, Cleopatra III. The mother and daughter, together with Ptolemy VIII, who was brother of one and uncle of the other, were lumped together as the rulers of Egypt. Polybius tells us of this Ptolemy that 'over and over again he let loose his troops on the people of Alexandria and massacred them'. In 311 he was driven out and went to Cyprus with Cleopatra III, where he murdered a bastard of his whom he feared as a rival. When the Alexandrians threw down his statues, he thought that they had been instigated by Cleopatra II. In revenge he killed the son she had borne him, cut the body into small pieces, and sent them in a box to her in Alexandria. Finally Cleopatra II was driven out herself and went to the Seleukid court where her daughter Cleopatra Thea, wife of Demetrios II, was probably living in separation from her husband. She induced Demetrios to attack Egypt, but he was in the end defeated by a pretender whom the Antiochines were backing. He fled to Ptolemais where his wife shut the gates in his face; then he made for Tyre where he was killed—at his wife's orders, it was believed. Cleopatra Thea further killed one of her own sons, Seleukos V, who did not prove amenable enough; then associated a second son with herself on the throne. Detected in an attempt to poison off this son, she was herself forced to drink the deadly cup. Meanwhile her mother, Cleopatra II, had returned to Alexandria to live once more with her brother as ruler.

By the time our Cleopatra was born, Rome had long been intruding into Greece and Asia Minor. Despite some massive resistances, such as that by Mithridates, the whole eastern Mediterranean was falling under her control, whether the regions were directly organised as provinces or carried on as client-kingdoms and the like. Now only Egypt, weakened as she was, could at all claim to be independent. She was continually threatened by a Roman annexation, but was saved, not so much by powers of defence as by the inability of Roman politicians and generals to agree as to who should take so rich a booty. The court was torn by intrigues and divided into cabals. Cleopatra turned this situation to her own advantage, managing to emerge as supreme ruler despite the existence of an elder brother and sister, and to hold this position despite the existence of a younger pair as well. Chance played its part, but she was always present with her quick and ruthless mind to make the most of whatever happened.

Thus she found herself the one ruler of any importance surviving from the world of Alexander the Great, west of the Euphrates. From the outset she set herself to fight for the continuance of Egypt as an independent State. Egypt could not challenge Rome as a military power; but Cleopatra hoped to find ways of using the inner divisions and conflicts of the Roman world in order to prevent the plain confrontation in which she could not possibly

Cleopatra

succeed. Here it was that her feminine charm was to play its part. She captivated both Julius Caesar and Marc Antony, the two greatest soldiers of her age. Not that she was a mere schemer using feminine wiles to achieve her aims through the men with whom she formed alliances. Her role was far more positive and active than that. She always brought to bear on any situation her vigorous outlook, her deeply considered views on how the world should be reorganised at this moment of crucial change, and how the immediate issues should be tackled. Thus she advanced from the struggle to ensure the survival of Egypt to plans for regaining the full extent of the early Ptolemaic Empire—and then to plans for domination of the whole Roman world as the consort of Marc Antony. She failed, but there have been few failures in history on a grander scale. Part of the aim of this book is to show how deeply she affected the minds of the men of her age, especially in the eastern half of the Mediterranean where Christianity was soon to be born. The glamour with which Shakespeare was able to surround her, as both a fascinating and many-faceted woman, and as a character of incisive and resolute action in the sphere of world politics, is the product of the skills of a great poet; but we feel that he is bringing out and revealing elements which were there, realised afresh within his rich and penetrative vision.

Cleopatra is thus one of the complex figures who, playing a key-role in a crucial moment of historical change, demand continual inquiry and re-examination. An historian needs no more motive in returning to her than a hope of seeing a little more deeply into her character and its motivations, and of setting her a little more fully in her entangled circumstances. I have tried here in particular to analyse and get inside the extremely involved web of propaganda that enveloped all the actors in this period of violent clashes, and to bring out the roles of religious and poetic ideas in that propaganda—fears and hopes of world-end, world-renewal, redemption by a mother-figure or a divine child or a sun-hero, and the advent of a happy earth in which the lion could lie down with the lamb. Not that all these ideas and emotions, which produce many god-masquings among the main actors, were by any means the result of deliberate manipulation; for all their political effects and purposes they cannot be reduced to politics in the narrow sense. Many of them came up from deep down in the life of the era and were spontaneous reactions of the suffering and yet aspiring peoples. Indeed it is the complicated relation between the conscious manipulations and the deep spontaneous responses which makes much of the fascination of the inquiry. In a world where only the politics of the upholders of the *status quo* found any direct theoretical elaboration, we need to turn to the sphere of religious and poetic imagery or symbolism to grasp what was humanly at stake in the minds and emotions of the people and of the protagonists themselves.

As it seems to me that much of the interest of the events derives from the quest for their meanings and for the facts behind the blurring veils of charge and counter-charge, I have not tried to palm off on the reader what I consider the likely interpretation as the only one. I have taken him into my confidence and done my best to show all the difficulties, all the opposing views and statements,

Cleopatra

which have to be unravelled before we can hope to get at the facts themselves. I trust that this element of detective research provides its own interest and yields a better sense of history than to present conjectures as a firm ground of narrative.

JACK LINDSAY

Cleopatra and the World of her Youth

Cleopatra was born in 69 B.C., the daughter of Ptolemy XII who had become king of Egypt in 80. The whole Mediterranean world, especially the eastern half, was undergoing crucial changes. The system founded by Alexander the Great was in its last stages of breakdown, and Rome was busy with the conquests and annexations that were soon to lead to her complete control of the area. Of the Hellenistic Kingdoms only Egypt remained intact, though in a weakened condition. Cleopatra, in her capable but desperate attempt to revive its power, became the stormcentre of the conflicts that ended with the creation of the Roman Empire. She was the last of a long series of ruthless and energetic women of the Ptolemaic line, Cleopatras, Berenices, Arsinoes, who were driven by a passion for power.

Many of the Ptolemies had married their sisters as part of the trend to divinise Hellenistic kings; and there was at least strong precedence for this custom in Pharaonic Egypt. Cleopatra was thus mainly, though not wholly, of

Cleopatra

Macedonian blood; her grandmother, mistress of Ptolemy IX, seems to have been an accomplished Greek *hetaira* or courtesan; she certainly had no Egyptian blood in her veins. We meet only one mistress of a Ptolemy, who seems an Egyptian. But at this phase of Egyptian history there is much obscurity, and we are not sure who was Cleopatra's mother. In 78 Ptolemy XII had married his sister Cleopatra Tryphaina, who bore Cleopatra VI and Berenice, then is said to have died in 69. She probably bore our Cleopatra as well. In the papyri her name goes after 7 August 69. However, an Edfu inscription, recording the work done by Ptolemies on the great temple, states that the site was completed in Ptolemy XII's 25th Year when the doors of bronze-plated cedar were set up in the entrance-pylon or gateway on 1 Choiach (5 December 57); and the names on the pylon were 'Ptolemy Young Osiris with his Sister Queen Cleopatra surnamed Tryphaina.' (Ptolemy XII had in fact fled the country by that date, but his flight did not affect the legal date.) If Tryphaina had died in 69, it is hard to see why the priesthood, sure to be well informed on such matters, named her as still alive eleven and a half years later.

The problem is further confused by Porphyrios later declaring that the Cleopatra Tryphaina, whom the Alexandrians recognised as co-ruler with Berenice (IV), was the eldest daughter; but he may have made a mistake and she may have been the wife. It is odd if mother and two daughters were all called Cleopatra; it is easier to assume that Berenice was the elder girl and we meet her name linked with that of her mother, not of a sister, Cleopatra Tryphaina. If that is so, Ptolemy XII would seem to have put his wife away in 69: a not unlikely

Table 1 THE PTOLOMIES

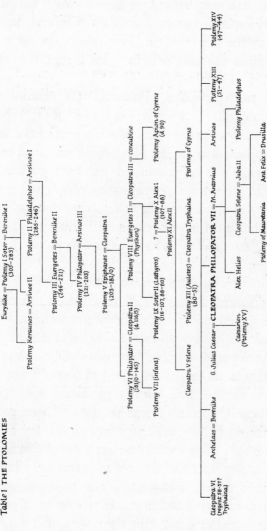

event in this court of confused intrigues and entangled
rivalries. She may have been at odds with him in some
way that explains her exclusion from official datings, as
shown in the papyri. The Edfu priests, perhaps taking
advantage of the king's flight from Egypt, then ignored
the ban.

After our Cleopatra, Ptolemy XII certainly begot
another daughter, Arsinoe, and two boys. Who their
mother was, we cannot tell. Many writers have assumed
that Cleopatra was the daughter of an unnamed mistress;
but since she was never taunted with having a concubine-
mother in the furious propaganda-charges and insults of
her later years, we are safe in rejecting that assumption.
Her mother must have been properly married to Ptolemy
XII, and so appears to have been Cleopatra Tryphaina,
his sister.[1]

As she grew up, she became familiar with every aspect
of the disordered court, with its efforts to preserve the
customary ceremonials and the pretences of a greatness
that had passed away. Her father, nicknamed Auletes
(Piper or perhaps more correctly Oboe-player) and
Bastard, was an incapable ruler, who could not control
the situation or find means to arrest the economic
worsening. The coinage was so debased that coins had
only a third of silver in their composition; the burden of
tolls and taxes grew steadily heavier. Rome had refused to
recognise the Piper on his accession; and he had no policy
except to humour the Romans as best he could, while they
went on conquering and dominating ever more regions of
the East, with Pompey taking the main role. Egypt was no
threat; but the politicians at Rome could not decide what
to do with so valuable a territory. Its resources were so

great that no leader or group wanted the others to lay their hands on it.

At Rome itself the last burst of successful expansion under the Republic was linked with a deepening of the inner conflicts. The peasants were being more and more driven off the land as the influx of money and valuables went on, and as political power was being concentrated in the hands of the great generals. Ever since the Gracchi the discontent of the populace had evoked radical leaders who used the situation for their own ends or tried to find

Coin of Cleopatra daughter of Ptolemy VI, and Antiochos VIII Gryps with Eagle on reverse. Coin of Ptolemy XII the Piper.

solutions such as the allocation of land to the dispossessed —while the commoners discovered a new source of power or income in the disposing of their votes. The old system of clientship which bound noble and commoner together was breaking down; and victorious generals became the centres of conflicting groups or united to impose what was in effect a sort of dictatorship. For a while Pompey was the dominating character. Then in 65 G. Julius Caesar and Marcus Crassus were allied with him, and the project was mooted of Caesar taking Egypt over. However, discords arose and nothing came of it. In late 64 a tribune of the *plebs* promulgated an agrarian law under which a Board of Ten, with military powers, would decide what land belonged to the State and would be entitled, if necessary, to annex Egypt. Cicero in three speeches mustered the opposition and managed to get the law held up. Next year the Piper turned to Pompey, who was in Judaea, and sent him a heavy gold crown with an offer to pay 8,000 cavalry and a request that he would intervene to restore peace in Egypt. Pompey took the crown and did nothing. Caesar had now turned his thoughts to Gaul; but as consul in 59 he had a resolution passed which recognised the Piper at last as the Friend and Ally of the Roman People. Suetonius says, 'He squeezed out of Ptolemy alone near 6,000 talants in the name of himself and Pompey.'[2]

The Piper celebrated the occasion by granting his people an amnesty. Diodoros of Sicily, who visited Egypt about this time, records an incident he witnessed. He is discussing the veneration shown by Egyptians to their sacred animals. 'So deeply implanted in the hearts of their common folk,' he says, 'is a superstitious regard for these animals and so ineradicable are the emotions each man cherishes as to their due honour, that once, at a time when Ptolemy their King had not yet been given the appellation of Friend and the people were courting with all possible zeal the favour of the Embassy from Italy then visiting Egypt, and in their fear were preoccupied with giving no pretext for complaint or war—yet when one of the Romans killed a cat and the mob rushed in a crowd to his house, neither the officials sent by the King to beg the man off, not the fear of Rome felt by all the people, was enough to save him from punishment, even though the act had been an accident.' Diodoros adds, 'And this second was warned off by Gabinius, governor of Syria. The Berenice party then found a man Seleukos who claimed royal connections, probably as the bastard of some Seleukid king; but he turned out to have such vulgar looks and manners the Alexandrians nicknamed him Saltfishmonger. Berenice tolerated him a few days as husband, then had him strangled. Finally there came Archelaos, a Greek, whose father, after being one of Mithridates' marshals, had gone over to the Romans. Archelaos indeed claimed to be the son of Mithridates (and so distantly related to the Ptolemies), and Pompey had made him priestking of the Temple of the Great Mother at Komana in Pontos. Berenice married him. To get rid of the Piper, the Alexandrians sent a deputation of a hundred men under the philosopher Dion to the Senate at Rome. The Piper hired murderers to deal with some of the envoys when they'd landed in the Bay of Naples, at Puteoli; and Dion, afraid of appearing before the Senate, was promptly murdered in Rome. The Piper, scared of accusations or assured that his affairs would now be favourably dealt with, went east to Ephesos, where he boarded in Artemis's sacred precinct. In September 57 the Senate ordered P. Lentulus Spinther, consul and prospective governor of Cilicia, to restore him. The Piper's great asset was now the vast debts he had accumulated at Rome, where the businessmen were pledged to put him back on the throne so that they, his debtors, might bleed Egypt at leisure.

But before Lentulus could act, Pompey, who wanted to counteract Caesar's successes in Gaul, thought it would be a good idea to restore his client himself; he was, however, deflected by the tactics of his fellow triumvirs,

Crassus and Caesar, who wanted to stop him getting hold of Egypt's great wealth. Then, in January 56, the statue of Jupiter in the Alban Mount was hit by a thunderbolt; and the Board of Fifteen, who dealt with such omens, consulted the Sibylline Books. They announced that they had found the prophecy: 'If the King of Egypt comes asking for help, don't refuse him friendship—but don't go to his aid with a host or you'll meet with troubles and dangers.' Such oracles could only be published with the Senate's assent; but in this case the senatorial opposition to the triumvirs was only too glad to authorise a warning that could be used against the ambitious generals. Cato as tribune led the Fifteen to the Forum and ordered them to read the oracle out. The Greek verses, done into Latin, were posted up on all sides. There can be little doubt that the opposition, among whom the Fifteen would be included, had fabricated the neatly-apposite statement. Such a setback to the Piper's plans would have been eagerly discussed at Alexandria, and Cleopatra must have heard about it. Perhaps she did not forget the effective political use that could be made of prophecies.

The situation was now complicated, with Pompey and even Crassus aiming to supplant Lentulus. A Committee of Three was proposed. But should the three be private citizens or army-commanders? The Senate gained time by arguing indefinitely over procedures. Crassus employed Clodius (an aristocrat turned a sort of anarchist gang-leader) to impede the claims of Pompey. A letter from Cicero to his brother gives a good picture of the state of things at Rome; on 6 February 56 Milo, the conservative gang-leader, 'again came up for trial. Pompey spoke—rather, he tried to. When he rose, Clodius's hired gangs

started yelling and that was what we had to put up with
throughout his speech. He was interrupted, not only with
shouts, but with insults and abuse. At last he ended—he
showed great fortitude in the situation, never quailed,
said all he had to say, and now and then compelled a
silence by his impressive personality—but as I said, at last
he ended and up got Clodius. We'd made up our minds to
give him as good as he gave. So he was met with such a
deafening roar from our side that he lost all control of
faculties, voice, features. Such was the scene from the time
when Pompey had barely finished his speech at noon,
right on till two o'clock, when every kind of scurrility
was vented on Clodius and Clodia, even doggerel of the
filthiest sort.'

Clodia, sister of Clodius, was the Lesbia of Catullus's
love and poetry; the anti-Clodians made many malicious
jests about her supposed incestuous relations with her
brother. Cicero goes on, 'Maddened and white with rage,
he asked his partisans—he was heard above the shouting
—who was the man who starved the people to death? His
rowdies answered, "Pompey!" Who was so anxious to get
to Alexandria? They replied, "Pompey!" Whom did they
want to go? They yelled back, "Crassus!" (Crassus was
there at the time, with no kindly feelings for Milo.) Then
about three o'clock the Clodians, as if at a signal, began
spitting on our men. We resented it in a paroxysm of rage.
They tried to hustle and get us out. Our men charged
them and the roughs took to their heels. Clodius was flung
off the rostra. Then we too dodged off for fear of serious
results from the tumult. The Senate was summoned to the
Curia. Pompey went home.'[4]

The Senate forbade Pompey to intervene even without

soldiers; they forbade interventions of any kind. But
tribunes vetoed the resolution. The impatient businessmen, however, wanted action. Lentulus was now in
Cilicia, and Pompey went to Ephesos, where the Piper
pleaded with him. Cicero wrote to Lentulus advising him
to carry on despite everything and restore the Piper; he
was always ready to accept or press for unconstitutional
acts when they fell in with his own interests—or to be
deeply shocked when they were the work of opponents.
But Lentulus lacked the nerve. Not till 55 was a man
found, with Pompey's aid, who was ready to defy the
Senate: Aulus Gabinius, proconsul of Syria. The Piper
promised him 10,000 talants. For a while Gabinius shrank
from the desert-march and the hazard of forcing the
frontier-fortress Pelousion; but his commander of cavalry,
Marc Antony (Marcus Antonius), a dashing young fellow
of some twenty-seven years, had no hesitations. He
hurried ahead, took Pelousion by sudden assault, captured
its garrison of Egyptian and Jewish soldiers, and cleared
the way for the Piper with the main Roman force.

Alexandria was easily taken. The Piper at once executed
his daughter Berenice and took revenge on her supporters.
Antony, however, gave honourable burial to her husband,
Archelaos, who had died fighting amid mutinous troops,
and he took under his protection the men of the Pelousion
garrison. With his prominent part in the war and its after-
math he could not have escaped the eyes of young
Cleopatra, who must have been deeply excited by all these
events, especially the execution of her elder sister. Now
she was the next in the line of inheritance; and the fact
that she was not involved in the punishments proves that
she had kept well out of all complicity with Berenice's

actions. Later tales declared that already she impressed the vulnerable Antony. He may indeed have noticed her and paid her some compliments, but neither he nor she could have guessed how closely their lives were to be entwined.

Antony soon left, though enough Roman soldiers remained to ensure that the Piper kept his throne and the Roman creditors were paid. Rabirius was appointed *dioiketes*, chief financial minister, to facilitate the looting of the land. Ships set sail for Puteoli laden with gold, glass, linen, paper, and other valuable commodities. The citizens of Alexandria and the peasants of the *chora*, or countryside, were alike angered. If we may judge by the Thebaid there had been competent magistrates who carried on as well as they could despite all the disorders, confusions, and corruptions of the court. Thus, Kallimachos, *epistrategos* (viceroy), seems to have been in charge there from July 78 to February 51, covering almost all the Piper's reign. He combined with his other titles that of Commander of the Red Sea and of the Indian Sea: he controlled the trade with Arabia, India, and the coastal stations to the south. He was perhaps the father of another Kallimachos, with the rank of *epistates* (governor); if so, he was raised at the start of Cleopatra's reign to the post of *epistolographos* (secretary) at Alexandria. In March 75 the court had written to the City of Ptolemais (apparently to its councillors) to tell them that the king had conferred the privilege of *asylia* (asylum) on a temple of Isis built by the *epistrategos* Kallimachos in the city's territory; and a *stēlē* set up in 43–2 (or perhaps 39) in honour of the *epistates* of the Theban division of the Pathyrite nome, Kallimachos, gives us further insight into the work done by the family. The stone monument was erected by the priests of Amun Rē Sonther and other heads of the community, who said that the *epistates* had been devoted paternally to the care of Thebes 'ruined as it was by a variety of grievous circumstances'—probably a reference to the damage inflicted by Ptolemy IX in 88 as retribution for revolt. In a recent year of famine and in the following year of pestilence he had done all he could to lessen the extreme distress; above all he had ensured that the rites in the temples were duly and properly carried out; thus the festivals of the gods had been worthily celebrated 'from the time when Kallimachos's grandfather' died (or made some restoration?). So there seem three of the line and name who had done constructive work as magistrates.

Now, as Rabirius and his colleagues put their squeeze on the finances of Egypt, there was a return of rebellious attitudes among the farmers, who demanded protection and threatened to stop maintaining the waterways, the dams and dykes; discontent appeared in Middle Egypt and in the nomes (large districts) of Oxyrhynchos and the Fayum. A report mentioned a group who 'do not practise the same cult'—who were apparently refusing to take part in customary rites. Rabirius as *dioiketes* insisted that the magistrates in the nomes were not taking strong enough steps against the troublemakers. But at last the anger against the Roman plunderers burst out beyond control. Rabirius had to make a hasty escape by ship for Rome. There in 54 he was put on trial, charged with his share in Gabinius' unauthorised invasion and with his holding of an administrative post under a king. Cicero defended him, pleading that his acts had been dictated by magnanimity of heart and that the Piper had forced him to wear Greek dress and act as his minister. Gabinius was also impeached for disobeying the Senate; but the corrupt legal system enabled him to gain acquittal by bribery. At a second trial, for extorting 10,000 talants from the Piper, his bribery was less efficiently carried out; and despite Cicero's advocacy he was found guilty. Even a letter from the Piper declaring that he had only paid the costs of the campaign did not help.

Surrounded by disaffected subjects and kept in power only by Roman legionaries, the Piper pondered how best to strengthen his position and that of his dynasty. He made a will, asking the Roman People to see that he was succeeded by his elder son and his daughter Cleopatra. He doubtless realised that Cleopatra was too strong a character to be ignored, while to give her pre-eminence might well annoy the Alexandrians, who had had enough of wilful domineering queens in previous reigns. A sealed copy of the will was sent to Pompey in Rome to be deposited in the State Archives. In the spring of 51 the Piper died.

Cleopatra was now queen, though saddled with a young half-brother as co-ruler. We may assume that they were married as was the custom. She was in her eighteenth year; her husband was about nine or ten, while Arsinoe was fourteen to seventeen and the younger brother was about eight. Each of the children was a likely claimant to the throne, gathering a cabal of hopeful supporters, while Egypt itself was in a bad way. Apart from the looting by Rabirius, there had long been a decay in trade and agriculture. The dependencies of Syria, Cyrene, Cyprus were gone; the dignity of the royal house had fallen about as low as it could go. Cleopatra was now acutely aware of all this decline and of the problems besetting her position; she must already have worked out in a general way how she meant to set about bettering things and reasserting Ptolemaic power in the face of Rome's overwhelming might. She had seen the Romans at close quarters, the strength and skill of the army in the person of Marc Antony, the infinite greed and callousness of its leading families and businessmen in the person of Rabirius. She felt that with a mixture of guile and force, with the aid of Egypt's still great resources, she could hold her own and perhaps somehow find the way of reversing the movement of fortune.

But meanwhile she and her brother-husband were caught up in the court-system, its close and smothering tangle of fierce intrigues and underhand tricks. The struggle that promptly arose between the two young rulers gives us a clear enough glimpse of the way they had been brought up, and of the forces surrounding them. The most powerful man in the court seems to have been the eunuch Potheinos. His name is Greek, his origin unknown; he might have come from any of the eastern regions. (The first eunuch at the court of whom we know was Aristonikos under Ptolemy V, a man of energy with an aptitude for military matters, says Polybios.) Potheinos may have had the post of Chairman of the Regency Council, which set him above the regular *dioiketes*; this interpretation is better than trying to fit him into an unfilled gap in the list of *dioiketai* in 48. With him was Achillas whom Plutarch calls an Egyptian; he may have been a native or a man of mixed Greek and Egyptian blood. He was not commander-in-chief as later writers assumed; Caesar says plainly that he was only *praefectus regius*,

Captain of the king's guards, at best the superior of the military tribune Septimius who seems in command of the Roman section of the army later at Pelousion. Achillas became commander-in-chief only when young Ptolemy recalled him to Alexandria to attack Caesar, as we shall see in the next chapter.

The third man of importance at court was a Greek, Theodotos, from Samos (or Chios) who was the *tropheus*, nurse or fosterer, of the prince, responsible for teaching him rhetoric.[6] The term was traditional at the court; an inscription at Crocodilopolis speaks of a man who was '*tropheus* and *tithenos* of the Son of the King'. Both Theodotos and Achillas were *tropheis*; Plutarch says they were the heads among the chamberlains or *valets de chambre* and the advisers of the council. We see then that originally Achillas was a sort of major-domo presiding over the court-domestics. Some *tithenoi* were mere servants, though they could be men of literature like Theodotos or like Kretaros of Antioch, who, after his functions as *tropheus* ended and his royal pupil was married, was called 'chief doctor of the king and chief man-midwife of the queen'. It is no doubt hairsplitting to distinguish *tithenos* as the fosterfather looking after the prince in the cradle from *tropheus* the teacher who had charge of the growing boy; in legal texts the two terms are put together so as to cover all possibilities; and in the inscription they are merely combined for an impressive effect. But it is relevant to note the Dionysiac overtones. *Tithenos* was a poetic term, with female form *tithenē*. In the *Iliad* the Naiads are *tithenai*, and Seilenos is *tithenos* of Bacchos in an Orphic hymn. The *tropheis* of the god appear on sarcophagi and in pictures (such as the stucco panels of

the Fornesina) where the theme is a child's initiation, with
Seilenos unveiling the holy things in the winnowing
basket; this scene is followed by one of the initiate's
felicity in the Dionysiac Paradise. A corresponding theme
is the consecration of a young woman by the revelation
of the penis, which precedes the depiction of the joyous
revels of the *thiasos*, the Bacchic confraternity. The child is
Dionysos Mystes.[7]

The Dionysiac cult had long played an important part
in the divinising of Hellenistic kings, especially in Egypt.
The Piper had certainly responded strongly to it. His
nickname was not merely derogatory; it expressed his
devotion to the Dionysiac revel. Like Ptolemy IV he was
represented as Neos Dionysos, the New Dionysos; in
hieroglyphic texts, the Young Osiris. His head on coins
was shown as that of the god, garlanded, with
thyrsos (ivy-wreathed wand tipped with pine-cone) at its
side. The earliest reference to his role as the New Dionysos
was made in 64–3. He strengthened the king-cult in certain forms. Official acts had referred to Our Lord the
King; now records and petitions spoke of Our God and
Lord the King. In 52 the Alexandrians consecrated a
precinct to him and his children as Our Lords and
Mightiest Gods, so that Cleopatra was used to being
called a deity even before she became queen. Even in
Rome, where the imagery of the Dionysiac Procession
had affected the Triumph, the Hellenistic cult of Dionysos
had long been making inroads. And in our epoch it had
been taking on a new colouration, suggesting a Saviour
who would rescue the eastern masses from the Roman
yoke. The great Mithridates VI of Pontos, who gave
Roman power such a setback and whose daughter had

been betrothed to the Piper, was greeted as the New
Dionysos by the Greeks and other eastern folk.

These ideas and practices deeply influenced Cleopatra,
who brought them to a head in her final struggle against
Rome. Though the first two Ptolemies had evolved
Sarapis as a sort of dynastic god uniting Greek and
Egyptian elements, Dionysos had become in many ways
more truly the god representing and sanctifying the line.
Ptolemy IV wanted to show himself in some sort as the
very god from whom his house claimed descent; he seems
to have been often called Dionysos by the people or the
courtiers; and to mark his devotion he had the Bacchic
Ivyleaf tattooed on his body. He was nicknamed Gallos
after the devotees of the Great Mother who in ritual
frenzy castrated themselves. A tale about the Platonic
philosopher Demetrios shows how the drinking-parties
of the Piper were seen as Dionysiac revels. A sober man,
he disliked these bouts, drank water, and attended
Dionysiac festivals without first changing into female
clothes. So every morning he was summoned and made
to drink and dance before the king in a gown of trans-
parent Tarentine material. On the walls of Philai we see the
Piper represented as a pharaoh smiting his enemies to the
ground—an ancient Egyptian motive—and not far off is
an inscription stating that someone (Strothein, Strouthon?)
'the *kinaidos*' has come. Also, 'With Nikolas, I Tryphon
the *kinaidos* of the New Dionysos have come to the Isis
who is in Philai.' Both names suggest lewdness; *strouthos*
(sparrow) was used for lecher and *tryphon* is linked with
tryphe, softness, wantonness. *Kinaidos* also means lewd or
lascivious fellow, especially a passive homosexual, though
it was further used for some sort of public performer,

probably a man performing obscene dances. The inscription thus brings out the more dubious side of the Piper's Dionysiac fervours.[8]

An Egyptian inscription, cut under Cleopatra's reign by Pshereni-ptah, highpriest at Memphis, is worth citing; for it describes the Piper's coronation in March 76 as the Young Osiris and mentions the 'royal children'—though Cleopatra was not among them, as she was yet unborn. It gives, however, a good picture of the sort of Egyptian rites in which she often took part:

> I lived 30 years in the presence of my Father. There went forth a Command from the King, the Lord of the Land, the Fatherloving Sisterloving God, the Young Osiris, Son of the Sun, Lord of Diadems, Ptolemaios, that the high office of Chief Priest of Memphis be conferred on me. I was then 14 years old. I set the adornment of the Serpent Crown on the King's head on the day when he took possession of Upper and Lower Egypt and performed all the customary rites in the chambers appointed for the Thirty Years' Festivals. I was leader in all the Secret Offices. I gave the instruction for the Consecration of the Horos [the divine king] at the time of the Birth of the [Sun] god in the Golden House [the spring equinox].
>
> I went to the Residence of the Kings of the Ionians [the Greeks] on the Shore of the Great Sea to the west of Rakoti. The King of Upper and Lower Egypt, the Master of Two Worlds, the Fatherloving Sisterloving God the Young Osiris was crowned in the Royal Palace. He proceeded to the Temple of Isis, the Lady of Yat-udjat. He offered to her many and costly sacrifices.
>
> Riding in his chariot forth from the Temple of Isis the King himself caused his chariot to stand still. He wreathed my head with a beautiful wreath of gold and all manner of gems, except only the royal pectoral on his own breast. I was nominated Prophet and he sent out a Royal Rescript to the

Capitals of all the Names, saying: I have appointed the High-priest of Memphis Pshereni-ptah as my Prophet. And there was delivered to me from the Temple of Upper and Lower Egypt a yearly revenue for my maintenance.

The King came to Memphis on a Feastday. He passed up and down in his Ship that he might behold both sides of the place. As soon as he landed at the Quarter of the City called Onkhtawy, he went into the Temple escorted by his Magistrates and his Wives and his royal Children, with all the things prepared for the Feast. Sitting in the ship, he sailed up so as to celebrate the Feast in honour of all the Gods dwelling in Memphis, according to the greatness of the goodwill in the Heart of the Lord of the Land, and the White Crown was upon his brow.[9]

The assignment of revenues suggests that Memphis at this time had a primacy over the whole Egyptian priesthood, of which elsewhere we know nothing: it is odd also that there is such stress on the White Crown (of Upper Egypt) at Memphis, the capital of Lower Egypt. Pshereniptah refers to his own 'goodly harem', though priests were supposed to be strictly monogamous; his reference to the Piper's 'Wives' may be merely a carry-over of Pharaonic phraseology or may mean 'the Queen and the Ladies of her Court'.

A complicated system of differences in prestige and status had evolved at the court. In the early reigns we find persons called Friends and Members-of-the-Bodyguard attached to the palace. With Ptolemy V a definite hierarchy was established, with orders conferred as a personal dignity on officials throughout the kingdom or on others whom the king wanted to honour. The highest order was that of Kinsmen, whom he addressed as Father or Brother (as a modern sovereign addresses his peers as

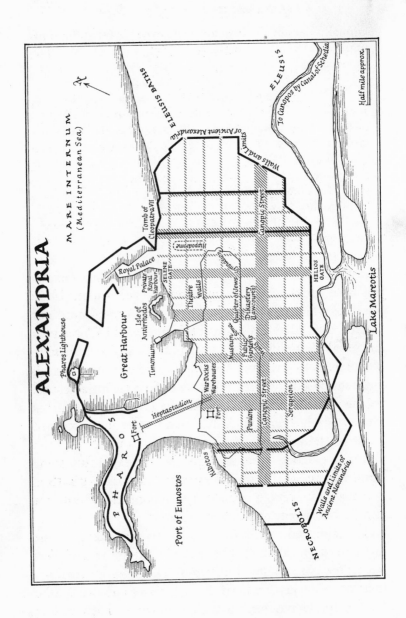

ALEXANDRIA

MARE INTERNUM
(Mediterranean Sea)

Pharos Lighthouse

Great Harbour

Port of Eunostos

PHAROS

Fort

Heptastadion

Kibotos

War Docks
Warehouses

Timonium

Isle of Antirrhodos

Private Royal Harbour

Royal Palace

Tomb of Cleopatra VII

Hippodrome

Theatre

SELENE GATE

Walls

Museum Square

Fort

Paneum

Canopic Street

Canopic Street

Public Baths

Argonauts

Quarter of Jews

Dikastery (Lawcourts)

Canopic Street

HELIOS GATE

Serapeion

NECROPOLIS

Walls and Limits of Ancient Alexandria

ELEUSIS BATHS

Walls and Limits of Ancient Alexandria

ELEUSIS

To Canopos by Canal of Schedia

Lake Mareotis

Half mile approx.

Cousin). The second order was that of Commanders-of-the-Bodyguard; the third was that of First Friends; next came mere Friends, and after them Successors (originally no doubt a reserve body of men ready to move up into the order of Friends when there came a vacancy). Later under Ptolemy VII a new order was inserted after the Kinsmen: that of those Honourably-Associated-with-the-Kinsmen, and a similar one after First Friends. These dignities were not hereditary and did not carry any duties beyond those which the bearer already had; they probably involved a distinctive dress, since we find that in an analogous system among the Seleukids the First Friends wore a gown of purple and the Kinsmen wore a golden brooch bestowed by the king. Since court-hierarchies do not easily yield up their rights and privileges, even if the court itself has lost much of its splendours, we may assume that all the orders still flourished in Cleopatra's time, jealously clinging to their insignia and priorities in etiquette. And we must imagine her court as composed, not of men and women in the sort of Egyptian costumes that we see in the paintings, reliefs, and statutary of the Pharaonic periods, but of courtiers in Greek robes and wreaths and officers in Macedonian mantles and high boots. Egyptian priests might be present for some particular reason, in their linen robes and with their shaven heads; but they were the exceptions and did not in any way set the style of the court.[10]

We gain a glimpse of the decorated dignitaries of the late period in some lines of a funerary verse-inscription from Edfu, which mention Ptolemaios, commander of the local contingent—here called the Army of Phoebus (the Edfu god, Horos-Behdety). The rulers had given him 'the Splendour of the Fillet, Sacred Appanage of the Glory belonging to the King's Kinsmen': he has been granted the title of *syngenes* (which does not seem conferred on governors of nomes earlier than 120 B.C.). We also meet Egyptians of the same period with the title *sn-niwt*, brother-of, the king, which seems the equivalent of *syngenes*. They are a cavalry-chief and two commanders, and at least the fathers of two of them. So natives like these, Pashu son of Pamenkhe and Pashu son of Khor, might be present at the court, like Ptolemaios, with their fillets, but they would be dressed like him in Greek fashion.[11]

Caesar in Alexandria

Shortly after Egypt became a Roman province at Cleopatra's death, the geographer Strabon visited Alexandria; his account is thus of the city that she knew. The ancients liked to compare landscapes with objects: the Peiraios had its Vase, Alexandria its Box, and the Town of Rhodes was seen as a Theatre, with its rounded port as the Orchestra. Alexandria in its layout was likened to *chlamys* or short mantle, worn properly by horsemen though the cloak of footsoldiers was also given the name. Pliny says the city was made 'in the image of Macedonian *Chlamys*, circular in shape, notched along the edges, and jutting out to left and right'.[1] Strabon declares, 'The shape of the city's area is like a *chlamys*. The two long sides are those washed by the two waters' of the Mediterranean and of Lake Mareotis, 'with a diameter of some 30 *stadia*'—a *stadion* was just over 606 feet—'while the short sides are the isthmuses, each 7 or 8 *stadia* wide and pinched-in, one by the sea and the other by the lake'. Philon adds that the city was cut into five sections, each called after a letter:

Alpha, Beta, Gamma, Delta, Epsilon. Beta seems to have included the Palaces, the Museum, the Sema, and other such buildings; Delta was the Jewish Quarter.[2] Strabon continues, 'The place as a whole is intersected by streets practicable for horse-riding and chariot-driving, and by two that are very broad, extending to more than a *plethron* in breadth'—a *stadion* was 6 *plethra*—'which cut one another into two parts, at right angles. And the city contains most beautiful public precincts as well as the royal palaces, which make up a fourth or even a third of the whole circuit. As each of the kings out of love of splendour used to add some fresh adornment to the monuments, so also he invested himself at his own charge with a residence besides those already built. Thus, to cite the poet [Homer], "There is building on building." All, however, are linked with one another and the Harbour, even those that lie outside the harbour,' on the Lochias promontory. 'The Museum is further a part of the palaces. It has a public walk, an exedra with seats, and a large house in which is the common mess-hall of the learned men who share the Museum. This group not only holds property in common, but also have a priest in charge of the Museum, formerly appointed by the Kings, now by Caesar.' (An exedra was a hall or arcade with seats or recesses, suitable for lectures and discussion.)

We may compare the structure described by Vitruvius: 'spacious exedras with three porticoes plus seats, where philosophers, rhetoricians, and all others who take delight in studies can engage in disputation.'[3] The *Souda* suggests that the Exedra was a separate building. 'They live near the Museum and the Exedra.' Part of the palace-area was also the enclosure where Alexander the Great and the

Ptolemaic kings were buried. 'In the Great Harbour,' says Strabon, 'at the entry on the right are the Island and the Tower Pharos; on the left, reefs and the promontory Lochias with a palace on it. Sailing into the harbour, you come, on the left, to the inner palaces which are continuous with those on Lochias and have groves and many lodges painted in various colours. Below lies the man-made harbour, hidden from view, the private property of the kings, and also Antirrhodos, an isle lying off that harbour, with its own harbour and palace. The name means that the isle is a Rival of Rhodes. Above the man-made harbour comes the Theatre, then the Poseidion, an elbow, as it were, sticking out from the Emporion, as it's called, and holding a shrine of Poseidon. . . . Next you meet the Kaisarion [Caesareum] and the Emporion and the warehouses; after these the ship-houses, extending as far as the Heptastadion,' the great mole joining the Pharos with its Lighthouse to the mainland.

'After that you come to the Harbour of Eunostos, and, above that, to the man-made harbour called Kibotos [Box]; it too has ship-houses. Further on there is a navigable canal leading to Lake Mareotis. Beyond the canal is left only a small part of the city, then we come to the superb Nekropolis, where are many gardens, graves, and halting-stations fitted for corpse-embalming, and, inside the canal, to the Sarapion and other sacred precincts of ancient times, now almost abandoned through the construction of the new buildings at Nikopolis. Thus, there's an amphitheatre, and a stadium, at Nikopolis, and the Five-Yearly Games are held there; but the ancient buildings have fallen into neglect. In short, the city is full of public and sacred structures. But the most beautiful is the Gymnasion, with porticoes more than a stadion in length. And in the city's middle are both the Court of Justice and the Groves. Here too is the Paneion, a high point raised by man; it resembles a rocky hill, in the shape of a fircone, and is climbed by a spiral road. From the top you can see the whole city spread out below on all sides: the broad street running lengthwise,' west to east, 'from Nikopolis past the Kanopic Gate. Then you come to the Hippodrome, as it's named, and to the other parallel streets which reach as far as the Kanopic Canal. Passing through the Hippodrome, you come to Nikopolis, with its settlement on the sea no smaller than a city, 30 *stadia* from Alexandria.'

The Kanopic Gate was the Gate of the Sun on the East; the road ran on to the Gate of the Moon on the West.[4] The Gymnasion was particularly noble because of its importance in Greek education and way-of-life; to belong to it was the jealously-guarded privilege of the Greek population. Throughout Egypt the Old Boys, Those-from-the-Gymnasion, of the local organisation were the élite.[5]

Cleopatra must have known sites like the Paneion; but we see that even without leaving the palatial complex she had a city of her own to wander over, a vast extension of noble buildings, with gardens and accesses to the sea, and with the Museum if she wished to listen to the greatest scholars of her world at their disputations or lectures. The great Library supplied her with the whole of Greek literature; agents had gathered more than 400,000 rolls. Medicine, mathematics, physics, geography, astronomy were studied in the Museum. There Eratosthenes had calculated the circumference of the earth and Aristarchos had demonstrated that the earth went round the sun, Herophilos had laid the basis of anatomy and Ktesibios had constructed catapults worked by compressed air. Meditating in the gardens and porticoes, Cleopatra could realise the greatness of her inheritance and determine at all costs to arrest and reverse the decline of Egypt and her

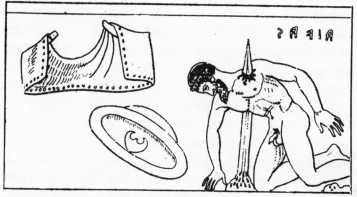

Suicide of Ajax (on Greek vase B.M. F480) with Chlamys hanging on wall and showing how its shape was attributed to Alexandria (as also to the world, the *oikoumene*).

dynasty: to wrest the initiative from the Romans despite all their military energies and powers of organisation.

Her exact relation to her co-ruler Ptolemy XIII is obscure. She never included him, or the younger half-brother whom she later married, on the legends of her coins. She alone, Queen Cleopatra, is named. Indeed the whole question of her regnal years as given on monuments or documents is difficult in the extreme. There may have been troubles at her accession or soon after. The troops left by Gabinius, mostly Gauls or Germans, were still encamped near Alexandria. Left without any signs of recall, they naturally wanted to settle down and marry the local girls (whether pure Egyptians or descendants of earlier bands of settlers, Macedonians, Greeks, Persians, Thracians, Asianics). When Marcus Bibulus, proconsul of Syria, did try to recall them, they murdered his two sons who had brought the order. Cleopatra, seeking to avert Roman wrath, had the killers arrested and sent to Syria. Caesar thus describes the royal troops whom he confronted in 46: 'Gabinius' soldiers had now become used to the licentious ways of Alexandrian life and forgotten the name and discipline of the Roman People; they had married wives there, by whom the majority of them had children. To these were added a host of highwaymen and freebooters from Syria, the province of Cilicia, and adjacent lands. Also many convicts and exiles had joined them. For at Alexandria all our runaway slaves were sure of finding protection for their persons if they gave in their names and enlisted as soldiers; then if any of them was arrested by a master, he was rescued by the mob of his fellows, who, involved in the same guilt, repelled at the hazard of their lives every violence offered to anybody. By a privilege of the Alexandrian Army, they had the habit of demanding the execution of royal favourites, pillaging the properties of the rich to swell their pay, investing the palace, banishing some men from the realm, recalling others from exile. There were also 2,000 cavalry, who had gained the skill of veterans by participating in several Alexandrian wars. Those who had restored Ptolemy the Father [the Piper] to his kingdom, killed Bibulus' two sons and engaged in wars against the Egyptians. Such was their experience in military matters'.

The events he lists seem to be put in chronological

order, so that the death of Bibulus' sons was apparently followed by native uprisings of some sort. We see what a tumultuous situation Cleopatra had to grapple with from the outset. Caesar writes of the royal army rather contemptuously; perhaps he didn't like to admit how recklessly he got himself into a difficult position at Alexandria. But it seems in fact that the Piper, to his credit, had built up the Gabinian forces into an effective army which gave Caesar more trouble than Pompey did.

Some of the Gabinians may have been posted up the Nile to guard the southern frontier. A document dated 'year 4, 5 Phaophi' (8 October) may belong to Cleopatra's reign. It deals with wine-distribution and we find such names as Antonius, Quintus, Vibius, Gaius, Marius, Decimus, Aurelius, Pompeius, together with names that seem Hebrew: Lotkis, Euieis, Zannais, Abdelos. The men may have belonged to the three cohorts that Octavian, after his conquest of Egypt, sent to do garrison duty at Elephantine and Syene: but the mixture of Latin and oriental names better suits B.C. 48. The Piper may well have taken recruits of various races to fill gaps in the Gabinians.[6]

We do not know the exact date of the Piper's death. On 1 August 51 (in fact 30 June) M. Caelius Rufus wrote to Cicero from Rome: 'It has been reported to us, and is now accepted as true, that the Alexandrian King is dead. Please write fully and thoroughly what you advise me to do, what is the situation in the kingdom, who is vice-regent.'[7] Cicero, now proconsul in Cilicia, was considered to be well situated for getting news from Egypt. Caelius had been accused, through his cast-off mistress Clodia, of murdering Dion who led the embassy to Rome against the

Piper. We can therefore understand his interest in Egyptian matters, though just what sort of advice he expected from Cicero is not clear—unless the question of annexing Egypt was thought likely to come up once more. We may note that some time seems to have elapsed since the first arrival of the news, and that no official notification had been made. How fast would such news probably travel from Alexandria to Rome? In a complaint about his distance from Rome Cicero remarks that an express-letter took forty-seven days to reach him in Cappadocia; so we may perhaps estimate a month for tidings from Egypt to reach Italy. The Piper was then probably dead by 15 May—though he may have died earlier, even in February. Clearly Cleopatra was doing her best to keep things quiet.[8]

All extant documents with dual dates (of both Piper and Cleopatra) were made out after his death, all but one (dated 24 May) at least a month after the latest possible date of the event. By 22 March, *stēlē* 13 of the Boucheion at Memphis shows Cleopatra as queen. By then the Piper was almost certainly dead. Allowing for a slow dissemination of the news, we should reckon him dead at least two months before the date of 11 Mecheir at Philai, and perhaps one month at most before 14 Mecheir in the Herakleopolite nome. We may deduce that he was still alive on 15 January and that he died sometime between that date and the 15 May which we have worked out from Caelius' letter. Cleopatra was on the throne by 22 March, but whether or not there was yet a regency we cannot say for sure.

Note that Caelius infers a state of vague rumours which he wants clarified. The lack of official reports is shown by his ignorance as to who now controls Egypt. Nothing had come directly from the court. Since any ruler of Egypt at such a moment of change had good reasons to suspect agitation for Roman intervention, there was certain to be a strong attempt to hush things up till the new rule was firmly established. If a struggle for power was going on at the same time inside the Alexandrian court, the need to keep Rome in the dark would be even more acute. Of one thing we can be sure: Cleopatra was fighting to gain the strongest position possible. She may have had a short period of co-regency with her father, or she may have hidden the fact of his death and put out a statement of co-regency. The inscription which refers to his children as *Neoi Theoi Philadelphoi*, New Gods Brothers-and-Sisters-loving-one-another, may have been an attempt by the Piper to set his children in a safe position which made interference by Rome more difficult; his will, we have seen, made the same sort of attempt. He may also have hoped to minimise the struggle among them, which he could not but have foreseen.[9]

An examination of earlier Ptolemaic documents suggests that where we meet two rulers linked in a dating we are dealing with an actual joint rule. None of the double datings at this time, however, can be shown to deal with a time when the Piper was still alive, and at least one (14 Epeiph, 15 July) was certainly written after his death.[10] There are indeed three types of dated documents for this year: (1) those dated simply by the Piper's 30th year; (2) those with the dual enumeration 'year 30=year 1' for 52–1 B.C., starting as early as Pharmouthi (though that date may be regarded as supplementary) and certainly covering from 24 May 51 to 15 July; (3) documents merely dated the 1st year of Cleopatra—the earliest is 6 July, then comes one of 12 August. No document solely dated by the Piper's year interrupts the second series. The material is not abundant enough to make an irrefutable case; but it is highly suggestive that single dates of the Piper are not attested after the later part of Mecheir (February); then with only one dubious exception we meet the dual dates till Epeiph (July); after that we find Cleopatra alone.[11]

We can now turn back to the inscription of 22 March in the Boucheion. On 19 Phamenoth (22 March) 51 she seems to have taken part in the rite of installing a new Bouchis Bull at Memphis. The usual stereotyped phrase of the monument runs: 'He was installed by the King himself'—which is not to be taken literally. But this time it is followed by the statement: 'The Queen, the Lady of the Two Lands, the Father-loving Goddess, rowed him in the Barge of Amun.' This is without parallel and must have some special significance.[12] The precision of the novel phrase suggests that Cleopatra was there in person and that she or the priests wanted to make sure that this was brought out by the intrusion of the unusual formula. Against this interpretation it has been argued that she would not have had time to arrange a royal procession up the Nile in such a rite so soon after her accession.[13] But the arrangements may have been made some time before, or Cleopatra may have felt that a special effort was worth while to impress her Egyptian subjects. In any event the inscription shows how quickly she dominated the situation; there is no reference to a co-regent.

Much as she was necessarily absorbed by the situation in Egypt, she must have been watching as closely as she could the events of Roman politics. Much had changed since the time of the Piper's restoration. The coalition of the three great men had broken down. Crassus had been killed in his Parthian campaign in 53; and Caesar and Pompey were becoming the leaders of the two main opposing factions. After a long political argument with the Senate, Caesar invaded Italy in January 49. Pompey collected his forces in Macedonia and sent round for aid to all the eastern lands, where his influence was still powerful. In 49 his elder son Gaius was in Alexandria asking for corn. Cleopatra was in no position to refuse; and perhaps she had not yet got her bearings in the new phase of conflict. She dispatched sixty transports with corn, together with five hundred men from the Gabinian force. If Pompey failed, she was liable to meet trouble. No doubt she kept her aid down to a minimal level, uncertain what would be the outcome of the civil war.

We gain some further glimpses of her attempts to remain the sole ruler of Egypt in these years 51–49. A contract dated 29 Mesore (29 August) 51 names her in the prescript as queen without co-regent. As we are there at least six months after the Piper's death, the omission of her brother cannot be due to ignorance or carelessness.[14] From Abusir-el-Malaq there are a fair number of papyri, but they throw no light on the struggle she was waging.[15] However, in her third year we find some evidence. In an Abusir papyrus the first three lines include an unusual form of dating, which seems to read, 'In the 1st, which is also denominated the 3rd year.' It opens, 'To Queen Cleopatra and . . .'[16] The odd formula here is not to be equated with a form of dual dating, 'in the last year which is also the 1st', where the second term is always 'year 1'.[17]

Here the '1st year' cannot be Cleopatra's genuine first year, which ran from February 51 to 4 September 51: the end of the Egyptian year. We cannot imagine any circumstances in which that year would be called her third (which in fact ran from 5 September 50 to 3 September 49). The year here called the first must be equated with that third year. But why the latter was renumbered as her first, we have no clue. As her name stands first in the first line, and as in any combination she would come out as the dominant partner, 'year 1' must here represent some alternative reckoning of her regnal years. Various suggestions have been made to get out of the difficulty, for instance that the rulers mentioned are rather Cleopatra Tryphaina in her co-regency with Berenice IV.[18] But as they ruled together, the dual dating makes no sense with them. Again it has been suggested that behind the strange dating lies the fact that the brother-consort Ptolemy XIII had been expelled from the throne after being nominally accepted. But if the Cleopatra is our queen, as seems certain, then the missing name may well be that of Arsinoe her ambitious younger sister, or even the younger brother who became Ptolemy XIV. As it is hard to imagine Cleopatra accepting Arsinoe on any terms we are driven to conjecture that at some phase of her struggle with Ptolemy XIII she displaced him and put his younger brother at her side on the throne as someone more amenable to her will.[19]

This analysis has been forced to resort to guesswork; but we can safely deduce from the peculiar dating systems that some sort of internal dynastic struggle was going on, in which Cleopatra found herself at loggerheads with Ptolemy XIII. A text from Bacchias shows that the new arrangement came about some time before Pauni in her third year; another text shows that it lasted on till the beginning of her fourth year. That year ran from 4 September 49 to 3 September 48; but before it ended, the system that Cleopatra had devised had broken down and she was driven into exile. The fact that now we definitely find her in violent antagonism with the elder brother, Ptolemy XIII, is a strong support for the analysis made of the obscure datings.[20]

At last some clear light falls on the embittered wranglings of the children of the Piper and on the cabals they had gathered. Ptolemy XIII, backed by Potheinos, Theodotos, and Achillas, was able to drive his sister out of Alexandria, over the border eastwards into the desertlands. Caesar tells us that the expulsion took place 'a few months' before Pompey was murdered on 28 September 48 (in the Julian calendar, 24 July).[21] She may even have been dethroned as early as 20 Tybi of her fourth year (21 January 48); for a papyrus from the Herakleopolite Nome of that date lacks the dual dating.[22] We also have a royal *prostagma* or proclamation that may belong to the period of crisis: it orders all cargoes of wheat and pulse from Middle Egypt to be diverted to Alexandria, and its heading cites 'the King and Queen'. Its date is 23 Phaophi, year 3 (apparently 27 October 50), and here also there is no equation with a year 1.[23] Efforts have been made to overcome the difficulty by assigning the order to the date 3 November 79 (under the Piper and Cleopatra Tryphaina); but when being re-edited it was found to have been written on a reused papyri, which in its first form mentioned a *strategos* Heliodoros and cannot have been as early as 79.[24] Another point is that the king is cited before the queen, and always in Cleopatra's reign the queen comes first.[25] The order then seems to have been issued by Ptolemy XIII at a moment when he had briefly gained the upper hand before Cleopatra was actually expelled, or when, after expelling her, he married his sister Arsinoe.

The implication of some sharp crisis runs through the document. The penalties for disobedience are death and confiscation of property: informers are to get up to a third of goods seized—if they are slaves, they will get a sixth and be freed. There was indeed a low flow in 48, but we do not know how the Nile behaved in 50. Pliny tells us of the 48 disaster: 'The largest rise up to date was one of 27 feet in the principate of Claudius, and the smallest $7\frac{1}{2}$ feet in the year of the war of Pharsalos, as if the river were trying to avert Pompeius' murder by a sort of portent.'[26] The attempt made by the *prostagma* then to control the food supply suggests that already in October 50 Cleopatra had been pushed off the throne and that her opponents were trying to cut her off from needed provisions. Ptolemy XIII would also himself want to get in foodstuffs for his own forces. Malalas, we may note, states that, when thrown out of Alexandria by her brother, she at first took refuge in the Thebaid. (The Boucheion inscription suggests that like her father she had popularity in this area.) Malalas' account harmonises with our interpretation of the *prostagma*, where the areas to which supplies are forbidden, the Delta and the Thebaid, would be those held by Cleopatra or her sympathisers.[27]

It seems certain then that Cleopatra had been in a difficult situation since 50 and that Egypt from the Roman viewpoint was in a rather chaotic state. Caesar says of the Piper's will, 'one of the copies was taken to Rome by his ambassadors to be deposited in the Treasury; but the public troubles held this up and the copy was lodged with Pompey; another was sealed up and kept at Alexandria.'[28] There is a likelihood that the Senate conferred on Pompey a *tutela* or guardianship over Egypt— possibly in 49 at Thessalonika. If so, the step may have been connected with a feeling that conditions in Egypt were getting out of hand.

However we interpret the often vague and circumstantial evidence, it is clear that Cleopatra had a stormy time from the moment of her father's death, using various devices, doubtless a mixture of force and craft, to depreciate the claims of Ptolemy XIII (and perhaps of Arsinoe) and to concentrate power in her own hands. The strength of the palace-cabal that united against her is the measure of the extent to which her claims and tactics angered and alienated the rest of the court. Now, in 48, not yet twenty-one, she was driven decisively from her throne. As her ancestress Cleopatra IV had done in 113, she set about gathering an army. Though she must have had a core of Greek-Egyptian supporters, she recruited men from the Arab tribes outside the eastern frontier and camped at Mount Kasios about thirty miles from Pelousion. Her opponents in turn mustered their forces and marched with Ptolemy XIII to the frontier-fortress to prevent her from invading Egypt. What would have happened if the two groups had been left to fight it out on their own is doubtful; certainly Ptolemy XIII had the main Egyptian forces at his disposal. But now they were all suddenly drawn into the mainstream of the conflicts in the Roman world. Caesar defeated Pompey at Pharsalos in Greece. Pompey took boat and set sail for Egypt, where the Piper had long been tied to him in a sort of client-ship; he had good reason to think that Ptolemy XIII would wish to continue the relationship established by his father and would agree, freely or under pressure, to put at his disposal the yet-considerable resources and treasure of his land. He would thus be able to make Egypt his base for a renewal of the struggle with Caesar.

By chance or intention, he did not sail for Alexandria. Hearing somehow of the civil war between Ptolemy and Cleopatra, he turned for the point on the coast where he could appeal directly to the king in arms. In September 48 he reached the spot near Pelousion where the latter was encamped. The king's council discussed this new problem. The whole situation was transformed. There would be little use in defeating Cleopatra if they took the wrong side in the wider conflict. Theodotos argued that Cleopatra had already compromised herself by sending aid to Pompey; Caesar had shown himself Pompey's superior and his favour at all costs must be gained. 'Dead men don't bite.' His arguments triumphed and the council decided that their compromising visitor must be got rid of. Achillas with two men (one of them a Gabinian officer, Septimus) went off in a small boat to bring Pompey ashore; the shallows prevented the latter's ship from coming close in. As they rowed away for the shore, Pompey recognised the morose taciturnity of the group, felt uneasy, and tried to draw them out. Then, as the boat came in towards the royal party which stood in welcome on the sands, Septimus struck. Pompey's head was hewn off and taken as proof of his death; the trunk was left bleeding on the beach.

However, they gained little by their treachery. Soon after, on 27 October (27 July) Caesar arrived with some 35 ships and only 2 legions: 3200 men with 800 cavalry.[29] Theodotos brought him Pompey's head and signet-ring. Caesar wept. Then he made what he himself seems to admit was a tactical error. 'At his landing he heard an outcry among the soldiers left by the king to garrison the city, and saw a crowd gathering his way, because the *fasces* were carried before him.' The *fasces* were the bundle of rods and an axe carried before a Roman magistrate. 'The whole multitude considered this act an infringement of the king's dignity. Though the tumult was appeased, frequent disturbances were made for several days in succession by a crowd of the populace, and a large number of his soldiers were killed in all parts of the city.'[30] He was short of money, and made things worse by attempting to get his debts in. The Piper had paid only half of the 6000 talants promised in 59; and Caesar now asked for ten million denarii, offering to write off what further money was owing. Potheinos retorted that he had better depart and deal with his duties at Rome. Caesar ignored his pertness. Then Potheinos, required to provide supplies for the Roman troops, sent musty grain and remarked that the men would be pleased to be fed at the cost of foreigners. At the same time his agents stirred up the touchy populace. Ostentatiously the royal table was laid with wooden or pottery vessels, and the gold and silver plate was handed over to Caesar to make him appear as the plunderer and polluter of sanctuaries. What policy Pothenos and his friends were following is unclear. They had killed Pompey and made enemies of the Roman senatorial party; now they were preparing to kill Caesar in turn.

Caesar ordered Ptolemy and Cleopatra to end their disputes, disband their forces, and accept his arbitration; he was the representative of the Roman People whom the Piper had enjoined to carry out the provisions of his will. Ptolemy in response came in person to Alexandria, but left his troops intact under Achillas to bar Cleopatra from Egypt. Her problem now was to reach Caesar without being murdered on the way. One of her adherents, a Sicilian merchant Apollodoros, conveyed her by boat past the guard-posts to Alexandria, then smuggled her into the palace inside a bale of carpet or bedding.

What happened at her meeting with Caesar we can only guess. No doubt she knew how to turn her unexpected and unconventional way of arrival to advantage, while Caesar was the man to be charmed with a bold stroke carried out by an attractive and intelligent young woman. He was now fifty-two, at the height of his powers, the military master of the world, but not a professional general in the way that Pompey had been; he was essentially an adroit man of the world with his own highly developed culture, a politician, yet not swayed by the vanities and simple power-lusts of his fellows, a gallant lover of many ladies, said to have given Servilia (mother of Brutus) pearls worth 1,500,000 sesterces, but a lover who never lost his head. Saviour of Mankind according to recent acclamations at Ephesos, Offspring of Ares and Aphrodite, God Incarnate, and yet a cool well-balanced character who found such praises in no way heady or disturbing.[31] And there was Cleopatra, no conventional beauty with her big mouth and her hooked nose, but with all her warmth and wit of charm, her imperial pride and ease of manner, her glistening assured body with its rich smell, her awareness of having been called divine even as a child, her readiness of intellect, which had enabled her to learn something of so many languages and to master the complex inheritance of Alexandrian culture. Plutarch informs us, 'Her beauty was not in itself quite incomparable, we are told, nor such as to strike all beholders; but converse with her had an irresistible charm. Her presence, combined with the persuasiveness of her discourse and the character which was somehow diffused about her behaviour towards others, had something stimulating about it. There was a sweetness also in the tones of voice; and her tongue, like an instrument of many strings, she could readily turn to whatever language she pleased, so that in her interviews with barbarians she seldom had need of an interpreter, but mostly made her replies unaided, whether the men were Ethiopians, Hebrews, Arabians, Syrians, Medes or Persians. It is said that she even knew the speech of many other peoples as well, though the [ptolemaic] kings of Egypt before her had not even made an effort to learn the native tongue and some even gave up their Macedonian dialect.'

It is likely that by the end of the interview, or soon after, she became his mistress. Caesar, able to recognise fully the precious quality of her charm, had fallen under her spell—to the extent that he could fall under any woman's.

Next day he called Ptolemy in and ordered him to be reconciled with his sister. In rage the lad rushed out into the streets, called on his people, and threw off his diadem. The crowd demonstrated outside the palace. Caesar made concessions, giving his decisions at a solemn ceremony. Ptolemy and Cleopatra were to rule jointly over Egypt; Arsinoe and the younger brother were to take over

Cyprus. Caesar thus on his own sole responsibility gave away a ten-year-old province. Cleopatra had her first triumph. We may be sure that she would have preferred Caesar to depose Ptolemy XIII and put her alone on the throne; but at least she had ended the desperate situation in which she had been as an exile, and had good hopes of strengthening her support from Caesar. Ptolemy XIII was brought back into the palace, but was unreconciled. Potheinos, acting on his behalf, recalled the troops under Achillas: some 2,000 foot with 2,000 cavalry. Alexandria was surrounded. Ptolemy, at Caesar's order, bade them depart; but the army knew that he was merely obeying Caesar's instructions and ignored the mock-command. The two envoys were insulted and sentenced to death, one killed on the spot, the other carried off to die of his wounds. Achillas entered the city and the populace rose behind him. Caesar was closed inside the palace with inadequate forces.

In his *Caesar*, Plutarch compresses all these events. 'She took a small boat, with only one of her confidants, Apollodoros of Sicily, and landed near the palace in the dusk. She was at a loss how to enter undetected, then thought of wrapping herself in a bed-coverlet, stretched out at length, while Apollodoros tied it up and carried it through the gates to Caesar's apartment. Caesar was first captivated by this proof of Cleopatra's bold wit and afterwards overcome by her charm, so that he made a reconciliation between her and her brother on condition that she was his co-ruler in the kingdom. A festival was held to celebrate the reconciliation, where Caesar's barber, a busy eavesdropping fellow, whose extreme timidity made him pry into everything, discovered a plot against

Caesar carried on by Achillas, general of the royal forces, and the eunuch Potheinos. Caesar, being told, set a guard on the hall where the feast was going on, and killed Potheinos. Achillas escaped to the army.'[32] The banquet here mentioned seems that described by Lucan:

> Great was the bustle as Cleopatra displayed
> a magnificence not yet adopted in Roman ways.
> A temple-size hall, too costly for an age
> corrupted with pleasure-spending. The ceiling-panels
> blazed wealth, the rafters hidden in thick gold.
> Marble the walls shone, not with mere veneers,
> agate in its own right, not just decoration,
> and porphyry; on alabaster they trod
> throughout the hall. Meroe's ebony
> replaced mere wood, not a thin cover of doors;
> structural, not for a show. The porch was ivory;
> Indian tortoise-shell, hand-coloured, stood,
> inlaying doors, with emeralds in its spots.
> Gem-gleamed the couches, jasper-tawny cups
> [loaded the tables, the sofas bright with hues]
> of coverlets, mostly steeped in Tyrian dye
> of many soakings, others richly embroidered
> with gold or fiery scarlet in the way
> Egyptians mingle leashes in the web.
> A swarm of attendants too, a ministering mob,
> differing in age and race. On some was seen
> African hair, on others hair so fair
> Caesar declared the Rhineland lacked such reds.
> Dark skins and woolly heads, with hair receding
> back from the brow; unfortunate lads whose manhood
> was cut away; and older lads whose cheeks
> were scarcely darkened yet by any down.

He described Cleopatra as laden with Red-Sea pearls, her white breasts showing through fine Sidonian stuffs, silks 'woven by the shuttle of the Seres [Chinese] and pulled-out by the Egyptian needleworker, who loosens the threads by stretching out the stuff'.

To return to the situation after the death of Potheinos: the Alexandrian mob tried to storm Caesar's area; but he had cohorts picketed in the streets and drove them off. At the same time an attack was made on the port, where much street-fighting went on. The assailants wanted to seize the fifty ships sent to aid Pompey, which had now returned home, together with twenty-two decked guard-ships of the port. If they gained these ships, they hoped to hem Caesar in from the sea and complete the encirclement. He had to take quick steps. He set fire to the ships in question as well as others in the docks; his force was too small to protect them. In his own ships he carried a detachment over to the Pharos, the lighthouse-island sheltering the two harbours; he thus held a point from which he could contact any supplies or reinforcements arriving by sea. Street-fights continued in various parts of the city without decisive gains for either side.

Caesar tells us, 'He secured the most necessary points and fortified them in the night. In this quarter of the town was a wing of the palace, where Caesar was lodged on his first arrival, and a theatre next to the house, which served as a citadel and commanded an avenue to the port and other docks. These fortifications he strengthened in the next few days so that he might have a rampart in front and not be forced into a fight against his will. Meanwhile Ptolemy's youngest daughter [Arsinoe], hoping the throne would fall vacant, slipped out of the palace to Achillas and helped to carry on the war. But they soon quarrelled over the command. So each gave more and more gifts to the soldiers, seeking by great sacrifices to gain their devotion. While the enemy was thus occupied, Potheinos, the young king's tutor and regent of the realm who was in Caesar's part of the town, sent messengers to Achillas, encouraging him not drop the enterprise or despair of success. But his men were detected and caught, and he himself was put to death by Caesar. Such was the beginning of the Alexandrian War.'[33]

And the end of Caesar's account of it. His commentaries were carried on by a staff-officer Hirtius, though some ancients thought the author was Oppius. The fire which Caesar started destroyed many of the warehouses for corn and papyrus-rolls as well as the ships; Livy says that 40,000 volumes were destroyed, but it is not clear if these were of unused paper or were completed books. In any event a tale grew up that the great Library had been burnt.[34] The actions of Arsinoe, Ptolemy, Potheinos, and Achillas suggest strongly that the brother and sister were acting in collusion; they thus support our conjecture that the pair had previously acted together to expel Cleopatra. Arsinoe was now only about fifteen, or a little older, but her vigorous and wilful behaviour during the war shows that she was no novice in the struggle for power.

Caesar must now have realised how rashly he had acted in pushing ahead and allowing himself to be blockaded in Alexandria. He himself makes only the weak excuse that he was 'detained against his will by the Etesian Winds which are wholly unfavourable to persons voyaging out of Alexandria.'[35] He seems for once to have miscalculated the forces he was up against; perhaps after the defeat and death of Pompey a certain euphoria had invaded his mind, making him unusually reckless, and perhaps his encounter

47

with Cleopatra had strengthened this mood. Master of the world, he came close to ending his career in a trivial side-adventure. However, when he recognised his danger, he promptly sent round for aid to the fleet at Rhodes, in Syria and Cilicia, and called for archers from Crete and cavalry from Malchos king of the Nabataeans. Gn. Domitius Calvinus, left to settle affairs in Asia, was ordered to send at once as many troops as possible and then to march the rest to Egypt via Syria. Calvinus sent the 37th Legion by sea and it did join Caesar at Alexandria; another legion, coming overland, arrived only after the war and was left by Caesar to garrison the city. Meanwhile Caesar also sent to Mithridates of Pergamon to levy troops in Syria and Cilicia, and bring them by land.[36]

Caesar went on making the best of his cornered position, getting in corn, setting up war-engines, and perfecting the defences. His aim was to fortify effectively a small section of the city, which was cut off by marshlands on the south. He was helped by dissensions among the besiegers. Arsinoe clashed yet more with Achillas; and with the aid of the eunuch Ganymedes, under whose care she had grown up, she had him put to death. The eunuch took command of the army and pressed Caesar hard. At one moment he seemed about to deprive him of the fresh water brought in by conduits from Lake Mareotis; he dammed the main canals, blocked up the lesser ones, and pumped sea water into the system, so that the basins and cisterns in Caesar's area were of no use. But Caesar knew that all beaches have veins of sweet water; he set his men digging and found what he wanted. Soon after came the first reinforcements, the transports with the 37th Legion and with supplies. Caesar turned to the offensive. The

Egyptians had collected their fleet in the western harbour. He attacked them; but their surviving ships took refuge under the artillery of the city. Caesar then attacked the mole and island from the sea and the eastern harbour. The village of Pharos and the near mole-end were taken. Next day he seized the mole-end on the mainland and tried to barricade it off. But the Egyptians landed in strength on the mole behind him. His warships began to push off. In dismay his troops saw themselves being left on the mole. They rushed for the ships, some of which, overloaded, sank. Caesar stayed with his men till the end, then climbed aboard a ship. But seeing that too many men were following his example, he jumped over and swam to another ship while the first one went down. The enemy got his purple general's cloak. In the action he lost 400 legionaries and many more sailors.

He had tried, unavailingly, to use Ptolemy's authority against the attackers; now he felt that he must gain time by negotiations and he let the lad go. His exact motives are hard to make out. However much Ptolemy had pro-tested that he'd try to stop the war, his word was clearly not to be trusted. Hirtius says that the Alexandrians petitioned for his release, saying that they were weary of being governed by a woman (Arsinoe) and were ready to obey their king and make peace. He adds, unconvincingly, 'Though Caesar knew the breed to be false and perfidious, seldom saying what they really thought, he judged it best to comply with their request. He even flattered himself that his condescension in sending the king at their request would work on them to be faithful—or, as was more in accord with his character, that if they only wanted the king to head their army, at least it would be more to his

a

credit and honour to have to deal with a monarch than with a band of slaves and fugitives.'[37] So, after exhorting the lad and taking his hand, Caesar sent him off. Ptolemy wept and begged Casesar not to send him. 'Caesar, moved at his concern, dried up his tears, told him they'd soon meet again if those were his true sentiments, and dismissed him. The king, like a wild beast escaped from confinement, carried on the war with such acrimony against Caesar that his farewell tears seemed to have been tears of joy. Caesar's lieutenants, friends, centurions, and soldiers, were delighted at the event: that his easiness of temper had been imposed on by a child, as if in fact Caesar's behaviour on this occasion had resulted from mildness of character and not from the most consummate prudence.'

Where the prudence or craft lay is not clear. We feel that Hirtius' account reflects the bewilderment of the Romans at Caesar's behaviour, or attempts to hide something. We must remember, though we get no hint of it from Caesar's own or from Hirtius' comments, that he was acting throughout in concert with Cleopatra. She for one would have had no illusions as to the results of freeing Ptolemy; she would not have trusted the plea of the Alexandrians that they were ready to surrender Arsinoe. But she may well have preferred to see her brother-rival exposed as an obdurate foe of Caesar than have him kept in a captivity where his true attitudes were suppressed. If Caesar won the war with Ptolemy still his prisoner, the latter could claim to have been on his side all the while and Cleopatra could not have got rid of him. The protestations by the Alexandrians that they hated Arsinoe were disproved by events; she seems to have gone on acting with her brother in command of the army against Caesar.

Dion's account is worth noting. He says that Caesar really thought the Egyptians had changed their minds, intimidated by their losses. 'Unwilling to seem averse from peace, though they might have treacherous intentions, he agreed to comply with their wishes, then sent Ptolemy along, thinking he had nothing to fear from one so young, with such a neglected education. He hoped also that the Egyptians would agree to a peace on his own terms; or if they refused, he could with more justice defeat and subject them, and they would further furnish him with a plausible pretext for conferring sovereign power on Cleopatra. For he never conceived he could be defeated by them, especially after the recent increase to his army.'[38] We see here again a jumble of conjectures. Also, Dion's chronology differs from that of Hirtius; he dates the release after the fall of Pelousion when Caesar knew help was near and might well have thought that Ptolemy's irruption into the camp of Arsinoe and Ganymedes would beget rivalries and confusions. His suggestion that Caesar was thinking of Cleopatra is unlikely to be correct, but may spring from a story of Cleopatra's counsels. Hirtius definitely puts the event before the decisive arrival of reinforcements. 'A report went about that a large body of troops were marching by land from Syria and Cilicia to help Caesar, though he himself had received as yet no news of them; but still they [the Alexandrians] resolved to intercept the convoys that came to him by sea.'

At last, however, the relieving army did arrive. It included 3,000 Jews under the Idumaian Antipatros, who on the news of Pharsalos had gone over to Caesar.

Mithridates, its general, was a man of mixed Greek and Gaulish parentage. He had laid claim to Armenia Minor, but the Senate had awarded it to the Galatian Deiotaros; perhaps anger at this decision had made him so ready to aid Caesar. He now crossed the desert from Palestine, stormed Pelousion, and entered Egypt; then he killed Dioskorides, who had advanced upon him in ambush.[39] Leaving a garrison at Pelousion, he followed the eastern (Pelousiac) branch of the Nile southward, probably moving over the marshy delta with its criss-crossing canals and streams. Josephos, who is mainly concerned to stress the role of Antipatros, mentions that that prince's influence brought about the surrender of groups of Jews encountered during the march (the Jews in the districts of Onias) and later of the Jews of Memphis. Mithridates fought a battle east of the Nile close to the Camp-of-the-Jews (now Tell-el-Iahoudieh, on the edge of the Arabian desert, 60,000 paces from Pelousion) where Onias IV had built a fortress and a temple for his Jewish Legion.[40] He won and Memphis fell. Then he crossed the Nile. Caesar had learned from a messenger of the approach of the relieving force; Ptolemy too knew of it. Both commanders set out, Caesar to join Mithridates, Ptolemy to crush him. Ptolemy used the boats he had on the Nile, but Caesar did not want a river battle. Mithridates could not have now been far off, for Caesar reached him quickly, sailing along the coast and landing west of Alexandria.

Our main sources, Josephos and Dion, mention only one battle fought by Mithridates. Josephos does so because he is only interested in showing that Antipatros played a crucial part in the campaign; he therefore deals solely with the first battle, though displacing it to the west bank of the Nile by a partial conflation with the second battle. Dion in his account is writing concisely; so he mentions only the major battle. This also is the action that interests Hirtius.

Hirtius says a narrow stream flowed into the Nile between Ptolemy's camp and the road along which Caesar advanced, at a distance of some seven miles from that camp. It may have been any of the countless canals or irrigation systems running into the Kanopic Nile. Dion, however, gives us a clue. Mithridates, he says, when he called on Caesar's aid, was in a tight corner in the vicinity of the Lake (Mareotis) between the river and a swamp. We can thus set the battle north of the lake, between the Nile and a marsh, and near enough to Alexandria for Caesar to march back there in one day and capture the city.

Ptolemy's cavalry, with a selected body of light-armed troops, at first managed to prevent Caesar from crossing the stream, which had very steep banks. Hirtius brings the scene up clearly before us. 'Our men, horse and foot, were badly mortified at the Alexandrians holding their ground so long against attack. Some of the German cavalry dispersed to look for a ford and managed to swim the river where the banks were lowest. At the same time the legionaries cut down several large trees, which reached across from one bank to the other, and soon heaped up a mound. Thus they got over. The enemy were so scared of their attack they took to their heels—vainly, for very few got back to the king. Almost the whole lot were cut to pieces in the pursuit. Caesar then advanced on the camp, which was well entrenched and ramparted. As the troops were tired, he camped near. Next day he attacked the fort in a village connected with the royal camp. Into the assault he put almost his entire force, so that they might follow up the panicked defenders falling back on the main camp, which was in a flurry of alarm. The attack could not be launched along the plain where the enemy were massed, or by a narrow pass between the camp and the Nile, from which the Alexandrians could harass the attackers by arrows and slingstones from both shore and riverboats. Caesar was held up, then noted that the topmost part of the camp was left unguarded. He ordered some cohorts to wheel round the camp' under Carfulenus, 'and assault the high part. The cohorts gained this point, then from several quarters rushed down into the camp. The Alexandrians, struggling to escape, threw themselves over the rampart in the section near the river. The first group tumbled into the ditch and were trampled into a causeway for the others. The king got away on to a boat, but so many fugitives crowded aboard that it sank and he was drowned.'

Caesar lost no time, marching back the same day to Alexandria. The citizens, dismayed at the news, made no resistance. They came as suppliants, 'preceded by all those sacred symbols of religion with which they were accustomed to mollify their offended kings'. Caesar confirmed Cleopatra in her power, but, doubtless to her annoyance, appointed the younger Ptolemy (XIV) as her consort. Hirtius remarks that she 'had all this while continued under his protection and guardianship', and suggests that he went off almost at once with the 6th Legion to Syria. 'He left the rest in Egypt to support the authority of the king and queen, neither of whom stood well in the affections of their subject on account of their attachment to

Caesar; nor could they be expected to have any firm foundation for their power in an administration existing for no more than a few days. It was also to the honour and interest of the Republic that if they went on being faithful, our forces should protect; or if ungrateful, they should be checked by the same power. After thus settling the kingdom, he marched by land into Syria.'

Three legions were left under the able command of Rufinus, son of a freedman. Such tasks were normally given to senators.[41] Caesar was perhaps showing his disregard of convention and was snubbing the Senate; but he may well have been also foreshadowing the later imperial policy that no man of importance should control such a land as Egypt and be tempted to use its resources for his own purposes. Ptolemy XIII had been got rid of, whether or not that had been the deliberate aim of his release; Caesar could hope for a trustworthy ally in Cleopatra, with the sources of discord eliminated from the royal family. Arsinoe, Hirtius says, was exiled; later she was made to walk in chains in the Triumph at Rome, behind Caesar's chariot. Cleopatra had certainly come well out of the war; and in her hatred of Arsinoe she must have exulted at the thought of her proud young sister humiliated in the streets of Rome. But in her own last days the image must have returned, now a thing of fear and shame, convincing her that death was better than surrender to the will of a Roman victor.

Ancient historians, dealing with this small but difficult war, saw for the most part only that Caesar acted through love for Cleopatra and thus fell into dishonour and dangers; the participant who wrote the *Bellum Alexandrinium* ignored all the problems. But it is extremely unlikely that Caesar was at any point swayed by emotion. He got himself into a fix at Alexandria before Cleopatra appeared on the scene at all. Then, finding that his furious pursuit of Pompey had involved him in unforeseen perils, he felt that he must trust his good luck and his quick grasp of situations to settle things without any ignominious retreat. As a result he learned to know and estimate Cleopatra, and decided that she was the right person to rule Egypt after all intriguing brothers and sisters had been disposed of. The brother with whom she was now associated was only about eleven, and she could surely manage him without political crises. As for Cleopatra, with the intimacy and understanding she had now established with Caesar, she must have felt that there was now a solid basis for her dreams of re-establishing Ptolemaic rule in Egypt and of reviving her line's past glories.

Caesar, with the winter gone, had to give his mind to consolidating his victory of Pharsalos. The Pompeians were gathering in Africa and Spain; street fights were going on in Rome and other towns of Italy; there was unrest among his legions in Italy which Antony, his representative, couldn't altogether allay; in Asia Minor, Pharnakes, son of the great Mithridates, had defeated a Roman army. At Rome there had been no news of Caesar for three months, and in such a situation rumours of all sorts proliferated.

The tales that he lingered amorously with Cleopatra are false. He did not stay till June (April in the Julian calendar), but left Alexandria two weeks after the battle, about 10 April (28 January) 47. No doubt he needed those two weeks to make a minimal amount of settlements

and dispositions.[42] Naturally Cleopatra made the most
of the time, providing gay festivals for the victor and
taking him along the Nile for some distance on a state-
barge. The Ptolemies had had a liking for big structures.
The barge in this instance was some 300 feet long, 45 feet
wide across the beam, and 60 feet high. Caesar had a
chance to get a glimpse of the Egyptian agricultural and
administrative systems. Ancient writers mostly do not
dwell on the two weeks after the war; we can perhaps
recognise the censoring hand of Augustus, who did not
want his 'father' associated with Cleopatra. However,
Suetonius gives us the dalliance-tradition. 'His greatest
favourite was Cleopatra, with whom he often revelled all
night till the dawn of day, and would have gone with her
through Egypt in dalliance, as far as Aethiopia, in her
luxury-yacht, had not the army refused to follow him.'

After the battle Caesar had had a search made for the
body of Ptolemy XIII. He knew that the Egyptians looked
on the Nile-drowned as Blessed in Osiris, and he wanted
no tales of the youth's survival to go round.[43] At last the
body was found in the mud, and the gold armour was put
on public view. On leaving Egypt Caesar marched rapidly
through Syria to Asia Minor. On 2 August (20 May) 47 at
Zela in Pontos he smashed the army of Pharnakes in a
battle lasting less than four hours. 'I came, I saw, I
conquered.' The strategic speed and skill he showed was a
token of what he was to do in breaking up the Pompeian
armies in Africa and Spain.[44]

Cleopatra and Caesar

We now come up against one of the many baffling problems in Cleopatra's life. Did she become with child by Caesar in their first encounter? It is often confidently stated that on 23 Pauni (23 June) 47 she bore a son to Caesar; but the matter is by no means sure or clear. Some historians indeed have denied that she bore a son to Caesar at all; others that the birth occurred in 44. We find no guidance of an unequivocal kind in any ancient writer; after the conflicts broke out between Antony and Octavian, propagandists were liable to say anything that suited their aims. At that time Octavian was basing his whole claim to political importance on the declaration that he was Caesar's heir and that Caesar was his adoptive father; it was therefore of the utmost importance for him to deny that Caesar had any sons of his own body, even illegitimate ones, as, in Roman law, any son borne to him by Cleopatra would be. The matter can thus be best discussed when we come to the year 44, and for the moment we shall leave it.

What is certain is that Cleopatra kept in continual touch

with Caesar till his death, that he felt warmly and strongly towards her, and that she soon followed him to Rome, where she lived for two years, or parts of them, in his Gardens across the Tiber. Here we may cite only one document: a grave inscription in demotic, Year Five, which calls 23 Pauni 47 a Feastday of Isis and Birthday of the King Caesar.[1] The king there would certainly seem to be the boy who was later called Caesarion, Little Caesar, and whom Cleopatra claimed to be Caesar's son. The identification has been denied on the flimsy and formal grounds that the child could not be thus addressed as king. But if the Piper's subjects could describe his children as gods, it seems unlikely that in a casual inscription a royal child, especially if the father was Caesar, might not be called king.

The connection with an Isis Festival is also not without significance. Cleopatra was worshipped as Isis, and she herself linked Caesarion with Horos. Coins struck in the now reunited Cyprus (though without a definite date) show her as Aphrodite-Isis holding Caesarion as Horos-Eros at her breast. The reverses depict the Ptolemaic cornucopia as emblem of the new age which she now feels confident of bringing about. In late Pharaonic times the pharaoh as Amun's son had his divine birth represented in detail as a ritual drama on temple-walls. Amun is shown as the king visiting the queen; after the birth the child is brought to the god who takes him into his arms and greets him as Horos; the babe is then suckled by cowheaded Hathor, by Isis, or by a Cow. In ancient times perhaps the king dressed up as Amun to copulate with his wife, and priests and priestesses wore masks and insignia to mime the divine beings considered present. Whether the

Ptolemies performed a birth-mime is doubtful; but it is of interest that later the Roman emperor Gaius, who cast back to Antony and Cleopatra, tried to make the birth of his girl Drusilla divine; he had her brought to Jupiter's Capitol Temple and placed her on the god's knees as if she were his child, then handed her over to Minerva for suckling. The Ptolemies, however, at least kept the imagery alive, not merely on temple-walls and in single rooms; they built special birth-temples, for which the Coptic term *Mammisi* (Birthplace) has been used. These annexes of the late period to the great sanctuaries were used for a yearly ritual representing the birth of the divine child; the best preserved are at Philai, Edfu, and Dendera, which are all architecturally alike. They show a peristyle enclosed to half its height by intercolumnar walls; on the abaci and the propylaea are reliefs showing gay and musical scenes, while the inner walls illustrate the divine marriage and the birth of the baby king. The child is always called Horos, without reference to an actual Ptolemy. It was in the birthtemple at Hermonthis near Thebes that Cleopatra had the birth of Caesarion depicted. That birth is set beside the birth of Horos, so that the principle of a purely symbolic representation is given up. She kneels in person, attended by goddesses; above her is her new name, Mother of Re (Sungod), in hieroglyphics; over the child stands the scarab to define him as the Rising Sun; on a couch apart sit two cowheaded goddesses suckling two babies, Horos and Caesarion. Not only is Amun-Re and the goddess Mut shown, but Cleopatra herself appears. The earthly counterpart of Re here would be Caesar, who, as the *de facto* ruler of Egypt, was the queen's consort in native eyes.[2]

In calling herself Isis, Cleopatra was not innovating. Cleopatra III had had priesthoods in her honour added to the eponymous priesthoods of the State-cult (whose names were used for dating purposes). After Ptolemy VI scribes used a shortened formula in Greek documents, but a demotic text of 112–1 B.C. shows four such priests who seem certainly hers. In the case of the first priesthood she is called, not by her own name, but 'Isis Great Mother of the Gods' (she had been mother of two godkings, Ptolemies IX and X); and the priest is called the Holy Foal—apparently because the name Foal, *polos*, is found for a priestess of Demeter in Greece, and in Egypt Demeter was at times identified with Isis. In the case of the other three priesthoods Cleopatra is called by her own official names, Cleopatra Motherloving Saviouress, and is served by priestesses called Wreathbearer, Firebearer, and Priestess, *hiereia*. A fifth priesthood of hers appears in a text of 112–8, with the name Lightbearer.[3]

For the king as Horos we may take a trilingual *stēlē* of Ptolemy IV found at Pithom, which records a resolution passed by a synod of Egyptian priests at Memphis in November 217 after his victory in Syria. It is dated 'in the 6th Year of the Young Horos, the Strong One, whom his Father caused to be manifested as King, Lord of the Asp Crowns . . . the Living Image of Amun, King Ptlumis [Ptolemy], Living for Ever, Beloved of Isis'. The *stēlē* also calls him 'the Avenger of his Father', a term commonly used for Horos, who avenged and justified his Father Osiris. (The phrase may have gained a new force for Caesarion after the murder of Caesar.) We also read, 'He arrived in Egypt on the Feast of Lamps, the Birthday of Horos', 12 October.[4]

But whether or not Cleopatra had already borne Caesar a son, he let her come to Rome in the summer of 46. She must have been working hard over the previous year to get her kingdom under control, make the administration effective, and conciliate her people. However anxious to see Caesar and renew her relations with him, she would not have been so stupid as to leave Egypt unless she were assured that there would be no troubles in her absence. And we hear of none. True, much of the spirit of resistance must have been shattered by the failure of the Alexandrian War and by the firm measures taken after it by Caesar; but there is good evidence that Cleopatra built up a considerable amount of goodwill in her kingdom before her death. Now that she was freed from the need to fight a daily battle of cabals in the palace, she was able to give full attention to administrative problems. Her young brother-husband she took with her to ensure that there was no revival of court intrigues while she was afar.

We know very little of her life in Rome. Dion says that Caesar 'incurred the greatest censure of all through his passion [*eros*] for Cleopatra: not what he had shown in Egypt, which was a mere matter of hearsay, but what was evident in Rome itself. For she had come to the City with her husband and settled in Caesar's own house, so that he too derived an ill repute on account of the pair. However, he was not at all concerned, but actually enrolled her among the Friends and Allies of the Roman People.'[5] So little was known of her residence in the capital that Suetonius, well read as he was in the byways of gossip and scandal, seems not to have known she was still there when Caesar was killed. 'He afterwards invited her to Rome, whence he sent her back loaded with honours and gifts, and gave her permission to call by his name a son, who, according to the testimony of some Greek historians, resembled Caesar in person and gait.'[16] It is possible that she broke her stay with a short home-visit to Alexandria in, say, summer 45, and that Suetonius did not know she came back to Rome. In any event it seems clear that Augustus managed to censor the accounts of Caesar's close relations with Cleopatra; and the paucity of information has led some writers to argue that he called her to Rome in order to have her under observation and to keep her well in the rear of his projected Parthian war. But that is hardly convincing. Caesar did not act in that sort of way, and there was no reason for him to fear treason from her when he fought the Parthians. He kept her at Rome, and in such a provocative way, only because he wanted here there.

True, he had his own wife Calpurnia at hand; but he was not faithful either to her or to Cleopatra. During his campaign of 46–5 he seduced Eunoe wife of Bogud, king of Mauretania. Also he was absent from Rome for long periods. In November 46 he was on his way to Spain and did not return till September 45: this was the interval during which Cleopatra may well have gone back for a while to Egypt. But he must have had strong reasons for summoning her to Rome and keeping her there so long. When we recall the suspicions, antagonisms, dire hatreds which surrounded him, especially among the big land-lords of the Senate, we cannot believe that he would have given his enemies such gratuitous cause for vicious gossip and insinuation as he did by keeping an eastern queen in his own Gardens, unless he had a powerful motive for his action. For a general to seduce a queen during a campaign

was an amusing peccadillo; to bring her to Rome was to
flout every possible moral and political convention. For a
man who in effect was now dictator of the Roman world
and whom his adversaries suspected of aiming at kingship, such a step was highly challenging and dangerous.
Foreign kings were no strangers at Rome; we have seen
how the Piper lingered there with his pleas and his
bribery-operations. But that was when they had clear
political reasons for their visit; and no such reason could
be adduced to cover up Cleopatra's presence. After the
Triumph of September (July) 46, she and Egypt must
have been objects of special interest. The people had seen
the princess Arsinoe led in chains; they had seen a large
statue of the Nile and pictures of the Pharos Lighthouse,
one of the world's seven wonders, and of the deaths of
Potheinos and Achillas. And we can be sure that the
soldiers marching jovially behind Caesar had taken the
chance of enlivening the scene by lewd songs about
Cleopatra in the style of the songs we know they sang at
others of his Triumphs:

> Shut up your wives, you men of Rome.
> We bring the baldhead lecher home.
> Your gold in Gaul you fucked away.
> So you come to borrow more today.

And, in reference to a libellous tale that when younger he
had submitted to the embraces of the King of Bithynia:

> Nicomedes bowed down Caesar
> who had forced the Gauls to bow.
> Caesar bowed down all the Gauls
> and gets his Triumph now,
> Nicomedes gets no Triumph
> though he made our Caesar bow.[7]

Table 2 M.ANTONIUS

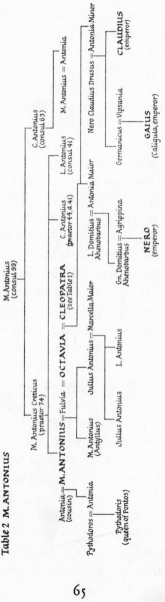

It seems unlikely that on this day of licence the bold-tongued legionaries would not have had songs about goings-on with Cleopatra.

Coins and statues give us a good idea of what Caesar looked like at this time. Some Greek coins tended to idealise, for instance on an issue of Nikaia, Bithynia, in 48–7, though even here we find touches of realism such as the long thin neck. On Roman coins, however, we expect Italian verism, and we find it. On one of the *Parens Patriae* coins, minted probably a month or so before his death, a profuse laurel wreath and forwards-combed locks attempt to hide the baldness; the massive brow is wrinkled; eyes are large with crowsfeet at the corners; the nose long and pointed; the head out thrust over the long scraggy neck with a pronounced adam's-apple; the cheeks sunken with deep creases and the chin-bones clear. After his death this strong unflattering version began to be modified; the head was made more monumental, and we even get touches of idealisation (as on a bronze from Gaul of 38). Of portraits, the head found at Tusculum (now at Turin) may have been made during his lifetime, or at least not long after; it shows less emaciation than many coins, and the characteristic features are lighted by an ironic smile. In profile it shows the hump at the top of the head. The Museo Torloni has what seems a Julio-Claudian copy, in which we see the Clement Caesar. Sculptors continued to use the genuine features, but in terms of a more balanced and monumental construction. As time went on (*e.g.* by the Trajanic period), Caesar was made into a symbol of sheer power in a colossal statue, while on coins he assumes a solid Vespasianic look.[8]

Suetonius gives us a detailed portrait. 'He was tall, it is

said, fair-complexioned, rather fullfaced, with dark piercing eyes; he enjoyed excellent health except near the close of his life, when he was given to sudden fainting-fits and disturbed sleep. Twice on active service he was seized by the falling-sickness. So nice was he in the care of his person that he not only kept the hair on his head close-cut and had his face smoothly shaved, but even had the hair on the rest of his body plucked out by the roots, a practice on which some persons rallied him. His baldness gave him much uneasiness through the many jibes of his enemies about it. So he used to bring forward the hair from the crown of his head; and of all the honours conferred on him by Senate and People there was none he accepted or used with more pleasure than the right of constantly wearing a laurel crown.' It is said he was particular in his dress. He used the *latus clavus* (a broad purple stripe in the toga's front), 'with fringes about the wrists, and always had it girded about him, but rather loosely. This habit gave rise to the expression of Sulla, who often advised the nobles to beware of "the ill-girt boy".'[9] The story of Sulla was no doubt an invention made up in Caesar's later days, but it truly enough shows how the ancients associated carelessness or oddity of dress with political discontent and rebellion.

At the triumphal celebrations he had dedicated the Forum Julium, built at great cost; in the midst of the open square there rose the temple to Venus Genetrix, Venus as the ancestress of the Julian *gens*, and beside the cult-image he set a golden statue of Cleopatra. When we recall that it was about this time, it seems, that Cleopatra was issuing Cyprian coins of herself as Isis-Aphrodite, there appears to be a definite intention in this dedication.

Caesar's procedure had its precedents in Egypt and other Hellenistic kingdoms, where it possessed a clear political and religious meaning. The Ptolemies and their wives had long been received into the sanctuaries as *synnaioi*, shrine-sharers; but in Republican Rome such an act was unprecedented. Caesar must have felt a close sympathy with Cleopatra to have thus gone out of his way to supply material of abuse to his opponents who wanted to make him appear an aspirant to kingship.[10]

Isis, we may note, was popular at Rome among the common folk, though her cult was now and then suppressed by the Senate. As for the link with Aphrodite (as Isis), there was already at Oxyrhynchos, in the reign of the Piper and Cleopatra Tryphaina, a Street of Cleopatra Aphrodite. We meet it in a lease of 73 B.C. and again in one of 44.[11]

Certainly Cleopatra would have encouraged Caesar in such acts as the gold statue. She would have considered that the only sensible thing was to convert Rome and its provinces into an Hellenistic kingdom brought up to date, making use of all the experiences of Egyptian bureaucracy and enshrining the ruler in a divine glow. But she was too shrewd to try to force Caesar along any such line faster than he was ready to go. She must early have discovered just how far she could push him and that his general ideas were merged with a clear realistic sense of just what was possible at any given moment. No doubt she often disagreed with him as to where that limit of possibility lay, but found that she could not budge him. One result of his murder is that we are left guessing as to what his ultimate plans were. Most likely he did not know himself. He knew however that there could be no return

to the old Republic dominated by a small group of arrogant and callous landlords; he knew that the imperial
expansion had created a new set of responsibilities which
the Senate could never shoulder, and that the provincials
must be steadily admitted to rights which the Senate
wanted jealously to conserve; he knew that the landless
peasants, now to a considerable degree gathered in the
legions, must be settled, and so on. But he had no crude
ambitions to become a dictatorial ruler, though at the same
time he could not see what forms might be evolved to
harmonise a maximum of possible freedoms with the
centralised controls necessary to hold the empire together
and make it effectively function. He may well have been
very interested in the Ptolemaic system without feeling
that it could in any simple way be imposed on Rome and
its provinces.[12]

If this view is correct, we can understand why he would
have found Cleopatra's views relevant and important
without accepting them in anything like their totality.
And he may well have felt that her mixture of feminine
charm and acute intelligence provided both relaxation and
stimulus for his leisure moments, when he turned from
the tasks immediate to his hands. His Gardens would have
given him a delightful setting for such intercourse. We
know only their general location, but may assume that
they were of the usual Roman type, in which lines of large
trees, especially planes, were set in regular order. Cypresses
too were much liked. The plane, imported from Greece,
was an emblem of unproductive leisure: 'unmarried',
'barren', 'widowed', 'giving shade to drinkers', and was
contrasted with the 'useful' elm, on which vines could be
trained.[13] There were alleys or walks of clipt yew-hedges;

the clipping art seems largely developed by C. Matius under Augustus, but ornamental gardening, *topiaria*, was certainly already well known. Other shrubs were box, laurel, bay, myrtle; and among fruit-trees were the peach and the cherry (recently brought in by Lucullus from Asia Minor). Amid beds of acanthus, rows of trees and vines, stood statues, pyramids, summerhouses, and fountains. Water indeed was an essential ingredient, water in fountain, *nymphaeum*, or artificial channel, for its glitter, its bright murmuring movement, its evocation of coolness and living nymph-presences.[14] Porticoes provided shelter from rain, as well as underground passages or a covered passage with windows. Flowerbeds of varying shapes might be bordered with shrubs or raised as terraces, the slopes planted with creepers or evergreens. The main flowers were roses and violets, but there were also lilies, crocuses, narcissi, gladioli, irises, poppies, amaranth and others. After Caesar's Gardens were bequeathed to the people, Augustus constructed a lake of some fifty acres which was used for naval displays. This fact gives us some idea of how extensive the Gardens were.

Indeed Caesar himself may also have dug there a lake for naval displays. Suetonius tells us, 'a lake was dug in the Lesser Codeta, and ships of the Tyrian and Egyptian fleets, with two, three, and four banks of oars, with a number of men on board, gave an animated representation of a seafight'. We may take this show to have been given at the time of Caesar's Alexandrian Triumph. *Codeta* means a meadow with mares-tail growing in it; and it seems significant that the site which Augustus chose in A.D. 2, at the time of his dedication of the temple of Mars Ultor was called Codeta Major. Codeta Minor has been taken to lie in the Campus Martius, or near it; but there is no proof of its location. Both the larger and lesser fields of mares-tail may have been in the same general region. Augustus tells us in his *Res Gestae* or *Achievements*: 'I produced a naval battle as a show for the people at the place across the Tiber now occupied by the Grove of the Caesars, where a site 1,800 feet long and 1,200 broad was excavated; there 30 beaked triremes or biremes and still more smaller vessels were joined in battle; about 3,000 men, besides the rowers, fought in these fleets.' Clearly it was an important event for him; he gives full details as he does for no other such matter in his account of his achievements. The battle of Actium was now some thirty-three years past; but he must have had in mind the great sea battle when, in his view, he proved himself the Son of the Divine One, the Avenging Mars of his 'Father'. (If this is so, he saw the crushing of Antony as the final act of retribution, though in the years after Caesar's death it was Antony who had been for the veterans the Mars Ultor of the murdered hero.) The parallelism between Caesar's 'Egyptian' sea battle and the Augustan show of the supreme sea battle, which 'avenged Caesar' and ended the Civil Wars, is too strong to be accidental. Since Cleopatra had lived in what Augustus calls the Groves of the Caesars, the setting would provide an added point of satisfaction. Whether she was at Rome during Caesar's celebration of his Triumph we do not know.[15]

In any event she had a charming place of residence at Rome, secluded, and yet within easy reach of the city and its busy streets. The Gardens lay south west of the Pons Aemilius and the Via Aurelia, and of the Tiber Island;

along the Via Campana. At this time the region was not strictly part of Rome; Cicero says in a speech that there was no legal reason why a colony should not be planted on the Janiculan Hills, just as in any other part of Italy. Augustus, however, made the area the 14th Region, the Transtiburina; but even so the jurists went on making a distinction between Rome and the *Urbs*, the city proper.[16]

In Alexandria Caesar may have briefly listened to what the scholars at the Museum had to say on such matters as the Calendar; for the new system he now introduced was based on that of the Alexandrian Sosigenes. He himself had some acquaintance with mathematics and astronomy; and at least in his reform he paid a compliment to Alexandrian science. The Roman calendar was lunar in basis, 355 days in a year (the lunar year of 354 with one day added), and in eight years of this sort the year became 90 days ahead of the sun. So, every second year, an extra month was put in. Then in a four-year period they had years of 355, 377, 335, 378 days respectively, giving an average year of 366¼ days (one day too many). The intercalary month was inserted after the 23 or 24 February. But the insertions did not occur automatically; they had to be prefaced by a formal notice from the College of Pontiffs, who had charge of the calendar (from the early days when it had been a patrician secret). During the civil wars nothing was done, and in 46 the year was two and half months out. What was celebrated as New Year's Day should have been 14 October of the old year. Harvest festivals were being held long before corn or grapes were gathered in. The lunar system with its intercalations also had the disadvantage of creating uncertainties, as the announcement by the pontiffs was sometimes made at last moment. When Cicero left Rome for his province of Cilicia in 51, he was alarmed that 50 would be one of the lengthened years and thus keep him longer away from Italy. In Cilicia, four days before the extra month should have begun, he still did not know what the decision had been.

Caesar resolved to end this state of things. The year 46, 'the last year of confusion', had three intercalary months and lasted 445 days; the Julian calendar was introduced on 1 January 45. In its leap-years the additional day was inserted between 23 and 24 February. Caesar may have also been thinking of Alexandria when he worked out plans for a great library at Rome under the polymath Terrentius Varro.

We must now pause to look in more detail at the world that Caesar was trying to understand and reorganise; for this was also the world that Cleopatra later set herself to subdue. Rome had risen to its great political position, a single city-republic now dominating the whole Mediterranean world, in large part through the mixture of strenuous class-war with an overall conservative and controlling system that held things together. The result was a strong expansive drive without a fall into the deadlocking confusions and breakdowns that overcame the Greek cities with their class-struggles. The main expression of the element of solidarity appeared in the network of clientships, the *officia* of all kinds binding men of the same class and men of different classes. The middle class (the *equites*) and the *plebs* expressed discontent, unrest, and rebellion at various times; about 130 B.C. the class-struggles entered a violent and unslackening stage of tension; and yet even then, in the last resort, the over-riding controls and interlinkages held and prevented a lapse into chaos. The *equites* and *plebs* did not ever attempt a direct all-out challenge to the power of the senatorial class; they fought on particular issues, but did not try to take over the government. The important role of personal relations checked the effective growth of a bureaucratic State; the opposition could not even carry out with any lasting effect the reforms they forced through. Still, Catulus, who died in 60, was the last of what we may call the natural *principes*, the leaders accepted in many ways unquestioningly by the society as a whole.[17]

The last century of the Republic thus saw strong cleavages and the emergence of conflicting groups: the *Optimates* (the Best Men, the senators) against the *Populares* (the upholders of the interests of the commoners). Yet this opposition never led to anything like the consolidation of definite parties. The reality of the situation was a shifting skein of social and economic interests or attitudes, in which one man might be upheld by different political sections although those sections did not arrive at any coherent or lasting connection.[18] The city-populace under the Gracchi became the dynamic force compelling rapid change, but its role was shared by the army after the decisive change in its social basis through Marius. The Marian reforms brought in the Eagle, the symbol and palladium of the new soldier; religion cemented the new kind of loyalties. The men swore to obey their general and not desert the standards. Also generals, going back to Scipio in 134, recruited their own clients.[19] Recruiting at this time was at first rural, then came the proletarianisation of the legions. We may note the hostility of the folk of the small towns to the army and the disaffection of the upper classes. Caesar doubled the men's pay (though it was often in arrears). After 50 came a new type of legion raised wholly in the provinces. The post-Marian soldier depended more and more on the largesse of generals, on loot, on rewards or land after his retirement. Despite all the hardships and miseries of the peasants, conscription had to be often used.[20]

In the rapid extension of Roman rule and the resulting social dislocations, many men got rich quickly among the middle classes as well as among the senators who could plunder the provinces; and among the groups with an increasingly subversive outlook can be counted both the professional soldiers and many of the newly-wealthy. The latter category, however, was complex and needs careful analysis; the greed for money and land could lead to all sorts of subserviences or of connivances with disorder. In the Italian municipalities the leaders included both the new rich and the old landed aristocracy, of whom many were ready enough to take office in Rome. Recruits from these strata were to modify the composition of the governing class under Augustus and the Julio-Claudians.[21]

The debt-situation more than any other factor enables us to glimpse the social changes and the discontents provoked. The Gracchan settlers and the later veterans were nearly all displaced countrymen who wanted to get back to the land without the disadvantages they had previously suffered.[22] The Gracchan work had no lasting effect; it did not touch the causes of expropriation, which went on with increasing momentum. The governing class of landlords, by the nature of things, were quite unconcerned with the outcries of the suffering peasantry; they were the men who were causing the suffering. Cicero cites the radical Philippus, 'There are not in the State 2,000 men possessing property.' He does not contradict the fact but merely objects to it being made public. 'A dangerous speech, aiming at a levelling of property: what can be a greater mischief? For commonwealths were established mainly so that men might hold what was their own.' He has no sympathy with the peasants who wanted to 'hold what was their own' but were driven out by men of greater economic and political power.[23]

Land was the main source of wealth and power. By the 40s the persons claiming the corndole in Rome had risen to 300,000. Rural workers were drifting in all the while, but the crucial moment seems represented by Clodius' Frumentary Law of 58, which provided for a free corn-distribution monthly to the poorer citizens. The poor city-folk had to rely on casual jobs in trades like building or on the liberality and bribes of the great houses; commerce and industry could not have absorbed many of them. The urban *plebs* of the late Republic and early Principate seems largely of servile origin; by manumission employers could make the Treasury pay for the upkeep of their workers, since they used the system of *operae* to extort much the same work from freed men as from slaves. These latter had little if any interest in agrarian reform and were rarely called up into the army. Free peasants survived best in mountainous and infertile regions and lived precariously on harvestwork and the like, which was put out to contract. With the big estates, tenant-farmers were on the increase.[24] The urban *plebs* could be stirred up to riot but had no stomach for revolution. They deserted Catilina when the fighting began; he found his support, says Cicero, in 'peasants, poor and needy folk'.[25] Bad harvests or other mishaps brought on such men a crushing burden of debt; the choice was to abandon the land or revolt. A creditor could keep a defaulter in custody or even work him as bondsman.

It is easy for historians to assume that these peasants or peasant-soldiers, whose voices rarely reach us, did not care about constitutional or political issues and ideals, and thought only in narrowly personal terms. The ancient writers, with their aristocratic bias, inevitably took up a contemptuous attitude, which makes it all the easier for the moderns to follow much the same line. Appian's summing-up is typical: 'The armies were not drawn from enrolment according to ancestral custom nor for the country's benefit; they did not serve the public so much as the individuals who brought them together; they served these not by force of law but by reason of private promises; not against a common enemy but against private foes; not against foreigners but against fellow-citizens their equals in status. All these things weakened discipline and the soldiers thought they were not so much serving in an army as giving aid by favour and judgement to leaders who needed them for personal ends. Desertion, formerly unpardonable, was now actually rewarded with gifts, and whole armies made a habit of it, including some illustrious men who did not consider it desertion to change over to a similar cause. For all parties were alike: none could be distinguished as battling against the common enemy of the Roman People. The familiar pretence of the generals that they were all striving for the good of the country made desertion easy through the consideration that a man could serve his country in any party. Understanding these facts, the generals tolerated the behaviour. They knew their own authority over the armies depended on donatives rather than on law.'[26]

All that has an element of truth; but in stating that 'all parties were alike' it simply ignores the nature of the deep conflicts going on, and it fails to note how the men's awareness that they were 'giving aid by favour and judgement' must have involved much thought and argument among them. Indeed the parties would not have so consistently and passionately poured out propaganda, and sought at all costs to prove their cause's justice, if such matters were of slight importance, if hope of gain and donatives was the determining factor. Clearly the common soldiers in their own ways struggled to understand and make sense of the events hurrying them along; perhaps they did so more persistently and honestly than their lords and masters. At Pharsalos, Caesar tells us that he had in his army 'a volunteer named Cratinus, who had been first centurion of the 10th Legion the previous year, a man of outstanding courage'. When the signal was given, he cried, 'Follow me, old comrades, and fight as hard for your general as you've made up your minds to do. This is our last battle. When it's won he'll recover his *dignitas* and we our liberty.' At the same time he looked back at Caesar and cried, 'General, I'll act today so that you'll be grateful to me living or dead.' Then he charged first on the right wing and some 120 selected volunteers of the same century followed him.[27] Later he was killed with a sword in his mouth. We can feel Caesar's own emotion in the account; he responded to these men and they responded to him. In their mouths the terms *dignitas* and *libertas* had a fresh and strong meaning. They were tough characters who had their own ideas and did not hesitate to answer the generals back. Caesar records how, early in the Civil War, in Spain, he refused to attack despite the complaints of his men, and again under his restrained prose we feel his admiration for the men he led. 'Caesar had hopes of ending the matter without an engagement, without a blow, as he'd cut off the enemy's supplies. Why hazard the loss of any of his men, even in a successful battle? why expose soldiers to wounds when they'd deserved so well of him? why, in short, tempt fortune, especially when it's a general's duty to conquer by tactics as much as by the sword. Besides, he felt compassion for those citizens whom he foresaw must fall. But this decision of his was not generally approved. The soldiers openly declared to one another that since such a chance of victory was let slip, they wouldn't come to an engagement even when Caesar wanted it.'[28] Caesar is certainly advertising there his *clementia*: which he had a right to do, since it was a genuine quality of his. But if he had wanted only to do that, he could have stated that his concern for his men's lives evoked their gratitude. Instead, he gives us the facts of their rough response.

As we go on, we shall see how often the soldiers played a decisive part in the conflicts between Antony and Octavian. An uglier aspect of the situation, however, came out in many episodes of bad behaviour. Cicero says that the entry of soldiers into a city of the provinces was not much different from an assault by the enemy. Caesar tried to spare Italy from looting and punished looters; even in the provinces he was scrupulous and, if he had to raise money, preferred to impose fines.[29] After his death, in the winter of 43–2 the Italian towns suffered from the

soldiers quartered on them; they had to provide free
board and put up with much rapine. The poor got the
worst of things. Jurists discussed the liability as between
landlord and tenant if passing armies carried things away,
or if, for example, the tenant fled from nearing soldiers
and removed window-frames and everything else from a
farmhouse.[30]

Sometimes the soldiers showed little sense of sympathy
for their fellow-peasants; but they could feel strongly for
other soldiers. Thus, in 41, 'They killed many of the
centurions and others who were partisans of Caesar'
(Octavian), 'and were trying to check them from riot.
Indeed they came near to killing him himself, making any
excuse serve their anger. And they didn't halt their agitation till their own relatives and the fathers and sons of
men fallen in battle had had restored all the land that any
of them had owned'.[31] As the civil wars worsened, each
side vied in offers to the soldiery of money or land. For
some time men had often settled in provinces where they
served, apparently buying land or just grabbing it. But
such behaviour was not so easy in Italy, with a Senate of
landowners watching the situation. Hence continual
conflict between the great generals and the Senate.[32]
When Caesar was murdered, one of the main fears working on the soldiers was that any regaining of power by the
Senate would jeopardise the land-allocations.

In estimating the revolutionary spur created by the
debt-situation, we must not forget how harsh were the
laws of debt and bankruptcy. Not only the lower classes
were involved.[33] The upper classes carried out public
services which were formally unpaid, and this incurred
heavy expenses. The cost grew worse as one went up the

scale. Yearly the temptation for the great men to gain money by illegal or dubious means increased. There was a huge influx of wealth into their houses, but they needed ever more to keep up their position, to make the necessary displays, to pay for the extravagant aedilician and other games, to carry out the corruption and bribery which their careers entailed. Laws against *ambitus*, electoral bribery, proliferated. A politician might try to make use of them against a rival; but they did not affect the situation. The great men had to borrow in a big way; especially at the start of his career a man of the senatorial class was often badly in debt; he had many chances of recouping as he advanced, but he had to face many risks. To fail in his obligations meant disaster; a senator needed both *existimatio* and *fides*, a good name and credit. The civil wars brought about a steadily worsening crisis in credit, helped by the political insecurity and the shortage of coin, a shortage caused in part by hoarding but also by the fact that there simply was not enough money in circulation. The crisis grew sharper through the problems of how to pay the vast armies. Estates fell in value. To sell on a falling market was to find oneself in a much worsened situation. Hence many rich men as well as poor felt the need to stake everything on social change, even on revolution. Once the open clash came, only the winners could hope to recoup themselves. Caesar found the question of debt a crucial one and took various alleviating measures; he himself had been pushed into a radical position by the weight of his own debts.[34] Debt lay at the heart of the civil wars, though not in any obvious way of a division between debtors and creditors. However, we may say that the senatorial side in general, the side of the big landowners, was the class that most profited from the situation, buying up or taking over land, and thus directly and indirectly crushing many debtors. How large the estates could be is shown by the fact that Pompey had so much influence in Picenum, with his land-holdings, that he could raise a private army in 83 in aid of Sulla; and Caesar tells us that L. Domitius Ahenobarbus, Cato's brother-in-law, owned such wide areas round Corfinium (north of Sulmona) that he could promise his levies 25 acres a man—and he had further estates on the Etruscan coast round Cosa, from which he took slaves, freedmen and tenants to man his warships.

To all extensions of privilege in any broad or significant way the senators or *optimates* put up a fanatical resistance, resorting to a dictatorship of murder if their position was seriously threatened in a constitutional way. Vatinius described them as a *natio*, tribe or race, which in such a context has much the same meaning as *factio* or *conspiratio*, faction or conspiratorial group: a set organised to resist the common interest by open or covert means.[35] Cicero tried to argue back that they were not a sectarian gang but the whole Roman People minus the Wicked (the property-less). There have always been, he said, two sorts of men seeking distinction in politics, the *populares* and *optimates*; the former in word and deed curry favour with the mob, the latter act so as to gain the approval of each best man (that is, their own class); they seek only *cum dignitate otium*, leisure with dignity.[36] In fact, as we noted, ever since the Gracchan threat to senatorial power, the *optimates* had had only one reply to any serious constitutional challenge: suspend the constitution and murder the popular leaders. Ever since Sulla they had drawn

horrific pictures of the 'demagogues', with the moral:
Kill them quickly. Cicero with all his bland constitutional
talk was one of the worst of them. His only solution was:
Kill them—as with Catilina, with Pompey, Caesar and
Crassus in the early days of their association, with
Antony after Caesar's murder. Caesar like all the popular
leaders since the Gracchi had had to go over the heads of
the Senate to the People; this was his unforgivable crime
in the eyes of the *optimates*, of men like Cicero.[37]

Part of the expansive dynamic of the Romans had come
from the concentration of power at Rome. They never
sought to work out systems of leagues, amphictyonies,
koinai, like the Greeks. They had no theory about it at all,
only a fierce sense of property and power; but if put to it,
they could have argued that the Greeks never made their
leagues truly effective and in fact had to fall back on the
kingship in order to develop large-scale political forms.
The *optimates* detested the kingship since it meant some
kind of control over their property and power; they
preferred to work through the Senate as a sort of ruling-
class committee. Now they were in a rage at Caesar's
admission of many of his partisans, often men of humble
origin, into that exclusive committee. Slogans were posted
on the walls: 'Good idea: nobody show a new senator the
way to the Senate House.' Verses were repeated:

Caesar led the Gauls in Triumph through the town,
Now in the Senate they drop their breeches down
and don instead the patrician gown—[38]

the *latus clavus*. When Fabius Maximus entered the theatre
for the first time as consul and his lictor demanded silence,
the audience yelled that he was no consul. Cicero in his

letters gives us the sort of bitter witticisms exchanged among the *optimates*. 'Tomorrow the Lyre [constellation] will rise.' 'Yes, by Edict.' (He is thinking of Caesar's new calendar.) Caesar had so many duties that he was not accessible, even to the *optimates*, as custom required of leading citizens. Once Cicero had to wait a long time before being admitted, and consoled himself by believing that Caesar had said, 'Can I doubt I am utterly detested when M. Cicero has to sit there and can't speak to me at his pleasure? And if anybody's easy-going, he is. I'm sure he hates me thoroughly.' In fact Caesar was growing ever more careless of forms which he felt to be meaningless and out of date. In October 45, on his return from Spain, he dropped the punctilio of earlier Triumphs, which pretended that the defeated armies had not been Roman.[39]

On the last day of 45, while he was presiding over the election of quaestors in the Comitia Tributa, news came that one of the conuls had died. He broke every precedent by appointing Caninius Rebilus consul for less than a day. Cicero records the incredible event, which had happened after lunch-time, and tries to joke.

'So I'd have you know that in the consulship of Caninius nobody had lunch. Still nothing wrong happened while he was consul. So marvellously wideawake was he during the whole of his office he never once went to sleep. All very funny, you think. Yes, because you're not here. If you were an eye-witness, you wouldn't hold back your tears. What if I tell you all the rest? There are countless cases of this sort and it'd be more than I could bear if I hadn't taken refuge in philosophy's haven . . .'[40]

One way in which senatorial discontent found an outlet

was in a cult of Cato as a sort of Republican Saint. He had dutifully committed suicide after being defeated at Utica; and now eulogies on him and his end were composed. M. Brutus wrote a funeral oration. Hirtius replied for the Caesarians; then Caesar was sufficiently irritated to publish an *Anti-Cato*, in which he attacked the saint for his personal vices such as drunkenness and meanness. Cicero weakly told Caesar that he liked the work, then wrote to one of the eulogists, 'Hold your hand, the Schoolmaster will be back sooner than we thought; I'm afraid we admirers of Cato are for the Lower World.' But Caesar was not the man to suppress such writings or their authors.[41]

The Cato-cult however had considerable effect on Brutus, who was haunted by the thought that he was descended from two great enemies of tyranny.[42] At the age of seven he had lost his father and had owed much of his upbringing to Cato, the half-brother of his mother Servilia. When Cato died, he left a son and a daughter, Porcia, who had been widowed in early 48 with one son. Brutus, on his return to Rome in the summer of 45, divorced his wife Claudia for no apparent reason except his wish to ally himself with Cato's family. Annoying his strong-minded mother, he married Porcia and became in effect guardian of Cato's grandson.[43] Meanwhile Cicero kept discontent alive by dropping murder-hints. The definite plans for action seem to have come from both Brutus (a Stoic) and Cassius (an Epicurean) also of tyrant-killing stock. Later, Antony said that Brutus was the only one who murdered from motives of principle[44]; certainly he provided the solid and respectable basis that made the conspiracy possible.

The *optimates* were sure that Caesar meant to set up a

kind of Hellenistic kingship; and they were at least right in their interpretation of the trend of events. Caesar did not, it seems, want to be a king, but circumstances made it impossible for him to relinquish power without allowing a general return to the old system of big landlords in complete control. If he had been left alive to carry on, the resulting imperial state might well have been much more based on the interests of the provincials, the small producers in Italy and elsewhere, the dispossessed farmers turned soldiers, the citizens of the small towns, and the like, than did the Augustan settlement, which gave as much power back to the big landlords as was commensurate with the secure rule of the *princeps*. Thus, though the murderers of Caesar brought many disasters on themselves and their class during the civil wars they provoked, they did perhaps ensure that the final point of rest was rather to the right of Caesar's positions. What, however, was brought about by the civil wars and their proscriptions was a large-scale change in the families and personnel of the ruling groups.

Meanwhile Caesar was working hard to get some order and stability into the situation he was administering. He suppressed the political clubs which he considered to have outlived their use and to express too narrow a set of metropolitan interests. He arranged for the settlement of some 80,000 poor citizens in colonies overseas, and had many other such plans. But all the while he was feeling the need for ready money. At his Triumph in 46 alone, each soldier got donations and each citizen got 100 denarii, 10 pecks of corn, 6 pints of oil; there were public dinners, distributions of meat, expensive games; and his partisans were pressing for offices, money, land. He was, however, determined to carry on without outlawry and proscription of opponents; he still hoped to win over a part of them to acceptance of the need for reform, or at least to disarm and neutralise them. His method was to get a maximum of reform with a minimum of dislocation and harsh measures. His feeling in all fields was the same as his attitude to literary style: no waste, no display, no effects for their own sake. In his treatise *An Analogy* he wrote, 'Avoid the rare and out-of-the-way word as the helmsman avoids the rocks.' But he had underestimated the enemy. The *optimates* took advantage of his clemencies without being in the least reconciled.[45]

Cleopatra must have argued strongly against his tolerances. With her inherited belief in her right to stamp on all opposition, she must have warned him against the consequences of letting men like Cicero and Brutus remain alive and carry on. Even if she stayed in comparative seclusion, she could not have helped meeting a fair number of leading Romans, and in her eagerness to understand the situation and talk it over with Caesar, she must have had agents and friends bringing her all the latest news and gossip. The important citizens, the great men of the Senate, must have puzzled her a lot, with their arrogant ways and their complicated affiliations that made any assessment of political trends a difficult matter. And we must not forget that she must often have met Marc Antony. In 47, while Caesar was in Africa, Antony was again left in control of Italy. Things were quiet there and perhaps he drank and indulged in enough love-affairs to cause some scandal; but it is certain that Cicero is wildly exaggerating when in his *Philippics* he draws a picture of extreme dissipation. If even a modicum of what he says was true, it is unlikely that Antony would have remained so high in Caesar's esteem. However, there seems to have been a period of slight estrangement with Caesar through the latter insisting that Antony pay for the confiscated property of Pompey he had taken up.[46] Antony did not go with the armies to Africa or Spain in 46; but in 45 we find him in full accord with Caesar, whom he went to meet in Narbo. In 44 he was consul with Caesar. There were therefore ample opportunities for him to grow acquainted with Cleopatra, whom he had met as a young girl in Alexandria. A man so much in Caesar's counsels must have often been at the Transtibertine Gardens; and it is more than probable that he took part in such restricted entertainments as Caesar thought fit to give Cleopatra, and in some of the discussions between them, whether politics or Hellenistic culture in general were the themes. (We do not know if Cleopatra with her gift for languages ever mastered Latin; but both Caesar and Antony would have spoken Greek with ease.) However, we must not think of any amorous approaches. Cleopatra was too completely bound up with Caesar the world's master; and Antony, however impulsive, was not a fool. He would not have courted a rebuff that would earn him Caesar's extreme displeasure. However, when we come later to the famous meeting of Antony and Cleopatra at Tarsos, we must remember that it was not an encounter of two strangers. Two experienced persons, who had already taken one another's measure at Alexandria and Rome, were at last coming together on a great ceremonial occasion, in the full light of history, with the world's eyes upon them.

Caesar's Murder

We have seen that while Caesar does not seem to have wanted any kingly title he was being forced into the role of a king; similarly, while he certainly did not aspire to the status of a god, there were strong popular trends demanding the deification of a world-conquerer. In 46 the base of one of his statues was found to have the inscription, 'He's a Demigod' (probably *divus est*), and he ordered the words to be erased. In May 45 the obsequious Senate decreed that his statue should be set up in the temple of Quirinus (the deified Romulus) on the Quirinal, with the inscription: 'To the Unconquered God.' Thus Caesar was defined as the second Founder of Rome with the halo of a Sungod. On 17 May 45 Cicero wrote to his banker friend Atticus from Tusculum, 'In other respects things were more tolerable at Astura. The thoughts that gall me are not more tormenting here, though, all the same, wherever I am, they don't leave me. I wrote to you about our neighbour Caesar because I learned the matter from your letters. I'd rather see him sharing a temple of

89

Quirinus than one of Salus' (Safety, Salvation). 'Yes, publish Hirtius' book' (on Cato). 'I had the same thoughts as you: that it revealed our friend's talent while its aim of blackening his character was proved ridiculous.'[1] Atticus' house and the temple of Salus were also on the Quirinal where Caesar had restored Quirinus' temple after its destruction by fire in 49. Cicero means that he'd rather Caesar was murdered, as in one legend Romulus was by the Senate, than left alive. Perhaps too the reference to Salus holds a side-glance at the way Caesar was being called a Saviour. Atticus among other things was a publisher with an establishment of slave-copyists; he seems to have been afraid to refuse to make copies of Hirtius' book and Cicero provides him with an excuse for complying. Nine days later Cicero asks, 'How do you suppose this messmate of Quirinus out of the procession will like my moderate letters?' *Ex pompa* refers to the Circensian Games at which images of the gods were carried; Caesar's image had been included.[2]

The month of Caesar's birth Quintilis was renamed Julius (whence our July). Royal birthdays had long been celebrated with popular festivals in the east; from the Hellenistic kingdoms came also the public prayers for Caesar's Safety (Salus), the oath sworn on his Genius, the striking of coins with his portrait. Caesar had reintroduced the prohibited cult of Dionysos, no doubt a concession to the common folk, but seen by the senators as one more link with Hellenistic court-cults. His statue, we noted, had been borne in procession with those of the gods, but he never claimed a cult. If he was voted a *flamen* or priest and Antony was named for the office, nothing was done to implement the vote.[3]

For long the entanglement of divine qualities with the conqueror had been going on. From the second century B.C. certain *gentes* (clans) tried to increase their prestige by linking themselves with a deity in vogue; and from Sulla on we meet the annexation of a deity by the leader of a political party. Sulla was already the object of a personal cult. Velleius Paterculus says, 'Sulla, having now arranged matters overseas, as chief of all the Romans, received ambassadors from the Parthians, some of whom were mages and foretold from marks on his body that his life and memory would be glorious.'[4] He called on Apollo at the battle of the Colline Gates. Caesar took over Venus; at Pharsalos he had Venus Victrix to oppose the Hercules Invictus of Pompey; he also invoked Venus at Thapsus under the name of Felicitas, and again at Munda. Dion says that he used her name as a rallying cry in moments of danger. The names of deities were also employed as watchwords or emblems by which one side could recognise itself.[5]

As a result, after each phase of the civil war, the winner had to break down, exorcise, or take over the religious propaganda of his rival. After Pharsalos Caesar merged Venus Genetrix with Felicitas, whom he had taken from Sulla. He thus exorcised Sullan taints and memories. Some of his followers were angry when he boldly changed the *Ludi Victoriae*, celebrated by Sulla over the Marians into *Ludi Victoriae Caesaris*. When he gave out *Felicitas* as watchword at Thapsus, he though of building a sanctuary to her on the site of the Curia Hostilia, says Dion, 'so that Sulla's name might not be attached to the monument'. The altar he raised before the Trophy of Pompey in the Pyrenees annulled Pompey's dedication and transferred the rights of the monument to Caesar, who thus supplanted his rival in the favour of the gods.[6]

The evidence we have for anything like a cult of Caesar comes from Dion, writing in the second century A.D. He it is that calls him Jupiter Julius with Antony as *flamen*, and adds to the statue in the temple of Quirinus another set next to those of the ancient kings of Rome. However, his statement that a temple was decreed to Caesar and his Clemency gets some support from literary evidence and from a coin-type. But apart from the link with Quirinus, Dion may be drawing on anti-Caesarian diatribes for his tales. That Octavian had to institute a cult of Divus Julius suggests that there was nothing at all like a cult during Caesar's life; and even the coins dealing with the temple of Clemency may have been issued after the murder.[7]

The coin-issues of early 44, which are decisive for evidence of Caesar's own views, may be thus summarised:

From 1 January: (Mettius as moneyer) Caesar as Dictator for the 4th time, with Juno in a two-horse chariot; (Buca) head of Venus and a representative of Sulla's Dream.

From about mid-February: (Macer) Venus, sceptre and shield; (Buca) Venus, sceptre; Venus seated; caduceus and *fasces* in saltire.

Uncertain date: Caesar as Perpetual Dictator, head veiled, with reverses: (Macer) Venus, sceptre and shield; (Maridianus) Venus, shield on globe; Caesar Parent of his Fatherland with reverses: (Macer) *desultor* or leaper from horse to horse at the games, (Maridianus) inscription in form of a cross.

After 15 March: (Macer) veiled head of Antony, and *desultor*; temple of Clementia, and *desultor*.

Moneta Castrensis: From 1 January (Mettius), Caesar Imperator with Venus, sceptre on globe. From mid-February (Macer), Venus and sceptre; (Buca) the same.[8]

This year, 44, a College of Four-men replaced the *Tresviri Montetales* (the Three Mint-directors). They were M. Mettius, L. Aemilius Buca, P. Sepullius Macer, C. Cossutius Maridianus. They worked closely together, as we see from the portrait of Caesar always laureate or veiled. Some points in their imagery are unclear: for example the substitution of the veil of the Pontifiex Maximus for the Triumphator's wreath on Caesar's head; the change of his title to *Parens Patriae*. We may note also how the *desultor*-reverse carried on after Caesar's death, linked with portraits of Antony as *flamen*, his beard expressive of mourning. But there is nothing in the whole series to suggest any wish on Caesar's part to be divinised. The prominence of Venus suggests that he was rather claiming to be her descendant and favourite.

On 26 January 44, as he was returning from the Latin Games, some people in the street shouted 'King!' (*rex*). He replied, 'I am not King but Caesar.' However, when he found two tribunes had removed a diadem set on his statue on the Rostra and had arrested some street-demonstrators, he bade another tribune to see to the deposition of the pair and himself expelled them from the Senate. But because he didn't like to see his humble admirers badly treated does not prove that he wanted their particular expression of admiration.[9]

There is no evidence he wanted the title of *rex*, which in Roman politics might be used as an insult. Thus Clodius called Cicero *rex* because of his lordly ways. 'How long are we going to let this man play the king?' he asks. 'I wonder you speak of *Rex*,' Cicero answered, 'since *Rex* [Q. Marcius Rex, Clodius' brother-in-law] didn't mention you.' Clodius had been dying to inherit Rex's money,

Cicero insists. (These exchanges went on in the midst of a lawsuit.) Cicero himself called Caesar king as a term of abuse. He was speaking of the reckless chatter of his nephew who had been telling people that he, Cicero, and Atticus, were irreconcilable enemies of Caesar: 'All this would have been terrifying if I weren't aware that the King knows I have no spirit left.' Cicero elsewhere states that Caesar used to recite a passage from Euripides: 'If you must do wrong, do it for tyranny's sake. Respect the divine laws in all other matters.' The anecdote does not ring at all true; but it shows what Cicero's set were thinking.[10]

On 14 February the Senate made Caesar Dictator for Life. Next day came the Lupercalia. He sat in a golden chair on the rostra and the half-naked Luperci made their fertilising race through the streets.[11] Reaching Caesar, Cassius, Casca, and Antony tried to crown him. The first two put the wreath on his knees, Antony on his head. But Caesar took it off and threw it among the crowd with orders that it be carried to the Capitol and put in Jupiter's temple. Historians, according to their prejudices, declared that the crowd cheered or failed to cheer, that Antony acted his part to gain Caesar's favour or to discredit his cause, that Caesar wanted or didn't want the crown, that he gave it up because he saw the people's disapproval. (Cassius indeed may have wanted to draw Caesar into an indiscreet act.) Lepidus, Master of Horse, was also on the platform and took the simple course of bursting into tears, which could mean anything.[12]

Next came the episode of the decree of perpetual dictatorship engraved on silver tablets, which the Senate was carrying in procession to the Capitol, led by Antony.

They passed the temple of Venus Genetrix in the new Forum where Caesar sat at public business, letting out State-contracts. The procession was on top of him before he had warning; he ignored it and went on with his business, not even rising. Later, he, or his followers, made the apology for his rudeness that he had been kept in his seat by a sudden attack of illness. If we have this odd event correctly recorded, it would seem that Caesar felt a sharp revulsion from the whole business of his glorification by men whom he knew detested him.[13]

It is of interest to turn from Roman to the eastern Mediterranean. Here we find in plain form the hopes of the provincials and commoners for a Saviour; and here we are in Cleopatra's world, which she understood and which she finally tried to lead against the Romans.[14] At Tralles Caesar's statue was raised with the epithets: archpriest, *autokrator*, benefactor (*euergetes*). Athens used the same terms plus *Soter,* Saviour; Karthaia or Keos had the same wording as Athens; Demetrias in Thessalonika called him *autokrator* and god, *theos—autokrator* anticipating emperor. We have only the pedestals; no statue or bust is known which can be dated in his lifetime; but the portraits struck on Greek coins probably derived from a contemporary Greek statue. Pedestals are known from Megara, Thespiai, Demetrias, Delos, Chios, Samos, Ephesos, Pergamon, as well as the places already cited. Probably the statues they held all looked to one famous original. They show the titles of imperator, pontifex maximus, consul for the second and the third time, dictator for the second and designate for the third time. We may presume that the statues were preceded by an honorary decree from some organisation, *boulē* or *dēmos* (council or people), or from both; and the body or bodies in question were responsible for the erection and appeared in the inscription as dedicator. Most of those for which there is definite evidence were set up by the *dēmos*; one by the Cities and Peoples of the Province of Asia. What is generally stressed is Caesar's role as benefactor and saviour. At Ephesos he was the Common Saviour of Human Life; in one Pergamene text he was the Common Saviour and Benefactor of all the Hellenes; in others the Dēmos called him their Saviour and Benefactor.

What we find is not a precise deification. But in three texts he is a god, *theos*, which is not a translation of *divus* as he was still alive. There is no connection with the deifying movement at Rome. At Tralles his statue was raised in the Temple of Victory in 48; an Ephesian inscription was of 48, and so were probably those of Karthaia and Demetrias.[15] Dion tells us that after the battle at Thapsos it was decided to set up there a statue of Caesar standing on the *oikoumenē* (world) and inscribed *hemitheos*, demigod. At Karthaia he was god and saviour of the *oikoumenē*, and Demetrias called him saviour of the *oikoumenē*. So we may assume that the statues at these two places imitated that of Thapsos. About the same time was the statue of Thespiai, where he was called benefactor and patron 'on account of *aretē*, *dikaiosynē*, and *andragathia*'—virtue (innate quality), justice, and manly virtue or courage. Here the dedication was to the gods. The Ephesos inscription called him descendent of Ares and Aphrodite, and suggests that he was viewed as a Neos Ares. Dion stressed his link with Aphrodite (Venus).[16]

We may add that in 1939 there was found at Thasos a head carved of local marble, which had Caesar's furrowed brow, deep set eyes, projecting cheek-bones, straight wide mouth, long neck and strong adam's-apple. The work is in eastern taste and its suggestion of defication may date it soon after the murder—though it may be a later copy of a work of that time.[17]

The imperial cult which we here see emerging round the figure of Caesar in the east had been heralded by the king-cults, the divinisation of Roman magistrates, and the cult of Rome there. A vogue for the worship of Roma seems to have grown in the first half of the second century B.C. She had her cult at Smyrna in 195, at Alalanda in 170, and soon after at Erythrai, Miletos, Elea, and elsewhere. In 161 Ariarthes of Cappadocia sent a crown of 10,000 gold pieces to the Goddess Roma, and Demetrios I of Syria followed his example. Festivals called Romaia were founded. The earliest known is that of Delphoi in 189; but at least a dozen more are recorded. An interesting testimony from the early period is a hymn in five Sapphic stanzas to Roma by the poetess Melinno. She sees Rome as resisting Time that destroys all else, and driving both land and sea in her (triumphal) chariot. She makes Roma a daughter of Ares. In Italy Rome was long connected with Mars, who was taken as father of Romulus and Remus, while in Greece Ares was father of the Amazon Penthesilia —Apollonios Rhodios makes him beget all the Amazons. So it was easy to make him the father of the warlike goddess Roma. It was usual indeed to connect a new deity with an old one. Marianos made Roma daughter of Asklepios the healer (and so connected with Apollo); at Athens she was worshipped with Dēmos and the Graces; the Rhodians in 163 set up a colossal statue of her in Athene's temple; in a paian sung by girls of Chalkis in

97

honour of T. Flaminius, Roma and Roman Faith (*Pistis*: *Fides*) were associated with both Zeus and the Roman magistrate. (When Q. Lutatius Catulus restored the Capitol he had a small figure of Roma put in Jupiter's hand.)[18]

We see then how many elements were seething in the east, ready to burst out in acclamation of a Saviour at the advent of anyone who at all seemed to fit in with the people's dream-picture. Cleopatra, steeped in Hellenistic tradition, was thoroughly aware of this sort of popular response and was to attempt to take full advantage of it as soon as her chance came. Meanwhile she must have been impatient at Caesar's indifference to the widespread demand for a saviour-champion. Not that he was ignorant of what was going on, or averse from using religious symbolism when it suited him. We may take the way in which the weariness and suffering, which large masses of people felt at the endlessly-dragging war-situation, was finding a partial outlet in the cult of the goddess Peace, Pax. Originally *pax* meant a pact. Hence Cicero could still pun in his *Phillipics*: '*Pax* will not be *pax* but a *pactio* of servitude'—with Antony as consular and Lucius his brother hoping to be consul. Long before, in 233, Q. Fabius Maximus, we are told, took to Carthage two tokens with representations of Spear and Caduceus (the herald's snake-twined staff), and asked the Carthaginians to choose War or Peace. The caduceus on coins is often just an attribute of Hermes-Mercurius, but it certainly emblematises peace on some coins of the Sullan age. Thus, we see Honos and Virtus on one side; on the other Roma with her foot on a globe and holding out her hand to Italia, who in turn holds a horn-of-plenty with a winged caduceus behind. Here is represented the pacification of Italy after the Social War. *Pax* appears as a political slogan and is not yet a goddess.[19]

As slogan *Pax* had two aspects: *concordia* for the citizens and peaceful order in the conquered rest of the world. *Concordia* among the citizens was one of Cicero's keythemes, much expatiated on after the break between Caesar and Pompey; in 49 he meant to write an essay on it, but failed to do so.[20] From 49 the winged caduceus was used on coins, often held by clasped hands. In connection with foreign land it signified pacification, the submission of the defeated peoples. Foreigners should be sensible enough to give in, the reasoning ran, and they would then have a quiet life guaranteed. Stoic philosophers like Panaitios and Poseidonios were impressed and took the idea up. Rome's *imperium* provided subjects with protection against external attack and internal disorder. Pay your taxes and you were given *pax sempiterna* together with *otium*, a quiet life. Tacitus finally, with his irony, turned the concept upside-down. *Imperium* is plunder and murder, *pax* is devastation.

The cult of Pax as a goddess was perhaps brought in by Caesar. A quinarius of about 44 has a female head and PAX, with clasped hands on the reverse. Another coin of the same moneyer shows Caesar's head, with winged caduceus on reverse, *fasces*, globe, and clasped hands. Pax is now the expression of the benevolent world-ruler. We may note also the Caesarian foundation of Pax Julia in Lusitania (Beja), while in Gallia Narbonensis was Colonia Pacensis or Forum Julii Pacatum (Fréjus). Such colonies probably had an altar of the new goddess; a later *as* of Pax Julia shows a head of Augustus, with a reverse of Pax seated with caduceus. Other colonies set up Tropaea or statues of Victoria. Caesar seems certainly to have wanted to spread the cult of Pax. Dion says that Antony in his funeral oration praised him as peacemaker, no doubt translating *pacificator* or *pacificus*, an epithet which Caesar himself had probably chosen and which had further the value of connecting him with Alexander the Great.[21]

In 44 the Senate decreed a temple of Concordia Nova with a yearly festival; on a denarius of about 42 Pax leans on a sceptre and holds a caduceus, with a reverse of Caesar's head. Other coins depicted the caduceus and clasped hands; and these emblems were used to express the reconciliation of Antony and Octavian in 40–39.

The concept of Peace was thus applied in different ways by different men according to their views of social order. Caesar used it to express the hoped-for end of the civil wars with a settlement which he considered most likely to overcome the post-Gracchan conflicts. Cicero as the supreme opportunist used it to define his scheme for the Good Men, the *boni*, the men of property, to close their ranks against the demands of the propertyless—in effect he wanted to draw in various groups from the *equites*, the *publicani* (tax-farmers), the owners of large and small estates, the worthies of the Italian towns, as supporters of the *optimates*; and as usual he employed a moral term to cover a political idea.[22] In a general way he moved from the notion of the Concord of Orders to that of the Consensus of All; perhaps in his middle period he used this slogan to gather round himself the political party or grouping which as a new man he lacked. Later, his programme, impractical enough in a period of violent change, did much to suggest to Augustus the doctrine of all good citizens working together under his control or guidance. The Ciceronian creed provided the imperial ideology and Pax lost its more radical Caesarian meanings.[23]

We may now return to the question of Caesar's alleged desire for the kingship. It has been argued that some coins with the legend DICT. QUART. (Dictator for the Fourth Time) show the knot of a diadem behind his head. But careful scrutiny has proved that the object indicated is not a diadem-knot at all; it is the lituus or augural crook distorted by a die-flaw.[24] Then another scholar thought that he had detected on coins, not a diadem, not a laurel wreath, but a stiff metal object: the golden crown of the Etruscan kings. Unfortunately we know nothing of such golden crowns; the contemporary idea of the headgear of ancient kings was a diadem: for example the diademed head of Numa on *asses* of Augustus.[25]

Then there is the tale that a prophecy was put about: Only a king could conquer Parthia. Even if the tale was true, there is no evidence for Caesar's connivance; we cannot imagine him using such a crude trick. Dion indeed merely says, 'There was a rumour of the existence of such an oracle,' and Suetonius states, 'There was a rumour that at the next meeting of the Senate, L. Cotta, one of the Fifteen, would make a motion' based on this prophecy. Such a rumour was safe enough, as Caesar was killed before the meeting in question. Cicero in *On Divination* says that there was no such rumour. Yet historians have argued that Caesar concocted the device after the failure of the crowning at the Lupercal.[26]

We get the impression that some of Caesar's supporters were sick of compromises and wanted to push him into some sort of Hellenistic kingship with an aura of divinity; and there were no doubt some spontaneous attempts to divinise him among the Greek and oriental sections of the Roman populace. But clearly also many of the tales have been invented, or coloured, by the propagandists among the *optimates* to discredit Caesar. To clarify the origins of the tales or rumours is generally impossible. Thus, Suetonius states, 'Helvius Cinna, tribune of the people, admitted to several persons that he had a bill ready drawn-up, which Caesar ordered him to get enacted in his absence, allowing him, in the hope of leaving issue, to take any wife he chose, and as many as he liked, and leaving no room for doubt as to his infamous character for un-natural lewdness and vice.'[27] The elder Curio in a speech declared, 'He was every woman's man and every man's woman.'

Curio's remark is a piece of pure vituperation; it embodies a formula that was liable to be used of any political character by his opponents, quite regardless of fact. Cinna, who had been Caesar's instrument in deposing the two tribunes in the diadem-episode, and who seems the sort of person that Caesar might indeed choose for some dubious tactic, is no more to be credited than Curio. His decree, the tale went, was to be brought up three days after the Ides of March, and so was never proposed; also Cinna himself was killed by bad luck five days after Caesar, being mistaken by the crowd for the conspirator Cinna. He thus could not contradict the tale, which clearly belongs to the same category as that of the prophecy about Parthia.[28]

The tale may, however, have arisen out of rumours that he was contemplating marriage with Cleopatra.

There must have been continual speculation as to her role in his life among the politicians at Rome, and her agents would have done their best to spread stories of her importance in his eyes. She may even have suggested, if she found a discreet and tactful way of raising the subject, that he should introduce some law legitimising their relationship. With her way of thinking, such a step would not be at all strange or unbecoming; Caesar, however, would have known how hopelessly it ran counter to all Roman traditions and conventions. Even if he had been ready to throw aside his wife Calpurnia—an act not in his character but typical enough of the callous way that *optimates* divorced their wives for any odd political reason in these times—he still could not have married the alien Cleopatra. Any legislation enabling him do so would have been highly repugnant to Roman custom, something almost as bad as an assumption of the title *rex;* but Cleopatra would have found it hard to accept that viewpoint.

Augustan censorship has so completely excised her from the accounts of these years that we might begin to doubt the evidence of Dion and Suetonius if it were not for the testimony of Cicero's letters. On 13 June 44 he wrote to Atticus from Antium, 'I detest the Queen. The voucher for her promises, Ammonius, knows I have every right to do so. Her promises were concerned with *philologa* and not derogatory to my dignity. I could have mentioned them even in a public speech. Sara, besides being a scoundrel, has also been impertinent to me, I've noticed. Once and only once have I seen him in my house; and then, when I asked politely what he wanted, he said he wanted Atticus. But the insolence of the Queen herself, when she was in the villa across the river, I can't recall

without great indignation. So no dealings with these
people. They don't credit me with any spirit or any
feelings at all.'[29] This outburst occurs without any
explanation, sandwiched between two statements about
his financial troubles, first some large payments to be
made to creditors (who include the people of Arpinum),
and then the lament: 'My departure from Italy I see is
hindered by the management of my affairs by Eros,' his
freedman. The whole of the letter, apart from the paragraph on Cleopatra, deals with money-matters, and that
paragraph must, it seems, have some link with his
anxieties in this respect. Atticus has clearly brought up
claims made against Cicero by Ammonius and Sara, agents
or officials of Cleopatra. *Philologa* is obscure. It means here
'something to do with questions of learning'. If it
means 'books', it is hard to see why he does not use the
specific term. He is certainly feeling uneasy; hence the
counter-attacking vehemence of his tone. On 21 December
44, writing to Atticus from Puteoli on a dinner, spent in
some perturbation, with Caesar, he also lapses into Greek
phrases: '*Spoudaion ouden* in the conversation, lots of
philologa.' No serious (political) talk, but much literary
discussion.

The letter about Ammonius and Sara was written after
Caesar's murder, when Cleopatra had been out of Italy
for some time. Cicero can let loose his rancour against her
without fear of reprisals; he wrote nothing about her
during Caesar's lifetime, though he must have felt much
indignation at her presence 'in the villa across the river'.
His letter gives away further the fact that, whatever he
now says, he had visited Cleopatra and tried to ingratiate
himself with her.

Certainly the other great men of the Senate would also have called and paid their respects, dissembling their hatred and suspicion, for reasons of caution and curiosity. Cleopatra would not have demeaned herself by some modest visit to Rome, with hardly any retinue; and she would have wanted to show as effectively as possible her inheritance of Ptolemaic culture. Philostratos, the philosopher, who had been in Africa with King Juba in 47, may already have attached himself to her; and the singer M. Tigellius Hermogenes, whom Horace satirised, may have been among the persons she patronised.

On the Ides of March, 44, the conspirators cut Caesar down in the Senate House. He was not afraid of such a fate; he seems to have expected an attack; and we may perhaps read his mood as a defiant and reckless sort of euphoria, like that which led him into the Alexandrian War—a mixture of careless daring and a wish to try out how far his luck and his mastery of events would go. All this mixed with a certain fatalistic despair, a sense of closing-in problems which were not soluble in what seemed to him rational ways. Death ceased to matter. He could perhaps even feel a distant malicious pleasure in thinking of the worsened mess that would be inherited by the men who were so eager to get rid of him. We must recall that in recent campaigns, at Thapsus and Cordoba, he had fallen ill at critical moments, apparently with epilepsy; he had been suffering in the last few years with headaches and fainting-fits. On the coins he looks old beyond his years. He refused the Senate's offer of a bodyguard of senators and *equites*; a month before his death he dismissed his Spanish retinue, despite the remonstrances of Hirtius and other friends, and moved about Rome without any protection. Suetonius and Dion, with the usual shallowness and incomprehension of ancient historians, attribute his action to a false confidence born

Relief of Mars Ultor, the Avenger, in full panoply; a sphinx supports his high plumes; military cloak flung across his back. On his right is Venus Genetrix (or Victrix), with a Cupid offering her a sword. The figure on his left has a hole in his head as if for a star to be fixed, but it is hard to see such a youthful person as Julius Caesar. The relief is from Carthage but seems a copy of a group from the podium of the apse in Mars Ultor's temple at Rome

of the honours voted in February; Caesar knew quite well that any increase in honours sharply increased his danger as well. He may have planned about this time to have all Roman citizens take an oath of allegiance to him, putting them in a sort of clientship with himself as a universal patron; and the Senate did in fact take the oath. Certainly the title, of no constitutional significance, *Pater Patriae*, with which he was now hailed, would harmonise with such a scheme. (Augustus later picked up the title, realising its implications.) But no doubt Caesar was looking round for some form of expressing his supreme position without overtones of kingship, rather than trying to establish his inviolacy.

A tale went round that, on the night before the Ides, the talk after dinner turned on death. He remarked that he hoped his own end would be sudden. The tale is probably an invention, though it is in character and he seems to have made much the same sort of comment some two years before. 'I have lived long enough for nature and for glory.' Cicero unwillingly heard this observation, and, six months after Caesar's death, applied it to himself.[30]

We hear of many abortive attempts to kill Caesar. In 47, in Asia Minor, after Zela, there was said to have been an attempt made by Deiotaros, which Cicero, in his speech on that king's behalf, did his best to laugh at. L. Cassius Longinus, who, like Brutus, surrendered to Caesar after Pharsalos and was pardoned, plotted to kill him at Tarsos, but waited on the wrong bank of the Kydnos. Again in 46 there were rumours of attempts at assasination. Two tales, however, by Cicero in his *Philippics* are certainly lies. He says that when Caesar was returning from Spain in the summer of 45, Trebonius and Antony planned to murder him, but Antony's courage failed. This story is used to explain why Trebonius detained Antony at the door while Caesar was being cut down inside the Senate House; but the real reason for that act was Brutus' insistence that nobody be killed but Caesar. Cicero was here speaking in Brutus' presence, so he dropped the theme he was always harping on, the sad error of not murdering Antony as well as his master. (The conspirators may also have feared

Antony's impetuous bull-strength.) Cicero further declared that a man was caught in Caesar's house with a knife and was found to have been sent by Antony. This alleged event is never mentioned in Cicero's day-to-day letters at the time it was supposed to have happened. As Caesar approached the Senate on the Ides, a Greek, once employed as tutor by Brutus, tried to speak with him and passed him a warning note, which remained unread in his hand.[31]

Caesar had certainly wanted to get out of the corrupt and feverish atmosphere of Rome into the wars on the frontiers, against the Dacians, against the Parthians via Armenia. Men said that he wanted to imitate Alexander the Great and Dionysos, to make a great triumphal march past the Caucasus to the Black Sea, then across the Balkans back to Rome. Perhaps he in fact felt that the prestige of a victory over the Parthians would make his political system more acceptable; perhaps he merely wanted to postpone a final showdown with its inevitable element of repression and open force. The *optimates* in turn were afraid to let him go. He might fail, but more likely he would return with vastly enhanced military power, with yet more veterans demanding land.

Cicero's letters give us further glimpses of Cleopatra. On 5 April he wrote, 'I see nothing to object to in the Queen's flight.' From the context with its scattered remarks we see that he is making a rapid survey of possible dangers in the immediate postmurder situation. 'You say Junia brought a letter written in a moderately friendly tone. Paulus tells me it was sent by his brother' (M. Lepidus, Junia's husband), 'and that at its end was a statement about a plot against him, which he had learned of an excellent authority. I was annoyed at it and he was still more annoyed. I see nothing to object to in the Queen's flight. I'd like you to tell me more what Clodia' (Clodius' sister), 'has done. You must look after the people of Byzantium like everything else and get Pelops to call on you. I'll look into all that pack of fellows at Baiae' (Hirtius, Pansa, Balbus: Caesarians suspected of hatching plans against the murderers), 'of whom you want to know, as you ask me, and will let you know all about them. I'm very anxious to hear what the Gauls, and the Spaniards, and Sextus [Clodius] are doing.'[32] It follows then that he considers Cleopatra might have been a centre of activities against the murderers and their supporters; her departure is a good riddance. On 11 May he wrote, 'I am sorry about the miscarriage of Tertulla' (Tertia, half-sister of Brutus and wife of Cassius—Tertulla is an affectionate diminutive). 'We want a crop of Cassii as much as one of Bruti. I hope it's true about the Queen and also Caesar's son.' Here Cicero, writing frankly to Atticus and not trimming up facts for propaganda purposes, accepts Cleopatra's child as the son of Caesar. If he had the least doubt he would have inserted some insulting term and developed some vituperative contrasts between the legitimacies of the offspring of the Cassii and the Bruti and the villainous trickeries of the Queen. This letter of his is then decisive for the fact that in 44 the men most in the know of things accepted without question that Caesar had begotten a boy on Cleopatra.

What is not so clear is the exact bearing of his comment. That comment is directly linked with the sad news of Tertia's miscarriage, and the general meaning is that we want the children of the Republican heroes to carry on their father's work in defence of our *libertas*, but we don't want the children of tyrants like Caesar. This point drives home the completeness with which Cicero recognises the child as Caesar's; but it is linked with the news that something unfortunate has happened to Cleopatra and the boy—what, we have no idea. Probably an unfounded rumour had come in that their ship had sunk or some accident had happened during their flight. He hopes that the mishap is as certain as Tertia's miscarriage. He seems to have at the back of his mind the thought: What a pity that Cleopatra did not have a miscarriage instead of Tertia, but anyway perhaps the mishap will serve equally well in destroying the child.[33]

The overtones of his statement thus make it seem that Cleopatra's childbed had been fairly recent, and this would support the argument that Cleopatra's child was born about the time of Caesar's murder, whether shortly before or after. However this deduction is not necessary. Even if the boy were a couple of years old, Cicero might still be moved to make the contrast by hearing about the same time of Tertia's miscarriage and of some mishap to Cleopatra and her child. The story about the mishap was much in his mind. On 17 May he wrote from Puteoli that he had been sounding Hirtius and finds that 'he is quite unreliable'. He ends: 'You say Brutus asks me to come before the 1st. He has written to me too, and perhaps I'll do it. But I really don't know what he wants. What advice can I give him when I myself need advice and when he has thought more of his immortality than of our peace of mind [*otium*]? The rumour about Cleopatra is dying out.'[34] On 24 May he wrote from Arpinum, 'Antony's plans as you describe them are revolutionary [*turbulenta*]. . . . So

ITALY

Verona
Mantua
Parma
Mutina
Bononia
Ravenna
Pisaurum
LIGURIA
ILLYRICUM
Salona
UMBRIA
Arretium
Igurium
ETRURIA
Perusia
Clusium
MARE ADRIATICUM
Epidauros
CORSICA
ROME
Ostia
Gaii
Lanuvium
LATIUM
Antium
SAMNIUM
APULIA
Brundisium
Capua
CALABRIA
Cumae
CAMPANIA
Puteoli
Neapolis
Pompeii
LUCANIA
SARDINIA
Tarentum
MARE
TYRRHENUM
Naulochus
Mylae
Rhegium
SICILY
Carthage
Syracuse
AFRICA
Miles 0 20 40 60 80 100

III

now I see it was folly to be consoled by the Ides of March. Our courage was that of men, but believe me, we had no more sense than children. We have only cut down the tree, not rooted it up. So you see how it's shooting out. . . .' As always he can't forgive Brutus for checking a massacre of leading Caesarians on the Ides. 'I wish it was true about Menedemus and I hope it may be true about Cleopatra. The rest when we meet, and especially what our friends must do, and what we must do, if Antony is going to surround the House with soldiers.'[35]

Menedemus was a Thessalian chieftain who was an upholder of Caesar. The latter writes of the period before Pharsalos: 'Menedemus, the chief man of those regions, on the side called the Free, came as envoy and assured him of the most devoted affection of all his subjects . . . Petreius, a young man of a most noble family, warmly supported Caesar with his own and his friends' influence.' In April 43 Antony wrote a letter detailing his grievances to Hirtius and Octavian; the latter sent it on to Cicero, who used it in a long and furious reply in the Senate, citing passages from it and then commenting on them. '*You approved of the execution of Petraeus and Menedemus, men who had been given the citizenship, guestfriends of Caesar.* We did not approve of what we had never heard. Certainly in such disorder of public affairs we should have given serious attention to two most rascally Greeklings [*Graeculi*].

'*You did not care that Theopompus* [a Caesarian of Knidos] *was stript and driven out by Trebonius, and took refuge in Alexandria.* A heavy charge against the Senate! We were careless about Theopompus, that eminent man, of whom, as to where in the world he is, what he does, in a word whether he's alive or dead, who knows or cares?'[36]

We may note the contempt with which Cicero speaks of mere Greeks. Brutus, it seems, had killed, or approved the killing of, the two Thessalian friends of Caesar during operations in north Greece. Cicero is lying when he says that nothing was known of Menedemus' fate and that the matter was of no interest, since in the above-cited letter he is much concerned about the man. But if Menedemus had been killed as early as May 44, Brutus was not directly responsible for his death. However, the linking of Menedemus and Cleopatra suggests that the rumour about the latter told of some disaster such as death by shipwreck. Cicero's interest in Cleopatra's flight and the stories about it show that he considered her a character of some significance in the whole tumultuous situation brought about by Caesar's death. Otherwise he would not have kept returning to it among so many pressing matters of extreme importance.

Despite the rumours Cleopatra and her son reached Alexandria safely.

Cleopatra and Caesarion

We can now return to the question of Caesarion. It has been pointed out that Caesar, though begetting a daughter Julia on his first wife Cornelia, never had any more children by his other wives. He was married fourteen years to Cornelia, six years to Pompeia, fourteen years to Calpurnia; yet, despite his wish for sons, Julia remained his sole child. The story that Brutus was his son—a result of his affair with Servilia, Brutus' mother—cannot be correct when we consider Brutus' age. Caesar had many known affairs, as well as many unknown ones, no doubt, but we do not hear of any children by them. So it is argued that he had somehow become infertile. This argument, however, is not wholly convincing. We have only to recall how many upper-class marriages were childless at Rome, probably in large part through lead-poisoning, which has more effect on women than on men in bringing infertility about. (The lead-poisoning came about mainly through the use of lead pipes for water and lead-lined utensils for cooking.)[1] For the vagaries of impregnation

we may further take from Egypt the case of Pshereni-
ptah whose funerary inscription we cited. He says, 'I was
a great man, rich in all riches, so that I possessed a fine
harem. I lived 45 years without a manchild being born to
me. In which matter the Majesty of this Glorious God
Imhotep Son of Ptah was gracious to me. A manchild was
given me.'² And if Caesar was not the father of Caesarion,
who was? We must suppose that Cleopatra was got with
child through carelessness by some casual lover, or that
she deliberately had herself impregnated in secret so as to
have a son to foist on to Caesar. Both these suppositions
are at variance with her character. There is not a shred of
evidence that she ever mated with anyone but Caesar and
Antony in all her life. The story that Gnaeus, the son of
the great Pompey, lingered at Alexandria when he came
to ask for help for his father, and had an affair with her,
has no likelihood. She could only have possibly taken him
as a lover if she were completely sure that Pompey would
win the civil war. The story is an invention of the period
when the description of her as a wanton had to be supported by supplying her with more lovers than she
actually had.

There is then no solid argument against Caesar's
paternity of her son. The fact that we have no gossip
about the boy before Cicero's letter of 11 May 44 proves
nothing. We have no sort of contemporary reference to the
whole of Cleopatra's sojourn at Rome, despite the amount
of comment it must have caused. All the references by
Cicero are after the Ides of March. This may be a matter of
chance; but it is odd all the same. The previous silence of
Cicero and his friends suggests that they felt it best to be
cautious about the Queen, however much they discussed

her in private. But the suggestion that the facts about Caesarion only came out after Caesar's death does not carry conviction. Cicero would surely speak of Cleopatra and the boy in different terms if the disclosure had been so late; he would not have accepted the child as Caesar's in the unquestioning way he does.[3] It seems to me that the setting up of the gold statue of Cleopatra in the temple of Venus must have marked some decisive moment in her relationship with Caesar.

But whether he set up the statue to express pleasure at the news of her impregnation or of the child's birth, we do not know. We are still as far as ever from finding out whether Caesarion was born in 47 or in 44. Plutarch definitely states that the boy was born in 47. 'After this he left Cleopatra Queen of Egypt, who soon after had a son by him, whom the Alexandrians called Caesarion, and then departed for Syria.' That is in the *Life of Caesar*; in his *Antony* he says, 'Caesarion was believed to be a son of the former Caesar, by whom Cleopatra was left pregnant.'[4] This suggests a birth after the Ides of March, and would agree with Cicero's letter if we could take it as meaning: I wish Cleopatra had had a miscarriage recently like Tertia.[5] The historians who hold to the date 44 or deny that Caesarion was Caesar's child at all are forced to suggest that the relief of the divine child, discussed above, was made after 44, and to date the Cypriot coins in a similar way.[6]

As we shall see the question of Caesarion's paternity became an important issue after Caesar's grand-nephew Octavius came forward as his heir and felt an urgent need to decry any claims to a closer relationship with the dead man. What was said then for or against Caesarion has little value as testimony, for it is throughout politically biased. However, the question as to what Caesar put in his will has more relevance to the inquiry. Drawn up on 13 September 45, it played a crucial part in the rise of Octavius. The latter had been born on 23 September 63, of a minor country family. He lost his father at the age of four and was brought up by his grandmother Julia. Antony jeered at him for having as great-grandfather a freedman ropemaker of Thurium, and as grandfather a usurer. 'His nursery,' says Suetonius, 'is shown to this day, in a villa of the family's, in the suburbs of Velitrae, a small place rather like a pantry. In the neighbourhood they say he was born there, "not on the Palatine at Rome". As a child he was called Thurinus "in memory of the birthplace of his family or because soon after his birth his father Octavius had been successful against the fugitive slaves in the country near Thurii".'[7] Caesar had the Octavian *gens* raised by the Senate in late 45 to the patrician rank. He had also helped the lad, his most promising near male relative, so that he was *pontifex* at the age of fifteen: an unusual advance for a young noble, though Caesar himself was *flamen dialis* at much the same age. This act, however, did not in any way designate him as Caesar's heir and successor (as Dion, wise after the event, stated).[8] Caesar indeed had considered his grand-nephew as an heir, but only in the last resort; he still hoped for a son of his own body, but not one born of a *peregrina* like Cleopatra. In his will the stress was on such a son. Suetonius tells us, 'At the instance of L. Piso, his father-in-law, his will was opened and read in Marc Antony's house. He had made it on the Ides of the previous September, at his Lavican villa,' south-east of

Rome, 'and handed it over for keeping to the head of the Vestal Virgins. Q. Tubero informs us that in the wills he signed, from the time of his first consulship to the outbreak of the civil war, Gn. Pompey was appointed his heir, and this was publicly notified to the army. But in his last will he named three heirs, the grandsons of his sisters: G. Octavius for three-quarters of his estate, L. Pinarius and Q. Pedius for the remaining fourth. Other heirs were named at the close of the will, in which he also adopted G. Octavius, who was to assume his name, into the family, and nominated most of those who were concerned in his death among the guardians of his son, if he had any; as well as Decimus Brutus among his heirs of the second order. He bequeathed to the Roman People his Gardens near the Tiber and 300 sesterces a man.'[9]

Calpurnia was still young enough for him to hope she might yet bear him a son. There is perhaps confirmation of his hopes in the fact that he allowed hereditary honours to be conferred on him, as Dion twice mentions. But in Dion's second passage there is reference to an adoptive son who cannot have truly been in Caesar's thoughts. The reference is more a piece of Augustan propaganda. On the other hand the bill which Cinna was to bring in to allow a multiplicity of wives, and which would have been a cruel blow at Calpurnia's feelings, was certainly a fiction; and we cannot stretch the hypothetical son of the will to cover Caesarion.[10]

We learn from Nikolaos that the contents of the will were kept secret from Octavius and thus also from the world at large. This secrecy is odd if Caesar seriously considered Octavius as his heir. Of ancient writers only Suetonius knows and records the provision for a possible son of his body; elsewhere Augustan censorship has done its work well. We see the same tampering with facts in the way in which a passage of Dion turns the *tutores* (guardians), intended for the possible son, into *epitropoi* (trustees) for Octavius, who was *sui juris* and did not need *tutores*. Caesar certainly never appointed any guardians for him; but in order to attribute more importance to him than he actually had at the time, the details of the will dealing with the unborn son are transferred to him.

A point of much importance for Octavius' claims was the legality or illegality of the clause adopting him. Suetonius mentions that it was in the *ima cera*, the last section, of the will. That was nothing against it as an expression of Caesar's wishes: the question was whether such wishes could be made legally valid by a will alone. Scholars like Mommsen have argued that the clause was a valid adrogation, which needed only a formal confirmation under a *lex curiata*. But it seems more than doubtful if a testator could adopt anyone. Ulpian states firmly that an adoption could not be made by 'someone not present or through someone else'.[11] No known law or legal expert accepts the testamentary procedure. It can then be argued that when Suetonius spoke of Octavius' adopting Caesar's 'family and name', he meant only that Caesar imposed on his *secundus heres* the *condicio nominis ferendi*, the condition that he took his name. This condition we know a praetor could allow a reluctant heir to ignore without losing his inheritance.[12] If this were so, the belated *condicio* of Caesar was of no great significance, except that it gave Octavius the chance of pretending that he had been named Caesar's heir in all things. So, when he appeared before the praetor G. Antonius in a *gestio* or action by which as extraneous *heres* he claimed inheritance of the appropriate portion of Caesar's property, the action turned (in Appian's account) into his formal acceptance of the adoption.[13] Appian goes on to describe the adoption of a man in *patria potestas* (still under the power of his father) and thus confirms our suspicion that the whole account was fictive and that no such ceremony was needed. For Octavius adopted the name and called himself (G. Julius) Caesar as soon as he heard of the will's contents. But he was too shrewd to think the name enough. He agitated for a *lex curiata,* which would make him truly the inheritor of Caesar's *clientela*—the large number of men owing him loyalty.[14] But there were too many resistances, both from Antony and the Senate, so that he didn't get his *lex* till he entered on his consulate in 19 August 43.

Still, if our argument is correct, no such *lex* could truly make him the heir. The *adrogans,* the person adopting, no longer existed. The pontiffs could not act on his behalf. We may, however, assume perhaps that under pressure they accepted the claim that a will could effect an adoption; they then acted merely as the scrutineers of the will's authenticity and so on, giving authority to the incorrect interpretation of the clause about the name as an adoptive act.

In fact Antony denied and obstructed Octavius' claim. About half a century later the conservatively-minded Tiberius refused to allow his mother an Altar of Adoption on the strength of a *condicio* in Augustus' own will.[15] Still, the important thing was that Octavius had something which gave him the right to call himself Caesar and thus lay claim to the loyalties surrounding his great-uncle.

(Henceforth we'll give him the name of Octavianus, the form used after his 'adoption' to express his origin in the Octavian *gens*. To call him Caesar as he himself did is confusing; to call him Augustus is to anticipate events.) In the confused situation, his claims could not undergo the careful scrutinies or meet the legalist objections that they would have roused in calmer times. He had his lever and with it he moved a world. Not only did he now manage to step in many ways into Caesar's political shoes; he also had a claim on large sums of money, which were necessary if he were to win over the soldiery.[16] Caesar's personal estate alone amounted to one-seventh as much as the whole Roman Treasury.

As for Caesarion, it proves nothing to point out that only after Caesar's death did the Senate debate the question of his existence. How could it have done so before? Antony made a report that Caesar had accepted the child as his own in talking with friends. There is nothing unlikely in such a statement. The only way open for Caesar to acknowledge a child born to him by a woman legally a *peregrina* was such an action. Suetonius follows the passage in which he says Caesar 'gave her permission to call by his name' their son, with the statement: 'Marc Antony declared in the Senate that Caesar had acknowledged the child as his own and that G. Matius, G. Oppius, and the rest of Caesar's friends knew it to be true. On this occasion Oppius, as if it were an imputation he was called on to refute, published a book to show that "the child which Cleopatra fathered upon Caesar was not his".'[17] We must remember that the one thing Octavian could not possibly permit was the suggestion that he was not himself truly Caesar's 'son' or that anyone else had a better claim to Caesar's heritage. No one could have gone on living in Rome or Italy who accepted Caesarion. Oppius' book would thus have been a simple act of self-preservation. G. Matius does not seem to have made a public statement—unless Oppius wrote his book in the name of all Caesar's friends who wanted to survive under Octavian.

Nikolaos of Damas denies, on the strength of Caesar's will, that Caesarion was his son. But that is no evidence. Even if Caesarion already existed in September 45, or Caesar then knew of Cleopatra's pregnancy, he could not name her children in a Roman will. Assuming that before his death he knew of Caesarion, he may have had plans for him of which we know nothing.[18] Finally there is the point that Dion mentions, in dealing with the period of conflict before Brutus and Cassius were defeated, a verification from the Triumvirs of Caesarion's legitimacy. 'The people of Tarsos were praised by the Triumvirs, who already were in control of Rome, and hoped to get some return for their losses. Cleopatra also, because of the aid she had sent to Dolabella, was granted the right to call her son King of Egypt; this son, whom she named Ptolemy, she pretended to be her son by Caesar, and she therefore used to call him Caesarion.'[19] Octavian must have known already that she claimed the child to be Caesar's, and it is strange to find him agreeing to any elevation of him to an important rank, which in effect acknowledged him to be legitimate in some sort of way. Perhaps Antony pressed for the recognition and Octavian did not feel strong enough to obstruct him at this stage. It is of interest to find Antony apparently favourable to Cleopatra's cause long before they met as lovers. Such

points help to confirm the suggestion that Antony and
Cleopatra had come to know one another in a sympathetic
if still distant way during her residence in Caesar's
Gardens.

The fact that she does not seem to have used Caesarion
in datings before Caesar's death, again proves little; for
she was not a free agent in the matter till March 44.
However a year's lease of katoikic land from Oxyrhynchos
was written on 27 Epeiph (the month also called Gorpiaios)
—26 July 44—'in the 8th Year of the Reign of Cleopatra
and Ptolemy, Fatherloving Gods'.[20] Who was this
Ptolemy: Ptolemy XIV or Caesarion? Dion mentions
that the former was at Rome with his sisterwife Cleopatra,
and seems to imply that he was later (41) put to death by
Antony with his sister Arsinoe in Ephesos. The latter part
of the account is clearly an error; the 'Ptolemy' of 41 was
a man pretending to be the Ptolemy who was drowned in
the Nile.[21] How then did Ptolemy XIV end?

He certainly died about this time. Cleopatra, no longer
impeded by Caesar, got rid of him. Josephos says that she
poisoned him at the age of fifteen; and though he is a
hostile witness we take his word in this matter. Porphyrios
states that the boy died in his 4th (and her 8th) Year as a
result of her *apatai* (guiles or treacheries). That puts his
death in 45–4. Since there would be no point in bringing
him back to Egypt to be murdered and in thus attracting
more attention to the deed, we may assume that she dealt
with him in the confused days immediately after the Ides
or that she had him killed and disposed of on shipboard.[22]
She would certainly have reached Egypt well before 26
July, and we would expect news of his death to have
arrived at Oxyrhynchos by then if he were dead at the

time she landed. However, such news could be late in moving across Egypt; and the protocol of the document in question may have been drawn up somewhat earlier in Epeiph, which in 44 began on 30 June.[23] So we must admit that we cannot draw any sure conclusions from the wording of the date.

The only definite records of co-rule with Caesarion belong to her 9th and 11th Years, 43 and 41 B.C.[24] Porphyrios states that in her Years 1–4 she was associated with Ptolemy XIV, in her Years 5–8 with Ptolemy XV, in her Years 8–15 she reigned alone, while her 16th–22nd Years correspond to Years 1–7 (of Antony). However, he was wrong in assigning double dates to her Years 5–8, since demotic *stēlai* of her 5th and 6th Year omit Ptolemy XIV, as does a coin.[25] The passage already cited from Dion about the Triumvirs giving her the right to call Caesarion King of Egypt makes clear that as soon as she got rid of her brother she planned to raise her son to the throne at her side. The temple at Dendera shows a colossal figure of her as Hathor with the boy dressed as an ancient Pharaoh. About the same time a Fayum Greek dedicated a *stēlē* on behalf of Queen Cleopatra, King Ptolemy Caesar, and 'their ancestors' (the houses of the Ptolemies and of the *gens* Julia), to the crocodile god, whom he described as the young king's great-grand-father. The *stēlē* of Turin begins its text: 'In the Reign of Queen Cleopatra Fatherloving Goddess and Ptolemy who is also Caesar Fatherloving Motherloving God . . .', though the rest can be only conjecturally restored.[26] Its date has been interpreted; 'In the 10th Year [of Cleopatra] which is also the 2nd Year [of Ptolemy Caesar],' that is 43–2. However it seems that this reading is an error and that the date of Cleopatra has been written out in full, completing the line; no year is then attached to Caesarion. Indeed it is usual for trilingual decrees, such as we find on this *stēlē*, to have the year set out in full in the Greek text. Further, a document, dateable 44–37, dealing with the cession of katoikic land [a military tenure], begins, '. . . Fatherloving and Caesar God Fatherloving, Motherloving.' The year-date is lost. It thus turns out that while there is clear evidence of Cleopatra associating Caesarion with herself on the throne, there is no known case where she gives him a separate year-date. The association suggests that the date 47 rather than that of 44 is preferable for his birth; but Cleopatra was quite capable of giving the title of king and co-ruler to a baby of a few months if it suited her.[27]

Back in Egypt, she had no lack of local problems, while all the while she was keeping her mind on the changing world-situation. She now knew all the main actors well, directly or through the unsparing gossip of Rome, and must have had agents and partisans who sent her further information from time to time. But it was not long before she had to deal with one of the periodic Nile failures which were followed by scarcities and famines. Seneca tells us, 'One knows that the Nile remained two years without overflowing. That was in the 10th and 11th Year of Cleopatra's reign. This irregularity, men say, indicated the fall of the two rulers. In fact Antony and Cleopatra did fall from power. Earlier, according to Kallimachos, the Nile did not overflow for nine years.'[28] He thus dates the difficulties in the years 42–1 B.C. It was indeed stretching portents to link the low Niles of those years with the fall of Antony and Cleopatra ten years later; but perhaps men remembered them as something darkening her reign. The Turin stēlē cited above was that on which Theban priests and leading citizens honoured the *epistates* Kallimachos—a monument we discussed in the first chapter. The magistrate, we learn, had done all he could to relieve the distress which the low flooding had caused.

The reason for the troubles, it has been argued, was to be found in the slow silting-up of the canals through neglect. No doubt under the later Ptolemies there was deterioration in the system; Augustus found it necessary to clean the canals out. But famines in Egypt came primarily from the failure of the Nile to rise above the Cubits of Death. Thus, under Ptolemy III, when the irrigation-works must have been in good order, there was a great famine. Cleopatra seems to have done her best to keep the agricultural system functioning as well as the circumstances of her day allowed. For one thing, she needed to foster and build up Egypt's resources for the moment when she would be involved, as she knew she must be, in the world-struggle; she lost no time in building up her fleet. Also, in her own way, she felt responsible for the well-being of her people; her whole concept of power implied a strong ruler who was the fountainhead of prosperity and happiness for those who carried out his or her will. Later, in 32, she was able to feed Antony's great army and navy, and supplied grain for his depots in Greece. She proclaimed her ideal by putting on her coins the double horns-of-plenty of Arsinoe II, Lady of Abundance.

As often, famine was followed by disease. Dioskourides of Anazarba, called Phakas (Freckled), who was at

Alexandria about this time or a little later, wrote the first medical treatise on the plague. He noted the symptoms (suppuration of the lymphatic glands, appearance of black blotches on the skin) which suggest bubonic. People were in dire need. A papyrus shows a woman contracting herself out as a servant for 99 years, that is, a slave; it was forbidden under the Ptolemies for free persons to sell themselves into slavery.[29]

The care which Cleopatra took over administrative matters, especially those concerned with agriculture, is indeed shown by a decree issued in her name and in that of Caesarion and found at Herakleopolis, dated 13 April 41.

Queen Cleopatra Fatherloving Goddess and King Ptolemy who is also Caesar Fatherloving Motherloving God, to the Stragegos of the Herakleopolite Nome, greeting. Let the subjoined Decree, with the present Royal Letter, be transscribed in Greek and in Native Letters, and let it be set up publicly in the Metropolis and in the Principal Places of the Nome, and let all else be done according to our Commands. Farewell. Year 11. Daisios 13, which is Pharmouthi 13.

To Theon [? *dioiketes*]. Whereas those from the City who do agricultural work in the Prosopite and Boubastite Nomes have addressed a Petition to us in Audience on 15 Phamenoth against the Officials of the Ten Nomes [probably those of Lower Egypt], setting out how these, contrary to Our Will and to the Orders repeatedly sent out in accordance with Our Decision, by those over the Administration, to the effect that nobody should demand of them anything above the essential Royal Dues, attempt to act wrongfully and to include them among those of whom rural and provincial dues, which are not their concern, are exacted,

We, being extremely indignant and considering it well to issue a General and Universal Ordinance regarding the whole

127

matter, have decreed that all those from the City, who carry on agricultural work in the country, shall not be subjected, as others are, to demands for *stephanoi* and *epigraphai* such as may be made from time to time, and on special occasions, in the Nomes. Nor shall their goods be distrained for such contributions. Nor shall any new tax be required of them. But when they have once paid the essential Dues, in kind or in cash, for cornland and for vineland, which have regularly in the past been assigned to the Royal Treasury, they shall not be molested for anything further, on any pretext whatever.

Let it be done accordingly, and this put up in public, according to Law.

Alexandrians had special privileges. Local officials had been harassing them for payment of various taxes that only the inhabitants of the *chora* (the country as distinct from the City) had to pay. Cleopatra, in response to a complaining delegation, sent round the strongly-worded decree given above, the last we have from a Ptolemy. She felt that it was necessary, no doubt, not only to keep the Alexandrians, with their readiness to protest and riot, in a good humour, but also to ensure that they would be available for agricultural work in the difficult year of 41. *Stephanoi* (wreaths, crowns) were in effect forced gifts by the people to the king, made on the fiction that they paid for his golden crown; some *stephanoi* seem paid on appointments to office or promotions in rank; they were made in irregular payments. If a cleruch, a holder of land by military tenure, failed to pay up, he lost his *kleros* or allotment, which passed over to someone who produced the money in his stead. Thus we find the lands of two men, each named Heliodoros, transferred to three others 'because they paid the *stephanos* on behalf of' the two defaulters. *Epigraphai* were imposts of a special kind, which, at least in origin, were designed to meet an emergency.[30] In ordinances of 118 B.C. aimed at the ending of unjust acts of the tax-collectors with regard to temple-estates we find:

> No one shall take away by force anything of what has been dedicated to the gods, nor apply forcible persuasion to the superintendence of the sacred revenues, whether derived from villages or land or any other temple-revenues, nor shall the tax on associations or the *stephanoi* or the artaba-tax be paid on what has been dedicated to the gods, nor shall the temple-lands by worked on any pretext, but they shall be left to be administered by priests.[31]

Stephanoi and *epigraphai* were clearly impositions that could be abused with particular ease by the officials.

Meanwhile in the great world Antony had been well placed to step into Caesar's place as his trusted lieutenant to whom the legionaries and veterans would rally. But he was a soldier rather than a politician and for a while felt lost in the confused situation following the murder. The force that upset all attempts at a new political compromise with the murderers came from below, from the populace and from the army. Herophilus, a veterinary surgeon who claimed to be a descendent of Marius, became a leading agitator on behalf of Caesar's divinity. Stirred by his apocalyptic preachings, the people set up a pillar on the site of Caesar's pyre, the place of his rebirth as a god out of fire. (In 52 the infuriated crowd had burned the body of Clodius in the Curia Hostilia, reducing the Senate House to ashes in the blaze.) Enthusiasts surrounded the pillar of sky-apotheosis with daily prayers and offerings, till

Antony, who at this stage saw such matters as a mere unsettling nuisance, arrested and executed Herophilus. Dolabella had the pillar thrown down.

The extent to which Antony seems trying at this moment to be all things to all men or to keep up a pretence of agreement between the *optimates* and the Caesarians is shown by a letter he wrote to Cicero on 17 April 44. He was restoring from exile Sextus, the devoted secretary of Clodius, and consulted Cicero, the most eminent anti-Clodian, with extreme politeness. He knew that Cicero could not prevent his act, but felt it a good thing to get his formal acquiescence. There was nothing bloodthirsty about Antony and he may well have wanted at this moment to bring about some sort of *concordia* that would avert another civil war; at the same time he remained firmly true to his Clodian loyalties. We do not know exactly when Antony married Fulvia, the widow of Clodius, herself as much a firebrand as her dead husband; but it was sometime before Caesar's death. He had divorced Antonia early in the year. 'You accused of misconduct a woman of the greatest purity. What can be said more? You weren't content with that. At a crowded session of the Senate on the Kalends of January, in your uncle's presence, you dared to allege this as your reason for hating Dolabella—your discovery of his attempted adultery with your cousin and wife.'[32] So declared Cicero in his second *Philippic* (never spoken but published in November 44). Fulvia had no doubt prompted Antony in the matter of the secretary's return.

The murderers had failed to develop any cohesive activity. A letter of Cicero recounts a visit to Brutus and Cassius at Antium in June 44. It reveals vividly the

mother-dominated Brutus, Servilia the active member of
the group, and Cassius, a man-of-action confounded by a
situation beyond his grasp. 'I reached Antium on the 8th.
Brutus was very pleased with my arrival. Then in front of
Servilia, Tertulla, Porcia, and a crowd of others, he asked
my opinion; Favonius was there too. On the way I'd
thought things out and I advised him to accept control of
the Asian corn-supply; no course was left to us except to
keep him safe—which meant keeping a bulwark for the
constitution as well. While I was in full swing with my
speech, in came Cassius. I repeated my remarks. At which,
with flashing eyes, a dragon of war indeed, he announced
that he'd refuse to go to Sicily.' Cicero goes on to give us
the very dialogue of the irresolute conspirators.

'Am I to bow to an insult as if it were a favour?'
demanded Cassius.

'What's your intention then?'

'I'll go to Achaia.'

'And what of you, Brutus?'

'To Rome if you suggest it.'

'It's the last thing. You wouldn't be safe.'

'Well, if it could be worked, would you agree?'

'I'd rather you didn't go to a province now or after
your praetorship, but I can't be drawn into advising you
to trust yourself at Rome.'

Cicero continues, 'That made them start lamenting at
length, and Cassius the loudest, their missed opportunities,
and they blamed Decimus bitterly. I told them they ought
to leave the past alone, but agreed with all they said,
when I went on to explain what should have been done—
saying nothing new, only what is the daily talk, and omitting altogether to question who else should have been

removed—merely mentioning that the Senate ought to have been called, the excited populace stimulated to a fury of partisanship, and the whole government taken over—your gossip Servilia burst out.'

'This is stuff I never heard from anyone,' she cried.

Cicero was unaffected. 'I shut her up. But I think Cassius will go; for Servilia promised she'll get the Corn-Supply Commission withdrawn from the senatorial decree, and our friend soon dropped his silly talk of wanting to go to Rome. So they've decided the Games are to be held in his name during his absence. It seemed to me they wanted to go straight from Antium to Asia. In short, nothing was satisfied by my journey save my conscience. I couldn't let Brutus leave Italy before I'd seen him. Omitting what I did as a duty owed to our affection, I found myself asking: Now what's the end of all your journey, seer? In fact I hit on a ship leaky or rather already breaking up. No plans, no reason, no system.'[33]

Meanwhile Octavian had arrived on the scene from Apollonia in Illyricum, where, in his eighteenth year, he had been undergoing some military training and where he had met M. Vipsanius Agrippa who was to prove so invaluable to him. On news of the murder he left for Rome with Agrippa and a few other friends, arriving early in May. Antony, not a vindictive man and temporarily out of his depth, as we saw, inclined to some sort of compromise. But he had Caesar's papers and money, and at once a conflict developed between him and Octavian. The soldiers were determined that Caesar should be avenged—or rather certain sections of the legions and the veterans, those who in the following months clamoured at the gates of Rome for the lands that Caesar had promised them, or who were settled in colonies, especially those in Campania and Samnium; those held under Lepidus as governor designate of Gaul and Hither Spain; those stationed in Macedonia, not far from Apollonia, who had been destined for the Parthian War; those stationed at Brundisium to maintain the Adriatic crossing. These men, partly out of a need to defend their gains and to claim what had been promised, and partly out of a sincere sense of loyalty, developed the *pietas Caesaris* which prevented any accommodation with the murderers and their supporters.[34]

What did much to confuse the situation and impede the growth of a simple avenging movement was the problem which these men felt as to who was to be the embodiment of their *pietas*. There were two figures who, each in his own way, stood out as the new leader: Antony, Caesar's comrade-in-war, and Octavian, the heir who had assumed the dead man's name. So Antony and Octavian had to outdo one another as Caesar's champion and at the same time to shake themselves free of any entanglement with the anti-Caesarians. Cicero, realising how demoralised were Brutus and most of the other conspirators, imagined that he could use the inexperienced Octavian against Antony whom all along he saw as the real enemy. Perhaps it was at this time that Antony testified to Caesarion's paternity in an effort to obstruct Octavian; he scoffed at the latter as a 'boy who owes all to a name,' an assumed name at that. Cicero launched his series of attacks on Antony in the Senate, called *Philippics* after the attacks by Demosthenes on Philip of Macedon (who was threatening the freedom of the Greek cities). He thus dragged the Senate into a war with Antony, who was defeated at

Mutina in April 43. Antony had to cross the Appenines without provisions and evacuate Italy. Such occasions of hardship and trial always brought out the best of him.

On the Senate's instructions, Octavian had joined the consuls in the attack on Antony. Both consuls died. The Senate wanted to appoint to the command Decimus Brutus, one of the more capable of Caesar's killers. But Octavian could not serve under him without losing his whole moral position, his basis of appeal to the legions and the veterans. He marched back to Rome and took the consulship by force in August, carried out a sentence of outlawry against the murderers, then went north to confer with Antony and Lepidus (Caesar's Master of Horse) near Bononia in October. The three men agreed to divide the world among themselves and marched on Rome. On 27 November their position was legalised by their appointments as Triumvirs for the Reorganisation of the State with unlimited powers for five years. At once they published lists of proscribed men; some 300 senators and 3000 *equites* lost life and property.

The thing which the ruling class most dreaded had happened; the logic of the situation, which Caesar with his clemencies had hoped to avoid, asserted itself. Behind the triumvirate and its policies lay the powerful pressure of the soldiers, who wanted to avenge Caesar and who brought the economic crisis to a head with their demands for pay, rewards, and settlements. Also the need to deal with the murderers of Caesar begot a sharp problem of raising ready cash.

Now the triumvirs, with assured army-support and with the resources for the war, turned to deal with the malcontents gathered under Brutus and Cassius in the east, where they were opposed by the hot-headed Dolabella. Cleopatra was naturally whole-heartedly on the Caesarian side, which was soon to recognise Caesarion as her heir; but Cassius was attacking Dolabella nearby in Syria and she feared to bring him upon her. Worse, the Egyptian fleet, stationed at Cyprus under the governor Sarapion, went over to Cassius. She used the genuine enough plea of famine and pestilence to avoid sending further help; and Cassius was meditating a march on Alexandria when he was called to Asia Minor by Brutus. Cleopatra put out with her fleet and met a storm off the Libyan coast; instead of going on to join Cassius, she returned home on a plea of seasickness. The first woman to command a fleet since Artemisia led a squadron of Persian ships against the Greeks, she was not likely to have been deterred by any bodily qualms if she had really meant to sail. However the Roman legions left in Egypt since 47 had earlier marched off under Allienus to join Dolabella, but in Syria they changed their minds and went over to Cassius. In July 43 Dolabella, pressed hard in Syrian Laodikeia, committed suicide. Then in the autumn of 42 Brutus and Cassius were defeated at Philippi and killed themselves. Octavian had fallen ill and the prestige of the victory went to Antony. The contrast of the two men also came out in their treatment of the vanquished. Octavian hacked off Brutus' head and sent it to be laid at the foot of Caesar's statue in Rome; Antony covered the body with his purple cloak and gave it worthy burial.

The triumvirs now divided the world. Italy was to be held in common; Octavian took Spain and Sardinia; Lepidus, North Africa; Antony, as the dominant leader, took both Gauls and the East. The man who had the East, the richest area, had also the task of collecting the money to be spent on the disbanded troops and thus played the superior role. Further, Antony was now in a position to carry on with Caesar's plans of attacking Parthia. But in fact his preoccupation with the East enabled Octavian to treat Italy as his domain, so that he held Rome with all its political importance and the crucial Italian recruiting-grounds.[35] He was thus able to supervise the assigning of lands and to deal with Sextus, son of the great Pompey, who had got control of Sicily. Of the 11 legions left, Antony had 6, plus 2 that he got from Octavian; he thus commanded 8 legions and 10,000 horse as against Octavian's 3 legions and 4,000 horse. Besides, he already had large armies in the Gauls, 11 legions under Fufius Calenus and 13 divided between Ventidius Bassus, Pollio, and Plancus—though he was beginning to lose touch with those generals. In the East he controlled the main sources of wealth and the big trading-centres, even if wars had impaired the productivity there; he thus was in turn strong in seapower. But as against all that Octavian had the strong tactical position of the man who seemed master of Rome, and to whom veterans had in large part to look for their allocations.

Leaving Greece, Antony landed at Ephesos where the people hailed him as the New Dionysos. As we have seen, Roman governors had long been given cults in Asia; the Ephesians were simply expressing the hope that Antony would be bountiful and beneficient; their cries in no way affected his actual position. But in the new situation the salutations as a god had a decisive new effect. They chimed in with his mood; he wanted to be taken as a philhellene, a man of deep culture, responsive to the rich symbolisms of the east. He rewarded Ephesos and some other towns that had suffered under Cassius, and began his Dionysiac career, hailed as the god sprung from Ares and Aphrodite and manifested as the Redeemer of Mankind. Welcomed by processions of revelling bacchantes and satyrs, ivy-wreathed, waving *thyrsi*, to the music of pipes and zithers, he felt that he at last knew what power was meant for. Everything in his expansive temperament, with its great powers of enjoyment, its sense of comradeship born out of the wars, responded to the imagery and its implications.

Marcus Antonius

We may now pause to look more closely at Antony, who was soon to be Cleopatra's lover. The Antonii, though plebeian in origin, had for generations belonged to the highest levels of the ruling class. His grandfather, an orator who specialised in pathos, had been killed by the Marians. His father decided to keep out of politics and squandered all the family wealth till only a mortgaged villa at Misenum, on the Bay of Naples, remained. Plutarch tells an anecdote that reveals his feckless nature. A friend came to borrow money, but as usual there was none in the house—or at least none that M. Antonius could lay hands on; for his wife Julia, a woman of vigorous character, kept strict control of the purse. So he said that he wanted to be shaved, and sent a slave for a silver basin. The slave, though bidden like his fellows to report to the mistress all extravagances of the master, did not suspect anything. M. Antonius dried his face, threw away the water, and presented the basin to the friend, telling him to pawn it. Later the basin was missed. Julia decided that some slave had stolen it, and began an inquisition of the household. Then her husband confessed. Though not ambitious, he had become praetor in 75, and next year used some friends to gain the command of the fleet mustered to sweep the seas clear of pirates. He basely used his position to plunder Sicily instead of defending it, and was badly defeated in his attack on Crete, where he died. He was called Creticus in derision. Sallust says that he was 'devoid of all cares but those of the moment.'

Our Antony was young when his father died—about ten years. His mother Julia, daughter of L. Julius Caesar, consul in 64, was distantly related to the great Caesar. She remarried; and Antony was brought up by his step-father Cornelius Lentulus, who in 63 was executed by Cicero as an accomplice of Catilina. That event must have had a considerable effect on Antonius, then about twenty. The youth shared his father's carelessness about money and soon ran into debt; but he was strongly built and had a restless energy. He was attracted by the anarcho-radical Clodius; but, in flight from creditors, departed to Greece and Syria, where we saw him serving as cavalry officer under Gabinius. After that he went, in 54, to fight under Caesar in Gaul. This connection determined his whole future. Caesar liked his vigorous capacities, his generous powers of devotion, and he admired in Caesar the intellectual breadth which he himself lacked, the scope of strategic vision, his stability of purpose, and the grasp of the epoch's throes of death and birth. He returned to Rome briefly, at Caesar's order, to carry on with the steps necessary for a Roman political career, and was elected quaestor. He then returned to Caesar, who sent him back to Rome again in 50, to become an augur and a tribune of the *plebs*. When on 1 January 49 the Senate ignored the veto of Antony and a colleague against the decree depriving Caesar of his command, the two tribunes considered their lives threatened and on 7 January fled to Caesar.

Caesar in reply marched on Italy and in a few weeks controlled the whole peninsula. Antony was made his legate in charge of it, while Caesar went to Spain; then in 48 he brought reinforcements to Caesar in Greece and fought at Pharsalos, commanding the left wing. In 47 Caesar, returning from Egypt as dictator, appointed him Master of Horse, again in charge of Italy, while he himself was fighting in Africa. During this time Antony had his affair with the actress Cytheris and did not shrink from appearing in public with her: a rehearsal on a small scale for his boldness with Cleopatra. As we saw he is said to have had a disagreement with Caesar over paying for Pompey's property; but the whole story of a break with Caesar is dubious. Antony may have been ill, or there may have been other reasons for his staying on in Italy, of which we know nothing. The fact that he did not accompany Caesar and yet held no office in Italy would have been enough for the anti-Caesarians to seize on the situation with innuendoes and slanders. The buying of Pompey's property appears to have been a political act, if we may trust Cicero's statement that no one dared to bid for the estate. Antony's act would then have been one of bravado, to show that he at least was not afraid of being marked down by the *optimates* for destruction. The story of the resulting quarrel with Caesar would be part of the whispering campaign against him, to show that his act

had been unlucky. The senators would be watching for
every hint of dissention inside the Caesarian party;
in 45, however, we find him in full harmony with
Caesar, whose fellow-consul he was at the time of the
murder.

He was a magnificent cavalry-leader, a downright,
jovial soldier, loved by the troops whom he understood
and genuinely cared for. He lacked any strong ambition,
valuing power for the way it enabled him to live blithely
and carelessly on the grand scale, helping his friends and
pleasing people in general. He was not a politician; but
Caesar must have thought well of his administrative
capacity as well as of his soldierly devotion, or he would
not have twice appointed him in charge of Italy at critical
times. When put to it, he could evaluate a situation with
shrewdness and carry out well-considered manoeuvres;
but he did all that, not with Caesar's comprehensive grasp,
but rather with a quick intuitive penetration and sense of
tactics, an understanding of people rather than of the
deeper forces at work. In the difficult time after Caesar's
death, for instance, he had to move very carefully and even
craftily to save himself from being isolated and to keep
on mustering the forces opposed to the Senate, a problem
complicated by the advent of Octavian. A good judge of
men, he could pick efficient subordinates, and he used this
intuitive sense of a man's value in such things as his
eastern settlements. In a corner he could be ruthless; but
as soon as the situation eased, he returned to his good
nature. He quite lacked the cold calculating foresights and
tenacious ambitions of Octavian. His greatness came out
in adversity; when things went easily, he slackened his
controls and wanted simply to enjoy himself and see

others also having a good time. By nature he was straight-forward and loyal, trusting others and not hard to deceive; he was incapable of standing up against a man like Octavian in long-distance schemes and complicated deceits. In one sense his loyalty did not extend to his relations with women, whom he saw as delightful creatures intended for his delectation in moments of leisure. Yet he was drawn to women of strong and even fiery character; and could subordinate his own aims and satisfactions to their demands in a more than temporary submission, in a transfer to their person of the emotions of comradeship that he normally kept for men. We know little of his first wife Fadia except that she bore him several children and was the daughter of a rich freedman.[1] She must have attracted him by an exceptional character or beauty, or by her money. His second wife, a cousin, is again lost in the shadows except for the charge that she had an intrigue with the impetuous Dolabella. The next woman with whom we find him connected was Cytheris, who had been freedwoman and mistress of Volumnius Eutrapelus. The latter was a friend of Antony, and seems to have surrendered the girl to him; at one time he was chief of engineers, *praefectus fabrum*, in Antony's army. After Antony, Cytheris was the mistress of the poet Gallus, who founded the Roman elegy and who complained of her fickleness.[2] With two other actresses, Origo and Arbuscula, she was the best known courtesan of the time at Rome; Gallus called her Lycoris in his poems. On 3 May 49 Cicero wrote to Atticus: 'Antony carries Cytheris about with him in an open litter as his second wife and has seven other litters of friends, male and female, as well. See what a shameful death we die, and doubt if you can that whether Caesar comes back victor or vanquished he'll stage a massacre.' Cicero was fond of suspecting that Caesar would take to the violences he himself would have liked to perpetrate on the radicals. But despite his hard words about Cytheris he was thrilled when he found himself near her at a dinner party. The date was around November 46 and the friend he addressed was L. Papirius Paetus, a rich Epicurean. He was at the house of Eutrapelus, with whom Cytheris was still on good terms, and who later on acted as Prefect of Engineers for Antony; and was scribbling in a notebook the text which would later be transcribed on *chartae*, papyrus-leaves. 'Are you surprised we've become so merry in our slavery? What then am I to do, I ask you, pupil of a philosopher, to advise me? Am I to suffer anguish? am I to torment myself? What good would that do me? and again, how long? Live, you say, in your books. Do you suppose I do anything else? Could I live at all if it weren't that I live in my books? But even with them, though I'm not fed up, there *is* a limit. When I've left them, though I'm not much concerned about my dinner—and yet this was the very theme of inquiry you put before the philosopher Dion—still I can't find out what I can do better, till it's time to go back to bed. But listen to the rest of my tale. Next below Eutrapelus reclined Cytheris. At such a dinner-party, then, you remark, was the famous Cicero.

He at whom stared the Greeks and to whose face
all turned their faces.

Hercules, I never suspected she'd be there; but after all even the great Socratic Aristippus didn't blush when it was thrown at him that Lais was his mistress. 'I have her,' he said, 'she doesn't have me.' It goes better in Greek: translate it if you like. As for myself, however, I was never tempted by anything of that sort even when a young man, much less now that I'm old. A dinner party is my joy. There I let go on whatever crops up, as they say, in the conversation, and convert groans into loud guffaws.' The citation was perhaps from Ennius' *Telamo*. Cytheris, Cicero says, reclined below Eutrapelus. She seems the only woman present and is no relation of the host; her reclining was thus the act of a loose woman. But in fact in the late Republic ladies ceased to sit discreetly on a chair and joined the diners; a graffito on a Pompeian dining-room wall bids the men keep their eyes off the other fellows' wives.[3] (We find however an odd touch of prudery applied under the Empire to the goddesses in a *lectisternium*; perviously they had reclined, now they were made to sit up.)

P. Volumnius Eutrapelus was a man of much wit and good humour. In writing to him, Cicero feels impelled to keep up a flow of flippancies. Here he is complaining that since he left Rome all the bad jokes are being attributed to him. 'Now the City is such a hotbed of vulgarity that nothing is so *banale* as not to seem charming to someone, unless you see at once that a *double entendre* is clever, an hyperbole in good taste, a pun smart, an unexpected conclusion comical . . . show your mettle and go so far as to asseverate that they're none of mine. Here we need the aid of your exquisitely refined discrimination and that esoteric erudition of yours, whereby you so often make me ashamed of myself when speaking.'[4] But in the *Philippics* the man to whom he had been so studiously polite a few years before is turned into a vile wallowing comrade and fellow-gambler of Antony, and Cytheris comes in for her share of abuse. Antony, 'a tribune of the people, was driven in a Gaulish chariot; laurel-crowned lictors preceded him; in their midst a female mime was carried in an open litter, a woman whom citizens from the towns, discreet persons, coming out perforce to meet her, saluted—not by her notorious professional name, but as Volumnia. There followed a travelling coach of pimps, a most iniquitous retinue; a mother, set in the rear, attended to her vicious son's mistress as though she were a daughter-in-law.'[5]

We see that Antony's mother Julia was present. A strong-minded woman, she later played a considerable part in the troubles after Caesar's murder. In the picture drawn by Cicero of Antony's movements the lictors are wreathed as for a Triumph. Plutarch tells us that a tribune could not claim any lictors at all, nor use a horse or carriage, nor wear a *toga praetexta* of the higher magistrates, nor indulge in any display. Cicero continues: 'You came to Brundisium. That's to say, into the lap and embrace of your mime-darling. How wretched to be unable to deny what's most shameful to confess. If you had no shame before the borough-towns, had you none even before your army of veterans? What soldier was there who didn't see her at Brundisium? who didn't grieve at being so late in finding out how scoundrelly a man he followed.' This picture of the shocked soldiery is somewhat ludicrous. Cicero adds, 'Then there was again a progress through Italy with the same mime as companion; in the towns a cruel and harassing drafting of soldiers; in the City a disgraceful pillaging of gold, silver, and especially of wine.'

Pliny says the carriage was drawn by lions, and Plutarch agrees. The latter draws on Cicero and other anti-Antonian propaganda for his account: 'They loathed his illtimed drunkenness, his heavy expenditure, his debauches with women, his days spent in sleep or in wandering around with crazed and splitting head, his nights in revelry or at shows or in attending the marriage feasts of mimes and jesters. At any rate we are told that he feasted at the nuptials of the mime Hippias, drank all night, and then, early in the morning, when the people summoned him to the Forum, came before them still surfeited with food and vomited into his toga, which one of his friends held at his service. Sergius the mime was also one of those with the greatest influence on him, and Cytheris, a woman from the same school of acting, a prime favourite of his, whom he took about in a litter on his visits to the cities, and her litter was followed by as many attendants as that of his mother. More, people were vexed at the sight of golden beakers borne about on excursions from the City as in sacred processions, at the pitching of tents when he travelled, at the laying-out of costly repasts near groves and rivers, at chariots drawn by lions, and at the use of respectable men's and women's houses as quarters for harlots and psaltery-players.'[6]

There were no doubt grievances at the quartering of soldiers and the like. But Cicero and his friends were watching with sullen vigilance all the while for any deviation, however slight, from traditional procedures and moral standards. And Antony was the man to give them many occasions for self-righteous headshaking. Still, as we noted, Caesar's continued trust in him is sufficient refutation of the tales of wild irresponsible behaviour. To have taken Cytheris round with him was enough to give the conventional moralists a sense of dire revolutionary changes portending all sorts of upheavals and disasters. Note how in the passage of May 49 Cicero interpreted Antony's open companionship with Cytheris as an obvious prelude to massacres: a train of thought not at all clear to us but plain enough for an upper-class conservative of the time. Also, Antony did have a pet dwarf, a creature about two feet high, with a sharp and cunning wit which earned him the name of Sisyphus, a mythical trickster. Horace mentions him:

> A father calls his squinting son
> 'a pretty leering rogue.' That lad's a 'chick,'
> who's an abortion, something to make you sick,
> like Sisyphus.[7]

Buffoons and dwarfs were however common in great households, though Octavian disliked such creatures. 'For amusement he'd at times angle, dice, play with pebbles or nuts, or with little boys he'd collected from diverse countries, particularly Moors and Syrians, for their beauty or entertaining chatter. But dwarfs or anyone at all deformed he abhorred as abortions of nature and evil-omened.'

Antony was certainly capable of much self-indulgence when he did not feel the need to gather his energies for action. He saw himself as Hercules and strutted in his heavy war-cloak, with big sword and hitched-up tunic. We feel a great physical force in his thick neck, bulky build, full curly beard and coarse pugilistic face with an unusual length between eyes and mouth: a great bullforce not entirely harmonious in its manifestations. But he was more than his bullforce. The fascination of his character lies in the extent to which he overcame and controlled the impulse to live in the moment as his father had done; to lift his great driving energies on to a higher level; to feel himself in the last resort the vessel of tremendous Dionysiac forces of redemption and renewal. Not that he ever wholly solved his inner conflict between the desire to live riotously in the moment and the need to serve some cause greater than himself, Caesar or Cleopatra, which at the same time brought about his own self-fulfillment.

We feel in the pattern of his life a repetition of the conflicts between his easy-going father and his strong-minded mother with her urge to control and manage things. But what in his parents remained an unresolved tension issuing in nothing valuable, was by him given a deep significance and raised to a new powerful level, at which it merged with the vast conflicts of his world. In seeking to overcome the parental kind of tension in his relations with Fulvia and Cleopatra he both enormously enlarged the pattern and drove passionately on in quest of a resolution, a harmony which was all the richer because of the conflicts it included and resolved. And this harmony he sought on a grand scale made him in turn the mouthpiece of the torn and suffering world's longing for happiness and peace.

After Philippi he struck coins with his own head and the radiate Sun. In his earlier years in the east he had probably encountered the theories that made the Sun the supreme deity, the leader or king of the universe: a view already known in Greece in the 3rd century B.C.[9] Now some Greeks were suggesting that all other divinities might merge in the Sun; Cicero declared that it was the

Sun who informed and ordered the universe, *mens* and *temperatio*; and this outlook was more fully worked out under the empire with its single ruler claiming the whole *oikoumene*.[10] The Sun, however, had appeared before on Roman coins; and Antony was not proclaiming himself the New Sun, as did his descendant and imitator Caligula.[11] His coins must be taken as merely meaning that there was a link between the supreme man and the supreme god: though he may have heard of the prophecy which connected the Sun with a Coming Golden Age; for instance, that of the Cumaean Sibyl in which the Sun's rule precedes the period of complete blessedness.[12] As for his Lion, that seems to have been his genethliac symbol. On the eve of his Parthian war he struck a coin with a Lion holding a Sword; over the Lion's back was a Star, the sign of the advent of the new dispensation. And in the Sibylline verses we shall later consider he is the Lion, the spouse of Cleopatra: 'You shall no longer be the Widow, you shall mate with the Lion.'[13] The Lion, too, we must remember, had links with the Sun.

Fulvia followed Cytheris in Antony's affections. Daughter of M. Fulvius Bambalio of Tusculum, she married the wild Clodius and used to go about with him, sharing his exploits and his plans; their daughter was later married for a while to Octavian. When Clodius was murdered and his body exposed in his house's atrium, with her angry lamentations she stirred the crowds to vengeance. She was an extreme example of the New Women, of whom Clodia was an outstanding leader. Cicero, who had wanted to marry Clodia, did his best to draw a scathing picture of her in his oration in defence of M. Caelius. 'You saw a young man become your neighbour. His fair complexion, his tallness, and his face and eyes made an impression on you; you wanted to see him more often; you were sometimes seen in the same gardens with him—you a woman of high rank.' He added. 'You have gardens on the Tiber and you set them in that particular spot where the young men of the city come to bathe.' Worst of all, she frequented a seaside resort like Baiae which all respectable people knew to be the scene of licentious goings-on. Cicero fulminated:

'. . . Lusts and loves and adulteries and Baiae and doings on the seashore and banquets and revels and songs and music-parties and water-parties. . . . If any woman without a husband opens up her house to every loose-liver and doesn't hide the whore's life she leads; if she makes a habit of dining with men who aren't her relations; if she carries on like that in the City, in her own gardens, and in that very jostling place Baiae; if in short she behaves in such a way that not only her way of walking, but also her clothes and those in attendance on her, her hot eyes and her free way of talking, her embraces and kisses, her beach-parties and water-parties and dinner-parties, all show here not only a tart but a very wanton and depraved tart at that, I ask you, if a young man happens to be seen with her, is it so much adultery as simply taking what's offered?'

The restless and vigorous Roman women of the period, often impressive with their strong powers of self-assertion, their effect of great energies unable to find a worthy outlet, have certain affinities with Cleopatra; but she, who did have her outlet whatever the difficulties she met, would perhaps have disdained their shadier aspects while still feeling a warm partisanship on their behalf.

Fulvia, after losing Clodius, married another man of her

set, G. Scribonius Curio, a slighter and more vacillating radical than the reckless Clodius, though a talented orator, who in 50 went over to Caesar. When in 49 he fell in Africa, she stayed a widow till she married Antony about 44. She bore him two sons. The tale went that she had lived dissolutely till this marriage, then devoted herself to Antony and his career. During the proscriptions she is said to have behaved cruelly and imperiously, delighting especially in the head of Cicero, who had been the bitter foe of Clodius as well as of Antony. Plutarch says, 'Antony put away his reprehensible way of living and turned his mind to marriage, taking to wife Fulvia, widow of the demagogue Clodius. She was a woman who gave no thought to spinning or housekeeping, nor would she deign to be the mistress of a man of private rank, but wanted to rule a ruler and command a commander. So Cleopatra was indebted to Fulvia for teaching Antony to accept a woman's sway; she took him over quite tamed and schooled from the beginning to obey women. Still, he tried playful ways and youthful tricks to make even Fulvia more light of heart. Thus, when many went out to meet Caesar after his Spanish victory, Antony joined them. Then suddenly a report burst on Italy that Caesar was dead and his enemies marching on the country. Antony turned back to Rome. He took the dress of a slave and came by night to his own house.'[14]

This tale seems a distortion of some masquerade of which Cicero gives a fuller account. 'You who imagined you'd been a Master of the Horse, who were a candidate, or rather a beggar, for the next year's Consulship, you, through the boroughs and colonies of Gaul—which we, when the consulship was canvassed for, not begged, used to canvass—you raced in Gaulish slippers and a mantle. But note the man's levity! When about the tenth hour of the day he reached Saxa Rubra, he lurked in a certain little tavern. Then, hiding himself, he went on boozing till dusk. After that, carried quickly in a gig to the City, he arrived home with head muffled. Doorkeeper: "Who are you?" "A courier from Marcus." At once he's taken in to the woman on whose account he had come, and handed her a letter. She read it with tears; for it was composed in amatory style and its gist was that he'd have nothing more to do with that mime of his, he'd cast out all love for her and transferred it to this other. And while she was weeping, this softhearted chap could bear it no longer. He unveiled his head and fell on her neck. O what a worthless character.'

Cicero and his group must have had a very efficient spy service if they could get such inside information about Antony's home life; but the story certainly sounds likely enough. There may well have been many angry and tearful scenes with Fulvia before Cytheris was finally discarded; and Plutarch was correct in seeing that these experiences played their part in curbing some of Antony's more wayward impulses and making him take a woman's claims with full seriousness.

After Philippi he gave Aigina and some small islands to Athens; Rhodes got Andros, Naxis, Tenos, Myndos; Lycia was freed from taxation and asked to restore Xanthos; Laodicia and Tarsos were made free cities, Tarsos being given a gymnasion. Antony called delegates from the cities to Ephesos; they represented the *Koinon* or Diet of Asia, the model for many other such Diets. Whether Antony founded the *Koinon* or gave it fresh

recognition is uncertain; its function as a vehicle of
Roman state-religion dates from Augustus. What the
delegates now found was that they had to raise money.
Antony praised the benevolence of the Roman (Seleukid)
system of taking a tenth of the harvest, which made the
government partners with the peasants, as against the
Attalid system of fixed payments; then he demanded the
same sum as they'd paid Cassius, ten years' taxes down.
Hybreas, orator of Mylasa, expressed the general despair.
'If you can take double tribute, doubtless you can give us
two summers and double our crops.' Asia had already
raised 200,000 talants. 'If the sum hasn't reached you, ask
your collectors for it. If it's paid and lost, we're ruined
men.' Plutarch comments acutely 'these words touched
Antony to the quick, for he was ignorant of most that
was going on, not so much through his easy disposition
as because he was simple enough to trust those around
him. There was a simplicity in his nature, a slowness in
perceiving things, though when he did see his mistakes
he showed keen repentance and made full acknowledge-
ment to the very young men who'd been unfairly treated;
and there was a largeness both in his reparation to the
wronged and in his punishment of the wrongers. Yet he
was thought to go past due bounds more in conferring
favours than in inflicting punishments. And his excess in
mirth and jest carried its own remedy with it. A man
might pay back his jokes and insolence; and he, Antony,
delighted in being laughed at no less than in laughing at
others. This vitiated most of his enterprises. He could not
believe that those who used bold speech in jest could
flatter him in earnest. So he was easily caught by their
praises, unaware that some men would mingle the piquant

sauce of bold words with cajolery to take away its cloying taste. Such men used their bold babbling over the cups to make their submissive yielding in affairs of State appear the action, not of men associating with someone merely to humour him, but of those conquered by superior wisdom.'[15] Antony reduced the demand on the Koinon to nine years' taxes to be paid over two years; but he probably never got all that. Cassius had exacted money all too efficiently.

Leaving Ephesos, he made the usual governmental tour of Asia Minor, holding courts in the chief cities. Those cities and the dynasts were both asked to supply money. As Plutarch says, he seems to have been lax in superintending such matters, and too generous in giving away what money he did get in. However he managed to carry on with fleet-building. The successes of Sextus Pompey in and around Italy had shown how the triumvirate was weak at sea. In Bithynia he met Herod. Hyrkanos, the highpriest governing Judaea, had earlier asked Cassius for the return of Jewish prisoners, and Cassius had agreed. Now the Jews, emboldened, sent to Antony the accusation that Herod, son of the dead Idumaian vizier Antipatros, was aiming at sole power in Judaea. Herod came to defend himself and impressed Antony as a capable and useful man. The complaint was dismissed.

In dealing with the many client-kings whom Rome at this time maintained in the east Antony made no changes till he had a good grasp of the situation in each area. Rome could not yet take in the whole east in the form of provinces; the client-kingdoms were needed as a transitional stage. They often paid tribute; they guarded frontiers and kept hilltribes in order; their armies were at

Rome's disposal. Their rulers could be changed if necessary, though the fixed custom was to choose the new ruler from the royal house. The two most important at the moment were Galatia (comprising also Paphlagonia and part of what was once Pontos, the area round Pharnakeia and Trapezos) and Cappadocia, where the kings, also ruling Armenia Minor, looked after the Euphrates frontier. The Galatian king, old Deiotaros, had aided Cassius; but his troops, under the secretary Amyntas, went over to Antony in time. Deiotaros died and Antony divided his realm between two grandsons. Galatian Pontos went to a grandson of the great Mithridates Eupator. In Cappadocia Ariarthes X succeeded in 42, but the priestkings of Komana had long claimed the crown. Komana was now ruled by young Archelaos (grandson of the Archelaos who was briefly king of Egypt during the Piper's exile), together with his mother Glaphyra, described by Dion as an *hetaira*. Appian says that Antony decided in Archelaos' favour because his mother 'appeared to him a beautiful woman'. But he also adds the unlikely story that he incited Archelaos against Ariarthes without dethroning the latter. The last thing he would have wanted, with a Parthian war in the offing, was to start civil strife in this region.[16]

As part of his settlements he had to call Cleopatra to account for her aid to Cassius. She was a ruler on a higher level than the petty kings of Asia Minor; and he set about summoning her with more tact and consideration.

Antony and Cleopatra

The man sent to summon Cleopatra was Q. Dellius, a clever fellow without any strength of character. Horace later addressed him in an ode in which with a touch of irony he advises him to do just what he knew that he couldn't do:

> Keep still in difficult days a mind
> unmoved; let easy times go by,
> all glad mad moods resigned,
> Dellius: you too must die.[1]

Plutarch says that, 'observing Cleopatra's looks and her subtlety and tricky wit in conversation, he at once knew that Antony would never think of doing such a woman any harm, and that in fact she'd have the greatest influence over him.' So he persuaded her to go. But, as we have seen, she must have known Antony well already; and even if she hadn't, she would certainly not have needed Dellius' persuasion to meet the man on whom Egypt's fate now depended. At last, after much preparations, she

set off. Plutarch's noble account of the meeting is familiar
through the use that Shakespeare made of it. 'Though she
received many summoning letters from Antony and from
his friends, she so looked down on the man and laughed
him to scorn that she sailed up the river Cydnus in a
barge with gilded poop, its sails spread purple, its rowers
urging it on with silver oars to the sound of the flute
blended with pipes and lyres. She herself reclined under a
canopy spangled with gold, adorned like Aphrodite in a
painting, while boys like Loves in paintings stood on
either side and fanned her. Also the loveliest of her
serving maidens, dressed up as Nereids and Graces, were
likewise stationed at the rudder-sweeps or else at the
reefing-ropes. Wonderful smells from innumerable incense-offerings were wafted along the riverbanks. Of the
inhabitants, some accompanied her on either bank from
the river's very mouth, others came down from the city to
share in the spectacle. Gradually the throng in the market
place drifted away, till at last Antony, seated on his
tribunal, was left alone. And a rumour spread on every
hand that Aphrodite was come to revel with Dionysos for
the good of Asia.'[2]

The rumour was surely started off by her agents; she
had indeed worked out the whole display with the aim of
spreading this interpretation. She knew Antony and his
salutations as the New Dionysos; she had set her mind
to stir his imagination and draw him close to her, using
symbols that appealed to them both.

'So Antony sent and invited her to supper; but she
thought it more suitable for him to come to her. At once,
to display his complaisance and amiable feelings, Antony
accepted and went. He found a preparation that beggared

description, but of all things was most amazed at the host of lights. We're told, so many of these were let down and set off on all sides at once, arranged with so many inclinations and adjustments to each other in patterns of rectangles and circles, that few sights were ever so beautiful or so worthy of being watched. Next day Antony feasted her in his turn, ambitious to surpass her splendour and elegance; but in both points he was left behind and vanquished. He was the first to make fun of the inadequacy and rusticity of his own arrangements. Cleopatra noted in his jests much of the soldier and the common-man, and adopted this manner now towards him without restraint, and boldly.'

Sokrates of Rhodes in Book III of his *Civil War* described the banquets. 'Meeting Antony in Cilicia, Cleopatra arranged in his honour a royal symposium, in which the service was wholly of gold and jewelled vessels made with exquisite art; even the walls were hung with tapestries woven of gold and silver threads. And having spread twelve *triclinia*,' the tables at each of which three guests reclined on couches, 'she invited him and his chosen friends. He was overwhelmed with the richness of the display; but she quietly smiled and said the things he saw were a gift to him. She invited him to come and dine with her again on the morrow, with his friends and his officers. On this occasion she provided an even more sumptuous symposion by far; the vessels used the previous time appeared paltry things; and once again she presented Antony with everything. As for the officers, each was allowed to take away the couch on which he had lain. Even the sideboards, as well as the couch-spreads, were divided among them; and when they went off, she supplied litters for guests of high rank, with bearers, while for the larger number she provided horses with silver-plated harness. For everyone she sent Ethiopian slaves to carry the torches. On the fourth day she distributed fees amounting to a talant for the purchase of roses; the floors of the dining-rooms were strewn with them a cubit-deep, in net-like festoons spread over everything.'[3]

The roses were thus one-and-a-half feet deep. Sokrates seems to have felt the Dionysiac implications of the festivities; for he further records that when Antony later visited Athens, he erected a scaffold in full view above the Theatre and roofed it with green boughs, like the caves or grottos built for Bacchic Revels. On it he hung tambourines, fawnskins, and other Dionysiac trinkets of all kinds, and in it he lay with his friends, drinking from early morning and entertained by Artists of the Dionysiac Guild who had been summoned from Italy—while Greeks from all parts gathered to see the sight. 'And at times he even shifted the sites of his revels to the top of the Akropolis, while the whole city of Athens was illuminated by torches hung from the roofs. And he gave orders that he should be proclaimed Dionysos throughout all the cities.' Athenaios, citing this passage, noted the similarity with Caligula's later behaviour. 'He was named the New Dionysos, and not only that, he also assumed the entire garb of Dionysos, and, thus arrayed, made progresses and sat in judgement.'

Cleopatra had no difficulty in explaining away her relations with Cassius. Antony was charmed. Sometime during the festivities they became lovers. At Cleopatra's insistence he had her sister Arsinoe put to death. Arsinoe had found asylum in Artemis' temple at Ephesos, where the highpriest or *megabyzos* was ill-advised enough to greet her as Queen. He escaped death through the appeals of the Ephesians to Cleopatra. With Arsinoe died the pretender who claimed to be Ptolemy XIV, and the governor of Cyprus, Sarapion, whom the Tyrians had surrendered.

Cleopatra was now about twenty-nine, an age, says Plutarch, when the Greek-Macedonian woman was at her best, both in mind and body. Her charm came from a mixture of intellectual and sensuous force; even the coins suggest her eager vitality. She had carried on the Ptolemaic tradition which had made the Museum (*Mouseion*, Sanctuary of the Muses) part of the palace, a place where the kings could discuss the universe with scholars.[4] We know of two philosophers who were in her entourage, Philostratos the Academician and Nikolaos of Damas, a Peripatetic. Of the former, called the Egyptian; we are told, 'Though he studied philosophy with Queen Cleopatra, he was described as a sophist—because he adopted the panegyrical and colourful type of eloquence: which came from associating with a woman who regarded even the art of letters [*to philologein*] as a sensuous thing [*tryphe*]. Hence the following couplet was made up as a parody aimed at him:

Acquire the temperament of that wise chap Philostratos, who, fresh from intercourse with her, takes on her colours.'[5]

A skilled organiser and woman-of-business, she had been reared in a corrupt court where the struggle for power was pervasive; she carried on the family-code and accepted no moral law but her own need as queen, as a woman (or goddess), who had at all costs to fulfil her destiny—though that destiny included making faithful subjects happy. It is unlikely that her two brother-marriages were ever consummated; they were forced on her as limitations of her power, something she resented and wanted to break from as soon as circumstances allowed; they were not part of a normal system of stabilising power like the earlier brother-sister alliances of the dynasty. She had two lovers whom she looked on as husbands, though in Roman eyes she was only their mistress. She was true to them; but it is unlikely she loved Caesar or even Antony in any ordinary sense of the term. Still, she loved them both in the sense that she needed them, not in any temporary or partial way, but as allies in the purpose that consumed her. Caesar she never came fully close to; she indeed came close to Antony, but while their union must have given her great satisfactions, it must also have irritated her. She must have chafed at his mingled weaknesses and resistant strengths, and at his final complete dependency on her. At the same time she gave herself and her hopes up to him with a passionate finality; he became a part of her as well as an inadequate instrument. There was no known case of a princess of the Macedonian dynasty ever taking a lover; they were all too proud and ambitious. What is surprising in Cleopatra, what makes her different from the others, is the element of sensuous femininity combined with an absolute determination not to be dominated.

As a woman of such varied capabilities, she had various works attributed to her. Naturally a book on cosmetics circulated later under her name, and Galen cites some of its recipes:

For bald patches, powder red sulphuret of arsenic and take it up with oak gum, as much as it will bear. Put on a rag and apply, having soaped the place well first. I have mixed the above with foam of nitre and it worked well.

The following is the best of all, acting for fallen hairs, when applied with oil or pomatum; acts also for falling-off eye-lashes or for people going bald all over. It is wonderful. Of domestic mice burnt, 1 part; of vine-rag burnt, 1 part; of horse-teeth burnt, 1 part; of beargrease, 1; of deer-marrow, 1; of reedbark, 1. To be pounded when dry, and mixed with lots of honey till it gets honey's consistency; then the bear-grease and marrow to be mixed [melted], the medicine to be put in a brass flask, and the bald part rubbed till it sprouts.[6]

A book of weights, measures, and coinage, went under her name; and more importantly a treatise on alchemy of great imaginative power, in which the imagery of death and resurrection is applied to metallurgical processes.[7]

It is often said that she was unpopular in Egypt. Certainly there was an Alexandrian faction which opposed her: and perhaps the Jews there disliked her for having excluded non-citizens from a distribution of grain to Alexandrians during famine. Much of the evil reports about her were the invention of Nikolaos who after her fall went over to her bitter foe Herod; they represent the gossip of his court. Outside Alexandria she was certainly popular among the Egyptians of the *chora*; there were no uprisings during her period of sole reign, and at the end the Egyptians offered to rise and fight for her. She forbade it, but after her death Upper Egypt did rise against the Romans. She seems the only Macedonian ruler who could speak the native tongue; she was a strong supporter of the native religion. The later Ptolemies had inclined in this direction; but she went further than the others. There was no truth in Dion's tale that she got her wealth by plundering the native temples.

When she left Tarsos, Antony agreed to visit her in Egypt.

All the east was watching. In Judaea, Antigonos of the Maccabees was disputing the government with Herod; the frontiers had to be secured against a possible new Parthian attack; a new governor had to be imposed on Syria. Antony did not spend much time in that province. He confirmed two dynasts on their thrones: Ptolemaios of Chalkis, who held central Syria with Damas (Damascus), and Iamblichos of Emesa. After consulting with the Jewish highpriest he made Herod and his brother Phanael tetrarchs; imposed heavy fines on the city Arados, which had revolted; tried to raise some quick funds by a cavalry raid on Palmyra, only to find that its people had gone off with their belongings to Parthian territory; appointed Decidius Saxa as governor of Syria with two legions made up of Cassius' men; and then hurried to reach Alexandria before winter. But he did not make Caesar's mistake. He entered as a private man, the queen's guest. She had in effect established herself as an independent ruler, not a client.

Once again there were rich banquets. 'She gave him a magnificent reception,' says Appian, 'and he spent the winter there without the insignia of his office and with the habits and way of life of a private citizen: because he was in a foreign jurisdiction, in a city under royal rule, or because he considered his wintering a festive occasion. He even put aside the cares and escort of a general, and wore the square-cut dress of the Greeks instead of his own country's costume, "the toga," shod with the white Attic shoe of the Athenian and Alexandrian priests, which they call the *phaikasion*. He went only to the temples, the schools, and the discussions of the learned, and spent his time with Greeks, out of deference to Cleopatra, to whom his stay in Alexandria was wholly devoted.'[8]

We saw how Cicero could not hide his contempt of the *Graeculi*. Antony's mode of life in Alexandria was something that the conventional Romans found disgraceful and disturbing. Plutarch gives us an especially full account of the period. He himself mentions one of his sources; and we know that he also drew for much of his information about Cleopatra from the memoirs of her physician Olympos. In the following passage we get one of the few intimate glimpses that ancient historians provide.

'Indulging in the sports and diversions of a young man of leisure, Antony squandered and spent on pleasures what Antiphon calls the most costly expenditure: time. They had an association called *The Inimitable Livers*, and daily they feasted one another, piling up outlays in bewildering profusion. At any rate, Philotas, physician of Amphissa, used to tell my grandfather Lamprias that he was in Alexandria at the time, studying his profession. Becoming well acquainted with one of the palace-cooks, he was easily persuaded, young fellow as he was, to have a peep at the extravagant preparations for a royal supper. So he was taken into the kitchens and there he saw eight wildboars roasting and a vast abundance of other provisions. He expressed his surprise at what must be the great number of guests. The cook burst out laughing and said, "The guests aren't many, only about a dozen, but everything set before them must be at its perfection, and that is spoiled in an instant of time. It might happen, you see, that Antony would ask for supper at once, and then perhaps after a little while put it off and call for a cup of wine or start off a conversation with somebody. So," he explained, "not one but many suppers are arranged, since the precise time is hard to hit".

'This tale, then, Philotas used to tell; and he said that as time went on, he became one of the medical attendants of Antony's son, the one by Fulvia, and that he usually supped with him at his house with the rest of his comrades, when the young man didn't sup with his father. And there, once, as a physician was behaving too boldly and annoying them a lot while they supped, Philotas shut him up with some such sophism as this: "To the patient who's somewhat feverish cold water must be given; but everyone with a fever is somewhat feverish; so to everyone with a fever cold water should be given."

'The man was confounded. Antony's son, delighted, said with a laugh, "All this I bestow on you, Philotas," pointing to a table covered with a large number of big beakers.

'Philotas acknowledged his good intentions, but was far from imagining that so young a lad had the power of giving away such valuables. After a while, however, one of the slaves brought the beakers along in a sack and bade him put a seal on it. And when Philotas protested and was afraid to take them, "You wretched fool," cried the fellow, "why hesitate? Don't you know the giver is Antony's son and he's got the right to give away such a heap of gold vessels? Still, take my advice and change them all with us for money. The boy's father might chance to miss some of the vessels—they're ancient workmanship and highly valued for their art." Such details, then, my grandfather used to tell me. Philotas would rattle off his stories whenever he had the chance.'[9]

Plutarch then turns to Cleopatra herself. 'But she, distributing her flattery, not into the four forms of which Plato speaks' in his *Gorgias*, 'but into many, and always mixing some fresh touch of delight and charm with Antony's hours of seriousness and mirth, kept him in constant tutelage and let him out of it neither by night nor by day. She played at dice with him, drank with him, hunted with him, and watched him as he took weapon-exercise. And when at night he'd set himself at the doors or windows of the commonfolk and scoff at those inside, she'd go with him on his round of mad follies, wearing the dress of a servant girl. For Antony would also try to dress himself up like a servant. He always reaped a harvest of abuse, and often of blows, before returning home—though most people suspected who he was. The Alexandrians took pleasure in his coarse wit and joined in his amusements in their graceful and cultivated way. They liked him and said that he used the Tragic Mask with the Romans, the Comic Mask with them.'

Sometimes Cleopatra must have tired of his sports and entertainments. It was all very well for him to deliver himself up so completely to her enticements; but she wanted him also to remember who he was and what was his destiny. At moments she must have been infuriated by his enormous capacity for enjoyment. 'To recount the greater part of his boyish pranks would be sheer foolery.

One example will serve. He was fishing and had bad luck; which vexed him all the more since she was watching. So he ordered his fishermen to dive down and secretly fasten on his hook some previously-caught fish; then he pulled up two or three of them. But the Egyptian saw through the trick. Pretending to admire her lover's skill, she told her friends about it and invited them to come and watch next day. So a large number of them got into the fishing boats; and when Antony let down his line, she ordered one of her own attendants to get ahead of him by swimming to his hook and fastening on it a salted Pontic herring. Antony thought he had made a catch and pulled the fish up. As you'd expect, there were roars of laughter. Cleopatra said, "*Autokrator,* hand over your rod to the fishermen of Pharos and Kanopos. Your bag is one of cities, realms, continents.'" The accusations of drunkenness aimed at both Cleopatra and Antony must be viewed within the perspective of their Dionysiac symbolism. Antony did get drunk in his times of relaxation; but the picture of him as a hopeless drunkard is an exaggeration seizing on his Dionysiac self-glorification and turning it against him. Cleopatra was treated in the same sort of way. She had a ring with *Methē* (Drunkenness) inscribed on it; so she was a devotee of hard drinking. In fact the point of the ring was the exact opposite. *Methē* was cut on an amethyst, the stone of sobriety; and an epigram of the period explains the allegory:

I, Drunkenness, well-engraved, on an amethyst stand.
Figure and stone each own a different will.
Cleopatra's sacred thing! On her queenly hand
even the drunken goddess must be sober still.[10]

We have here a reference to what became the neoplatonic paradox of sober drunkenness, a development of the theory of inspiration in Plato's *Phaidros*, which was especially worked out by Philon of Alexandria in the first century A.D. The idea thus seems a part of Alexandrian religious symbolism, perhaps elaborated in connection with the mysteries of Sarapis in his Dionysiac aspects. In Philon, Sober Intoxication is the Mother of Virtue, the expression of the mystic wisdom or divine joy of life; it thus represents a moralisation, in philosophic terms, of the Bacchic revel. Cleopatra's ring, which the epigram calls a sacred possession, strongly suggests that she was an initiate of Dionysos and that she kept the ring as one of the sacred symbols of initiation. Apuleius in his *Apologia* remarks, 'I have been initiated into most of the sacred rites of Greece. Certain of their tokens and insignia, given to me by the priests, I have carefully kept as memorials. I speak of nothing unusual, nothing unheard-of. You too, brother members of the college of that single god, Father Bacchus, who are here present, you, I say, know quite well what it is you keep so studiously treasured at home, and what it is that, after excluding the uninitiated, you venerate in silence.'

Though Antony and Cleopatra had certainly now come close together, there was still a continual fencing between them, a probing of each other's strengths and weaknesses. Cleopatra must have learned that he was malleable up to a point, but doggedly stubborn after that; and she too in her own way had qualities of easy accommodation and immovable decision. He wanted to get his hand on her treasure, and he failed; she wanted a much more definite statement of their relationship than she was able to extort.

In the last resort he was loyal to Octavian. She must have found that at a certain point he stiffened, drew away. So for the most part she merely played Aphrodite to his Dionysos. Each deeply stimulated the other. She must have recognised that if she were to fulfil her dreams it would be through this man; and he must have felt that here was a woman who supremely combined all the elements he had sought in Cytheris, Fulvia, and the others: unapproachable and yet all his, a true queen and yet a gay lover. He may have bedded Glaphyra; but mostly his women had not been particularly high in social status— Fadia a freedman's daughter, Cytheris a freedwoman mime, Fulvia of a country-town family. He was proud of his splendid queen; in a later letter to Octavian he wrote, 'Why are you changed towards me? because I lie with a Queen? She's my wife.'[11]

Closed in Alexandria, he did not know what was happening in Italy. With the early spring came bad news from west and east alike. Fulvia had stirred up trouble in Italy and the Parthians had broken into Syria, killed the governor and taken Jerusalem. Herod had saved his family and treasure in the fortress Masada among the mountains by the Dead Sea. Asia Minor seemed lost; many cities had joined the Parthians whose kings had absorbed Hellenistic culture and encouraged it at their court. In the civil wars they had sided first with the Pompeians, then with the anti-Caesarians; they preferred a Roman system that was not properly unified. Now they took into their service all the opponents of the triumvirs scattered about the east. Q. Labienus, whose father, once a general under Caesar, had gone over to the Pompeians, led the Parthian army and issued coins with his title,

Parthiacus Imperator, an odd mixture of Roman forms in a traitorous colouration. When the noisily-patriotic *optimates* were thus ready to join the deadliest national foe, what was there strange in Cleopatra's plans of drawing Antony in as her ally?

The situation was as bad in the west. Octavian was struggling with the job of settling some 17,000 men. As money was not available, he evicted farmers to make room for the men without compensation. Poets like Propertius, Tibullus, Virgil, lost their family estates and all their property. 'Everything was rent by factions,' says Appian, 'and the army indulged in insubordination to the faction-leaders, while famine began afflicting Rome, sea-supplies being cut by Pompey and Italian agriculture ruined by the wars. Any food produced was consumed by the troops. Most of them carried out robberies by night in the city, and acts of violence worse than robbery went unpunished. The men thought to commit them were soldiers. The people closed their shops and drove the magistrates from their seats, as if there was no need of lawcourts or useful arts in a city oppressed by hunger and infested by brigands.'[12] Many countryfolk had gone to Rome in hope of corndoles; some veterans had lost the taste for work on the land and wanted to sell their estates. Even in good times Rome needed imported food. Sextus Pompey, who held the sea, was being joined in Sicily by runaway slaves and uprooted men of all sorts. He put Neptune on his coins, and in his elation, 'believing himself in very truth Neptune's Son, he donned a dark blue robe and cast alive into the strait [of Messina] not only horses but also, as it's said, men as well.'[13] As a feckless champion of the disinherited he enjoyed wide popularity in Italy and at

Rome among the poor. Meanwhile Antony's veterans felt themselves neglected beside those of Octavian, no doubt with truth.

But Octavian himself was not having an easy time. 'It was of high importance,' comments Appian, 'that the five years' term of office was running out and the soldiers' goodwill was needed for its renewal; and so he was willing to overlook for the moment their insolence and swaggering. Once, in the theatre, in his presence, a soldier couldn't find his own seat; he then went and took one in the section reserved for the *equites*. The people pointed him out and Octavian had him removed. The soldiers were infuriated. They gathered round Octavian as he was leaving, and demanded their comrade; as they couldn't see him, they assumed he'd been put to death. Even when he was produced, they supposed he'd been brought from prison; but he denied that and told the facts. So they swore he'd been instructed to lie, and reproached him for betraying their common interests.'[14] Suetonius says that Octavian only escaped being lynched by the sudden appearance of the man. There was trouble about a meeting in the Field of Mars on the subject of land-division; a centurion who defended Octavian was murdered. The soldiers' cause was taken up by Fulvia and Antony's brother Lucius. Fulvia's portrait seems to have been stamped by Antony on coins as the head of Victory; if so, she was the first Roman woman to gain this honour while alive. Certainly such an act would suit Antony's character. Now in her energetic anger she decided that Octavian was playing Antony false, trying to get hold of the Gauls and treat Italy as his sole preserve. He had married her daughter Clodia in his reconciliation with Antony;

as his mother-in-law she felt that she had the right to dominate him. But he promptly sent the girl back, declaring her
still a virgin. Knowing him, we may surmise that he had re-
frained from consummating the marriage in order to be
able to throw her out when necessary. He then proceeded
to marry Scribonia, a connection of Sextus Pompey, to
help in coming to terms with him. This sign of a changed
political outlook would not have passed unnoted by
Fulvia, she would have seen the threat of an alliance that
might work much to Antony's detriment. Ancient writers,
always on the trail of some shallow personal motive,
declared that she wanted to get Antony away from
Cleopatra. It is indeed possible that she had been told of
Glaphyra and Cleopatra by Manius, Antony's procurator,
who seems to have played a large part in stirring her up.[15]
But the roots of the conflict went far deeper than any
impulse of jealousy on her part. Lucius Antonius had
begun to take up the cause of the oppressed Italians.
(Appian says that she rebuked him at first; then, hearing
of Cleopatra, inflamed him.) Manius boldly summed up
the charges of bad faith against Octavian. He had de-
frauded Antony by freeing Cisalpine Gaul; he had assigned
to the soldiers almost all Italy, not only eighteen cities;
thirty-four instead of twenty-eight legions had been
given a share in land and money; nothing had been done
against Sextus Pompey, who was causing famine in Rome,
and the money raised to fight him had been used to win
the favour of the soldiers; he was not so much selling
the confiscated properties to the soldiers as giving them
away; if now he wanted peace, he should render an
account of his past acts and in the future do only what was
decided by common consent. Civil war began. Lucius had

assumed the name Pietas; and he and Fulvia were trapped in the rockfort of Perusia. By the end of February 40, after hardships that begot a proverbial phrase, *Perusian Hunger*, they surrendered. Agrippa's capable activities had much to do with their speedy defeat.[16]

Some of the sling-bullers thrown into the town have been recovered. We find facetious inscriptions: 'Blessing,' 'Give it to Fulvia,' 'Hit L. Antonius on his bald head.' Others bear the names of Mars Ultor (Avenger) and Divus Julius, showing how the idea of a war of retribution on the murderers of the Saviour had sunk into the minds of the soldiers. Vicious reprisals were taken on the Perusians. Suetonius states: 'After the capture of Perusia he [Octavian] took vengeance on a very large number. To

Coin with Lucius Antonius on one side and his brother Marcus on the reverse; a coin struck by their young brother Gaius while proconsul in Macedonia, where he was captured by Brutus, who later killed him. The coin shows the head of Macedonia with a *kausia* cap.

all who tried to beg a pardon or offer excuses he returned a single answer, "You must die." Certain writers declare that 300 men of both orders were selected from those who'd surrendered, and were sacrificed like victims on the Ides of March at the altar erected to the Deified Julius. Some again have written that he took up arms on purpose, to uncover his secret opponents and those whom fear rather than goodwill held in check, by giving them a chance to follow the lead of L. Antonius, and, when they'd been overcome and their estates confiscated, to pay the rewards promised to the veterans.'[17] Dion has the tale of the altar and states that the city was burned down. He adds, 'So the story goes'. Seneca also mentions the human sacrifices. Appian is more favourable to Octavian. He says the fire was the work of Cestius, a Perusian; Octavian's soldiers on their own initiative killed several of his enemies; the town councillors were imprisoned and then executed (except for a man who had voted once for the condemnation of Caesar's murderers). Velleius, who always gives the Augustan account, says the cruelty was rather the work of the soldiers than the wish of the leader, and that a Perusian, Macedonicus, set fire to the place.[18]

The tale of the human sacrifices is indeed hard to believe, though it is not out of key with the slogan *Mars Ultor* and it chimes in with the account of Sextus' sacrifices. What seems certain is that the defenders of Perusia were treated extremely barbarously and that Octavian cannot be whitewashed as Velleius tried. No doubt he felt altogether rather desperate at this phase and wanted to give a severe warning to malcontents. L. Antonius, however, he let go free. Perhaps he felt that his execution would create a hopeless antagonism between himself and Marc Antony. Fulvia with her children and Munatius Plancus fled east, via Puteoli and Brundisium. On the death of Antony's commander in Gaul Octavian in flagrant bad faith took the province over; Fulvia could argue that her suspicions had been justified.

The Perusian War had clearly been accompanied by

much violent propaganda on both sides. After the failure of a meeting for arbitration at Gabii, Appian says, 'Octavian and L. Antonius determined to wage war and were already employing bitter edicts against one another.' Manius seems to have produced a forged letter from Antony calling for war. After Perusia surrendered Octavian said that Lucius had 'artfully made false accusations' against him.[19] Further, Martial has preserved six lines of an excessively coarse epigram by Octavian against Fulvia:

> *Glaphyra's fucked by Antony. Fulvia claims*
> *a balancing fuck from me. I hate such games.*
> Read six lewd lines that Caesar Augustus wrote
> (you read all Latin with a spiteful note).
> *Manius begs me: must I buggar him?*
> *No, if I'm wise, no humouring his whim.*
> *Fuck or else fight! she cries. But still I've found*
> *dearer than life my prick. Let trumpets sound.*
> When such strong downright Roman speech you try,
> Augustus, my sprightly works you justify.[20]

One recalls the slingstone: 'Give it to Fulvia.'

Charges were made that Antony had allowed Fulvia to attack Octavian, meaning to get the profit if she won, or to disclaim her if she lost; also that he did not dare to face the troops in Italy without the money he should have collected. (In fact he did face them without it a few months later.) Appian makes clear that he heard of the war only after he had left Egypt. 'In the spring he set out from Alexandria and went by land to Tyre, and then on by sea, touching at Cyprus and Rhodes, to the province of Asia. There he learned of the doings at Perusia and blamed his brother and Fulvia but most of all Manius. At Athens he found Fulvia, who had fled from Brundisium. His mother Julia, who had gone off to Pompey, had been sent by him from Sicily with warships and escorted by some of his party's leading men, by L. Libo his father-in-law, by Saturninus and others, who, attracted by Antony's capacity for great deeds, sought to bring him into friendly relations with Pompey and to form an alliance between them against Octavian.'[21] This alliance seems the plan of Julia, who had been playing her part in the political sphere for some time. At the time of Mutina (43) she had used her influence in the Senate to save Antony from outlawry. During the proscriptions she rescued her brother and interceded for many highborn ladies whose wealth was liable to bring disaster on them. Now she had been intriguing with Sextus as the best possible ally against Octavian. We may thus class her among the strong-minded women like Clodia, Fulvia, Servilia, and in her son's character we may trace the conflict and fusion of his two very different parents, the lazy pleasure-loving father and the capable politically-minded mother. His whole life, as we noted, was in one sense an effort to dramatise and resolve on a new level the parental antagonism.

The last thing Antony would have heard from Italy before winter held up navigation was the news immediately after the accord of Teanum, when everything seemed settled. There was no reason why he should have suspected the change for the worse; the problem of pacifying Italy was in Octavian's hand and he had no wish to interfere. But now he reacted vigorously. He at once set sail for Brundisium. By the time he reached Corcyra he must have heard how the inexperienced son of his commander in Gaul, on his father's death, had handed over the legions at Octavian's demand. Now indeed it seemed that Fulvia's insistence on the latter's treachery was verified. He had no choice but to join with Sextus.

Pollio, his supporter, had got in touch with Domitius Ahenobarbus, a Pompeian, and reported that he was ready to change sides. Antony with his usual generosity of spirit wanted to show that he trusted the outlaw, set off with only five warships, and encountered Ahenobarbus' large fleet. Plancus was afraid they'd run into a trap. Then the outlaw's flag came down and he turned his ship broadside to Antony's ram. They all went on together to Brundisium, where they found the gates closed. The governor there seems to have acted on his own initiative; after Perusia suspicions were natural. But Antony took it to mean that Octavian wasn't ready to listen to his perfectly good excuses. So he blockaded the town and sent word to Sextus, who at once attacked Thurii and Consentia, while four of his legions easily routed Octavian's small force in Sardinia. Octavian hastily marched south and camped opposite Antony. Agrippa rescued Sipontium and Sextus was driven off from Thurii. But a major clash seemed inevitable at Brundisium. Antony showed his mettle again with a brilliant cavalry skirmish near Hyria. Then came news that Fulvia, worn out by rage, bitterness, and anxiety, had died at Sikyon. At least her death simplified the situation. The veterans in both camps began fraternising. L. Cocceius Nerva, a moderate, went between the two leaders, trying to ease tension; the soldiers chose two more mediators. Antony made the first gesture of friendship, telling Sextus to go back to Sicily and sending Ahenobarbus to govern Bithynia. Maecenas was the envoy chosen by soldiers of Octavian, C. Asinius Pollio the one chosen by those of Antony. At last the two leaders were reconciled.

The result was the Treaty of Brundisium of autumn 40, which tried to patch up the triumvirate and devise new boundaries for the spheres of Antony and Octavian. The Mediterranean area was divided by a line that ran through Scodra (Scutari) in Illyricum: the same line was used centuries later to divide the breaking-up empire. West of the line went to Octavius; east of it to Antony—with Africa left to Lepidus. Italy was to be a neutral recruiting-ground, but in fact Octavius went on treating it as his territory. As Caesar had done, the triumvirs nominated consuls for years ahead to secure positions and bind adherents. Antony soon gave a signal proof of his good faith. He put to death his procurator Manius who had done much to start off the Perusian War. Then Salvidienus Rufus, who meditated revolt, sounded Antony, who at once informed Octavius. Salvidius was called to Rome on some pretext, accused of treasonous designs before the Senate, and condemned to death. Octavian now gave Antony the remaining five legions of the previous commander in Gaul—Appian implies that he handed over the whole army, which is impossible. The outlawry was removed from Ahenobarbus. Amid the troops' acclamations Octavian betrothed his sister Octavia to Antony; she was the widow of Marcellus. His daughter Julia was sent to Sextus. (When five years later she died, it deepened the split with Sextus.) As Octavian probably guessed that Antony, especially after his liaison with Cleopatra, would not prove faithful, he may have already been calculating the benefits that would accrue to him when the marriage with Antonia broke down.

Octavia was a year older than Cleopatra. Antony's gold coins show her fine head on a slender neck, large eyes and keen glance; Maecenas sang of her hair that owed all its splendour to nature. Gentle and devoted in character, she was no more a home-spinning matron than Fulvia. Like Cleopatra she was deeply cultured, though in a quieter and more modest way. She was patroness of the architect Vitruvius and aided the literary circle that Maecenas was gathering for Octavian's benefit. She had her philosophers too: Nestor, an Academic, who taught her son Marcellus, and the Stoic Athenodoros Kananites —his father being of Kana in Cilicia. Athenodoros had known Poseidonios at Rhodes, then moved on to Apollonia, where he attracted the notice of Octavian and followed him to Rome. He often gave him advice in frank terms. Claudius the future emperor was under him in youth. In old age, returning to Tarsos, he found it mis-governed by Boethos (who had been a favourite of Antony), had him expelled, and persuaded Augustus to remit the *vectigalia*-tax for the town. He died at eighty-two and left a memory kept alive by yearly festivals and sacrifice.[22] One of his works was dedicated to Octavia. Though not actively political like Fulvia or Cleopatra, she was no mean diplomat when forced to it; she never complained of Antony's treatment of her; and what is conclusive for her goodness, she took charge of his children by her rival and brought them up.

The law insisted that a widow should wait ten months before remarriage: presumably to give her time to bear a child if she were carrying one. The Senate now gave

Octavia remission. About the time of the Brundisium Treaty Virgil wrote his Fourth Eclogue which we shall soon consider in some detail. In it the hope of a redeeming hero found powerful expression; indeed it is because so many trails of dream-aspiration and prophetic insight into the patterns of history were concentrated into its few lines that after endless analysis it still remains perfectly clear and hopelessly enigmatic. We may note here however that the sort of ideas and emotions on which it draws had been stimulated by the advent of a comet in 44 about the time when Octavian gave games in Caesar's honour. The comet was taken as an apotheosis of Caesar, even if Octavian himself privately preferred to see it as expression of his own rebirth as the New Caesar. On 1 January 42, at his request, the Senate obediently decreed the deification of Caesar. Now Octavian was not Gai filius (son of Gaius) but Divi Filius (Son of the God); and he signalised the new name-title on his coins. Dion tells us that he set up a statue of Caesar with a star above its head in the temple of Venus.[23]

After Brundisium came a new type of coin, with the caduceus between two opposed horns-of-plenty on a globe. Caesar had used horns and caduceus on a globe to express the blessings to come from a world-ruler; the objects were emblems of power. In 46 he was portrayed at Rome with the *oikoumenē* (globe) under his feet. But Antony's two opposed horns had not been used before in the west. They cannot refer to a re-establishment of east-west trade, as much of the east was still under the Parthians; rather they represent the concord of the two rulers in their shared power. Probably he used the globe because neither he nor Octavian were claiming it separately; it was their united power that made up world-domination. Octavian did not dare to use the globe on his own till after Actium. We may note also a coin by one of Antony's moneyers which shows his head and a genius with sun-attributes while Jupiter amid other gods stands on a globe. Here the genius seems to represent Antony's power or good fortune; the sun-attributes remind us of the Lion and the coins struck after Philippi.[24]

Antony and the Return to Cleopatra

Soon after the peace-treaty Herod arrived. He had left Judaea when the Parthians put their nominee, Antigonos, on the throne. Cleopatra had given him a ship: an act that would bring her again to Antony's notice. Both the leaders liked Herod; Octavian recalled his father's services to Caesar; the Senate duly appointed him king of Judaea. This act was the first break in the custom of choosing a new client-king from the old line; it was done by Antony and Octavian together, but Herod felt his primary loyalty was to Antony—if only because he knew that Antony was taking over the east and thus would be his overlord.

Sextus, unappeased, tightened his hold on the corn-supply. The people blamed Octavian; and in October 40, when the cult-image of Neptune was borne in procession, they applauded. Despite protests Octavian had it removed from the divine company.[1] This episode occurred after his fleet had met a great disaster through storm and he cried out, it was said, that he'd conquer even against Neptune's will. Dion remarks, 'When on certain days the statue wasn't brought out, the people took stones and drove the magistrates from the Forum, threw down the statues of Caesar [Octavian] and Antony, and finally, failing to accomplishing anything in this way, rushed violently on the men themselves as if to kill them. Caesar, though his followers were wounded, tore his clothes and set about supplicating them, while Antony bore himself more forcibly; and when, mainly because of all this, the people grew wrathful and it was feared they'd commit some act of violence, the two leaders were forced against their will to make overtures to Sextus.'[2]

Tax-notices were torn down by the crowd after Octavian tried to tax slaves and legacies in order to raise money for war-preparations. Antony seems to have restored order and saved Octavian's life. The latter felt that at all costs he must reach some agreement with Sextus. The first attempt at Puteoli failed. Then in summer 39 the Pact of Misenum was signed. Sextus was permitted to hold Sicily, with Sardinia and Corsica (already in his power), and was promised the Peloponnese; he was to be compensated for the family's confiscated property, become an augur (like the other two), and hold a future consulship. In return he guaranteed to see to the delivery of corn, to stop taking runaways, and plant no garrisons on the Italian coast. All exiles in his forces were to be let go home to Italy with properties restored; proscribed men were to regain at least a quarter of their losses. Dion describes the scenes of joy at the Pact, which brings out the intense desire felt for an end of civil broils. 'After drafting these pacts and reducing them to writing, they deposited the documents with the Vestal Virgins, then exchanged pledges and embraced. At this a tremendous shout rose up from mainland and ships at the same moment. Many soldiers and civilians there suddenly cried out all together, terribly tired of war and strongly desirous of peace. Even the mountains echoed the cry. The result was a great alarm and panic. Many died from that alone, many others perished by being trampled or suffocated. Those in small boats did not wait to reach shore but jumped out into the sea; those on land rushed into the water. They clasped one another swimming and threw arms round one another's necks as they dived. There was thus a spectacle of varied sights and sounds. Some knew their relatives and associates were alive. Seeing them there, they gave way to unrestrained delight. Others, who thought their dear ones already dead, unexpectedly saw them and for long didn't know what to do. They stood speechless, distrusting their eyes and praying it might be true; they wouldn't accept the recognition till they'd called out the names and heard the answering voices. Then at last they rejoiced, as if their friends had been brought back to life; but, forced to yield to a flood of joy, they couldn't hold tears back. Again, some were unaware that their loved ones were dead; they thought them alive and present; they went round searching and asking everyone they met. As long as they could learn nothing definite, they seemed crazy and were reduced to despair, hoping to find the men, yet fearing their death, unable to abandon hope because of their longing or to surrender to sorrow because of their hope. When at last they found out, they tore their hair and rent their clothes, calling on the lost by name as if their voices could reach them, and giving themselves up to grief as if their friends had just died and were lying there before their eyes. . . .

They spent all day as well as most of the night in these demonstrations.'³

At the confirming banquet in shipboard Sextus made a jest that could have been bitter. Antony had taken his father's house situated in a region of Rome called the Carinae (Keels); so he now said that he was entertaining him and Octavian in the Carinae (on shipboard).⁴ His henchman Menas wanted to murder the guests, but was rebuked: 'You should have done it without telling me beforehand; now let's leave things as they are; perjury is not my way.' Julia, Antony's mother, with her special interest in Sextus, was probably present at all the proceedings.

Antony was made Pontifex Maximus, an office that Caesar had held. He sent his officer Ventidius eastward to deal with the Parthians. Plutarch tells a tale of one of Cleopatra's agents, an astrologer, at this time. 'Now there was with him a seer from Egypt, one who cast nativities. This man, as a favour to Cleopatra or in truthful dealing with Antony, used frank language with him. His fortune, he said, was most great and splendid, but obscured by that of Caesar [Octavian]; and he advised Antony to put as much distance as possible between him and that young man. "For your guardian spirit [daimon]," said he, "is afraid of his. Though it has an exultant and lofty force when it's on its own, yet when his comes near, yours is cowed and humbled by it.' and indeed events seemed to testify in the Egyptian's favour. We are told that whenever in diversion lots were cast or dice thrown to decide matters in which they were engaged, Antony had the worst of it. They would often match cocks or fighting-quails, and Caesar's would always win.'⁵ That is obviously derived from a piece of Octavian propaganda, though it is likely enough that Cleopatra had several agents or supporters planted in Antony's retinue. He stayed on in Italy till after the birth of Octavia's child, a girl, the elder Octavia, about August or September 39. We see in this his kindly nature; for there were many matters in the east he must have wanted to deal with. After the birth he took his wife off to Athens.

The years 39–7 were a lull. Antony was mainly at Athens. Octavian at last found a woman who suited him. Though Antony has come down in history as a great lover it was Octavian perhaps who merited the name, at least in terms of simple appetite. He had divorced his first wife, daughter of P. Servilius Isauriacus, for no reason except that he felt it politically advisable to marry Clodia; he discarded Clodia and took up Scribonia similarly for purely political reasons; the latter, a widow older than he, was discarded as she was near bearing a child. Aged twenty-four, he fell strongly in love with the nineteen-year-old Livia Drusilla, of the patrician Claudians, who was married to Tib. Claudius Nero, one of Antony's partisans. After Perusia, Nero fled to Antony, then came with him to Italy. Despite Scribonia's advanced pregnancy, Octavian forced the College of Pontiffs (of which he himself was a member) to dissolve both his marriage and hers. In January 38 he married her, with Nero acting as the father who gives the bride away. Next day, at the feast, 'one of those prattling boys that women keep around for their amusement, generally naked, saw Livia reclining in one place with Caesar, and Nero in another with a man. He went up to her and said, "What are you doing here, lady? Your husband"—pointing him out—

"is lying over there."[6] When Livia soon after bore a boy, Octavian sent the baby to Nero with a memorandum: 'Caesar returned to its father Nero the child borne by his wife Livia.' But before long Nero died and Octavian became guardian of his two sons. People gossiped and cracked the witticism, 'The lucky ones have children in three months,' a phrase that became a proverb.

Octavian was eager to have children by Livia; but all that happened was one miscarriage. Suetonius records that in early years he was much accused of being a passive homosexual. 'Sextus Pompey reproached him with being an effeminate; M. Antony, with earning his uncle's adoption by prostitution. L. Antony, Marc's brother, also charged him with being buggered by Caesar, that adding for the fee of 300,000 sesterces he gave himself in the same way to A. Hirtius in Spain; also that he used to singe his legs with burnt nutshells to make the hair softer. At a public diversion in the theatre, the following sentence was recited, alluding to the Gallic priest of the Mother of the Gods beating a drum: See with his orb the buggerboy's fingers play! At once the whole concourse of people applied the passage to him, with vast applause.'[7] But these tales mostly fall too much into the formulas of vituperation to carry conviction. There is more of a ring of truth in the accounts of his lechery. 'Even his friends don't deny that he was guilty of various adulteries; but they argue that he engaged in the intrigues, not from lewdness but from policy, to detect more easily the designs of his enemies through their wives.' Even if this unlikely excuse was correct, it makes his moral character even lower. 'Besides the precipitate marriage with Livia, Marc Antony charges him with taking the wife of a man of consular

rank from table, in her husband's presence, into a bedroom, and bringing her back to the entertainment with
her ears very red and her hair in great disorder; that he
divorced Scribonia for too freely objecting to the
influence one of his mistresses had gained over him; that
his friends were forced to pimp for him and that they
made matrons and ripe virgins strip so that their bodies
might be fully examined, as if the slave dealer Thoranius
was putting them up for sale. And before they came to an
open rupture, he wrote to him in familiar terms: 'Why are
you changed towards me? because I lie with a Queen?
She's my wife. Is this a new thing for me, or haven't I
been doing it these nine years? and do you take liberties
with Drusilla only? May health and happiness attend you,
as when you read this letter you're not playing about with
Tertulla, Terentilla, Rufilla, or Salva Titiscenia, or the
whole bunch of them. What matters where or on whom
you spend your manly vigour?'[8] Terentilla seems the
affectionate form for the name of Terentia, wife of
Maecenas, who was not unacquainted with later scandal.
The other women were doubtless the wives of other
associates of Octavian. We cannot take too seriously the
allegations made in Antony's vituperative exchanges. But
there seems little doubt that Octavian was given to
lechery in a large way. Suetonius adds, 'He kept his reputation for wanton behaviour and afterwards also (we're
told) he was rather inclined to violate maidens who were
sought out for him from every side, even by his wife.'
That cannot be a piece of abuse from the period of the civil
wars. Later, Tacitus, summing up the case against him,
says, 'His two favourites, Q. Tedius and Vedius Pollio,
were distinguished only for riot and debauchery; and to

crown everything, Livia ruled him with a boundless sway, a fatal empress to the commonwealth and a pernicious stepmother to the Caesarian family.'[9] He was much addicted to gambling, but otherwise kept his small-town attitudes, being careful and sparing in his habits. In appearance he was low-statured; his freedman Julius Marathus said he was five feet nine inches in height; his shortness was however hidden by the fine proportion of his limbs, so that it only showed up when someone taller stood by him. He had small ears, an aquiline nose, a complexion 'between brown and fair'; his eyebrows met and he had piercing eyes, the daunting effect of which pleased him, though in later years, his left eye grew weak. 'His teeth were thin-set, small and scaly, his hair slightly curled and inclining to a yellow tinge.'[10]

Livia was a matron of the older kind, unlike Octavia or Fulvia; averse to display and luxury, a housewife watching over her girls who spun and wove, dignified and discreet in public. Seneca says, 'She was a woman who guarded her reputation most carefully'. She had a shrewd common-sense and was firmly conservative. Behind the scenes she established a strong ascendency over Octavian, who consulted her on most things. Her great-grandson Gaius (Caligula) called her 'a Ulysses in a woman's frock'. She was useful to her husband as a standing example of the Good Roman Wife.

The new marriage however did not keep him at home. In 39 he went to Gaul to join Agrippa, whom he had put in Salvidienus' place, to deal with uprisings. A stern disciplinarian, Gn. Domitius Calvinus, had been sent to Spain to crush the tribal insurrections there. Agrippa remained in Gaul, crossed the Rhine, and secured the frontiers by settling the Ubii in the Cologne region. Octavian, returning home, was hailed as Imperator for the third time (Agrippa having done the work). He now dropped Julius from his name and took Imperator as his first name, no longer a title: Imperator Caesar Divi Filius. He had found a formula which got rid of his Octavian origins and expressed his unique position in terms which he thought were Roman.

Antony had not handed over the Peloponnese to Sextus; he wanted first to get in arrears of tribute. So Sextus had a pretext for fresh troubles. Holding Sardinia, he was in a good position for harrying the Italian coast. Octavian sent urgently to ask Antony to meet him at Brundisium. Antony at once hurried there, all the way from Syria, but no Octavian appeared. So Antony returned east and wrote to Octavian, advising him not to start a war. However, Octavian launched a naval campaign and suffered a heavy defeat. In 37 he recalled Agrippa, who, after considering the situation, began a largescale programme of constructing big ships with turrets and artillery. Along the coast 20,000 slaves were trained as rowers, and funds were levied from private property-holders.

Antony spent two winters with Octavia at Athens. Now it was that he proclaimed himself the New Dionysos. This procedure was something quite different from the mere salutation by the Ephesians. Oddly, he was applying Cleopatra's lessons in a situation without her; and sooner or later he was sure to feel that without her the situation was hollow. He now built the Dionysiac cave of greenery we noted earlier. The Athenians altered inscriptions on two colossal statues set up some years before to Kings

Eumenes and Attalos of Pergamon, and rededicated them to Antony: a cheap way of making their homage. We are also told that they proposed a ritual marriage between him and the goddess Athena on the lines of that of Demetrios in the 3rd century B.C. (Demetrios too 'used to make Dionysos his pattern more than any other deity, as the god was most terrible in waging war and on the other hand most skilful after the war in making peace minister to joy and pleasure'.[11]) The tale of the marriage with Athena however reads too much like a rhetorical exercise, based for instance on the story of the wedding of Antiochos IV and Atargatis. 'To woo Athena' was almost a proverbial phrase for the insolence of power. She was a Virgin who in myth had defied the attempts of gods to mate with her; and so the tale of Antony's marriage with her is certainly an invention of the Octavian party to express their belief that he was going too far in his god-claims.

The inventor of the tale showed a certain wit. He says that Antony thanked the Athenians and asked for a dowry of a million drachmai. A councillor riposted, 'Lord Zeus took your mother without a dowry'—he was referring to Danae, the mother of Dionysos; Antony at last agreed to take the sum in three instalments.

Coins show his Dionysiac role. They belong to a type on which is represented the god's mystic chest (*kista*), ivy, serpents; but they added Antony's head wreathed with ivy and a bust of Antonia on the *kista,* or jugate busts of the pair, with the *kista* holding a bust of Dionysos. The inscription puts the series after the Pact of Misenum in summer 39, when Antony was designate consul for 34 and 31, and before his second imperatorship at the end of 39.

That is, they were struck in the autumn of 39 when he first took Octavia to Athens. There is an alternative explanation also for the coins with opposed horns-of-plenty which we have discussed: the horns stood for the marriage with Octavia (which in a sense was a marriage or reconciliation of east and west). After Antony had gone east an adherent gave him the globe on his own: this was excessive and was probably not done at his direction. The horns-type did not last long, as about August-September 39 the child of the marriage was born and turned out a girl. After that, disappointed as the Hercules-Father of a Hercules, he turned to Dionysos and had the *kista*-series designed. (The coins thus give us important clues as to the date at which he consummated the marriage; the ceremony itself, carried out at Rome, must have been in early November 40 at latest.)

The Alexandrians were delighted with the pair, whom they extolled as gods and benefactors. Antony gave splendid feasts and dressed as a Greek as at Alexandria.[13] As gymnasiarch of the city, he defrayed the cost of the Panathenaic Games in August 38, the games being given the further name of Antonia. He went with Octavia to the lectures of philosophers.

All this was reported to Cleopatra; for when six years later she too was in Athens with Antony, she took care to be granted the same honours as Octavia. Her agents or bribed members of his retinue no doubt reminded him of her at the right tactful moments. He must have learned in late 40 or early 39 that she had borne twins to him; and after the birth of Octavia's girl he must have often recalled that he had at Alexandria a son whom he had never seen, the son of a queen. One of the epigrams flitting about

Athens ran: 'Octavia and Athena to Antony: keep your property!' Here we meet an old formula of divorce in Roman law, used to suggest Antony's levity—perhaps with a thought of Cleopatra lurking in the background.

Coin of Gn. Domitius Ahenobarbus struck to celebrate his naval victory in the Adriatic in 42. Coin of Labienus with inscription Q. LABIENUS PARTHICUS IMP.

P. Ventidius Bassus who had been sent to deal with the Parthians was a capable soldier, who had begun as a muleteer. Some verses stated:

> You augurs and *haruspices*, run to me.
> Lately has happened the oddest prodigy.
> A rubber-down of mules as consul you'll see.

The Senate had given Antony confirmation in advance of any measures he should take in the east. The Parthian successes had shown up weaknesses in the system of client-kings; Labienus, the traitor, had been helped by Tauros peoples. Antony took advantage of the precedent of Herod to pick two good men not of any dynasty: Amyntas of Galatia (former secretary of Deiotaros) and Polemon of Laodicea—and to set them over the tribes.[14] He also strengthened Tarkondimotos, dynast in unruly Amanos, by making him king with his capital at Hieropolis Kastabala; the new king called himself *Philantonios*.

Kleon, brigand chief who had defied Labienus, was confirmed in his rule of Mysian Olympos.[15]

In 38 Antony took to Asia the four legions in Epeiros, leaving seven still in Macedonia. Now came the invitation to Brundisium, where Octavian failed to show up. In 39 Ventidius drove the Parthians from Asia Minor and Syria. Herod did not profit by this success, as Antigonos bribed Ventidius and kept his throne. Labienus fled and was killed in Cyprus. Then again in 38 Ventidius won a great victory, at Gindaros in north Syria. This battle taught the Parthians not to rely on armoured cavaliers, cataphracts, against the legions, and thus in the long run was a disadvantage for the Romans. But for the moment the latter were jubilant. A Parthian prince had been killed and the defeat of Crassus at last avenged. The latter's head had been carried to the Parthian king, so now the prince's head was sent round the Syrian cities. The frontiers were again pushed back to the Euphrates.

Then Pakoros made a second invasion and turned Antony from his plans for invading Armenia. Fugitive Parthians had taken refuge with Antiochos of Kommagene; so Ventidius marched on Samosata, his capital, a stronghold on the Euphrates, Antiochos, following Antigonos' example, offered him 1,000 talants to mark time; the siege did not progress. This second scandal made Antony supersede Ventidius for all his military virtues; he set out in person to take charge of the wars, shaking off the spell of Octavia with her ordered civic outlook. Departing, 'he took a wreath from the sacred olive tree' in the Erectheion on the Akropolis, 'and, in obedience to a certain oracle, filled a vessel with water from the Klepsydra,' a sacred spring just below the Akropolis'

ancient portal, and carried it about with him. The olive-
wreath suggests a special relation to Athena, who in
legends was often the patron or protector of heroes, for
instance Herakles; perhaps from this relation sprang the
tale of the marriage.[16]

Samosata surrendered. Antony made Antiochos'
brother Mithridates king and was himself hailed Imperator
for the third time. Ventidius went to Italy for his deserved
Triumph, on 27 November 38 or 37, and was never heard
of again. After Gindaros he had sent a force to help
Herod; but Antigonos again bribed the commander.
Herod went to Antony before Samosata; and on that
town's fall Antony put in Sosius' hands the task of restoring him, with strict orders against bribery. Sosius sent
Herod on with two legions: a rare example of an alien in
charge of Roman troops. Herod beat his opponents at
Jericho and went on to besiege Jerusalem. Sosius came
up and the whole Roman army took part. In July 37 the
town was at last taken. Herod stopped desecration of the
temple and ransomed Jerusalem from pillage; he wanted a
kingdom, he said, not a desert. He had married Mariamme,
the last Hasmonaian princess, and now began his long
reign over Judaea. Soon some Jews rose against him, and
in the winter 37 Antony executed Antigonos to prevent
him being used as a focus of revolt.

Antony wintered in 38 at Athens with Octavia. He was
diverted once more from Armenia by an appeal, brought
by Maecenas, from Octavian after his naval disaster.
Antony was more than ever the dominant figure in the
partnership. Three of his generals had recently been
granted or had celebrated Triumphs, with that of Sosius
yet to come; Octavian had only his defeat by Sextus. Yet

again Antony kept faith. In spring 37 he sailed to Tarentum with Octavia and his whole fleet, to find that Octavian had spent the winter in building ships and didn't want any aid. Plutarch says that Antony sailed with three hundred ships for Italy 'once more irritated against Caesar [Octavian] by certain calumnies,' and that Brundisium again wouldn't let him in. This account suggests that Antony came in wrath against Octavian, whereas in fact he came at his request. Plutarch goes on that he sent Octavia to her brother, that she won over Agrippa and Maecenas, and begged her brother not to fight. As things were, all men looked on her as the wife of one imperator and the sister of another; 'but if the worse should prevail and there be war between you, it's uncertain which will win, which lose, but my lot in either case will be one of misery,' So Octavian came peacefully to Tarentum and a new treaty was signed.

Each leader pledged aid to the other. Antony, perhaps pleased at not having any further to look after the ships, handed over two whole squadrons and ten scouts for use against Sextus; Octavian promised him two legions, which in any event Antony claimed as his own and which in the end he never got. The triumvirate had been due to end by January 37; so in the autumn of that year they had it prolonged till the last day of 32. A final effort was made to strengthen family ties by betrothing Antyllus, Antony's son by Fulvia, to Octavian's little Julia.

On his way back to Korkyra, Antony brooded long and hard. Octavian had continually insulted and played him false. He, Antony, had been shut out of Brundisium in 40, though Italy had been defined as common ground. (And if Plutarch is correct. he had been shut out again this year.) He had been urgently called to a conference which Octavian didn't bother to attend; he had again had his help begged for, then his prompt response had met rejection. He had been treated in underhand ways; his Gallic command hd been stolen from him, even though he had loyally reported the treason of Salvidienus; his treaty rights in Italy were ignored; Octavian did not carry out his promises about the legions and he had got in the way of the prosecution of the Parthian war for two years. Now he, Antony, had provided ships according to agreement and had received nothing in return.

Suddenly his heart hardened; he would stand it no more. He told Octavia to go back to Italy: she was pregnant again and he said that he did not want her to suffer the hazards of sea and war. That he had arrived at his decision after the Tarentum meeting is shown by the events. If he had made up his mind to break before that, he would clearly have acted differently. The crucial moment was when he decided to discard Octavia.

As soon as he arrived at Antioch, he sent his friend Fonteius Capito to Alexandria for Cleopatra. Clearly he had made up his mind to stop all delays and concentrate his energies against the Parthians. For that purpose he needed Cleopatra's help, her Egyptian resources. But behind the resolve to turn to her was a gradual disillusion with Octavian and a distrust of his methods, his slow erosion of the basis of their alliance. He was weary of a pleasant life at Athens. He wanted action; and action now could only be the Parthian war. If successful, he took on the mantle of Caesar and finally outshone Octavian, who, thanks to Agrippa, had been catching him up and whose vantage-point in Italy made time his ally. The only

Table 3 G. JULLIUS CAESAR

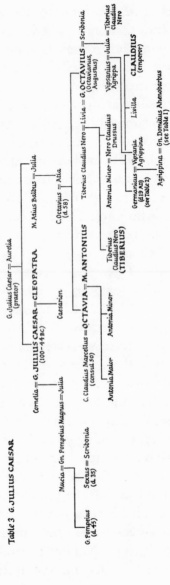

way that Antony could offset Octavian's strengths was by some great exploit like a victory over Parthia. No doubt his dislike of Octavian had introduced an uneasy element into his relations with Octavia; he could not but feel in her her brother's presence. Besides, he wanted a woman of force and passion, who combined Octavia's cultured range with the gay sensuousness of Cytheris and the fierce energy of Fulvia. He could not but recognise that he was piling many difficulties on his shoulders by turning to Cleopatra; but what else, he must have felt, was there for him to do, unless he were ready to decline into a hanger-on of Octavian, tolerated because of Octavia? He must concentrate on a crushing defeat of the Parthians and a further eastward extension of the empire; after that, come what will. For Parthia he needed Cleopatra's help, whatever problems it brought. It was perhaps after he turned to Cleopatra that the Lion reappeared on his coins, the Lion with Sword and Star, as an expression of his taking-up of Caesar's work.

We must realise the importance that Parthia had now assumed in Roman eyes and was to continue to hold for many centuries. Pompey had won Syria for Rome in 67; and apart from Egypt the more Graecised parts of the post-Alexander east were all firmly under her control. The question was whether the expansion was to halt more or less at the Syrian frontiers or to carry boldly on over the whole area that Alexander had conquered. Clearly, however large the words that were used, Rome was not really mistress of the *oikoumenē* (the civilised or settled regions of the globe) unless she embraced Iran and reached to North India. A continual tension thus existed from the days of Pompey till the time of the Arab invasions between the Roman and the Parthian world, which was ruled first by the Arsakids, then by the Sassanians from the second quarter of the third century A.D. At moments the tension led to war and the frontiers changed a little, then it slackened in periods of more or less peaceful coexistence. But all the while the problems of the Iranian east and what lay beyond it was present for the Romans. What would have happened if a commander like Caesar in the heyday of his power had tackled the Parthians, we cannot guess; Antony's failure to carry out his plans determined the shape that the Roman Empire was to take.[17]

Virgil's Fourth Eclogue

We had better pause now to examine Virgil's Fourth
Eclogue, for the problems it raises take us right to the
heart of our period's most deep, hidden, and powerful
aspirations. Without understanding something of it, we
cannot understand what was moving men to bring about
the full pattern of change in this revolutionary epoch, or
what unresolved conflicts they bequeathed to the future;
we cannot understand the emotions which Antony and
Cleopatra stirred in the masses and which they themselves in their own way shared. The Christians later took
the Eclogue as a prophecy of Christ. They were not so
amiss in their views as is often stated; for here we have
the first clear expression, in the open field of culture, of
a total world-renewal which will see the advent of a
saviour-child ushering in a Golden Age.[1] First then here
is the poem line for line, in a plain version:

> Sicilian Muses, a somewhat higher theme!
> Not all delight in shrubs and lowly tamarisks.
> If woods we sing, let the woods be worthy a consul.

The Last Age, told in Cumaean song, is at hand;   (*aetas*)
the great cycle of ages begins afresh.   (*saecla*)
The Virgin too returns, and Saturn's reign.   (*regna*)
Down from high heaven is sent a new progeny.

(*progenies*)

On the Boy soon to be born, who'll end the Race

(*puer, gens*)

of Iron and make the Race of Gold rise up,
smile, chase Lucina. Now your Apollo reigns.

Your Consulship will bring in this Grace of the Age,

(*decus aevi*)

Pollio, and start off the Great Months' round;
with you as guide, the last traces of our guilt

(*sceleris vestigia*)

will fade and earth will shed the undying fear.
He'll share the Life of Gods; Heroes he'll see
mingled with Gods, himself beheld by them:
he'll rule the peaceful Earth with his father's Virtues.
But, Boy, the Earth as her first offerings
will pour you untended, all round, wandering ivy
with baccar, colocase twined with smiling acanthus.
Goats of themselves will bring their milkswoln udders
home, and herds won't dread the mighty lions.
The very cradle will pour alluring flowers.
The Serpent will die, the deceitful plant of venom
will die; Assyrian spikenard will be common.
And as of Heroes' Glory, your Father's Deeds,
you read, and understand what Virtue is,
the field will softly yellow with gradual corn-ears
and reddening grapes will hang on the rough branbles
and stubborn oaks distil the dew of honey.
Yet some few traces of ancient evil will stay,

(*vestigia fraudis*)

to bid men try the sea with ships, enclose
cities with walls, and cleave the earth in furrows.
There'll be another Tiphys, another Argo

with chosen heroes, and wars will rise again
and great Achilles once more be sent to Troy.

When age confirmed has turned you to a man,   (*aetas*)
the sailor will leave the sea, the ship of pine
will barter no goods, all lands will yield all things.
The soil won't suffer the harrow, vineyards the hook,
the sturdy ploughman will loose his unyoked bulls,
nor will the wool learn counterfeiting colours:
the ram himself in meadows will tinct his fleece
with glowing purple or with saffron dyes.
Spontaneous scarlet will clothe the cropping lambs.

The Fates concordant in the established order
will sing to their spindles, 'Run on, unending ages;'
                                          (*saecla*)
Dear Offspring of Gods, great Progeny of Jove,
                        (*suboles, incrementum*)
move on to great Honours; for the time is near.
See the Universe nodding with its massive dome
the Earth, the Tracts of Sea, the Depths of Heaven;
See all things joyous at the approaching age.
O that my last days may prolong their course
with breath enough to celebrate your deeds.
Nor Thracian Orpheus or Linus shall top my song,
though his father aids one, his mother aids the other.
Apollo for Linus, Calliopea for Orpheus.
If Pan with Arcadia as judge should himself oppose me,
even Pan will fail, with Arcadia as judge.

Begin, small child, with a smile to tell your mother.
                                          (*parve puer*)
Ten months brought on your mother's length of pangs.
Begin, small child: he on whom no parents smiled,
no god has honoured with table, no goddess with bed.

First, some clear points. Pollio was consul in 40, and while
consul he played a major part in bringing Antony and

Octavian together. He acted for Antony as Maecenas acted for Octavian. The poem was written during his consulship, *te consule*; and it prophesies a great event in that period. The event is a birth that has not yet occurred, but is close at hand. It is going to produce a renovation of all things: the advent of human harmony or brotherhood is seen as inevitably interlinked with the ending of all violences, all predatory cruelties in nature outside man. The new earth of the poem is essentially in the key of all folk paradises: work is no longer necessary, the earth of its own accord produces all that we need, industry and trade disappear, and with them the whole network of divisions and exploitations that have carried on through history and in fact constitute, from one angle, the substance of history. Now history ends. There is no need of property and the mechanisms of power on an earth of spontaneous plenty. The easygoing Land of Cockaygne in which earth pours out all kinds of food automatically, is in a sense a variation of the image that appears in Dionysiac myth and ritual: the earth of revelry where milk and honey flow of their own accord. (We may note the rites of Bona Dea at Rome, restricted to women, where wine, called milk, was drunk from jars called honey-pots.) That the ancient folk-utopias where more or less identical with the medieval dreams is shown by passages from Attic Old Comedy. Take this from Telekleides:

> I'll tell you of the life I gave the dead
> in the first days when there was peace for all
> easy as scooping water with the hand.
> Earth brought forth then no fear and no disease
> but everything desired broke blossoming.
> The mountainsides were cleft with hurrying wine

and barleycakes were quarreling with loaves
which got the first bite from the mouths they wooed . . .
The fishes gliding homeward then would leap
fried from the water, flapping on the tables.
A stream of soup, with joints and chops still warm
and bobbing amid its savours, wreathed along
past the couched diners, while from pipes there dribbled
perpetual fronds of mincemeat richly spiced
for all to lick the luscious stalactites . . .
Those were the days when men were properly nourished
and thewed like giants.[2]

We may add the phrase from Petronius, 'If you were anywhere else, you'd say that roast pork walked in the streets here.'[3] The Romans knew this kind of folk-idiom as well as the Greeks. Its comic touches cannot disguise a close kinship with the Eclogue's world of spontaneous plenty. A version that links the unseen motions of nature-spirits (the Nymphs) with the use of machines to do away with manual labour and bring plenty is to be found in Aristotle and in Antipatros of Thessalonika (perhaps 1st century B.C.). The latter's little poem on the water-mills runs:

Cease from grinding, O you toilers, Women, slumber still,
    even if the crowing rooster calls the morning star.
For Demeter has appointed Nymphs to turn your mill
    and upon the waterwheel alighting here they are.
See how quick they twirl the axle whose revolving rays
    spin the heavy roller from overseas.
So again we savour the delights of ancient days,
    taught to eat the fruits of Mother Earth in ease.[4]

In the pure folk-utopia there does not appear any myth of redemption; no saviour is invoked to bring about the actualisation of the dream. The god-advent however does appear in the Dionysiac vision; and so we might say that a picture like Virgil's unites the folk imagery with the Dionysiac god-advent, especially as Dionysos is often represented as a child among the Nymphs. In one respect he is a vegetation-god, the babe-in-the-green; but the *eniautos daimōn* or year-spirit, who brings about the miraculous birth of the earth in spring, is now seen as a divine presence who makes the spring-miracle the constant basis of everyday life. There is no longer any need for conflicts or ravening violences; the age of plenty is the age of peace. Isaiah had linked the saviour-child with the golden age when the lion lies down with the lamb, long before Virgil. Indeed his prophecies were strong with the sense of an earth soon to be redeemed:

> Your sun shall no more go down; neither shall your moon withdraw itself; for the Lord shall be your everlasting light, and the days of your mourning shall be ended. Your people also shall all be righteous; they shall inherit the land for ever, the branch of my planting, the work of my hands, that I may be glorified. A little one shall become a thousand, and a small one a strong nation: I the Lord will hasten it in his time.[5]

Virgil no doubt did not know Isaiah, though we must not underestimate the extent to which the Greek version of the Hebrew sacred books, made at Alexandria under the early Ptolemies, were known in part or entirety by the more learned sections of the Hellenistic world.

These points we can deduce from the poem in a general way. We can also see how the image of the folk-paradise ushered in by a divine babe has become entangled with learned speculations. On the one hand there is the scheme set out early by Hesiod, of stages of men represented by the metals, gold, silver, bronze, iron.[6] On the other hand there is the notion of a Great Year or Cycle which was completed when the heavenly bodies in their complex

Monumental base from Sorrentum: Diana with torch, Apollo in flowing robes (like the Actian Apollon on coins) with tripod; Latona with what seems the Cumaean Sibyl at her feet (to express the removal of the Sibylline Books to the Palatine Temple of Apollo); a Couretes and Cybele with Zion; a Genius and Mars.

revolutions assumed at long last the same patterns or positions as they had held at the moment of their creation. At such a moment, it was thought, the universe entered on a new era and all things began afresh. We can see at a glance that Virgil has illogically combined two viewpoints: first, that the new era liberates men for all time from the conflicts and limitations of the previous years, and secondly, that the great year merely initiated an era which in all details repeats the completed cycle—men begin with innocence and paradise restored, but they fall again into sin, *fraus* and *scelus*, through the return of trade, competition, and war. *Fraus* and *scelus* were the typical horrors of the civil wars.[7] Horace cries, years later, when

Octavian has become Augustus and drawn about himself what he could of the saviour-nimbus, assuming the role of Apollo:

> What god shall we, the People, now beseech
> to prop the falling empire? Ah, what prayers
> will now avail the Virgin Choir to reach
>   Vesta who scarcely cares?
> Who'll end our crime? Jove gives to whom this task?
>
> (scelus)
>
> Augur Apollo, clouding from our gaze
> your gleaming shoulders, come, we humbly ask,
>   lead us to better ways.[8]

Virgil makes no attempt to reconcile the two different interpretations of the new start. But however the new cycle operates, it is to be inaugurated by the divine babe born in Pollio's consulship.

Before we go into the question of who that babe was, there are some general points about the poem, which it would be as well to look at, since they help us to understand the ideas on change, revolution, the pattern of history, in Roman minds at this time. First, then, the reference to the Cumaean Sibyl. In *Aeneid* VI, Virgil treated that Sibyl at length. He tells how Aeneas lands on the Italian coast and penetrates the vast cavern where she lives, inspired by Apollo. She prophesies that Aeneas will face many dangers in Latium, and uses terms that echo the Eclogue:

> Another Achilles already breathes in Latium,
> again the son of a goddess . . .
> again as before the cause of dire affliction
> for the Trojans will be a wedding . . .

The context is quite different. The New Achilles here is the enemy of the Romans (Trojans); but there is a link in the idea of a recurrent pattern in history. The changed role of newborn babe and of marriage may be mere chance or may have a deeper significance we shall discuss. For the moment what matters is the fact that the Cumaean Sibyl, on the threshold of Aeneas' arrival in the land of his destiny, initiates him into the future and provides the way down to the underworld, with the golden bough as guide, and that in the underworld the combined visions of past and future culminate in pictures of the two Marcelli: the successful patriot of 226 who defeated the Gauls in north Italy, and the nephew of Augustus, son of our Octavia, who in 23 B.C. died at the age of twenty. Anchises, explaining things to his son Aeneas, stresses the high hopes raised and then dashed by the second Marcellus:

> O piety O oldtime faith O hand
> unconquerable in war . . .
> Pitiful boy if you break harsh fates
> you too shall be a Marcellus. Give lilies from full hands . . .

Marcellus here, like the child of the Eclogue is *puer*, a boy of immense promise; but whereas Virgil in 40 was confident the *puer* would renew man and the earth, he now sees him as the bright image of lost hopes: a child who might have brought about a new era, but who was doomed. We need not press these points too far, but we can still feel there is a close emotional link between the Eclogue and *Aeneid* VI. Wild dreams, however, have given way to a sober view of history. The poet still believes in the fated glories of Rome, but in terms of a chequered pattern of hope and doom, achievement and setback. He is not consciously contrasting Eclogue and *Aeneid*, but the theme of Rome's destiny provokes in the epic various echoes of thought, imagery, even sound, from the past dream.

Another point is that in both cases the Cumaean Sibyl is connected with a prophetic outburst on Rome's destiny. The name *Sibylla* does not seem Greek, but its origin is obscure. It seems originally applied to a prophetess of the village of Marpessos in Troy's territory, though the town of Erythrai tried to claim the first Sibyl and there was much argument on the matter. Sibylla won Apollo's favour and he inspired her with infallible though riddling oracles. The name came to be used for a whole group of prophetesses: the Phrygian, Lydian, Delphic, Kimmerian (perhaps the same as the Cumaean), Erythrian, Samian, Cumaean (later called Amalthaia), Hellespontine, Tiburtine, Persian. A Jewish or Babylonian Sibyl was added (identified with the Marpessian–Erythraian one); and in her name a late collection of oracles are extant, in which we often meet Jewish or Christian propaganda.[9] We shall have more to say of that collection when we come to Cleopatra's version of the ways in which a redeemed earth was to be created. The Cumaean Sibyl too had her name given to a collection of prophecies in verse (*carmina*), kept at Rome under control of the Board of Fifteen. We have already met these *carmina* and their Board. How the collection was formed, it is impossible to say; but often we see that an oracle brought forward by the Board was a fabrication made to support or obstruct some political move of the moment. The oracles were stored in the temple of Jupiter Capitolinus, which in 82 B.C. was destroyed by fire; a fresh collection was formed, but again the sources are unclear.[10] We get a glimpse however of the way that oracles turned up and were incorporated or rejected in a story that Tacitus dates A.D. 32. 'A tribune Quinctilianus consulted the Senate about a book of Sibylline Oracles; and L. Caninius Gallus, of the Board of Fifteen for Religious Ceremonies, wanted the Senate to vote its inclusion in the Sibyl's Prophecies. The Senate agreed without discussion. But Tiberius wrote mildly criticising the tribune for his childish ignorance of traditional custom, and reprimanding Caninius. The latter's familiarity with religious lore and ritual should have warned him not to raise the matter in a poorly-attended Senate and on unreliable authority; he had not waited for his Board's decision or the usual reading and consideration by its executive committee. Tiberius also recalled that, because of many forgeries circulating with the prestige of the Sibyl's name, Augustus had required their notification to the city-praetor before a certain date, private retention becoming a crime. So the collection of oracles recommended by Caninius was duly referred back to the Board of Fifteen.'[11] A complex role was played by the Sibylline Books. On the one hand they were used with a lot of chicanery to support political moves, especially of the aristocrats who more or less controlled the legal use through the Board; on the other hand they were composed by various propagandists or enthusiasts among the people, at Rome or in the eastern provinces, to support all sorts of anti-governmental impulses or movements.

By introducing the Cumaean Sibyl, Virgil then gave both the Eclogue and *Aeneid* VI an aura of oracles dealing with Roman destiny. The Virgin of line 6, we may note, is not the Child's mother, as the Christians took her to be;

she is Astraea, Justice. In Georgics II, Virgil, looking at
the farmers of Italy, cried:

> O more than happy if they only knew
> their blessedness, who far from discordant arms
> see the most righteous Earth pour from her soil
> an easy sustenance . . .
> > on leaving the world
> Justice took her last steps among them.[12]

He links Justice with the plenteous earth of peace, and
suggests that the goddess lingers on among the countryfolk when she has long left the towns with their chaffering
and luxury-living. (Petronius in his poem on the Civil War
says that at the outbreak Peace departed: 'at her side goes
humble Faith and Justice with loosened hair, and Concord
weeping in her torn cloak.')[13]

Virgil combines the Hesiodic idea of successive ages,
peoples, races, and the astrologic idea of recurrent cycles
with specific Roman ideas, such as those drawn from the
Etruscan concept of the *saeculum*. The ritual in this relation included the driving of a nail into the wall of the
Capitoline temple: an act which, like the closing of the
lustrum, symbolised the expiation of past guilt and thus a
purified new start. Varro with his usual odd etymologies
declares:

> A five-year period was called a *lustrum*, from *luere* [more
> likely from *lavere*, wash], to set free: that is, *solvere*, to release
> —because every fifth year the taxes and voluntary tribute-
> payments were completely discharged, through the activity
> of the censors. A *seclum* [*saeculum*, ultimately from a root
> meaning to sow, seen in *semen*, seed] was what they called the
> space of a hundred years, named from *senex*, old man,

because they thought this the longest stretch of life for *senescendi* [aging] men. *Aevum*, eternity, is from an *aetas* [period, age] of all the years. From this comes *aviternum*, which has become *aeternum*, eternal—which the Greeks call an aion. Chrysippus says this is *aei on*, always existing. Hence Plautus: All *aetas* is not enough for thorough learning. And hence the poets; the Eternal Temples of the Sky.[4]

Livy records the nail-driving as an expiatory rite in 363 B.C. The Capitoline *Fasti* (calendar-lists) mention it for that date, and for 263 as well, as a *dictator clavi figendi caussa*—a dictator set up for the purpose of carrying the rite through.[15] It was one of the old rites underlying the Secular Games, a performance of which was being planned for 39 and would have been much talked about. The recorded holdings of the games in 249 and 149 (or 146) show the reckoning by a hundred years. But there was also a reckoning by a hundred and ten, and this was used to justify the Augustan Games in 17 B.C. We may compare the Jewish Jubilee kept every fifty years as a year of emancipation and restoration; and the Roman Catholic use of the term for a year of remission from the penal consequences of sin.[17]

Censorinus states that the closing of a *saeculum* was accompanied by prodigies: he is drawing on Varro and Etruscan Ritual Books. Varro says there were to be ten *saecula*; then would come the end of the Etruscan Name. Plutarch records a prodigy portending a *saeculum's* end in 88 B.C., and Servius tells how a *haruspex* took the comet of 44 as a sign of the end of the ninth *saeculum* and the start of the tenth.[18] Coin-types show that the notion of a *saeculum*-end was very much in men's minds.[19] The Etruscan idea of a *saeculum*-end did not necessarily imply a recurrence like the Pythagorean doctrine or the Stoic Great Year; but the link was easy to assume. Servius attributes to the Cumaean Sibyl the creed of ten ages, which he identifies with the astrologic world-cycle. 'When all the *saecula* are ended, the same things begin afresh.' And he connected this new start with the return of the stars to their original positions. In all this he seems to be correctly interpreting Virgil's own outlook.[20]

The Etruscan scheme of Ages had also come up in relation to prophecies attributed to the nymph Vegoia, which she had delivered to Arruns Veltumnus. She played a large role in Etruscan revelations; we have a Latin fragment of her pronouncements. *Libri Vegoici* as well as *Libri Sibyllini* were kept in Apollo's temple on the Palatine. As Egeria had inspired the Roman king Numa, so Vegoia had disclosed the secrets of Etruscan discipline to Arruns, who was a seer or prince from Clusium. Late in the Republican period a friend of Varro, the *haruspex* Priscus, who lived at Rome, produced a rhythmic version of Vegoia's mysteries. The fragment of her prophecies that we possess may well go back to him, though a Christian has tampered with it. It had a propaganda purpose. Arruns seems to be seeking a sacred protection for the Etruscan landlords against the Roman allotment system; and he may have issued this prophecy about 91 in the midst of the struggles against the tribune M. Livius Drusus, leader of the *populares*. It is based on the idea of the nation having its number of *saecula*; and three years before 88 fits in well with its statement that *Avaritia* (Greed—a term used by the propertied classes to express any measures of confiscation) was dominant 'almost at the end of the Eighth *Saeculum*'. The consul L. Marcius

Philippus called to Rome the Etruscans and Umbrians who were afraid of losing their public domain and of being disturbed in their private estates. They turned up, accompanied by huge *familiae* (retinues of followers and dependants) on the pretence of registering a complaint, but really to murder Drusus—as they duly did. The *haruspices* had been active that year, and the consul spread their omens, of which the worst came from Etruria: bloodstained bread, earthquake, two mountains moving against one another and crashing thundrously, bouncing forwards and receding with flames and smoke between them vanishing into the sky. A huge crowd on the Via Aemilia was said to have witnessed the prodigy. We see here both how the *haruspices* helped the conservatives and how the idea of world-end had long been politically manipulated. The Vegoia prophecy, if we correctly date it, was just fifty years before the Fourth Eclogue.

A document embedded in John Lydus' book *On Prodigies* shows us further how Etruscan methods of reading omens were being used by the big landlords. The text is ended by the statement, 'This daily Thunder-divination (*Brontoscopia*) Nigidius judged to be, not of universal application, but to concern Rome alone.' There is no reason why it should not be the work of Nigidius, 'Pythagorean and Mage,' as Jerome called him. A friend of Cicero, he was a bitter opponent of the forces making for a change in the *status quo*; against Catilina and Clodius he advocated the most violent tactics.

The *Thunder-Calendar,* based on a lunar system, treats of thirty-day months, starting with June, and indicates the significance of thunder on each day of the year; some lucky or unlucky event for agriculture or social life is foretold. A largely agrarian society is revealed, but there is a ruling City with various subject cities. This City is controlled by a powerful class, with whom the people are in constant conflict, and who have clients. A *basileus* (king) keeps coming up, often in tyrannical form; ceaseless dissension threatens the birth of a tyranny. A Senate dominates but the *plebs* seem always on the edge of revolt; the situation is one of murders. conspiracies, and the menace of civil war. Abroad, wars continually go on, severe, unexpected, costly of man-power; several times we hear of a King of the East, who experiences war and danger. Men are driven to crimes by avenging Furies, and they go to the stake; women are dangerous intriguers. We hear of crimes committed 'by women and slaves'. The slaves indeed cause much trouble. They breed diseases and are liable to break out into insurrection. As navigation opens (26 March), thunder announces the arrival of slave convoys.

The document may be based on some earlier Etruscan calendar of thunder-warnings, but in its Nigidian form it seems reordered to meet the Roman situation of the 50s and 40s B.C. The underlying idea is certainly old and belongs to a complex of ideas and practices which seem to show a strong link between certain aspects of early Etruscan culture and the Babylonian-Assyrian world of the 7th century B.C.; but the Nigidian adaptation, perhaps made with the aid of Etruscan *haruspices*, may be safely taken as dated to the age of Cicero. In 56 the omen-readers issued a statement that there was dire warning from the gods of political and social disaster. Cicero in his speech on the report declares: 'They warn us "to take care that slaughter and perils are not brought about for

the senators and chief men through the discord and dissension of the ruling class [*optimates*] and that our senators do not grow disheartened by lack of support: so that the provinces fall under the power of a single man, our armies be defeated, and a great loss of power result".'
He takes the opportunity to launch a violent attack on P. Clodius as a rabble-rouser. Among the omens he cites are 'a noise and a roaring' in the Latin district, and 'a certain obscure noise and a horrible rattling of arms' heard in a neighbouring suburban area. To interpret such matters, he says, they did not need soothsayers or 'that ancient system given, as men tell, to Etruria by the immortal gods themselves.' The way in which any strange occurrence in nature was seized on by the fears and hopes of men as a token of world-end can be exemplified from the Gnostic *Apocalypse of Adam*: 'Fire, pumice, asphalt will be cast on these people. And fire and dazzling will come over those Aions and the eyes of the manifestations of the luminaries [sun and moon] will grow dark. And the Aions will not see by them in those days. And great clouds of light will come down on them and also other clouds of light come down on them from the great Aions,' the Ages, the Rulers of the Ages. This passage is clearly based on reports of the great Vesuvian eruption that destroyed Pompeii. The eyewitness account by the younger Pliny described three phases: a rain of pumice and stone, flashing fires (? gas explosions), and a shower of white ashes coming down to cover everything.

A word for the plants mentioned in that Eclogue: ivy, colocase, acanthus. Ivy is a Dionysiac plant used by devotees for wreaths and as a tattooed initiation-emblem; baccar (Greek *baccharis*), often translated valerian, suggests

Bacchus and Bacchantes; colocase is the Egyptian bean, a lily-type of plant connected with revels and love-making.[21] In the *Georgics* Virgil links acanthus (as a feminine noun) with eastern products like frankincense and balm.[22] There is thus a strong Dionysiac colouration in the plants.

Pollio, to whom the eclogue is dedicated, was both a patron of poets and himself a poet. In Horace's ode opening the second book he is discussed as orator, historian of the civil war, and poet of tragedies.

> You treat of civil broils that burst,
> Metellus as consul: the causes, crimes,
>   fortune's dark game, the cursed
>   leaders'-pacts, the times,
>
> arms stained with unexpiated blood—
> a work that's dangerous and rash:
>   on lurking fires you tread,
>   under the treacherous ash.[23]

Virgil's Third Eclogue is a song-competition between two shepherds, into which Pollio is introduced:

Damoetas: Pollio loves my Muse though she's a peasant.
  Pierian Sisters, feed a heifer for your reader.
Menalcas. Pollio makes new songs. Feed the bull for him.
  Already it butts and sand with its hooves it scatters.
Damoetas. Let him who loves you, Pollio, reach honours he's
    glad you've reached.
  For him let honey flow, the prickly bramble bear amomum.

Here too, though in terms of poetic honours, we find the Dionysiac honeyflow and the transformation of bramble to an aromatic shrub (from which a balsam was prepared). The relation to Pollio makes more striking the link with the full paradisiac and transformative imagery in the next poem, addressed to Pollio.

We now turn to the question of the child and his identity. It has been argued that he is purely symbolic and that Virgil is merely expressing, in hyperbolic terms, the hope that the Treaty of Brundisium will start off a new epoch of world-peace and prosperity.[24] That such a hope is present cannot be denied; but it does not follow that the poem's content can be reduced to it. The poet is too specific about the birth, the child himself, the parents. He stresses the father's Virtues, the mother's actual gestation and pangs. After a careful reading no one could doubt that Virgil has some real birth and marriage of 40 in mind. *Modo nascenti* implies that the child is not yet born but will be in the near future.[25] By poetic licence it is assumed that the child will be a son.

The advocates of the purely symbolic meaning suggest that Virgil was basing himself on a genuine Sibylline oracle, perhaps even an official one. The *puer*, they say, is a sunchild; and it is pointed out that an *aureus* of P. Clodius at Rome, dated 42, has the head of Sol, with crescent and stars on the other side.[26] Or the *puer* is the child of Liber and Libera: hence the Dionysiac note. Or he is any child born at the great moment of change, who thus comes to typify the new age; or the Treaty itself; or the Poetry of Virgil—a point aided by the lines cited above from the Third Eclogue. The sun aspect we can indeed relate to the hope for a Sun-hero, which we found Antony taking into himself. But any interpretation is incomplete that moves on a single plane. There is certainly a symbolic level; but there is also an actual one, a mythic one (Argo, Tiphys, Achilles, Troy), a divine one (Apollo, Lucina the birth goddess, Jupiter), and an historical one (Pollio and the parents).

First then, because of Pollio's prominent role in the poem, it had been argued that the *puer* is his son. Ancient commentators, and some moderns, have held that there was a son, Saloninus, who may have been born after the Treaty, but before the end of 40, while Pollio was still consul and resident at Salonae on the Dalmatian coast. Most of this argument is however insecurely based. Macedonia was the province assigned to Pollio after the Treaty when he laid down his consulate; and Salonae did not belong to that province, where we know Pollio fought against the Parthini in the neighbourhood of Dyrrhachion and celebrated a Triumph for his victory. Salonae lies some 250 miles in a straight line across the sea, and much further off by land, reached by a difficult route. We know nothing of the son Saloninus apart from his presence in the scholiasts. And indeed Saloninus as a name has no connection with Salonae; it derives from the gentile name Salonius, which was ultimately of Etruscan origin. Pollio's family did use the name; Pollio's son Gallus had a son Saloninus, who was stepson of the emperor Tiberius. But it is possible that this grandson was turned by the commentators into a son of Pollio; and they got rid of him by saying that he died very early, apparently before the *dies lustricus*, the ninth from birth, when a male child usually got his *praenomen*—or at least within the first forty days. But the tale of an early death seems an assumption from the poem's third last line. The baby smiles, so it dies. Philargyrius argues that it was a fatal sign if a smile appeared before the fortieth day. But even if there was such a belief about the smile, the tale makes nonsense of the poem. Virgil, we are told, wrote a poem on a world-saviour, then inserted the omen because he knew the child was doomed to an early death. As to Pollio's presence at Salonae, it is barely possible that Pollio called in at the port while coasting down from the north to meet Antony at Brundisium; but it is extremely unlikely that he would have been carrying his wife around with him. (Commentators have been driven to suggest that she sought refuge there during the Perusian war.) Pollio had been near Altinum in 41, vainly defending Venetia against Octavian's armies; by coming to terms with Domitius Ahenobarbus, who held the Adriatic, and winning him over to Antonius, he gained a route southward that enabled him to avoid Octavian's men.[27]

A plausible suggestion is that the whole Saloninus-idea arose much later, in the 3rd century A.D. under Gallienus. The coinage of that emperor and his two sons, Valentinian II and Saloninus, is full of imagery of the golden age: Jupiter Crescens, the young prince whose early years are like those of Zeus in Crete, the gods watching over his growth, *dei nutritores,* the lowly generation that is fit to inherit the redeemed earth (*Pietas Saeculi*). Either then the Eclogue was already considered what Servius calls it, the Genethliacon (Birthdaypiece) of Saloninus, and was therefore applied to Galienus' son; or the golden-age imagery associated with Saloninus brought forth the thesis of a son of Pollio with the same name as the third-century prince.[28]

Though there is not the least suggestion in the poem itself that Pollio was the babe's father, his prominent position there seemed to stress the claims of his family; and his son Asinius Gallus told Asconius Pedianus that he was the saviour-child. But we need not take that statement seriously.[29]

If then we drop Pollio's sons or son, who is left? We need a child who was near his birth in late 40 when Virgil wrote the poem. Virgil might, it has been suggested, have written it in early 39, projecting himself back into the days just after the Treaty. That is unlikely in view of the nature of the poem; but in any event it does not alter the problem. We know of two important ladies who were both pregnant and connected with one or other triumvir: Octavia and Scribonia. First then Scribonia, the less suitable candidate. She had borne a son and a daughter to C. Cornelius Scipio; Octavian married her because her brother was father-in-law of Sextus Pompey, and she bore him a girl, Julia. However, Julia was born on the very day when Octavian callously divorced her so that he might marry Livia; and it follows that the gestation and birth were too late for the poem.[30] (The fact that the poem is a wedding-song as well as a birth-song—a point soon to be examined—also puts Scribonia out of the running.) But what above all discredits any identification of the father with Octavian is the dedication to Pollio, who was at this time a strong partisan of Antony.

Here we may glance at Virgil's own affiliations in 40. After Philippi, among the areas assigned to the veterans was Cremona; but as its territory proved insufficient, the soldiers were also awarded, or merely grabbed, the lands of neighbouring Mantua. Virgil's father lost his farm at Andes. Virgil applied for help to Pollio, then Antony's legate in Transpadane Gaul for 41. Pollio took up his cause. Virgil regained his estate. Octavian played no essential part in the whole thing; at most he accepted the decision for the poet made by Pollio. The other men besides Pollio who played a part in the matter were Cornelius Gallus, the poet, and Alfenus Varus. Gallus protected the folk of Mantua, including Virgil, and brought an accusation against Varus for unjustly measuring out the land. He had been appointed by Octavian to deal with the land-distribution in the north. Virgil then had reason to be grateful to Pollio and Gallus, but not to feel any special reverence for Octavian at this phase; he was however likely to desire strongly that amity should prevail among the two outstanding leaders. In the First Eclogue, apparently written before the Fourth, he has been considered to describe Octavian as a *deus*, who had taken up his cause and to whom he will always owe reverence. 'A god has given us this peace-and-quiet [*otium*]; for me he will always be a god; his altar will often be stained with the blood of a tender lamb.' The speaker is a shepherd Tityrus who has been seen as Virgil; but he describes himself as shaving a greyish beard and a case had been made out for considering him Eros, the old freedman-secretary of Virgil, who is expressing his gratitude to his master for freeing him. The other shepherd Meliboeus addresses him as 'Fortunate Oldman', and repeats the address. This fellow makes a lament for the way that the soldiers are taking the land; while Tityrus says that he gained his *libertas* in Rome and now keeps his property. Whether or not these identifications are accepted, we must not build too much on seeing Octavian as the Young God of the poem. Certainly in 41–40 Virgil was in no way a committed partisan of Octavian, as he later became. The nature of the *deus* is deliberately left unclear; he might be Terminus, Silvanus, Apollo; he might stand for all Virgil's benefactors. In reading the poem we must not use the perspective of Virgil's later years. The fact that he chose Pollio for such a work as the Fourth Eclogue proves that he did not at this time have any hard and fast affiliations. The whole point of the Eclogue is that such affiliations were unnecessary, as an age of concord was being born; the choice of Pollio shows that he is approaching the issue from the Antonian angle.

We must then turn to Octavia for the child's mother. But first let us consider the attempts that have been made to date the treaty and the poem with precision. The treaty seems signed on 5 or 6 December 40.[31] Some scholars however, have tried to link the poem with the start of Pollio's consulship on 1 January 40; the poem would then have been written in late 41. The reasoning here is weak. It has also been asserted that in 40 a New Moon coincided with the Sun's Birthday on 25 December; but even if that were so, we are not brought much nearer to an event likely to produce such a strong reaction as the poem reveals.[32] Again, the two Alexandrian festivals of the Sunbirth have been cited; by splitting the difference between their dates we get 1 January.[33] But that does not help much either. A further attempt at a precise date has been made by pointing out that a new *saeculum* was thought to have been begun in 149 B.C.; and as a *saeculum* was properly reckoned as 110 years, not 100, a new *saeculum* would begin on 1 January 40. So 40 would be the year of destiny. But unfortunately the arithmetic holds an error: the new *saeculum* was really due on the first day of 39.[34]

Scholars have worked out yet another argument for clinging to 1 January 40. At this confused period there

were often two or more pairs of consuls in one year; so
Virgil didn't really know if Pollio would be consul till he
actually assumed office. Pollio could not have done that
on 1 January or any time near it, on account of the
Perusian war; yet Virgil must have written with the first
possible day (1 January) in mind. But all this is super-
fluous and implausible. Again it is argued that the Eclogue
preceded Horace's Epode XVI, that the Epode is of the
time of the Perusian war, so the Eclogue goes back to the
turn of 41–40. But there is in fact no proof as to which
poem came first. The epode is however an important work
for the moods, the fears and hopes, of the period, and we
had better look at it.

> Now civil wars have worn another age away.
> By her own powers Rome falls and finds decay.

What barbarians had failed to do, the Romans were themselves doing. The only hope was to leave the polluted
scene, going wherever the southern or the boisterous
southwest wind drove the ships.

> The encircling Ocean waits for us. Let's seek afar
>   where the blest fields, the isles of richness are.
> Ah, there the crops each year come bursting out, untilled,
>   with grapes are all the unpruned vineyards filled.
> Ah, there the unfailing olive sprouts amid the green
>   and dark upon the boughs the figs are seen.
> From hollow oaktrees honey drips, from craggy steeps
>   with rustling feet the nimble water leaps.
> Goatbitches with no shepherd to the milkpail come,
>   with udders plump the friendly herd trots home.
> Growling about the fold no bear of dusk is found,
>   no viper-broods are heaving in the ground.

More marvellous things we'll see. No soaking eastwind drops
  a storm of rain upon the shattered crops.
No parching glebe destroys the life that seeks to teem,
  the king of heavenly ones forbids extremes . . .

The Argonauts, the Sidonian mariners, the crew of
Ulysses never got there.

God hid for faithful folk these secret shores of old
  when he debased with brass the age of gold,
with brass, with iron he hardened the ages; yet there'll be
  a happy flight for the good. My prophecy.

We have here a version of the folk-paradise where the
untilled earth brings forth plenty; but the blessed islands
will not be gained through some saviour. They must be
found by effort, by a mass-flight across the water. A clue
to the date is given by the names of the winds, Notus and
Africus, that are to be encountered. Horace is describing
a seavoyage westward which avoids the Sicilian Waters
held by Sextus. The poem was thus written during a food-
panic at Rome, when Sextus held the southern seas. The
route that the exodus is to take is that along the Etruscan
coast; the ships must face the squally Gulf of Lion instead
of sailing between Sardinia and Sicily. Anything rather
than meet the invincible navy of Sextus. The other
danger that threatens Rome and Italy is a barbarian attack.
The best date then seems the spring of 38 when Sextus
was doing very well and the Parthians had overrun Syria
and parts of Asia Minor.

Horace's Epode is thus definitely later than Virgil's
Eclogue; but the two poems are closely related. Horace is
making a sort of savage parody of Virgil's work. Where
the latter saw providence, Horace sees a curse; The curse

has now come home. To the Pythagorean mystique of fate he opposes a tragic view of history, stressing human responsibility. His mood is that of an earlier Epode on the civil wars, but, thanks to his bitter response to Virgil's Eclogue, he sets out the disastrous situation in a more complex perspective. The earth that could have been a paradise is hopelessly discordant; the dream has left the immediate world of experience, where it persists in the Eclogue, and retreated into the distance of fantasy. Yet what remains but to go chasing it?

Here is the earlier angry Epode:

> Whither, curs'd rabble, do you rush? why show
>   swords that were sheathed a while ago?
> Has not on land and Neptune's waste been spilt
>   enough of Latin blood in guilt?
> Not that proud Carthaginian towers should feel
>   the might of Roman fire and steel,
> or that the Sacred Way should witness lamed
>   with fetters Britons yet untamed,
> but that the Parthian prayers should win at length
>   and Rome be stabbed with her own strength.
> No wolves or lions are so fiercely blind,
>   they do not fight with their own kind.
> Is it a madness, ravening energy,
>   or urge of sin? come answer me.
> There is no answer. Pale and horror-eyed,
>   men shrink with misery stupefied.
> I see. The old curse harries Rome, again,
>   penalty for a brother slain.
> The innocent blood of Remus from the earth
>   taints generations ere their birth.[35]

To return to the Eclogue. The phrase, *te consule* (with your aid, with you as consul) suggests that Pollio played an important part in the events leading to the new hopes. Also, the modification of the picture of total peace by the statement 'wars will rise again' can be explained as coming from the idea that the civil wars are over for ever, but it may be necessary to deal with the Parthians. (To see the wars-to-be as those that were in fact to occur between Antony and Octavian is to miss the whole point of the poem.[36]) The wars will be afar, against barbarian enemies of the Romans, quite unconnected with internal dissension. Further there is the point that Pollio's work as a peace-maker in itself cannot be the deed creating the universal change, however much it may be a necessary prelude to the great event.

All analyses bring us back to the period close to the Treaty of Brundisium; and when we consider the poem carefully we see that it is a disguised marriage-song as well as a birth-song. Virgil carefully introduces from Catullus' poem on the wedding of Peleus and Thetis, which is to produce the semi-divine hero Achilles. He takes over its refrain about the turning of the spindles of the Fates.[37] The saviour-child is thus linked with the marriage of divine or semi-divine human beings; and no one else fits this description but Octavia and Antony. The marriage has for Virgil the great virtue that in honouring it he can rightly claim to be honouring both of the triumvirs: Antony directly, Octavian through Octavia—while by concentrating on the offspring of the marriage rather than on the two great men in person he lifts his tribute above any suspicion of servility. What fascinates him is the hope of concord between the two men and its concrete expression, not either great man in separation.

Next we may note that the child of Octavia here cannot

be her Marcellus, who was born not later than 42.[38]
Besides in 40 nobody could have selected him as a possible
world-ruler. Propertius tells us of his death at Baiae in 23
B.C., apparently through excessive bathing:

The lake there, shut from Avernus' shady waters,
dashes up to the smoky ponds of heated Baiae;
there Misensus, Trojan trumperer, has his grave
and Hercules' work, the causeway, murmurs with waves;
there the cymbals clashed in honour of Thebe's god
while he was winning men's cities with strong right hand . . .

What avail then his high birth and his manly worth,
his excellent mother, his status in Caesar's family,
the awnings waving in the crowded theatre
and everything managed by his mother's hands?
He is dead with his twentieth year but just begun . . .[39]

The Theatre of Marcellus had been built by Augustus
in his nephew's name; and Octavia had carried out her
son's duties as aedile when he was too ill to attend to
them.

We are then left with the child that Octavia was bearing
at the time of the Treaty or was to bear. Was this child
begotten by Marcellus or by Antony? was she pregnant
at the time of the betrothal and marriage, or had she
already borne the child she was left pregnant with at the
time of her widowhood? Dion tells us that she was pregnant at the time of the treaty; but this seems an incorrect
deduction from the fact that she gained a marriage-dispen-
sation from the Senate. Marcella minor however may have
been born a few months after her father's death, and the
readiness of the Senate to give Octavia permission to
remarry before her ten month's period was over may well

have been based on the fact that her child was thus already born. The Eclogue certainly celebrates the marriage of Octavia and Antony. To do that together with a prophecy glorifying the child she was bearing to another man would have been the limit in bad taste. Besides, it would make nonsense of the two references to the child's father. The poem could only have been written as it was if the poet was expressing the great hopes that he and other men had in the child which would ratify the reconciliation of the two opposing leaders and embody in his single existence their now-united power and will.[41]

The historians do not stress the hopes of a stable peace that the treaty aroused; but they knew that it was only the prelude to a worsening situation. Dion says that the people felt great delight, 'for they thought that harmony between these men meant peace for themselves,' though they also wanted the war with Sextus to stop. Tacitus with his ironies uses the occasion to bring out the hollowness of the hopes and the insidious treacheries of Octavian that lurked behind the apparent accords.[42]

Once we accept the thesis that the parents are Octavia and Antony, and the saviour-babe is the child they are to produce, almost all the poem can be easily explained. The New Achilles then refers to the hero who will defeat the Parthians—an Antonian touch like the Dionysiac imagery. The 'great progeny of Jove' is an odd phrase, since Jupiter seems to have no part in the system—but perhaps it refers to Hercules. The child is to be Herculean like his father Antony. (There is a certain ambiguity and lack of a distinguishing line between father and son: both are the heroes of the Parthian war, both are incarnations of Hercules. But this is no doubt the sort of thing that could

not be avoided in such a brief and yet complex concatena-
tion of symbols.) Hercules certainly appears again in the
last line; his is the *mensa*, the Table of Hercules, and the
mensa-image links with 'sharing the life of gods' in line 15.
The line of thought is that the child's ancestor became a
god through his great deeds, and so will the child himself.
The end of the poem means: Smile at your mother, don't
weep, or you'll never be a Hercules. In his *Herakles Idyll,*
Theokritos has the line, 'that suckling babe at nurse who
never knew tears'.[43] Achilles thus merges with Herakles,
as the two heroes did as ancestors or prototypes of
Alexander the Great. The child will be a New Alexander
and conquer the whole east (the Parthians). The imagery
of Alexander had long been invading the Roman Triumph;
Pompey had liked to think of himself as an Alexander;
and Antony covering the body of Brutus at Philippi had
been making the gesture of Alexander over the body of
Dareios.[44]

We must also take into consideration the likelihood
that the poem has been revised. Possibly Virgil, while not
wanting to exclude Pollio altogether or to obliterate the
atmosphere of the Brundisium days, blurred a few points;
he may have lessened the role of the father so that the
increased stress on the child of a new era would make
readers think the work referred to the coming Augustan
system. The belief that the Fourth *Georgic* once ended with
praises of Cornelius Gallus, which were excised after that
poet and official fell from favour, seems certainly errone-
ous; but there is nothing unlikely in the idea of censoring
or changes in poems to suit a new political climate. By
his later work Virgil in any event altered the perspective
through which his Eclogues were viewed.[45] As early as

the First Book of the *Georgics*, lines near the beginning suggest Octavian as the god-king of the new dispensation:

> And chiefly, Caesar, you whom it's not revealed
> which company of gods will welcome: whether
> you design to visit cities or care for states
> and the mighty globes receives you, giver of fruits,
> ruler of seasons, binding with your mother's myrtle
> your temples, or god of the boundless seas you come
> and seamen worship your deity alone . . .
> Whatever you will be . . .
> grant me an easy course, my bold design
> favour, and pity the ignorant farmers with me,
> begin and grow used now to invoking prayers.

He even suggests that the Scorpion constellation is drawing in its claws so as to leave room for the new god in the skies. In *Aeneid* VI Augustus is directly proclaimed as the bringer of the Golden Age:

> This is Caesar, this the whole progeny
> of Iulus, who'll rise to the great sky-axle one day.
> This, this the man you've heard promised to you,
> Augustus Caesar, a god's offspring, who'll found
> the Golden Age in Latium through those lands
> where Saturn reigned of old, and shall extend
> his empire to Garamantes and Indians. . . .[46]

We feel that in writing such a passage Virgil was clearly recalling the Eclogue and going out of his way to transfer its meanings to Octavian. As if he were saying: I was right in my sense of great impending changes, but I did not see distinctly the figure around whom the ideas, images, and symbols were gathering. Perhaps he hopes by such a passage to make it even appear that in the Eclogue he was

thinking somehow of Octavian, not of Antony; and
perhaps in such a mood he inserted the phrase 'now your
Apollo reigns'—the one statement in the whole poem that
does not seem at all to belong to the Brundisium situation. Apollo cannot be Antony; he definitely suggests
Octavian. And yet to set up Apollo-Octavian in the midst
of the idyll of Octavia and Antony with their saviour-babe
is to strike a hopelessly jarring note. If such an Apollo
reigns, we are already at the situation set out in *Georgic* I
and *Aeneid* VI, and there is no need of the Dionysiac babe.
So, unless there is some point in the phrase which now
eludes us, it would appear to be an intrusion, the result of
a revision by which Virgil wanted to bring Octavian in
as a god-presence without making a thorough reconstruc-
tion of the text. Apollo here can be taken, however, as the
god of poetry, the brother of Diana identified with
Lucina the birth-goddess. The phrase then means: 'Here
the spirit of poetry and inspiration controls everything.'
This meaning is made easier by the fact that Apollo was
the patron and inspirer of the Cumaean Sibyl. Virgil might
have reflected: Apollo is the inspiring god and so no one
can object to his presence; but he is also Octavian and thus
his appearance modifies the strong Antonian colouration.
Thus the poem could be said to make the best of two
worlds: that of Apollo-Octavian and that of Dionysos-
Antony.

But when did Octavian definitely assume the Apollo-
image? In establishing himself as the son of Caesar, he
became *Divi Filius*, the Son of the Divine One, and thus
in some sort himself *divus*. After the defeat of Sextus in 36
he enlarged his programme to make himself the mission-
ary of Peace. The people went with garlands to meet him

and escorted him to Rome and the temples. In his speeches (never published) he set out his new slogans. 'He announced Peace and Prosperity.'[47] A soldier put a sword at the feet of Jupiter Capitolinus, to express the fact that swords were no more needed. The Senate set up a gold statue of Octavian for restoring Peace on Sea and Land; later he and his followers used to refer to the closing of the Temple of Janus in these terms.[48] But so far his claim to divinity, such as it is, depends on his relationship to Caesar; if he is the *deus* of the First Eclogue, it is as the *Divi Filius*, not as Apollo.[49]

The precedent for turning to Apollo went back to Sulla with his prayer to that god in the midst of civil war at the Colline Gate.[50] This prayer in turn was linked with an ancestor of his who in 212 had introduced the Ludi Apollinares. Octavian was early associated with laurel. Early in 40 the Roman citizens gave themselves up to merrymaking, conveyed him in his triumphal clothes into Rome, 'and honoured him with a laurel crown, also with the right to wear it when anyone else, celebrating a triumph, wore it.'[51] But here the association is with the Triumph and Jupiter, not with Apollo. However, the martyred Caesar had been linked, two years before, with the Games of Apollo and with laurel. 'They laid the foundation of a shrine to him as Hero, in the Forum, on the spot where his body had been burned, and caused an image of him, together with a second image, that of Venus, to be borne in the procession at the Circensian Games. And whenever news came of a victory anywhere, they assigned the honour of a Thanksgiving to the victor by himself, and to Caesar, though dead, by himself. And they forced everyone to celebrate his Birthday by wearing

laurel and by merrymaking, passing a law that those
neglecting these observances should be accursed in the
sight of Jupiter and of Caesar himself, and, in the case of
senators or their sons, they should forfeit a million
sesterces. Now it happened that the Games of Apollo fell
on the same day, and they therefore voted that his Birth-
day-feast should be held on the day before, on the

Relief from Amiternum of late Republican or early Augustan date,
showing a funeral procession, with strong Etruscan influence in the
symbolism of the Journey to Hades (seen on late Etruscan urns); the small
attendant at the rear has a *situla* and palmbranch for rites of the Journey.

grounds that an Oracle of the Sibyl forbade a festival on
Apollo's day to any god but Apollo.'[52]

Dion links laurel with Augustus in 37, telling a tale of
many omens; but there is no hint of a connection with
Apollo. Rather, the laurel has triumphal associations. 'A
host of dolphins battled against one another and died near
Aspis, the African city. And near the city blood flowed
from heaven and was carried in all directions by the birds.
When at the Roman Games no senator gave a banquet on
the Capitol (as had been the custom) this too was taken
as a portent. Again, the incident that happened to Livia,

though giving her pleasure, scared everyone else. A white bird, bearing a laurel-sprig with berries, was thrown by an eagle into her lap. As this seemed a sign of no small moment, she cared for the bird and planted the laurel, which took root and grew—so that it supplied those who later on celebrated Triumphs, and Livia was destined to hold in her lap even Caesar's power and to dominate him in everything.'[53] In 36 a laurel crown was awarded to Octavian, but again the associations are triumphal. Still there is at last an overt connection with Apollo, though the appearance of a thunderbolt is odd, since Jupiter was the hurler of such things. 'The people resolved that a house should be presented to Caesar [Octavian] at public charge. For he had made public property of a place on the Palatine which he bought with the aim of erecting a residence there, and, after a thunderbolt fell on it, he consecrated it to Apollo. Hence they voted him the house and also protection from any insult by word or deed.'[54] Suetonius does indeed tell us that Octavian's mother dreamed of being raped by a snake and for this reason he (strangely) was taken as Apollo's son. The story came from 'the theological books of Asklepiades of Mendes' in Egypt. 'Awakening, she purified herself, as usual after her husband had mated with her. At once appeared on her body a mark in snake-form, which she never could efface and which obliged her for the rest of her life to avoid public baths. Augustus, it was added, was born in the tenth month after and thus was thought to be Apollo's son. The same Atia, before her delivery, dreamed that her entrails stretched to the stars and expanded through the whole circuit of heaven and earth. The father, Octavius, likewise dreamed that a sunbeam issued from his wife's womb.' Such a story would certainly be late, well after the Battle of Actium, and seems to take Apollo as a solar deity. (It is odd to find an Egyptian favouring Octavian's cause.)[55]

As we shall see later a satirical epigram does suggest that by the time of the marriage with Livia Octavian was beginning to link himself with Apollo; but it is more than unlikely that in these years he had staked any clear claim to the god. In B.C. 40, there can have been nothing to make *tuus Apollo* in the Eclogue recognisable as him. The direct reference is to Lucina-Diana, and, perhaps behind her, the figure of the Cumaean Sibyl. Apollo reigns as god of prophecy; the Sibyl's oracle, coming true, vindicates the god who inspires her. To suggest that already some ruler in god-guise is in charge of things is to rob the prophecy of any point; what the poem deals with is the saviour-babe as the future ruler or redeemer, and, linked with his work, the preluding achievements of his father. By the time of *Aeneid* VI Octavian's laurel-bough had become the golden bough which the Sibyl gave to Aeneas, ancestor and prototype of Octavian as a guide into history, in the past and future revealed in the spirit world. In 40 what absorbed Virgil was the hope of healing the world's wound by the union of the two great men; Octavian for his purpose was amply represented by Octavia, and if the marriage had succeeded there would have been nothing incorrect in this way of putting the issues.[56]

In our analysis of the Fourth Eclogue we have had to make many devious twists and turns; but the quest has been necessary. The various facets of thought and belief that it had revealed all throw a light on the minds of Antony and Cleopatra, and on the goals that that pair ultimately set themselves. We have learned much of the underworld of ideas and emotions in their world: ideas and emotions which at first glance may seem far removed from the forces that were actually shaking and re-making that world, yet which, on being probed, give us an insight into the passions, the needs, the fears and the hopes, powerfully agitating men and driving them on past partial solutions and temporary compromises. Any analysis of the general forces, economic, social, and political, which were at work throughout our period, gives us only an abstracted and narrow view if we fail to add the human dynamic, the terror and the exaltation bringing men up against the final questions of life and compelling them to face deep questions of choice. There may often seem pathetic or ridiculous contrasts between the tremendous emotions and their symbols, and the return to old oppressions in a new form, or on a new level, which is what actually happens. And yet the emotions and the symbols were not a mere waste, a mere illusion. They may seem to flare up and then die out, effecting little or nothing. Yet they survive in men as something essential for human life, something driven deep but never annihilated, ready to revive and reassert itself, satisfied with nothing less than entire freedom, peace, union in worthy ends.

We have seen Antony in a momentary blaze of Dionysiac glory as the father of the child who will save the world, himself mysteriously entangled in the fate of his son. A great poet has penetrated, for a flash, into the human truths behind the noisy façade of an historical event. Antony in his own way had a feeling for those truths. The years following Brundisium seemed to be dissipating his forces, severing him more and more from the deep satisfactions he knew when he was being carried on the crest of a great wave of life. He decided that he was being baffled and sidetracked, made a mere cipher, by Octavian: there lay the element of truth in the propaganda tale of his spirit being cowed by the nearness of Octavian's.

To break from a way of life that he felt dwarfed him, he had to break from Octavia too. And that meant turning to Cleopatra for a union that would bring the miraculous transformations true after all.

Cleopatra Again

Arriving without Octavia in Antioch, he sent his friend Fonteius Capito to fetch Cleopatra.[1] The promptness of her response suggests that there had been some previous exchanges and that she was not surprised at the summons. They met after a separation of three and a half years. While married to Octavia, he was not free to marry again, and in any event he could not marry an alien. How far he underwent a formal marriage with Cleopatra, we do not know; he may have wedded her with Ptolemaic forms; in any event he henceforth acted as if they were man and wife. In the Hellenistic east there was nothing strange in a ruler with two wives; Ptolemy VIII had married both mother and daughter.

We have seen that she bore twins some time after he left her in March 40. It seems that only now they were given the names by which they came to be known, Alexander Helios and Cleopatra Selene.[2] The boy was to be a great conqueror, a Sun-king who would inaugurate the golden age; the girl was his female counterpart, Cleopatra-Isis.

The pair together thus took over the Parthian king's title of the Sun and Moon and symbolically deprived him of it. The naming of the twins in these terms represented for Antony the parting of the ways; the Brundisium-vision was taken away from its Italian setting, its links with the triumvirate, its hopes of a sun-hero born of Octavia, and was transferred to Cleopatra and her children. A third child, a boy born in 36, was named Ptolemaios Philadelphos; he was to be the Egyptian ruler who would restore the Ptolemaic heritage inside the new world-system created by the twins. (No doubt Cleopatra saw the twins as ultimately marrying.) This third child could walk and salute his parents, even if with guidance, in the autumn of 34, so that he was then at least two years old; he must have been conceived during the Antioch meeting. Attempts have been made to show that Antony visited Cleopatra in 38; but this visit, inherently more than unlikely, is based on an error in Josephos, who puts 'Egypt' instead of 'Athens'.[3] The child's birth may be dated August–September 36.

If Antony had backed Fulvia with all his stength, he could no doubt have destroyed Octavian and become sole master of the Roman world; but his sense of loyalty and decency prevented him. If he had patiently stuck to Octavia, he might have held the eastern provinces, but at the cost of becoming a sort of warden in a system increasingly dominated by Octavian. By turning to Cleopatra he put himself in a position where he must challenge Octavian, but in an open way, with the issues brought clearly out. He must have known this, and perhaps he chose his new path because he wanted to have a showdown with Octavian, but not in a dubious situation where the legal issues would be complicated and the real basis of the struggle could be obscured. What he did not realise at this moment was the extent to which the terms of the new confrontation would be more and more determined by Cleopatra. The names for the twins must have been hers, giving her version of the sort of aspirations uttered for the Roman world by Virgil. She had no doubt been biding her time, sure that Antony would come back, before she thus set out her programme; without his support the significance of the names would be much lessened and her act might have led to unpleasant reactions from Italy. Antony in his defiant mood accepted the names without seeing quite what he was letting himself in for.

To maintain his position against Octavian, he needed to defeat the Parthians; the carrying on of the war would be made very much easier if he had the resources of Egypt. He could have claimed Egypt and invaded it; and even if formal objections had been made, many Romans would have applauded and admired him. But he could not treat the mother of his son in such a way; he needed Cleopatra at his side; and he may well have rationalised his resistance to any adherents who advised an invasion, by saying that such an action would stir up prolonged Egyptian unrest and in any event would cause much trouble and delay—the last things he wanted—whereas with Cleopatra's co-operation he would make the best use of Egyptian resources with a minimum of trouble. But if he thought that she would simply meet his demands, he soon found himself mistaken. She probably refused to see the Parthian war in his terms or to agree that it was essential for his position in the Roman world; she knew that the main enemy was Octavian and wanted to keep her resources for the day when he had to be fought. She had none of Antony's scruples about the basis or pretext for the coming struggle.

First of all, she wanted to regain substantially the empire which Ptolemy II had held; and with some truth Octavian regarded her as the counterpart of that ruler. She asked for the territories as a wedding gift, as a token to all the world that she and Antony were united by a pact and purpose transcending any rites, Roman or Ptolemaic. He executed Lysanias for his treason of 40 and gave her Chalkis at the foot of the Lebanon, together with all that lay between Chalkis and Herod's realm—it was the old Koile Syria in a narrowed sense, an area covering central Syria: its inhabitants had joined the Parthians.[4] He also gave her Cyprus, or perhaps merely confirmed Caesar's gift; he gave most of the coast of Palestine and Phoenicia from Egypt to the river Eleutheros (the original Ptolemaic boundary). Tyre and Sidon alone were left out, as free cities. So that she might ship timber from the Tauros, like Arsinoe II, he took what had once been Roman territory, Cilicia Tracheia, from Polemon, and gave it to her, less the city of Seleukeia. She also got Cyrene in the west. Now she had all the former Ptolemaic possessions except some islands in the Aegean, Judaea and Galilee (under Herod), and the kingdom of Nabataia. The part of these territories she badly coveted was Herod's area; but all she gained was his profitable balsam-gardens and date-plantations round Jericho—and with them, his hatred. Also, the part of Nabataia that Ptolemy II had held, the land east of the Dead Sea with its monopoly of the bitumen fishery. The Arab Malchos, who ruled there, was not truly a client-king, but he dared not resist any decision made by Antony. Cleopatra shrewdly embroiled the two rulers whose lands she wanted, by arranging for Herod to collect the yearly rent of 200 talants from the region she rented back to Malchos.[5]

She began a new system of dating from the time of the gifts by the addition of a second number. Thus her 16th Year (1 September 37 to 31 August 36) was also called the 1st Year. Plutarch says that Antony cited Herakles to justify his actions. 'He used to say that the greatness of the Roman Empire was manifested, not by what the Romans took in, but by what they gave out, and that noble families were extended by the successive begettings of many kings. Thus, at any rate, his own progenitor was got by Herakles, who did not confine his succession to a single womb, nor stand in awe of laws like Solon's for the regulation of conception, but gave free course to nature, and left behind him the beginnings and foundations of many families.'[6] He was able to make his Donations in part because of the confusions brought about by the civil war and the Parthian irruption into the system developed by Pompey: a cordon of client-states from the Black Sea alone the Euphrates to the borders of Arabia, which protected provinces like Asia, Bithynia, Syria. A new system was needed; and Antony's dispositions were felt as a new era. Not only Cleopatra expressed this in her datings: the city of Chersonnesos on the Black Sea introduced in 37 a new era on its coins; Herod used two dating systems, one from 40, the other from 37 when he re-entered his kingdom with Antony's help and began building a fort commanding the Jerusalem temple-area, called Antonia.

Antony was popular in Alexandria. Men recalled how he had stopped the Piper from killing off his prisoners and how he had behaved gaily and un-Romanly. Cleopatra began building him a temple, unfinished at her death and turned then into a temple to Augustus. She and Antony put one another on coins. She was the only Ptolemaic queen who coined in her own right. Now she was able to carry on more effectively the mating of her Aphrodite with his Dionysos; for the Egyptians they became Isis and Osiris. There can be no doubt that she took herself seriously as Isis and saw the role as far more than a useful masquing for political purposes. She wore an Isis-robe on State-occasions; and in disputes in other regions she sided with the woman, with Aba in Olba and with Alexandra in Judaea. Her ideal of herself as queen is the picture we find in the Aretologies of Isis of the late period. Here is the version from Kyme:

> I am Isis, the Mistress of Every Land, and I was taught by Hermes, and with Hermes I devised Letters, both the Sacred and the Demotic, so that all things might be written with the same [letters].
>
> I gave and ordained Laws for men, which no one is able to change.
>
> I am eldest daughter of Kronos. I am wife and sister of King Osiris. I am She who finds Fruit for men. I am Mother of King Horos.
>
> I am She that rises in the Dogstar. She called Goddess by women. For me was the City of Boubastis built.
>
> I divided the Earth from the Heaven. I showed the Path of the Stars. I ordered the Course of Sun and Moon. I devised business in the Sea.
>
> I made strong the Man. I brought together Woman and Man. I appointed to Women to bring their Infants to birth in the tenth month. I ordained that Parents should be loved by Children. I laid punishments on those disposed without natural affection towards their Parents.

I made with my Brother Osiris an end to the Eating of Men. I revealed Mysteries to Men. I taught [men] to honour Images of the Gods. I consecrated the Precincts of the Gods.

I broke down the Governments of Tyrants. I made an end to Murders. I compelled Women to take the love of Men. I made the Right stronger than Gold and Silver. I ordained that the True should be thought Good. I devised Marriage-contracts.

I assigned to Greeks and Barbarians their languages. I made the Beautiful and the Shameful to be distinguished by Nature. I ordained that nothing should be more feared than an Oath. I have delivered the Plotter of Evil against other men into the hands of the one he plotted against. I established Penalties for those who practise Injustice. I decreed Mercy to Suppliants. I protect [or honour] righteous guards. With me the Right prevails.

I am the Queen of Rivers and Winds and Sea. No one is held in honour without my knowing it. I am the Queen of War. I am the Queen of the Thunderbolt. I stir up the Sea and I calm it. I am in the Rays of the Sun.

Whatever I please, this too shall come to an end. With me everything is reasonable. I set free those in bonds. I am the Queen of Seamanship. I make the navigable unnavigable when it pleases me.

I created Walls of Cities. I am called the Lawgiver [Thesmophoros, an old epithet of Demeter]. I brought up Islands out of the Depths into the Light. I am Lord of Rainstorms. I overcome Fate. Fate hearkens to me.

Hail, Egypt that nourished me.[7]

Now let us look more closely at the name Alexander Helios. 'Alexander' needs no commentary, with its explicit glance at Alexander the Great. Attempts have been made to link 'Helios' with two yearly festivals at Alexandria, the Birth of the Sun on 25 December and of Aion on 6 January.[8] (The fact that both festivals used almost identical formulas suggests that there was in fact only one festival: a point supported by the fact that the early Christian church used both dates for the Birth of Christ. We see incidentally how much ,of Christian mythology had its roots deep in the period we are treating, with its hopes of a saviour-child.) What evidence we have for these festivals is later than Cleopatra's time, and must be used with caution; but in any event a yearly rite in one city cannot explain the widespread belief in a cosmic event such as a golden age to be ushered in by a sun-child. Rather, the rite is part of the wider sphere. Besides, as we saw, it is not likely that the boy was called Helios at first; the name, like that of Cleopatra Selene, seemed to have been conferred at Antioch as part of Cleopatra's strategy for the whole post-Brundisium situation.

Closer to the roots of the Fourth Eclogue and to her own personal mythology was the *Potter's Oracle*, a Greek document of the Ptolemaic period, which shows that in Egypt the king of the golden age was expected to come from the Sun. We may compare an oracle (Jewish at least in part) in the Sibylline Leaves:

> And then God will send a King from the Sun
> who will make evil War stop all over the Earth. . . .[9]

But these passages link the Sun with the Warrior King who is to precede the King of the Golden Age and to pacify the earth with his word. The two kings seem merged or confused in Virgil. ('From the Sun' however might mean only 'from the land of the Rising Sun', from the East.) The origin of the *Potter's Oracle* is obscure, but there are certainly original Egyptian elements. The text tells of the troubles of Egypt under foreign soldiers, who are expelled by a king from the South.[10] The golden age is restored—marked by the destruction of the City by the Sea (Alexandria) and the return of the gods to their abode at Memphis. What we see is not a work produced under Jewish or Persian influence, but a modernising of ancient Egyptian prophetic literature in which we find many outbursts dealing with foreign invaders (for instance the Hyksos). The form is however popular rather than priestly-scholarly. The Greeks are named as the foe and the situation is Ptolemaic.[11] Alexandria is to become a place 'where the fishermen dry their nets' (as happened with the Arab conquest). But in its first form the work was probably a translation of an Egyptian prophetic text adapted, for example, for the Helleno-Memphite community in the 4th century B.C. when Greeks and Egyptians there were joined against a common Persian enemy. Then a new version was used to express the hatred and jealousy felt by the Egyptians for the Greeks as a ruling class with their stronghold Alexandria. However those emotions were also held by the poorer sections of Greeks and Greek-Egyptians, who did not belong to the Greek citizens and their *politeumata* or citizen-bodies. The rescension we have may perhaps date soon after the battle of Raphia, when the Ptolemies found themselves driven to make concessions to the native population and their cults, with a following century of racial and social tension, unrest, rebellion at home and lessening power abroad.[12]

The *Oracle* tells how the king coming of the Sun (as a representative or incarnation of Re, the sungod) will be a giver of all good things. Prosperity will be effected by a return to a lost natural order—not simply the restoration of the Egyptian Wandering Year to a coincidence with the solar year.[13] (The Egyptian calendar had fallen in a state of even worse confusion than the Roman calendar before Caesar's reform; and there was an effort to get it into order under Ptolemy III.) No doubt the contradiction of the natural year with the priestly calendar was felt as a sign of cosmic disorder, and men hoped that with the seasons set back in their proper calendar-places there would be no more low Niles. The sort of dismay caused by calendar-dislocations appears in a prayer to Amun of the New Kingdom: 'Come to me, Amun, deliver me in this year of misery. It has come to pass that the sun does not rise. The winter is come as summer, the months are reversed (?), and the hours are disordered. The great cry to you, Amun, and the small seek after you. Those in their nurses' arms say: Give us breath, Amun.'[14] But the calendar-issue is only one aspect of a situation of total disorder and injustice. The Sun-Hero is to right all wrongs and send the famine off to the Persians; he is to bring about a resurrection of the righteous. 'And the City by the Sea shall become a place where fishers dry their nets, because the Good Daimon and Knephis shall have departed to Memphis, so that certain who pass by shall say, "This City was a univeral nurse [*pantotrophos*], every race of men settled in her.' And then Egypt shall be blessed, when the King who is benevolent for 55 Years shall come from the Sun, a giver of good things, established by the Greatest Goddess Isis, so that those who are alive and survive shall pray that they who have died shall rise again to share in the good things.'[15] The Oracle exists in three texts, and there are two related texts. In one of the latter the Jews are named as the hated enemy.[16] We meet also an allusion to King Bocchoris of the Saite era and his magic Lamb which prophesied the invasion of Egypt from the Land of Choir (Phoenicia) and the final recovery of the gods carried off to Syria (perhaps to Nineveh); the story ends with the burial of the Lamb. Pseudo-Plutarch says, 'The Lamb has spoken to you; Egyptians have recorded a Lamb speaking with a human voice. It was found to have on its head a royal winged serpent and it foretold the future to one of the kings.'[17] The *Souda* adds that the serpent was four cubits long. The crown here described is based on the Egyptian royal uraeus, four cubits long, with ostrich feathers on the sides.

The *Oracle of the Lamb* goes far to confirm the thesis that the term *Potter* (which as such has no links with prophecy) is a rendering into Greek of the Egyptian words that mean Potter and are titles of the ramheaded god Khnum, the creator of Sun, Gods, and Men on his potter's wheel. The original prophet would then be Ramheaded Knum.[18] The lamb prophecy has a reference to a Golden City, which may be Aphroditopolis, the city of Hathor, who had her link with gold; but may also be Heliopolis, the city of the Sun, as gold and sun were often associated.[19]

Isis had a connection with both Justice and the Sun. Justice is at times found as her name in inscriptions. Apollonios son of Ammonios at Alexandria, with his wife Timokrion and his children, dedicated an image on behalf of Ptolemy IV and Queen Arsinoe, Fatherloving Gods, to Demeter, Kore, and Justice—presumably Isis.[20] In Aretologies we read, 'I made Justice mighty.' Proklos declares that 'In the shrine of the Goddess', Isis—Plutarch says, on her throne at Sais—she claims to have borne the Sun.' That is, she has borne it once for all, not at a yearly festival, even though a festival might be said to express or reaffirm an eternal event.[21] (An inscription at Aigina, much later, probably referring to Elagabalus, runs: 'To the New Dionysos from the Sun, a great god who hears prayers.'[22]) We might then argue that Cleopatra as the New Isis bears the Sun, who is incarnated as Alexander Helios. Her great forerunner Arsinoe II had been Isis, and Ptolemy III (officially but not in fact her son) had on his gold coins his head decorated with sun-rays: which makes him a good candidate for the 'King from the Sun established by Isis' of the *Potter's Oracle*, a phrase that must have meant something more specific than that every Egyptian king was a son of Re. The horn-of-plenty on the coins' reverse is also crowned with sun-rays, representing a prosperity come from the Sun. We have already noted that Ptolemy III made a calendar reform.[23]

So we find a considerable basis in Egyptian and Greek-Egyptian ideas for the name of Cleopatra's son; and the suggestions here made will be confirmed when we come to the prophecies set out later in her reign. For the moment we may however point out the link of sun and utopia in the romance by Iamboulos, which played a part, together with Stoic ideas, in stimulating the revolutionary attempt to found an egalitarian City of the Sun at Pergamon nearly a century before the time with which we deal. The romance's utopia was on Islands of the Sun, where the Sun was honoured above all other gods.[24] The Ethiopians, who sent the narrator to the islands, believed that he would there enjoy a golden age of peace and happiness for six hundred years. Six hundred is Berossos' figure for the lesser of the two great years, the cycle called Neros; and it was adopted by the Jews as the basis of their

great year. Josephos says on the long life of the patriarchs:
'God afforded them a longer time of life on account of
their virtue and the good use they made of it in astro-
nomical and mathematical discoveries; they would have
lacked the time for foretelling [the star-periods] unless
they'd lived 600 years; for the Great Year is completed in
that interval.'[25]

So on the Islands the whole coming world-cycle was to
be golden, with no deterioration. Here the utopian con-
cepts must be further linked with two Hellenistic ideas.
First, the Sun as the just god, the watcher over Justice.
This attitude had wide extensions in the ancient east.
Malachi speaks of the Sun of Righteousness; the Persian
Acts of Pusai refer to the sun as Judge of the whole
Earth, who sees righteousness and pronounces judgement;
a Babylonian hymn calls the sungod Shamash, 'Judge of
Heaven and Earth', before whom 'righteousness raises its
head'. Pythagoras connects sun and justice with the mystic
number 4; the Orphic *Hymn to the Sun* calls the all-seeing
orb 'the Eye of Justice'. We see then why the Virgo
Justice has fled the impious earth but returns with the
golden age in Virgil's vision.[26] In ancient Egyptian
thought, Justice or Truth (Maat) was the daughter of Re
the sungod; Osiris as Judge of the Dead had his throne
set on a flat pedestal shaped like Maat's hieroglyph; the
blessed live on the *maat*-plant, which forms the body of
Osiris. Here are fused the notions of rebirth, justice, and
blessedness; and we see that there was also an Egyptian
basis for the Eclogue's ideas and imagery.[27]

Secondly, the Hellenistic king as animate law shared in
the power of the Sun as supreme deity; in the State he
concentrated the radiant sun-power and was lord of

justice.[28] The Christians took over these concepts to glorify the emperors who supported the church. Eusebios, drawing on sources like the *Kingship* of Diotogenes, said that as God to the Cosmos, so the King to his Polis; he is incarnate law, *nomos empsychos*, and imitates the *syntaxis* and *harmonia*, the order and harmony, of the cosmos; as incarnate law he 'is transformed into God among Men.'[29]

It is clear then in the naming of the twins Antony and Cleopatra were bringing together a number of mythical and prophetic ideas that had great importance for both the learned and the simple of their world. Antony was in part reacting against the failure of the Brundisium aspirations and expressing his gratitude to Cleopatra for having, unlike Octavia, given him a son. Virgil's Eclogue, we must realise, would have been well known to him as to all the leading characters of the Brundisium Treaty. Octavia would certainly have been presented with a copy; and we may assume that Virgil, introduced by Maecenas or Pollio, read his poem to the two triumvirs, Octavia, and others. The poem would then have been much talked about, though we need not consider it as circulating in manuscript till the Eclogues were published, about 39.

The Parthian War

Antony spent the 37–36 winter at Antioch, furiously preparing for war. First he had to secure his rear. Syria and the regions further south were secure in the hands of Cleopatra and Herod; but Asia Minor was still to be settled. At last he made his decisions, basing his system on three capable men without dynastic claims, Amyntas, Archelaos, Polemon. Amyntas, in addition to his existing territories (Pisidia and the nearer parts of Phrygia) was made king of Galatia; he also got Lykaonia and some of Pamphylia. The whole of central Asia Minor was thus under one man. The Galatian cavalry was the best in the Roman east and important to Antony. Two Galatian chieftains were given areas—Adiatorix, the Roman section of Herakleia; Ateporix, a part of Zelitis. Ariarthes was executed for his treason of 40; his Cappadocia was handed over to Archelaos of Komana, but not Armenia Minor. Archelaos was a student and author of the type of Juba II of Mauretania; previous kings of his region had called themselves Friends of Rome, he called himself

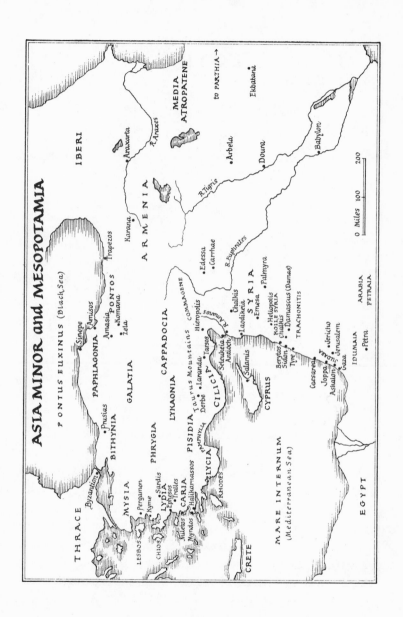

ASIA MINOR and MESOPOTAMIA

THRACE

Byzantion

MYSIA
Pergamon
Kyme
Sardis
LYDIA
Ephesos
Tralles
CARIA
Miletos
Halikarnassos
Mydnos
LESBOS
CHIOS
RHODES
LYCIA
PAMPHYLIA

PONTUS EUXINUS (Black Sea)

PAPHLAGONIA
Sinope
Amisos

BITHYNIA
Prusias

GALATIA

PHRYGIA

PISIDIA
Derbe
Loranda

LYKAONIA

PONTOS
Amasia
Komana
Zela

CAPPADOCIA

Taurus Mountains

CILICIA
Tarsos
Seleukeia
Antioch
Soluanis

COMMAGENE
Hierapolis

CYPRUS

ARMENIA

Karana

R. Araxes
R. Araxata

IBERI

MEDIA
ATROPATENE

to PARTHIA →

Ekbatana

Arbela

Doura

Babylon

R. Tigris

R. Euphrates

Edessa
Carrhae

Palmyra

SYRIA
Chalkis
Laodikeia
Emesa

Heliopolis
KOILE SYRIA
Chalkis
Damascus (Damas)

Berytos
Sidon
Tyre
TRACHONITIS

Caesarea
Joppa
Askalon
Gaza

Jericho
Jerusalem

IDUMAIA
Petra

ARABIA
PETRAIA

EGYPT

MARE INTERNUM
(Mediterranean Sea)

CRETE

0 Miles 100 200

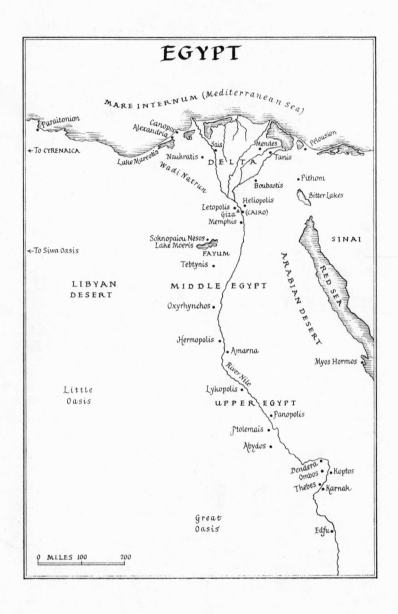

EGYPT

MARE INTERNUM (Mediterranean Sea)

Paraitonion

←To CYRENAICA

Canopos
Alexandria

Lake Mareotis

Naukratis

Sais

DELTA

Mendes

Tanis

Pelousion

Pithom

Bitter Lakes

Wadi Natrun

Boubastis

Letopolis
Giza
Memphis

Heliopolis

(CAIRO)

SINAI

←To Siwa Oasis

Soknopaiou Nesos
Lake Moeris

FAYUM

Tebtynis

RED SEA

LIBYAN
DESERT

MIDDLE EGYPT

Oxyrhynchos

Hermopolis

Amarna

ARABIAN DESERT

Myos Hormos

Little
Oasis

River Nile

Lykopolis

UPPER EGYPT

Panopolis

Ptolemais

Abydos

Dendera
Ombos
Thebes

Koptos

Karnak

Great
Oasis

Edfu

0 MILES 100   200

Friend of his Country, *Philopatros*. Polemon had had to surrender Cilicia Tracheia to Cleopatra; Antony sent him in compensation to Western Pontos, where the throne seems to have been vacant. Polemon now had the reconstituted old kingdom of Pontos, stretching from Armenia to the Halys; he thus took over part of the Roman province of Bithynia and Pontos, with Armenia Minor added. At Olba in Cilicia Cleopatra saw to the restoration of Aba, a Teukrid by marriage, to the priest-kingship which had been usurped by a local tyrant not of the royal line.

Of the four major appointments by Antony—Herod, Amyntas, Archelaos, Polemon—all had successful reigns from the Roman viewpoint, and long reigns as well, apart from Amyntas who was killed in war in B.C. 25.

In spring 36 Antony went to join his army. Cleopatra, expecting Ptolemy's birth, went with him to Zeugma. then back to Egypt. On the way she called in on Herod to arrange about her monopolies, perhaps amused at knowing that he would have killed her but for his fear of Antony. (After Antony's failure in Media, Herod got little of her rents from Malchos.) In his *Memoirs* he stated that she tried to provoke him into love-making, so that, if he made a false step, she could incite Antony to kill him. This tale is certainly untrue; for if she had had any such plan, she could have easily lied to Antony with a tale of Herod's advances to her. He escorted her to the Egyptian frontier.

He had appointed Ananel as highpriest, but Alexandra asked Cleopatra to use her influence on behalf of her son, Aristoboulos, grandson of Aristoboulos II and last male of the Hasmonaians. Early in 36 Herod did make the young man highpriest, at Antony's request or to win over the Hasmonaian adherents. Alexandra seems to have gone on intriguing to gain the throne for her son; and that autumn she decided that she and her boy were in danger, or thought it politic to say so, and Cleopatra sent a ship for them. But their escape in two coffins was prevented. Later in the year, with Antony distant, Herod decided to have the lad murdered—drowned in a swimming party. But he left Alexandra alive, perhaps through fear of Cleopatra. Again Alexandra appealed, now for revenge. In January 35, Cleopatra meeting Antony in Syria, tried to get Herod punished. Antony went so far as to summon Herod, but had no intention of removing so valuable a vassal; he accepted the argument that as he had made Herod king he must let him act as such. Josephos says that Herod wrote to Jerusalem, stating that 'when he came to Antony he soon regained his footing with him, by the presents he'd brought; and soon, after conversing with him, he induced him to drop his indignation. So Cleopatra's persuasions had less force than the arguments and gifts he used to win back his friendship. As Antony said, it wasn't right to ask a king to give an account of his government; for then he wouldn't be a king. Those who gave him that authority should let him use it. He also said the same to Cleopatra: that it would be best for her not to meddle so actively with the acts of the king's government. Herod narrated these events and enlarged on the honours received from Antony: how he sat by him while he was hearing law-cases and daily ate with him, and how he enjoyed these favours despite the reproaches so sharply laid against him by Cleopatra—wanting, as she did, to get hold of his country and earnestly entreating

Antony to give her his realm. She laboured with the utmost thoroughness to have him put out of the way but he still found Antony just to him.' Herod clearly overstated Cleopatra's discomfiture, but Antony stood by him despite her pressure.[1]

However, before this encounter, much had happened. In Parthia there was a new king. Orodes, crushed by the death of his dear son Pakoros, had made another son, Phraates (IV) his heir; and Phraates, annoyed at his father lingering on, murdered him. He killed also some protesting nobles, while others fled. Behind the turmoil there seems to have been conflicts between nobles and commoners, cataphracts and horse-archers. The noble cavaliers had done their best against Ventidius and been badly beaten; Phraates meant to base himself on the archers. An adherent of his, Monoaeses, warden of the western marches, a man of great estates in Mesopotamia, was marked out for the command. He pretended to be opposed to Phraates, fled to Antony, was welcomed and given a small kingdom, with a promise of the Parthian throne. But he told Antony nothing of the change of tactics being worked out by Phraates; and in the spring of 36, having learned what he could, he slipped back to Parthia, where he took command of the army.

Antony, a dashing cavalry commander, had never so far had to plan a whole largescale campaign. He had Caesar's papers and must have known how he meant to strike: to reduce Armenia and build an advanced base there, then take Ekbatana, the Parthian capital, cut off Babylonia, annex it and make it the new frontier. However, after two years of delays not of his own creation, he was over-impatient and wanted to do too much in one year. Canidius Cassius had been sent, perhaps late in 37, to make a preliminary conquest of Armenia, in imitation of Alexander's winter campaigns. Canidius defeated Artavasdes, Parthia's ally since 53, who submitted and returned to alliance with Rome. The act of submission seems to have been considered sufficient; there is no evidence of guarantees being exacted, hostages taken, towns garrisoned. In spring 36 Canidius moved on, and, like Pompey, reduced the Albani and Iberi of the Caucasus. Antony struck coins with the Armenian tiara as if he securely held the kingdom; he seems to have relied on the way that Armenian policy tended to play Rome and Parthia off against one another, and to ignore the fact that Armenia's deeper bonds were with Parthia. The other Artavasdes, of Media Atropatene, had joined Parthia, and in the situation Armenia was sure to feel a strong impulse to follow his example.

Antony's scheme was bold and might well have succeeded. Instead of invading from the west across the Euphrates and the desert, as had previously been done, he chose a long circling movement via the north. Crossing Armenia, he would occupy Media, attack the Parthians in the rear, and thrust to their heart. While the Parthians awaited the usual attack, he turned north to Karana (where Ezerum now is). On the Armenia plateau he was joined by his army from the Caucasus. The sources suggest that he was late in carrying out his plan; but clearly he had to make a rendezvous with Canidius. Though he had left seven legions in Macedonia and one at Jerusalem, he now reviewed the largest army he had led: sixteen seasoned legions of about three-quarters, strength, some

60,000 men, with 10,000 Gallic and Spanish horse, 30,000 Asianic auxiliaries (including Artavasdes with 16,000 cavalry and the forces of the client-kings). Among the light troops were slingers with bullets that carried further than Parthian arrows and could pierce armour. Canidius and Ahenobarbus were among his legates, and his quaestor was Plancus' nephew, Titius.

Now came the decision that wrecked his scheme. Eager to press forward, he divided his troops. Oppius was left with the baggage-train guarded by two legions, Polemon, and Artavasdes, to take the easier but longer route along the valley of the Araxes. The train included a column of three hundred wagons with siege-engines: essential machines that could not be replaced in a land without heavy timber. He himself with his main force hurried on by the shorter mountain-route. With Lake Urumia on the right, they struck across the plain for the capital of Media, Phraaspa. Marching blind, he had no idea where the Parthians were; he relied on his surprise tactics to leave them bewildered. In fact Monoaeses knew all about his movements, doubtless through Artavasdes, and was quite close with 40,000 archers of his own and 10,000 more under the Median king. Somehow he had worked out a system of arrow supplies. Now he bore down on the isolated baggage-train. Artavasdes, whose horsemen made up most of the escort, rode off before the attack. The two legions were destroyed; their Eagles were added to the Parthian collection; Polemon was captured by the Medes; the siege-train was burned. When in mid-August Antony reached Phraaspa, he had no means of taking such a strong well-garrisoned fortress; and so he had nowhere to winter. However he refused to retreat without an attempt on

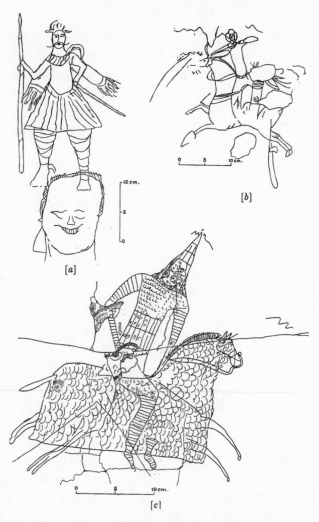

Graffiti from Doura-Europos (a) a Parthian foot soldier with heavy spear,
long sword, baggy trousers; note his characteristic helmet; he perhaps
stands on the cut-off head of an enemy (b) a Parthian horseman shooting
an arrow; his hair-arrangement suggests a noble (c) a Parthian knight or
cataphract in full armour on a horse covered with chainmail; he has metal
helmet with vizor, a coat of chainmail and (apparently) metal greaves,
sword, and long spear; no stirrups.

the town. He built a mound against the walls and improvised engines. Soon his foraging parties, forced to go far
afield, were being shot down. In desperation he offered
battle. Monoaeses tried one attack, but finding how
strong the legions were, withdrew with only some eighty
dead. Antony claimed a victory, but meanwhile the town
garrison had sallied out and burned his few machines.
October was coming on, and the cold weather; he had no
choice but to retreat.[2] Luckily he found a guide who
offered to lead the army back through the difficult hills to
Tabriz and thus avoid the plains where the Parthians
could have annihilated them. This man had been made a
prisoner when Crassus' army was cut off; but as this change
in his condition hadn't altered his feelings, he came by
night to a Roman outpost and warned them not to keep
to the intended road, but to slip off through a wooded
part of the country. This proved the salvation of M.
Antony and his legions (Velleius).[3]

The retreat over 280 miles took twenty-seven ghastly
days. Despite the terrain the legions marched in square.
The Parthians swarmed at their rear and rushed in at every
chance. The heavy legionaries closed ranks and raised
shields. Plutarch's detailed account clearly draws on the
account of someone who shared the march, and needs to
be cited in full. It shows how hardships and difficulties
brought out the best in Antony. 'On the fifth day Flavius
Gallus, an efficient and able soldier in high command,
came to Antony and asked for more light-armed troops
from the rear as well as some horsemen from the van,
confident he'd win a great success. Antony gave him the
men; and when the enemy attacked, Gallus beat them
back. He didn't then draw back and lure them on to the

legionaries, as had been done before, but fought on and engaged them more hazardly. The leaders of the rearguard, seeing that he was being cut off, sent to call him back, but he wouldn't listen. Then, they say, Titius the quaestor laid hold of the standards and tried to turn them back, abusing Gallus for throwing away the lives of so many brave men. But Gallus returned his abuse and exhorted the men to stand firm. Titius withdrew. Gallus forced his way among the enemy facing him without noticing that large numbers were enveloping him in the rear. But when missiles began to fall from all sides, he sent for help. Then the leaders of the legions—among them Canidius, a man of the greatest influence with Antony—are thought to have made no light mistake. Instead of wheeling their whole line against the enemy, they sent only a few men at a time to help Gallus; and then, when one detachment had been broken, sent out others. Before they knew it, they came near to plunging the whole army into defeat and flight. But Antony himself came quickly with his legionaries from the van to confront the fugitives, and the third legion soon pushed through against the enemy and checked any further pursuit.'[4]

Some 3,000 men had been killed and 5,000 wounded were carried to the tents, among them Gallus, pierced in front by four arrows. He died, but Antony went to visit the others, encouraging them with tears in his eyes. 'The wounded men however with cheerful faces grasped his hand and exhorted him to go away and take care of himself, and not to be distressed. They called him *Imperator* and said they were safe while he alone was unharmed . . . . And so, by sharing in the toils and distresses of the unfortunate, and by bestowing on them whatever they wanted, he made the sick and wounded more eager in his service than the hale and strong.'

The Parthians were exhilarated. They bivouacked for the night nearby, expecting soon to plunder the empty tents and baggage of men in flight. Next morning they gathered for attack, some 40,000 horsemen, the king having sent along his bodyguard to be in at the death. (The Parthian king himself was never present at a battle.) 'Then Antony, wanting to harangue his men, called for a dark robe, so as to appear more pitiful in their eyes; but his friends objected and he came forward in the purple robe of a general and gave his speech, praising those who'd been victors, reproaching those who'd fled. The former shouted to him to be of good courage; the latter, as an apology, offered themselves for decimation, if he wished, or for any kind of punishment; only they begged him not to be wretched and vexed. Antony in reply lifted up his hands and prayed the gods that if any retribution were to follow his former successes, it should fall on him alone, and that the rest of the army might be granted victory and safety.'

Next day the Parthians attacked; but they were met with such a vigorous response that they were disheartened. However, they assailed the Romans during the descent of some steep hills. The latter formed the *testudo* or tortoise. The shield-bearers wheeled about, enclosed the light-armed troops, and, dropping on one knee, held out their shields; the second rank held their shields over the heads of the first, the third over those of the second, and so on. The Parthians thought the Romans were sinking down with fatigue, laid their bows aside, and rushed in with spears. The Romans sprang up with their full battlecry and thrust with their javelins, killing the fore-most Parthians and driving off the rest. The same tactics were used on the following days.

'But now famine assailed the army. Raids provided little grain, and the men lacked grinding implements for what there was. Such things had been left with the dying beasts-of-burden; what beasts remained were needed to carry the sick and wounded. The men had to put up with roots and vegetables; and some of them ate a herb that produced madness and then death.' Many perished thus and the Parthians wouldn't desist and Antony (we're told) often cried out, 'O the Ten Thousand!' He was expressing his admiration of Xenophon's army, which made an even longer march from Babylon to the sea, fought with many times as large a number of enemies, and yet came off safe. The Parthians began peaceably mingling with forage-parties, pointing to their unstrung bows, and saying that they were going away. A few Medes still followed the Romans, not molesting them, but merely protecting the outlying villages. Antony began to think it would be feasible to go down to the plains. But a man from the enemy camp, Mithridates, came and asked for someone who spoke Syrian or Parthian. Alexander of Antioch, a close friend of Antony, talked with him and was told that the Parthians hoped to lure the Romans down to the plains, where they would ambush them under the hills. The Mardian guide agreed with the deserter. Antony decided to take the rough road through the mountains. The main problem there was lack of water, so the soldiers filled their few vessels and used helmets or skins. The Parthians replied by setting out in pursuit, against their custom, at night. Just as the sun was rising they came up with the tired-out Roman rear, who had marched 240 furlongs in the dark. Disheartened, with their thirst growing worse, the legionaries struggled on till the van reached a river. The water was clear and cold, but salty and poisonous; whoever drank it had his bowels cramped and his thirst inflamed. The Mardian warned the men, but they could not resist the water's appeal. Antony rode round, begging the men to wait a while; not far ahead was a river with good water. He called back the men who were fighting and ordered the pitching of the tents, so that they might at least rest in shade.

During this lull, Mithridates came up again. He said that the river was near and that the Parthians would not pursue the Romans beyond it. Antony had a large number of golden bowls and cups brought out, and Mithridates took as many as he could hide under his clothes. Then, while it was still day, they broke camp and moved on. The Parthians did not attack again, but that night was the most dreadful in all the march. Looting broke out. Men with gold and silver were murdered; even Antony's baggage-carriers were seized and beakers or costly tables were smashed or shared out. Soldiers who did not know what was going on thought the enemy had broken in. There was great confusion, straggling, skurrying about. 'Antony called a freedman of his body-guard, Rhamnos, and made him swear to thrust his sword through him at the word of command and cut off his head, so that he wouldn't be taken alive or recognised dead. His friends burst into tears. The Mardian tried to encourage them, insisting that the river was near; a breeze blowing from it was moist and a cooler air on their faces made breathing more pleasant. He also said the time

they'd marched made his estimate of the distance conclusive; for little of the night was now left. At the same time
others brought word that the tumult was the result of
their unrighteous and rapacious treatment of one another.
Wishing to get order into the crowd after their wandering
and distraction, Antony ordered the signal for encamp-
ment to be given.' Day was now dawning and order was
being restored, when Parthian arrows fell on the rear
ranks. The Romans took up their tortoise-position, but
the enemy did not come close. Little by little the front
ranks moved on, till the river was sighted. Antony drew
up the cavalry to face the Parthians while the sick and
wounded were taken across. When the Parthians saw the
river they unstrung their bows and called to the Romans
to cross over, praising them for the fight they'd put up.

The Romans marched on, not trusting the Parthian
assurances, but six days later they reached the Araxes,
which formed the boundary between Media and Armenia.
The river was deep and violent, and a rumour had got
about that the enemy were in ambush, ready to attack
as soon as the crossing began. But no attack was made. As
the army reached Armenia, they saluted the earth and
wept and embraced one another for joy. However, as they
advanced through the fertile country, they fell sick with
dropsies and dysenteries. Antony held a review and found
that 20,000 infantry and 4,000 horsemen had died, more
than half by disease.[5]

The Parthians had finalised the tradition of their
invincibility that lasted till Trajan. Phraates was represented later in Greek poems from Sousa as Omnipotent
God, a title not in the key of Mazdean religion. Meanwhile
Antony decided to press on for the Syrian coast. In the

snowy highland he lost another 8,000 men. The loss of so many veteran fighters was a heavy blow. But he could not winter in hostile territory. He stayed with his men as long as there was any fear that Artavasdes might attack, then pushed on ahead, leaving Canidius and Ahenobarbus to shepherd the army home. For all he knew, the Parthians might have overrun Syria and all the cities be in revolt In his message to Cleopatra he therefore did not call her to a big seaport, but to a village, Leuke Kome, where, if need be, she could force a landing. He found Syria safe, but was worried about the temper and condition in which his army would arrive. Day after day he rushed from the dinner-table to scan the horizon for Egyptian ships. But he need not have feared that Cleopatra would fail him, perilous as winter sailing was. She arrived in time with the badly-needed supplies, clothes and comforts for the wintering troops. So the army was got into its quarters without much difficulty. Antony had little money. But he somehow got a sum together, at least enough for a small donation to each man. Rumours against Cleopatra circulated. She hadn't brought any money; when Antony distributed it in her name, it was to save her face. She was the one responsible for holding him back so that the war wasn't started in time. She it was who had lured him back to Syria, when it would have been much better to have wintered in Armenia and resumed the war in the spring.

What must have most depressed Antony was the loss of the veterans; with Italy barred, he could not replace them. Meanwhile Octavian, who had at last defeated Sextus with Agrippa's aid and who had removed Lepidus from his place in the triumvirate, had 45 legions at his call. Secretly pleased at Antony's failure, he formally accepted the report sent to the Senate, which claimed success since there had been no defeat in battle. Festivals were held at Rome. Octavian meditated what would be his next step against Antony. He realised that for the moment he needed to do nothing; as Antony entangled himself more with Cleopatra, he would put himself hopelessly in the wrong in Roman eyes.

Deepening Divisions

Back in Alexandria with Cleopatra, Antony set himself to reconsider the situation. If only Octavian kept his word and sent the promised four legions, he'd be able to recoup his losses to a fair extent; but Octavian was not the man to help a rival whom he saw going downhill. In early spring 35, instead of the legions, he returned 70 ships out of the 130 Antony had lent him; he knew that, cut off from Italy, Antony would find his effective manpower dwindling. Cleopatra used this further example of Octavian's bad faith to underline the arguments she was urging. For her the Parthian war was a side-issue; Octavian was the main enemy who must be faced and dealt with sooner or later, and the sooner the better; what needed to be done now was to organise for the final confrontation; when Octavian was defeated, everything was possible and Parthia could be easily subdued. She was right enough in her contention, but did not, in Antony's eye, understand Roman ways and methods. If he had himself been ready to force the issue, the Perusian war had been the moment

271

for action; he should not have stayed aside while Sextus and Lepidus had been eliminated. He could not now merely challenge Octavian as a rival he disliked; that would be to put himself utterly in the wrong, for all Romans except his few close adherents, as a wanton aggressor—and worse, one who was weakly obeying the will of an alien queen. He knew, as Cleopatra did not, how much the people of Italy wanted an end of civil wars and how much Octavian could now pose as the champion who had brought that end. On the other hand, if he had decisively beaten Parthia, and even if he were still to do so, his prestige would grow enormously; he would achieve a great popularity and a renewed support in Italy and elsewhere; he would have the resources for donatives, gifts, settlements; he could make demands on Octavian that could not be ignored.

But even then, as he no doubt tried to shrug out of his mind but was forced to recognise in lucid moments of withdrawal, he would have the compromising presence of Cleopatra at his side, which would belie all his efforts to set himself out as a good Roman. Increasingly he was getting into the position where he could not act without Cleopatra, without her material aid and her strong reassuring presence, and where that presence made all the plans illusory or at least complicated things to an embarrassing and confusing extent. This dilemma was to beset him more and more from now on.

Meanwhile Octavian was immeasurably strengthening himself. There had been a lull in his struggle with Sextus, who however went on claiming the Peloponnesos, plus the dues of tribute that Antony had been promised. Appian says 'Sextus, angry (as Octavian said) about these

matters or out of his general fickleness or through
jealousy of the others with their big armies, or because
Menodorus incited him to look on the agreement as a
truce rather than a durable peace—Sextus was constructing ships and gathering rowers, and he once harangued
his troops, telling them to be prepared for everything.
Secret piracy again troubled the sea and the Romans got
little or no relief from the famine. They cried out that the
treaty had brought no relief from starvation, but only the
imposition of a fourth tyrant. And when Octavian caught
certain pirates and tortured them, they said that Pompey
had sent them out. This statement Octavian proclaimed
to the people and wrote to Pompey himself, who dis-
avowed it and made a countercharge about the Peloponnesos.'[1] Appian further comments that Octavian needed
the alleged confession of the pirates 'as the belief was still
prevalent that the war was in violation of the Treaty.' He
wrote to Rome and himself told the army that it was
Sextus who was the treaty-breaker. His witness was a
deserter from Sextus, Menodorus; and he added that
'Antony knew it and for that reason would not give up
the Peloponnesos.' This last remark was certainly
untrue. Through his freedman Philadelphus he persuaded
Menas, freedman and lieutenant of Sextus, to hand over
Sardinia, Corsica, three legions, many light-armed troops
and perhaps sixty ships.

In a series of converging attacks, Octavian, Agrippa,
and Taurus advanced on Sextus from Italy, while Lepidus
acted from Africa. Off Mylae on the north Sicilian coast
(where there had once been a great victory over the
Carthaginian fleet) the big warships of Agrippa at last
overwhelmed Sextus. Octavian, trying to land in eastern

Sicily, was badly beaten. Saved by the dusk, he managed to get back to Italy in a boat. Unnerved for a moment, he begged his companion to kill him. But in September 36, Agrippa in a second sea battle off Naulochos crushed Sextus' fleet. Sextus fled in a few ships to Asia, hoping for Antony's aid.

Lepidus now thought it was time he made some self-assertion and claimed Sicily. Octavian was eager for a chance to get rid of him. Winning over his troops, he deprived him of his triumviral office and left him to retire as *pontifex maximus*. He himself now had Africa as well as Sicily, Italy, and the West. 'I cleared the sea of pirates. In that war I captured about 30,000 slaves who had run off from their masters and taken up arms against the republic, and I handed them back to their masters for punishment.'[2] In fact, it was Agrippa who had won the war. Disbandment now began. Some veterans were sent to colonies overseas; others were put on land for which a proper price or compensation could at last be offered: thus Capua was given land in Crete and a new aqueduct in return for land taken. Many honours were showered on Octavian by the Senate; a statue of gold on a pedestal set about with ship-prows was raised in the Forum, inscribed, 'After prolonged unrest he restored peace by sea and land'. Coins used the monument, with his new name, *Imperator Caesar*.

We may note how the traditional system of names was changing.[3] Caesar and Antony were among those who were dignified enough to attempt no name-jugglings. In such a custom-bound society a breakdown of the name-system shows a wide and deep convulsion. Normally a Roman had his personal name (*praenomen*), a name proper (*nomen*) of his *gens* or clan, and a *cognomen* (surname, family-name): to which could be added his filiation and tribe. Now personal names tended to be dropped except in formal statements or in daily familiar use. In writing a man was often designated by *nomen* and *cognomen, e.g.* Julius Caesar (with Gaius dropped). Variations cropped up according to a man's social status or the literary form involved. *Cognomen* was put before *nomen, e.g.* Balbus Cornelius: a practice starting at a low social level and rising up. In 38 Agrippa dropped his lowly *nomen* Vipsanius. The *praenomen* was adhered to most of all among the aristocrats, *e.g.* Gaius Caesar, with the family-name reaching the level of a *gens*-name. Sometimes names were manipulated to give an effect of noble birth to which a man was not entitled; freedmen and clients took the gentilic name of their patron. Hence the *nomen* lost its exclusive quality and the family-name or the surname tended to be stressed. There arose hosts of Cornelii, descendants of the dictator Sulla; after Caesar, hosts of Julii. With Caesar himself we saw that the surname Caesar, tended to become the *nomen*; it was used as such by Augustus' adopted sons from 17 B.C. on. But the Julian name was kept by princesses of the line as well as by freedmen and men granted Roman citizenship; in the next generation of the ruling house it re-emerged, as we see by the names on the arch of Ticinum. Tiberius' sons (one real, one adopted) were called Drusus Julius Caesar and Germanicus Julius Caesar; and the two sons of the latter were Julii. Agrippa's posthumous son was given the *gens Julia*; but he, Agrippa Julius Casar—note how his father's surname, turned into a *nomen*, has now become a personal name—was relegated and thus omitted from the Ticinum arch. But apart from the royal family there was tendency to drop Julius. Thus, an *eques*, L. Julius Vestinus, had a son who was consul in 65 A.D. and who called himself M. Vestinus Atticus.[4]

The class-conflicts of the late Republic intensified the pride of nobles in their birth; we find unusual *praenomina* chosen to express the high claims of individuals. Sulla began to use Felix as surname, but gave to his son the personal name of Faustus (auspicious, lucky). Faustus Sulla then called himself on coins simply Faustus. Antony gave his son of 43 the name Jullus; the Antonii were of the plebian nobility, while Jullus was anciently of the patrician Julii—though Antony was not trying to upgrade his son but to show loyalty to the dead Caesar. Later, two heirs of the Claudii Nerones were stepsons of Augustus. Nero was an ancient family-name (Sabine like Appius); but while the elder youth used the correct form, Tiberius Claudius Nero, his brother put the *cognomen* as his personal name and became Nero Claudius Drusus, dropping his original *praenomen* Decimus. Pompey's elder son, who fell at Munda, took the surname assumed by his father (Magnus, Great) and called himself Gnaeus Magnus; 'Great' has now become his *nomen*. His brother Sextus began correctly, but dropped his personal name Sextus as well as the *nomen* Magnus, and turned himself into Magnus Pompeius Pius Son of Magnus in a Lilybaeum inscription; but he preferred to be simply Magnus Pius, the Pious (Fatherloving) Great Man.[5]

We see a trend among the mighty to a kingly sort of name. Magnus was used of eastern monarchs or heroes like Achilles. Octavian had been Gaius Octavius Thurinus; taking over Caesar's name he became Gaius Julius

Caesar Octavianus; but to get rid of associations with the mere Octavii, he called himself Caesar Divi Filius (Son of the Divine One)—as soon as Casar was consecrated by the Senate in early 42. Dropping Gaius and his Julian *nomen*, he now took as his official name Imperator Caesar. Imperator here was not a title but a personal name, and Caesar had supplanted Julius as *nomen*.[6]

Imperator derived from, and referred back, to the army-salutations; and the new use of it had a slight precedent in the unusual way that Caesar had treated it, putting it at the head of his titulature. Octavian's first acclamation by the soldiers seems to have occurred in April 43 (Mutina); his second came at some unknown time; his third was first recorded on Agrippa's coins of 38; then came Imperator as personal name. A magistrate or pro-magistrate, hailed as Imperator, seems to have felt a certain incompatibility between that title and his other one, whatever it was; the more splendid term tended to obliterate, for the moment, the lesser. During the civil wars, under Caesar or the triumvirs, generals on all sides liked to add the title of imperator, and when the triumvirs asserted themselves better, they tried to stop this practice. Thus, in 36 Octavian forbade the wearing of purple cloaks by commanders not of senatorial status. Imperator further had an old sense of simply leader or commander; so, as a personal name, it expressed and flaunted Octavian's claim to be the military leader over all others. He seems to have asserted this claim as a compensation for his own bad defeats in 38. The complex surrounding Pietas had been taken over by Sextus; and to keep on being an imperator in the ordinary sense was not distinctive enough. Also, Imperator may have been a

277

counterblast to the Pompeian use of Magnus. Though it was a name in the style of Faustus Sulla or Magnus Pius, it went beyond the other self-glorifying names and suggested a dominating power without attempting to define it. Augustus' successors did not use it as a personal name, except for Nero near the end of his reign. Then Vespasian, keen to suggest his legitimacy as successor, took it as *cognomen*, with Augustus; after him it became the very title of the ruler.[7]

To return to Octavian: after the defeat of Sextus, some emergency decrees were revoked. His great point was that he had ended the civil wars; anyone who caused further trouble would be in the position of a vile aggressor. He declared that he'd resign the triumviral powers before their expiration if Antony did the same. As the man holding Rome and Italy, with an obsequious Senate, he knew that he could always find some new form or pretext for maintaining his power, while Antony, if he resigned, would become a genuinely private person. The Senate gave him the rights that Caesar had had: personal sacrosanctity and a seat with the tribunes of the *plebs*. Refusing some lesser honours, he accepted these. 'It was ordained by law that I should be sacrosanct.' The yearly-elected tribunes were champions of the *plebs*, armed by statute with the right of 'rendering aid' and of veto against all official acts of magistrates; they could pass measures in Senate and popular assemblies; any assault by word or deed on their persons was a crime worthy of death. By becoming a sort of perpetual tribune, Octavian demonstrated how he could always find a basis for his continuing power, while, as soon as the powers conferred by their past accord ran out, Antony would be powerless.

At the same time Octavian was vying with the New Dionysos by putting Apollo, the god of song and order, on full-weight coins of silver. In 36 he vowed a Temple of Apollo adjoining his own house on the Palatine, where in tradition the house of Rome's founder Romulus had stood. And he decided not to rest idle at Rome while Antony fought in the east. No doubt he acted on Agrippa's advice. It was a good thing to keep his armies in fighting trim and to see that his reputation as Italy's defender did not grow dim. So he set about gaining the Alps as boundary and bringing the mountain tribes into subjection. At the same time, by controlling the Ocra pass and the upper Save he eliminated any possibility of invasion from the east and prevented further raids on Italy. Hence the Illyrian wars of the next three years. Halting-stations were founded and existing towns were made into frontier-points. The first steps were taken to opening up Dacia: something that Caesar had had in mind. Octavian took part in the fighting, which was unusual for him; once he was wounded in the knee by a stone missile. By securing the east Adriatic coast he was also gaining new recruiting-grounds for his navy and areas for settling veterans. Finally he was able to recite a long list of conquered tribes and deposited some recovered standards in his Porticus Octavia.

As the news of his actions came in, Cleopatra was able to point out how right she was in her interpretation of events and tendencies. Antony was depressed; his heart was not in the internal struggle for power; he agreed with Cleopatra without being able to carry her ideas into action. But she, however averse from eastern wars that dissipated the forces needed for war with Octavian, could not but admit that Artavasdes of Armenia must be punished for his treason. Since her plans involved the mustering of the eastern world against Rome, it would never do to leave such a traitor secure in the rear, destroying the Asian unity she wanted. So both she and Antony agreed that first of all they must deal with Armenia. Octavian too knew that Antony had further work to do in the east. With his permission or urging, Octavia set out in March 35 to bring supplies of clothes and other materials, together with 2,000 picked men—a force large enough not to be negligible, but not sufficient to set Antony on his feet again. When she reached Athens, she was met by a message from Antony bidding her to return to Rome. She at once obeyed after inquiring where to send the troops and stores.

Dion's account shows that Antony heard of her voyage when he was on his way north to deal with Armenia after having failed to lure the King to Alexandria: 'Learning on the way, however, that Octavia was coming from Rome, he went no further, but returned, in spite of his then and there ordering her to go home and his later accepting the gifts she sent, including the soldiers she had begged from her brother for this purpose.'[8] Plutarch has a ridiculous account of Cleopatra being thrown into a panic at the news of Octavia's departure. Antony, he says, heard of the voyage through a friend Niger, whom Octavia sent to him. 'But Cleopatra realised that Octavia was coming into contest at close quarters with her, and feared that if she added to the dignity of her character and Caesar's power her pleasurable society and her assiduous attentions to Antony, she would become invincible and gain complete control over her husband. So she pretended to be passionately in love with Antony herself and reduced her body by a slender diet. When Antony drew near, she put on a look of rapture, and one of faintness and melancholy when he went away. She contrived to be often in tears, then quickly wiped the tears away and tried to hide them, as if she didn't want Antony to notice. And she practised these arts while he was intending to go up from Syria and join the Mede. Her flatterers too were busy on her behalf. They kept on abusing Antony as hard-hearted, unfeeling, the destroyer of a mistress devoted to him and him alone. Octavia, they said, had married him as a matter of public policy and for her brother's sake, and enjoyed the name of wedded wife; but Cleopatra, queen of so many people, was called Antony's Darling, and she didn't shun or scorn the name as long as she could see him and live with him; but if she were driven away, she wouldn't survive. At last they so melted and enervated him that he grew afraid for Cleopatra and went back to Alexandria. . . .'[9] This account, which reads more like a passage from a love-romance, must come from an Octavian source with its glorification of the charms of Octavia. It also holds some inner contradictions. Antony is preparing to go north, join the Median king and carry on the war afresh, and Cleopatra is using her wiles on him. Then we find him going back to Alexandria—a phrase that suits better the account in Dion, where Cleopatra is nowhere about when he hears from Octavia and at once makes his decision, ordering her to go home.

When Octavia returned to Rome, Octavian was enraged at the callous treatment she had undergone, and bade her leave Antony's house: which she refused to do, since she was still legally his wife. There is no reason to disbelieve that Octavian was fond of his sister and angry at the way she had been treated. But we have seen his own way of marrying off himself or his relatives, including Octavia herself, to suit his political advantage; and we can be sure that so acute a judge of men must have known perfectly well that Antony would refuse to receive his wife. The dispatch of Octavia to the east can only have been a considered move on his part to bring out the break between him and Antony in a dramatic way—in a way most calculated to arouse hostility to Antony among all Romans. The great propaganda-card that he had to play against his rival was the latter's alliance with Cleopatra; he certainly wanted to use it and force it out into the open, in the west as well as in the east. Before the dismissal of Octavia, men might have merely smiled at tales of Antony's playing-about with Cleopatra; now the argument that he was seriously embroiled and had thrown in his lot with an eastern queen against his own people, was given a piece of convincing evidence.

Octavian made the most of the indignation aroused at Rome. He had both Octavia and Livia granted privileges which were normally only the right of the Vestal Virgins guarding the sacred fire of Vesta. They were pronounced inviolable, freed from the legal position of tutelage that weighed down on other women, and were authorised to set up pictures of themselves. The honours enhanced Octavian's own position. Octavia remained in Antony's house at Rome, looking after his children—her own daughters and Fulvia's two sons, though the boys soon went to Antony. She also did what she could to attend to her husband's interests. We can absolve her of acting any part in her brother's schemes; she was doing her wifely duty as she saw it; but the sight of her long-suffering devotion and her sacrosanct status helped Octavian's cause.

Vessels of *terra sigillata* made about this time in the big ceramic centre of Arretium in Etruria show the sort of propaganda that was being directed at Antony and Cleopatra. He is depicted as Hercules in woman's dress, seated in a chariot drawn by centaurs; one of his attendants holds a parasol over him, a section has a fan, while others bring a ball of wool and a spindle. Opposite him sits Omphale, who has bewitched him. His lionskin is thrown over her; she holds his club in her left hand and stretches out her right for a bowl of wine. Plutarch reflects this sort of satire: 'Antony, like Herakles in paintings where Omphale is seen taking away his club and stripping off his lionskin, was often disarmed by Cleopatra, subdued by her spells, and persuaded to drop from his hands great undertakings and necessary campaigns, only to roam about and play with her on the seashore by Kanopos and Tahosiris. And at last, like Paris, he ran away from the battle and sank on her bosom: though to be more precise, Paris ran to Helen's chamber after his defeat, while Antony ran off in chase of Cleopatra and thus threw victory away.'[10] Propertius carried on the imagery:

> Omphale, a Lydian girl, who'd surely been dipped
> in the Gygaean Lake, so lovely was she,
> made the man who'd reached Columns at end of the
>   conquered World
> spin wool, too soft a task for his hard strong hand.[11]

There may have been an Alexandrian basis for these jeers. We saw how, at the Piper's court, a philosopher was expected, like the other courtiers, to dress in woman's clothes in the Dionysiac festivals. Ovid in the *Fasti* links such transvestism with festivals of this kind:

> In such array they feasted and went to sleep;
> apart, in beds set side by side, they lay,
> preparing in purity for a festival
> of the vine's finder, held at break of day.[12]

He is dealing with Hercules and Omphale. We may here cite Velleius for one more testimony to the Dionysiac revels of this period: 'His passion for Cleopatra daily increased as well as the strength of those vices always fed by wealth, license, flattery. So he resolved to make war on his homeland. Previously, however, he had given orders to be called the New Father Bacchus, after riding through Alexandria with an ivy-chaplet on his head, a gold-hued robe, a thyrsus in his hand, and buskins on his feet.'[13] To such masquerades we may allot the dance-mime by Plancus, also described by Velleius. 'The queen's meanest flatterer, more obsequious than any slave, Antony's letter-carrier, the prompter and actor of the vilest obscenities, venal to all men and for all purposes, at a banquet he depicted Glauchus [seagod] in a dance, naked and painted green, wearing on his head a chaplet of reeds, dragging a tail after him, and crawling on his knees.'

Nothing however could have been further from the facts than the depiction of Cleopatra as lewdly drawing Antony away from action. She may have disagreed with him as to which enterprise should be given priority; but even more than he, she wanted bold plans and actions. If either of them lagged, it was Antony. But though he liked to forget the world's problems in festivals, there came a point where such things bored him and he felt an urgent need to break off and fling himself into furious activity. Nor did he ever tamely accept her objectives and desires. He carried on with the Parthian war against her wishes; he refused to let her persecute or unseat Herod.

Now it was Sextus Pompey who was causing him trouble and impeding his war-plans. First Sextus wooed the Parthian king, hoping to become a second Labienus. Then he offered to join Antony against their common foe, Octavian. Despite his defeat and his wilfulness, he was not an ally to be scorned; he still had much backing among the commoners of Rome and Italy. (Later his murderer Titius was hissed by the crowds at the Games he held in Rome.) But Antony had no taste for a war waged on such a character's behalf; and to link up openly with him would give Octavian a good pretext for a crusade against the drugged servant of a lecherous eastern queen and the piratic champion of runaway slaves. Cleopatra however thought the alliance might well be a good idea; she wanted the showdown to come as soon as possible and saw no reason for not using Sextus as a popular figure on the anti-Octavian side. But Sextus spoiled such chances as he had by refusing to come to Alexandria. He gathered troops in Asia Minor, caused a lot of trouble, and seized one of Antony's lieutenants. Antony sent the legions from Syria against him, under Titius, a personal enemy; and Titius hunted him down and killed him at Miletos, with or without Antony's assent—most probably without it. At Rome Octavian held celebrations: he could do no less for the destruction of an adventurer who had so long been a thorn in his flesh; but he managed to insert a sting in the honours voted for Antony, who had a statue set up in the temple of Concord, with permission to dine there with his wife and children: that is, with Octavia. Later on, he hypocritically reproached Antony for cruelty in killing Sextus, while he himself had spared Lepidus—ignoring the fact that Sextus was a wild and reckless firebrand, and

Coin of Arsakes XIV under whom Labienus served, inscribed 'King of Kings, Euergetes, Epiphanes. Philhellene'. Coin of Polemon II, son of Pythedoris.

that Antony did not seem to have ordered his death, whereas Lepidus was a harmless person with no particular support, whom Octavian brought down only because he wanted the province of Africa. The changed role of Antony now appeared in the way that the surviving murderers of Caesar, Turullius and Cassius of Parma, who had been with Sextus, came over to him.

It was too late to do anything on a large scale in 35; once again Antony was held up through no fault of his own. He went on with his preparations. He now had 25 legions, but 7 were in Macedonia and many were low in numbers while 3 were mixed legions taken from Sextus. However he somehow raised 5 more. He got some Italians from Caesar's colonies and the scattered groups of traders; but inscriptions show that he enlisted many Asians and Greeks, who assumed Latin names. Following Caesar's examples, he did not use new recruits to fill gaps in the old legions, those of the Parthian war, but built up new legions out of them. He brought over six of the veteran legions from Macedonia and sent new legions to fill their place. He also began building ships on a big scale. Thirty series of coins were struck, each with a legion's number; on the reverse, a flagship. And he married his daughter Antonia (by his first wife) to Pythodoros of Tralles, a rich man with more than 2,000 talants, who had been a friend of the great Pompeys. This marriage of a highborn Roman girl with a Greek, coming on top of his liaison with Cleopatra, gave much offence to *optimates* at Rome. (Antonia's daughter, Pythodoris, married Polemon and became queen of Pontos; on her husband's death she kept hold of both Pontos and Colchis, though she lost the Bosporos; she married Archelaos of Cappadocia; then on his death in 17 B.C. she went back to Pontos, which she administered till she died. Strabon the geographer, who was born in Pontos, at Amasia, says that she was a woman of great virtue and business capacity, so that her dominions flourished under her rule. Of her two sons, Zenon became king of Armenia; Polemon, after helping her administration, became king of Pontos.[14])

Meanwhile Medes and Parthians had quarrelled over their booty; the Median king let Polemon go free as emissary to Antony with an offer of alliance. There was also trouble inside Parthia, where Phraates' dated tetradrachms disappear from 36 till April 34. The first thing Antony wanted to do was to settle accounts with Artavasdes of Armenia, whom, no doubt unnecessarily, he suspected of being in conspiracy with Octavian. First he sent Dellius to him with a proposal of betrothing Alexander Helios to his daughter; but the king was too canny to come along to a ceremony where he would be at Antony's mercy. However, when Antony, who on 1 January 34 had taken up and laid down the consulship, arrived by forced marches before his capital, he went to the Roman camp, where he was told to surrender his treasure and his fortresses. His commanders proclaimed his son Artaxes king in his place. Antony then sent Artavasdes in silver chains to Alexandria, and defeated Artaxes, who fled to Parthia. Two younger princes were captured and the land pillaged. Antony gave part of Armenia to the Median king and betrothed Alexander Helios to his daughter, Iotape. This act, together with the marriage of Antonia to a Greek, showed a definite turn from Roman attitudes, customs, and prejudices, an acceptance of Greek and eastern ways of life in harmony with his marriage to Cleopatra. The betrothal of the sun-child is of especial interest; it proves that Antony saw him as a king of the east (the Orient, the land of the sun), a king whose realm would be much larger than the Roman eastern provinces and spheres of influence. A marriage with a Median princess only makes sense if Alexander was marked out to rule Media, Parthia, Armenia, Mesopotamia, and, beyond those kingdoms, the more distant lands that Alexander the Great had conquered. His territories would be part of a yet greater empire, extending westwards as well, under Antony and Cleopatra, Hercules-Dionysos and Aphrodite-Isis.[15] The betrothal was then a device for much more than keeping Media loyal, though that was the immediate motive.

In autumn 34 Antony was back in Alexandria. He had left his legions to winter in Armenia, which for two years was a Roman province, open to the depradations of Roman businessmen and traders. Antony's prisoners included the two princes and Artavasdes himself; in his loot was the solid gold statue of the goddess Anaitis from her temple in Akilisene. Octavian ignored the conquest of Armenia as if the conqueror were no longer an authorised Roman general. This silence represented a sharp change from the thanksgivings that followed the rounding-up of Sextus. Antony, who had not turned up to dine with Octavia in the temple of Concord, was henceforth in effect being considered a renegade, even if Octavian was not yet ready to bring the issues into an open conflict. Soon after his return he held a formal Triumph in Alexandria; but we do not know if this was his defiant reply to the silence at Rome, or whether that silence was caused by rumours of his intention to celebrate his successes in Egypt. In any event his action was an important step in his turning away from Roman tradition; for a Triumph proper could only be held at Rome, ending at the temple of Jupiter Capitolinus. Ventidius had had to go to Rome to enjoy his Triumph over the Parthians. Antony could have done few things more likely to alienate the Roman populace and all men who clove to Roman custom, to the ancestral ways. He seemed to be putting Alexandria on a level with Rome and thus gave substance to the Octavian propaganda that he and Cleopatra meant to make Alexandria the new world-capital. He dressed for the occasion, not as Imperator, but as Dionysos: wearing the god's insignia as he rode in his chariot. It was probably of this procession that Velleius was thinking when he wrote the account of Bacchic guisings cited above. The Armenian king in golden chains went in front; the troops and the booty, behind. The goal was the temple of Sarapis whom Ptolemy I had chosen or rather created as the god of his house and realm. (Sarapis as a sort of chthonic Osiris had his Dionysian aspects.)[16] But the person presiding over the ceremony was Cleopatra-Isis, who sat high on a golden throne while Antony presented his captives. Artavasdes, by oriental custom, should have prostrated himself; but, proud of his Hellenistic culture (he had written poems and tragedies), he merely greeted Cleopatra by name. He was not slaughtered, as he would have been at a Roman Triumph, but was kept prisoner. In the whole glittering show Antony perhaps meant no defiance of Rome, no mockery of a Roman Triumph, but was thinking of such great Dionysiac processions as that of Ptolemy II. He could not, in the existing political situation, go to Rome to claim a Triumph if he wanted to; he consoled himself then with a display which he felt to be in the Alexandrian tradition.[17]

The procession was followed a few days later by another ceremony, the Donations, which was certainly a proclamation of a new sort of empire that could not but clash with the Roman. A huge crowd assembled in the spacious gymnasion; there was no city-senate or it would have played a prominent part. On high sat Cleopatra once more as Isis, but this time Antony was throned at her side, and, a little lower, on lesser thrones, their three children and Caesarion. Antony addressed the people, no doubt speaking in Greek. He declared that Caesar had been Cleopatra's husband (there is no need to conjecture what ceremony or system Antony had in mind as defining the marriage); and that Ptolemy Caesar was their legitimate son. Therefore what he proposed to do was a tribute to Caesar's memory; his action was justified as something done in Caesar's name, carrying on Caesar's own intentions. He called Cleopatra Queen of Kings and Ptolemy Caesar King of Kings, joint monarchs of Egypt and Cypros, and overlords of the kingdoms and suzerainties of the other children. To Alexander he gave Armenia as his realm, with suzerainty over Parthia and Media (or of all lands east of the Euphrates). In preparation for this moment, the boy had been dressed like the Achaimenid kings, with a tiara (a high Persian cap wound round with a white turban and decorated with peacock feathers) and given an Armenian bodyguard. To Ptolemy Philadelphos in his Macedonian dress (*kausia*, bonnet with diadem; *chlamys*, little purple cloak; *krepides*, small boots), amid his Macedonian bodyguard, he gave the Egyptian possessions in Syria and Cilicia, with suzerainty over all client-kings and dynasts west of the Euphrates 'as far as the Hellespont'—the most westerly dynast seems to have Kleon in Mysia. To Cleopatra Selene he gave Cyrenaica and Lybia.[18]

To commemorate these Donations he struck coins with his own head, tiared, 'Armenia Conquered,' with Cleopatra on the reverse as Queen of Kings and of her Sons who are Kings. She was thus made supreme ruler of the whole system. His own position is not stated. For his troops and Roman supporters he was simply a Roman magistrate; for the Greeks and Asians he was Antony-Dionysos-Osiris married to Cleopatra-Isis Queen of Egypt. This unresolved dualism was what finally destroyed him; and indeed it is hard to see how he fits into the scheme displayed by the Donations—just as it was hard to see what role he had in the Fourth Eclogue except to father the saviour-child and provide him with an example of *Virtus*. Here he is the begetter of the system, but disappears inside it, with the actual dominance left to Cleopatra. Further, Caesarion is given a larger role than that of his own children by Cleopatra. The latter are to extend the Cleopatra–Caesarion Empire east and west, but they remain something like vassals of the sovran pair.[19] We may note that the legionaries of Cleopatra's bodyguard bore her badge or name on their shields; Servius tells us that Augustus in his *Memoirs* stated, 'Antony ordered his legions to keep guard at Cleopatra's palace and to obey her nod or command.'[20] Octavian did not mind the appointment or deposition of client-kings; he did that sort of thing himself; but the system set up in 34 at Alexandria was indeed unprecedented and did in fact challenge all Roman conceptions and methods. If it survived and succeeded, a new sort of world-State would emerge.

Some coins represent Cleopatra as the New Goddess and give her Isis-attributes. In the Ptolemaic period Isis had gained a world-role, which was to increase under the Roman empire. A mystery-goddess, she had a clearly defined daily ritual, an Egyptian characteristic carried into the Graeco–Roman world; and with her life-giving Nile-water she had a power to evoke deep personal devotion, as we see from *The Golden Ass* of Apuleius. Cleopatra seems now to have taken to public appearances as Isis, with golden sistrum or rattle. As a universal mystery-goddess, Isis had assumed the marks of a saviour-deity, with a cosmic significance and claims to have originated social values, as we saw in the Aretology cited earlier; she provided the criterion of the good life and was the pledge of eternal existence. At Rome she had long aroused the suspicions and dislike of the ruling class; in the years 59 to 48 the Senate on five occasions ordered the destruction of her chapels. But in 43 the triumvirs allowed the building of a temple to Isis and Sarapis in Rome. In spring 32 a Roman officer, C. Julius Papeius, probably a *praefectus fabrum*, visited the shrine on her island Philai which Ptolemy II had begun; in his dedicatory inscription he did reverence to the goddess, adding the names of his children and attendants. His name shows that he was by birth a Greek, admitted to Roman citizenship by Julius Caesar; among his companions were several Greeks; the centurions under him were partly Greeks, partly Romans.[21]

At Alexandria, we saw, a temple was being built to Antony; but he did not take the diadem and title of king, not even on coins where Cleopatra is Queen of Kings. Other coins keep his Roman titles and call him triumvir. His position was strong but vague. It could be inherited, for already in early 34 he struck the first of coins with his own head and that of his eldest son, Antyllus (Little Antony, the Alexandrian nickname to pair with Caesarion), officially Marcus Antonius the Younger. Much argument has gone on as to whether he appeared in the regnal datings, where however he is never mentioned by name. The first instance known of the new system appeared in 34, the year of the great inauguration of Cleopatra, yet it assumes 37 as its starting-point. If the system were found only in Syria, we could refer it to the year she was given Chalkis; but it is found also in Egypt and so must have a wider basis. Perhaps it was not meant to be too precisely understood. If need be, it could be explained as referring to Cleopatra's territorial expansion; yet for her and Antony it signified the time of their definite union and compact. At least for Cleopatra that time was intended to be the foundation-date of a great new world-system, and we cannot wonder that she wanted it out clearly in her regnal datings even if she could not yet explain openly what 37 and 34 meant to her.

As the grantor of Cleopatra's high titles, Antony was certainly above her in his odd unstated role, since the granting of the titles did not involve any abdications on his part. He was still the ultimate dispenser of status and the inaugurator of the golden age. It would be hard then for him to counter Cleopatra's contention that there could be only one world-ruler, and that, since Octavian would never accept a minor role, he must soon be fought and destroyed. What were his exact schemes, if he had any, we can never know. No doubt there was nothing clear-cut. As a Roman, he was doing his best to carry on Roman institutions in a phase of violent change and to find how to make them function somehow inside the new evolving systems; at the same time he was learning from Cleopatra the accumulated lores of the Hellenistic kingdoms and the ways that those lores clarified the problem of organising a world-State with a bureaucracy under a single rule. The precise balance of Roman and Ptolemaic that he would use would depend on circumstances. His political thinking had become as full of incompatibles as his personal life in which he had to keep on assuming that Cleopatra could be both the wife of a Roman triumvir and an eastern Queen of Kings. To the argument that the situation was impossible, he could reply: Yes, but it works—and similarly the world-system that will come up out of the present welter will also be full of incompatibles and yet work.

For Cleopatra the theoretical issues were comparatively simple. Roman traditions might have been useful in their time and place; but they had done their job and were now out of date. What was needed was something like the imperial system of Alexander the Great, modernised, more powerfully established and worked out, with the divine kingship as its centre. But the oath that the Romans attributed to her, 'As surely as one day I'll give judgement in the Capitol,' is certainly an invention: part of the propaganda meant to frighten the west after 34. We have no evidence that she was given to boasting, and she was not fool enough to provide her enemies with such useful anecdotes.[22]

Antony with his genial hopeful temperament was indeed liable to blur dream and reality. He had celebrated the conquest of Armenia on a coin two years before he achieved it. How far he and Cleopatra shared the great dreams which they stirred up, and which found expression in cults and prophecies, we cannot say with any precision. Not much was needed to arouse the hope of Rome's total defeat among the folk of Asia, Syria, Egypt; old prophecies and revelations were revived and revised. Some Jews foretold that Cleopatra's victory would be the signal for world-end and the following reign of the Messiah; and not only Jews. She on her side must have been aware of much of what was being said and chanted, and her agents would have done their part in spreading and strengthening all oracles that helped her cause. She certainly saw herself as the Isis of a new dispensation of Justice, as

Antony saw himself as the Dionysos of a new liberation
of joyous energies; there was an obvious point of
convergence between these cult-forms on the upper levels
and the prophetic agitations going on among the masses.
But there was also a clear point of divergence. Cleopatra's
ideas of justice were not the same as those of a city
artisan or a poor peasant. She wanted a hierarchical society, in which each class or individual has rights and duties,
with herself keeping the balance and ensuring that no
encroachments or oppressions went on within the given
structure; the artisan or the peasant, caught up in the
apocalyptic dream, wanted to see that structure quite
shattered—even if he used the term king, queen, or god,
for the leader, the force, that brought about the shattering.

Octavian was also trying to build up a religious background for his cause, which would provide morale and
inspiration for his followers. This meant that he had to
combine a piety towards traditional Roman forms with a
belief in himself as the Apollo of a new order. Being
master of the capital, he was able to express his creed of
Rome in architectural edifices that helped to compact the
loyalties of the citizens. He rebuilt the Porticus Octavia
and put in it the recaptured Eagles of Gabinius; in 32 he
restored the Theatre of Pompey without adding his own
name; L. Aemilius (on his staff in the Sicilian war)
completed the work begun by his father on the Basilica
Aemilia, which Pliny considered among the most
beautiful buildings in the world; Statilius Taurus, after an
African Triumph in 34, started rearing a great stone
amphitheatre in the Field of Mars; Maecenas, in charge
of Rome during the Illyrian wars, turned a burial-ground
on the Esqueline into a fine park with walks. Agrippa,

as we'd expect, did yet more. In 33 he took on the
unwanted, because costly, office of aedile, restored a
century-old aqueduct and built another, provided hun-
dreds of new fountains and basins decorated with marble,
and thus made water plentiful. He also renewed the
drainage-system, relaid streets, repaired public buildings,
and was generous with free baths and theatre shows.
Octavian restored the hallowed temple of Jupiter
Feretrius, where the *spolia optima* dedicated by Romulus
were thought to have been deposited; he thus helped to
stimulate the image of himself as the second Romulus.
Adherents rebuilt the ancient Regia, for which he provided statues, and restored the temples of Hercules of the
Muses, and of Diana on the Aventine. Horace could now
write of Octavian as a man whose cause was to protect
'Italy and the shrines of the gods', and could advise a
parvenu freedman to use his money on decaying temples.

Octavian also paid attention to the priesthoods. In 33
he was given the power to create new patrician families
for the purpose of filling priesthoods; thus be able at the
same time to do much in reviving aristocratic power and
prestige. He himself was an augur, and he rewarded the
ex-republican Messalla Corvinus for services in the
Sicilian war by getting him, *extra numerum*, into the
augural college. He revived in 40 the Game of Troy, a
rite (of supposed great antiquity) of horse-manœuvres in
maze-forms.[23] And when he felt the time had come to crush
Antony he acted out the antique ritual of the fetial priest.
By using this procedure he made himself the defender of
the most deeply traditional aspects of Roman religion and
also stressed the alien character of the enemy. He suppressed, or lent no favour to, eastern cults in Rome—

though he allowed himself to be initiated, while at Athens, into the august mysteries of Eleusis. In 33 by edict he expelled all astrologers, fortune-tellers, and magicians

Altar from the Vicus Sandalarius (now in Uffizi): Augustus officiating as augur with *lituus*; note the chicken pecking at his foot to represent the auspices of the *tripudium* (good omen); on one side Livia, on the other one of the young princes (perhaps Lucius Caesar).

(such as Horace described). The date is significant. The final crisis was maturing; and the prophets were dangerous men.[24]

We saw how Octavian took care to become an augur.

Such readers-of-omens played an important part in the civil wars. Polybius in the second century B.C. had known the Romans as the most religious-minded of men; but by our period, while superstition remained and even increased, there was a wide scepticism, at least among the educated classes. In the distracted times the alarmed and suffering masses became ever more responsive to tales of prodigies and to apocalyptic exhortations. Leaders in the struggles had more and more recourse to omens and oracles. Sulla made much use of a dream in which Bellona, goddess of war, put a weapon into his hands, of promises of victory said to come from Jupiter, and a message from Bellona brought by an inspired slave. He explained the successes of his lieutenant Lucullus with a similar kind of story. Thus the ruthless pillager of Greek sanctuaries became devoutly concerned about signs from the gods which helped him in his work of killing fellow-citizens in 83-2. Caesar, in a rationalist way, excluded the gods from his account of the Gallic War. There was however perhaps a contradiction between the appeal to his military skill on the one side and to his Fortuna or Felicitas on the other—though it may have been the Pompeians who stressed the role of Fortuna to explain how he won against Pompey. When however he crossed the Rubicon and began a civil war, he turned to presages. These were again invoked in the Pharsalos campaign: 'It was noted at Elis, in the temple of Minerva [Athena], on calculating and counting the days, that on the very date of Caesar's victory the image of Victory, set before Minerva and facing her statue, turned about towards the portal and entry of the temple; and the same day, at Antioch, such a shout of soldiers and sound of trumpets was twice heard that the citizens ran in arms to the walls. The same thing happened at Ptolemais; a noise of drums was heard at Pergamon, in the private and secluded parts of the temple, where only priests were admitted (parts called *adyta* by the Greeks), and again at Tralles in Victory's temple where stood a statue consecrated to Caesar. A palm tree at that time was shown: it had sprouted up from the pavement through the joints of the stones and shot up above the roof.'[25] Sulla had pioneered in turning into a personal divine some priest or *haruspex* selected from those accompanying troops in war, and in stressing his function. A rebellious general needed some way of answering his enemies at Rome, who could put pressure, for instance, on the Fifteen who controlled the Sibylline books. Fear of the chicanery of augurs and the like lies behind Cicero's comment, 'Let's deal with priests so that they produce from their books anything whatever rather than a king.'[26] Octavian asked the Vestals to use their influence with the gods to stop the desertion of slaves to Sextus.

The strictly national character of Roman religion made it difficult for a rebellious general to claim any religious powers or rights. The decree of the Senate changing the name of the month Sextilis to August states: 'He has thrice triumphed on Rome, thrice set out from the foot of the Janiculan Hill, leading the legions under his Auspices and Faith. In this same month he has submitted Egypt to the power of the Roman People, and in this month has put an end to the Civil Wars. . . .'[27] That was the ideal thing: to lead with all the correct auspices of the State religion, which gave the troops complete confidence in the leader. The scepticism of the period was entangled with an extreme scrupulosity as to forms. To be deprived of augural powers was a severe blow to a general; Cicero deplored the way in which army chiefs were being deprived of auspices, and in the civil war the two great legal questions that kept on cropping up were the right of this or that general to take auspices and the validity of his *imperium*. When Sulla was declared *hostis* (enemy) by the Marians, he put the augural *lituus* or crook on coins issued in Greece; back in Italy he at once took steps to legitimise his rights as augur. Marius also was an augur and seems to have made political use of his priesthood. Caesar put the *lituuus* on coins after Pharsalos, thus claiming that he too had the gods' sanction. It is noteworthy that he waited till this moment to assume a priestly role on which Sulla and the Pompeians had rested their religious politics. But he had had all along his position as *pontifex maximus* to exploit; it was not merely as a matter of privilege that Lepidus asked for the same rank after the Ides of March—he wanted some outstanding role that he could set against Octavian's claim to be Caesar's adoptive son, and the conspirators tried to win him over with a promise of the office. In fact, however, the pontificate had waned in importance; what the triumvirs were concerned about was augural power. In a *Philippic* Cicero cries: 'Which of the two then will we more willingly sanction as Augur of Jupiter the Best and Greatest of Gods, whose interpreters and messengers we are? which of the two will the Roman People choose? Sextus Pompey or Antony?' The way in which the augurs could be used to foster morale is shown in an anecdote of Octavian. 'At Perusia the sacrifice gave no favourable intimations; rather the contrary. So he ordered fresh victims. However the enemy in a sudden sally

carried off the sacred things. The augurs agreed that all
the perils and disasters threatening the sacrificer would
fall on the heads of those who'd got possession of
entrails; and so it happened.'[28]

For Octavian the *lituus*-claim was connected with his
imaging of himself as Romulus. But that does not explain
why his rivals attached so much importance to the *lituus*
and put it lavishly on their coins. For Antony the role of
augur guaranteed his Roman character; for Sextus it gave
an official seal that counteracted his life as an outlaw
leading slaves and desperadoes. After the pact of Misenum
was broken, Octavian and Antony hastened to deprive
him of his briefly-held priesthood. In 32 Octavian tried to
do the same with Antony, and Antony refused to accept
the validity of his act. More than ever he asserted his
augural role.

The *haruspices* were Etruscan soothsayers who foretold
the future through inspecting the entrails of victims, as
the augurs did by observing the notes or flight of birds,
lightning, the feeding of sacred fowls, certain appearances
of quadrupeds and so on. They were traditionally
connected with the most reactionary circles of the ruling
class, but they became for soldiers the true ministers of
the national religion. Sulla, fighting Marius, had his
haruspex Postumius, who played an important part in
urging his master on. Here we find the *haruspex* linked
with the general rather than with the army. How the
optimates themselves could give massed support is shown
by Octavian's own accounts of the battle of Actium:
'More than 700 Senators served under my standards,
including 83 who before that, or afterwards, were
appointed consuls, and about 170 of whom were appoint-

ed priests.'[29] But the diviners who came up out of the people might be attached to the radicals or rebels; Marius had a Syrian prophetess Maria with him in the Cimbrian war. Pompey had many augurs in his camp before Pharsalos; Cassius had diviners active in his army at Philippi; in 44 there were many at Rome, but Caesar mocked at their warnings and predictions of his death.[30]

Cleopatra's Egypt

For a man like Antony the preparations for a world war did not preclude festivities. Entertainments were lavishly staged; pantomimes gave their scenes from myth. The tale of Plancus, a close friend allowed to use Antony's signet-ring, who dance-mimed the part of the seagod Glaucos, suggests a parody of the true pantomime, a drinking-party improvisation. We may contrast the situation at Rome where Caesar had had to restore to the poet Laberius the rank of *eques* which he forfeited by appearing in one of his own mimes. At a banquet Cleopatra is said to have worn in each ear a pearl worth ten million sesterces; she dissolved one of the pearls in vinegar and drank the liquid. Pliny tells the story at length in a passage where he is stirred to a rare personal reminiscence by his detestation of ostentatious luxury. 'I have seen Lollia Paulina, who became consort of the Princeps Gaius, not at important or solemn ceremonial celebrations, but actually at an ordinary betrothal-dinner, covered with emeralds and pearls alternately interlaced and shining all over head, hair, ears, neck, and fingers, the sum total valued at 40,000,000 sesterces, she herself ready at a moment's notice to produce documentary proof of her title to the lot. Nor had they been presents from an extravagant prince. They were heirlooms, got in fact with the spoils of the provinces. Here we see the final outcome of plunder. Here we see what it was that M. Lollius disgraced himself for, taking gifts from kings all over the east; for what he had himself cut out of the list of friends of G. Caesar, son of Augustus; for what he was driven to drink poison. All that his grand-daughter might be on show in the lamplight, covered with 40,000,000 sesterces. Now let someone reckon up on one side of the account how much Curtius or Fabricius carried in his Triumph, and picture to himself the spoils they displayed, and on the other side Lollia, a single little lady reclining at the emperor's side—and would he not consider it better they should be dragged from their chariots than have their victories with this result?'

Then he goes on to Cleopatra. The pearls in question were, he says, the largest ever known, come down through the hands of the kings of the east. 'When Antony was daily gorging on exquisite dishes, she with a pride both lofty and insolent, queenly wanton as she was, poured scorn on all his pomp and splendour. When he asked what further magnificence could be devised, she replied that she'd spend 10,000,000 sesterces on a single banquet. Antony was keen to learn how it could be done, though he doubted its possibility. So bets were laid. Next day, when the wager was to be settled, she set before him a banquet splendid enough, so that the day wouldn't be wasted, but of the kind they had daily. He laughed and mocked at its niggardliness. But she swore it was a mere extra-confectionery and that the banquet proper would round off the account: that her own dinner would cost 10,000,000 sesterces. She ordered the last course to be served. Following their instructions, the servitors put before her only a single vessel with vinegar, the strong rough quality of which can melt pearls. In her ears she was wearing that remarkable and truly unique work of nature. Antony was curious to see what on earth she'd do. She took one earring off and dropped the pearl into the vinegar; and when it was melted, swallowed it. L. Plancus, umpiring, put his hand on the other pearl, which she was preparing to destroy in the same way, and declared that Antony had lost the battle—an ominous remark that came true.'

He adds that when Cleopatra was captured, the remaining pearl was cut in two, and the halves were set in each of the ears of Venus in the Pantheon at Rome. Macrobius tells the same story, also at length, with his own rhetorical elaborations. 'Everything that lives in the sea, on the earth, in the air, seemed to Antony fated to solace his voracity; he delivered it up to his jaws and teeth. And it was in this obsession of his that he wanted to transfer to Egypt the seat of the Roman Empire.' He describes the two halves of the second pearl as 'enormous in size'.[1]

The whole thing sounds circumstantial enough— though the way that Pliny uses it as an omen of Antony's defeat should make us pause. In fact the story is an invention. Vinegar does not dissolve pearls; an acid strong enough to do so would eat through the stomach's lining. An ingenious explanation is that Cleopatra deftly swallowed the pearl and later defaecated it. But we find the theme of pearl-swallowing to be a conventional motive in the literature directed against luxury. Pliny goes on to say that Cleopatra was outdone by Clodius the son of the tragic actor Aesopus, who died very rich. As a prodigal epicure, Clodius wanted to know the taste of pearls. Dissolving one in vinegar, he found it 'marvellously acceptable', and so, 'in order not to keep the knowledge to himself, he gave his guests also a choice pearl to swallow'. So, Pliny thinks, the whole episode of Cleopatra's pearl was degraded; for Clodius, 'virtually an actor', outdid her, 'not for any wager, which would make the matter more royal, but to discover by experiment, for the honour of his palate, what is the exact flavour of pearls'. In the version given by Horace, who appears not to know the tale about Cleopatra, Clodius takes the pearl from the ear of his wife Caecilia Metalla, whom he had married after she was divorced for an affair with the libertine Dolabella:

> Aesop's son from Metella's ear once drew
> a pearl; to swallow a million at a gulp
> he dissolved it in vinegar: wiser than if he threw it
> in a rapid river or the common sewer.[2]

And Suetonius says of Caligula (Gaius), 'He surpassed all the prodigals that ever lived. He invented a new kind of bath, with strange dishes and suppers, washing in precious unguents, warm and cold, drinking pearls of immense value dissolved in vinegar, and serving up his guests loaves and other victuals modelled in gold, often saying: A man should be a good economist or else an emperor.' The act was then a commonplace of epicure behaviour in the diatribes of the moralists. The vituperation against Antony as a drunken gorger ensured that the story would be connected with him. The explanation of recovery-by-evacuation can hardly apply, we may note, to Clodius and his guests.

The association of Inimitable Livers was still functioning in some form or other; for we have an inscription by a man calling himself Parasitos, who describes Antony as his God and Benefactor (*euergetes*), also the Great Inimitable, and attaches to the last word *aphrodisiois*, which refers to matters-of-Aphrodite, sexual enjoyments.[3] *Ta Aphrodisia* is common in Plato for such pleasures; but the term is also used for a festival of Aprodite, for a woman's genitals, and for brothels. We meet *aphrodisia* as pleasure resorts in a decree dated 140–39 B.C., houses of Aphrodite, of which the temple in question, or temples in general, claimed to have a monopoly; private persons, the priests complain, are setting up such brothels and diverting the fees from them.[4] The dedication is then saying that Antony is an inimitable performer in brothels or in any business of Aphrodite. The date of the inscription is 28 December 34 (with the double dating: Year 19 also Year 4, Choiak 29). Parasitos is here a proper name, but with a play on its double meanings: the comic reference still preserved in our word 'parasite', and the earlier priestly connotation. Anciently the *parasitoi* had been priests who ate their meals at public expense; then the word had gradually come round to mean any cadger who dined at someone else's table, a buffoon and a flatterer—an important type of character in the comedies. Our dedicator is saying in jest that he is a parasite at Antony's table and at the same time a priest of Antony the great god.

Athenaios in his *Dinner of Scholars* has a long passage
showing that the contrasted meanings of the word were
discussed by the smiling learned. We find *parasitoi* often
connected with Herakles. 'In the temple of Herakles at
Kynosarges is a tablet with a decree proposed by Alcibi-
ades, the clerk being Staphanos son of Thucydides. With
regard to the term's use, the decree's words run: The
priest shall sacrifice the monthly offerings in company
with the *parasitoi*, who are to be drawn from the men of
mixed descent and their children, according to ancestral
custom; and whoever declines to serve as *parasitos* is to
be cited in the courts on precisely this charge.'[5] Persons
of mixed descent were those like Themistokles at Athens,
who had a citizen-father and a foreign mother, and for
whom the gymnasion called Kynosarges was specially
reserved. Kleidemos in his *History of Attika* states,
'*parasitoi* also were chosen to honour Herakles'. On
tablets dealing with the Delian Sacred Mission, the two
heralds from the House of Heralds connected with the
Eleusinian Mysteries 'shall serve as *parasitoi* for a year in
the precinct of Apollo'. *Parasitoi* were thus not regular
priests, but were co-opted to act with those priests in
sharing the sacrificial meal. As a typical passage from the
comedies we may take the following from *The Heiress* by
Diodoros of Sinope in which we find both Zeus and
Herakles stressed:

> The Parasite's life was the invention of Zeus,
> the God of Friendship, admitted the Mightiest God.
> For this god enters our houses, makes no distinction
> of rich and poor. Wherever a nicely spread couch
> he sees, with the table beside it holding all
> that anyone could desire, he lies at once

decorously with the guests and feasts himself. . . .
And after enjoying everything that's served
I go back here like Zeus the God of Friendship. . . .
When the State gives out a sumptuous honour
to Herakles and celebrates festivals
in all the demes, never to this day
has it chosen by lot parasites for these feasts
and never has it selected ordinary citizens.

The *Table of Herakles* appeared in the last line of the
Fourth Eclogue, looking back to the phrase about
sharing the life of the gods. Antony in his banqueting
certainly felt himself as Herakles Epitrapezios (on or at
the Table). In archaic art we see Herakles as the heroic
toiler, at times the great eater and drinker; then he turns
to the devoted hero seeking for the right course, redre-
ing wrongs and gaining immortality; he becomes the
world-saviour. 'Conquered is Chaos,' says Seneca. In
Hellenistic art we find representations of the heavy strain
of his struggles, as in the Collossos of Tarentum; as
Epitrapezios he has reached immortal life, all pains gone,
only the rejoicing left. At this point he takes on Dionysiac
qualities.[6] Technically, a *trapeza* was a table consecrated
to the gods on which are set viands and offerings. The
idea of Herakles as guardian of the banqueting table grew
up and found much expression in the Latin poets.[7] The
Latin term for the ritual table is *lectisternium*, and there
were fewer rites more common at Rome than the offer
of a repast to a deity. Before a table, the sacred *mensa*,
where the dishes were set, was a cushioned bed; on it the
image or symbolising object was placed to receive the
offerings. (Oddly, at Rome, with its many *lectisternia*, the
rites of the Ara Maxima excluded the full ceremony from

the temple of Hercules; there a worshipper might only offer a *mensa* at the statue's foot.) Hercules, as part of his Bacchic connections, was among the deities to whom the Romans used to give thanks at the beginning and end of banquets; he was thus ranged among the Lares and became Hercules Domesticus. Hence the need for small figures of him to ornament the tables of festivals. Alexander the Great seems to have set the style by ordering from Lysippos a foot-high statuette. The Dionysiac *thiasos* was associated with Hercules in banquet scenes.[8]

Some satirical remark by the party of Octavian on Anthony as Heracles-at-the-Table seems to have led to an Antonian six-line riposte:

When lately in a dinner-masquerade
Twelve Gods in well-matched pairs had Mallia puzzling.
The part of Phoebus Caesar foully played;
in new adulteries the gods lay guzzling.
From earth depart the outraged deities.
and from his golden throne Jove headlong flees.[9]

The scene is one of a *lectisternium*, with human actors. Who Mallia was, we do not know; nor what factual basis lies behind the squib. That Octavian is described as taking Apollo's role is of interest. Critics have objected that Octavian would not take part in a masquerade where someone else was Jupiter to his Apollo. *Lectisternia* did not always include Jupiter; the first of which we hear occurred in B.C. 399, at time of pestilence, and had three pairs on the couches, Apollo and Latona, Diana and Hercules, Mercury and Neptune; but the full ceremony with six pairs, as in 217 after the disastrous battle of Trasimene, no doubt normally had Jupiter and Juno.[10]

311

Suetonius, citing the verses, adds, 'What made this supper more obnoxious to public censure was its happening at a time of great scarcity, almost famine, in the City. Next day there was a cry going round among the people, "The gods have eaten up all the corn, and Caesar is indeed Apollo, but Apollo the Torturer", under which name the god was worshipped in a quarter of the City'—possibly in the Suburra where Martial says that torturing scourges were sold.[11] The verses, like the cry about Apollo Tortor, may have been the work of Antonian agents or partisans: though we must recall that at this time Octavian was embroiled with Sextus Pompey, who also had his noisy adherents. The feast, described as a god-charade or parody of a lectisternium, seems very likely to have been that at which Livia was betrothed by her former husband to Octavian, probably about December 39 or early January 38.[12] We are told that Octavian was suspected of adultery with Livia before her divorce, so that her son, Drusus, born three months after her remarriage, was in fact his child. But even without that suspicion the scandalously hasty method of Livia's divorce and remarriage were enough to provoke the charge of *adulteria*. If this dating is correct, then already by this early period Octavia was associating himself with Apollo.[13] We may note also how the epigram adroitly reverses the picture drawn in the Fourth Eclogue. There the gods return to earth, associated through the Child with the *mensa* of Herakles; Justice (the Virgin or Astraea) comes back to the redeemed scene. Here the gods take flight, Justice with them as is normally stressed in the account of their rejection of a polluted earth.

Antony as Herakles Epitrapezios was also accused of

blasphemous dinners. The tale of Plancus as the god Glaucus (no doubt told by himself after his desertion) perhaps belongs to the counter-charges on Octavian's side. At any rate the comparison of Octavian with Apollo Tortor links with the comparison of Antony with Dionysos Omestes. Plutarch tells us of Anthony in 41 with his first full Dionysiac display: 'Lute-players like Anaxenor, pipe-players like Xanthos, Metrodoros a dancer, and suchlike rabble of Asiatic performers who surpassed in impudence and effrontery the pests from Italy, poured like a flood into his quarters and held sway there. It was intolerable that everything was devoted to these extravagances. All Asia, like the famous city [Thebes] of Sophocles, was filled alike with incense-offerings. "Alike with paeans too and sound of heavy groans." Anyhow, when Antony made his entry into Ephesos, women dressed like Bacchanals and men and boys like Satyrs and Pans led the way before him, and the city was full of ivy, *thyrsos*-wands, harps, pipes, and flutes, with the people hailing him as Dionysos Joygiver and Beneficient. Such he was without a doubt to some, but to the greater number he was Dionysos Carnivorous and Savage.'[14]

But now we may turn for a while to Egypt itself. We need to know something of its government, its social and economic systems, since the world-state that Cleopatra envisaged was certainly based ultimately on her Egyptian forms, however much she may have recognised the needs for modifications in any expanded version. All the post-Alexander monarchies developed well-organised systems; but the Ptolemies, working on inherited Pharaonic principles, came nearest to creating a planned economy.

In Cyrene, Syria, or Asia Minor, they acted like Seleukids; but in Egypt they based themselves on the existing scheme and made no effort to turn the Egyptians into townsmen. A careful survey divided the land into various categories; the best land, directly under the king, was leased to natives with the status of crown-peasants, who could not leave the land till harvesting was done. The course of the farming year (the times for sowing and harvesting, the kind of grain, generally wheat, to be sown, and so on) was all laid down in the terms of tenancy. The harvest was measured on the fields or the threshing-floor, and scribes worked out the amounts to be delivered as rent or kept as seed-corn. The headman or village-secretary knew local conditions and superintended the proceedings according to instructions handed down through a graded hierarchy of officials. Over him were the district officials and their bureaus; over these in turn the military governors of the Nomes, Greeks, with their advisers. In Alexandria was the central government under the *dioiketes*. Crops were rotated with two harvests a year; foreign vines and livestock for breeding were brought in. The same methods were applied to the small scattered estates given to Greek or Macedonian soldiers. Contributions were levied even from the sacred land controlled by the priests for the maintenance of their cults. An edict stated, 'No one has the right to do as he pleases, but all is ordered for the best'.

A monetary economy was created to a considerable extent, with a well-developed system of banking: though for royal lands rents and some salaries were paid in kind, and barter was by no means ended. State granaries, collecting the grain, were used like the banks as repositories of private accounts. There was an extensive system of state monopolies. Banking was one, though besides the royal banks there were private ones leased by the government. We know most about the oil monopoly, oil being made from many plants such as sesame, croton, linseed, safflower, colocynth. There was strict control of cultivation, and the State fixed the area of land in each nome for such crops. The government supplied seed to farmers, who paid a quarter of the product as tax and handed over the rest to the contractors at fixed prices. The oil was extracted at factories under state-control; the workers were free but might not leave their homes during the season. Only temples could own private mills, and they could use them for making oil only two months a year; for the rest of the time their mills, like the crown-mills, were sealed. The right to sell the oil was let out to wholesalers and retailers, who had to sell at fixed prices. The royal profit seems to have ranged from 70 per cent to 300 per cent or more. There was an import duty on olive oil of 50 per cent. Other monopolies were of textiles (linen, wool, hemp); the temples were allowed to make the fine linen worn by priests, while supplying the king with a fixed amount for export. Cleopatra had a Roman senator, Q. Ovinius, as supervisor of her woollen mills and carpet factories.[15] (Octavian later put him to death for it.) There were also monopolies of salt, natron, beer—though doubtless home-brewing was permitted. From these monopolies, plus the rent of domain-land, a vast revenue, swollen by the many taxes, tolls and customs dues, was gained. Taxes, save those paid in kind, for which officials were responsible, were got in by private agents, who bought the rights at yearly auctions; but these agents were closely supervised and watched at every point and in the later period bidders were not easy to find.

Money was carefully channelled into royal hands and kept as much as possible from the Egyptians by means of a thorough control of the prices paid to producers. Products were bought or requisitioned for the royal storehouses. Benefits in money from the export trade stayed with the king and the intermediaries; they did not reach the producers. And what little cash the latter got was brought back to the king through taxes, *e.g.* on salt. Such money as circulated was among the Greeks in Egypt, and they could not put much of it into the land on account of the royal and priestly controls. Interest rates were high, legally 24 per cent; the entry of capital was restricted or controlled by the toll-bar; foreign coins were restruck into Ptolemaic types. The high interest kept money dear and work cheap; it helped the Greeks to maintain their superior status and to hold the Egyptians down. The customs dues protected the royal monopolies and made foreign products expensive. The peasants were thus in effect pegged down to an existing system of needs and satisfactions; the countryside stayed almost economically static and closed against outside influences. Some technical changes were however introduced: the use of iron tools in agriculture, the saqqieh. The planting of vines, olives, fruit-trees was encouraged; but in general all Egyptian techniques that were effective in the situation were carried on. Despite the precedent of Tachos (a late native ruler), the Ptolemies never issued coins with Egyptian hieroglyphs on them, though in other Hellenistic areas the coins ended by showing legends in the national tongue, Indo-Greek, Arab, Parthian. Greek was the administrative language; the legal system was Greek—though private rights, protected by language, notarial tradition, and separate tribunals, long kept to their own evolution based on Egyptian customs and attitudes.

Though the Greeks remained the ruling class and Alexandria had a strongly privileged position, the Ptolemies were forced to rely more and more on the natives. A levy of Egyptians, trained in the style of the Greek phalanx, made possible the victory over the Seleukids at Raphia in 217. There were many risings. In 166 a revolt led to a Pharoah, Harmachis, ruling for a while the region between the first and second cataracts. By the end of the 2nd century B.C. we find some Egyptians in high administrative posts. Only eight years before the Piper came to the throne, there was heavy fighting in the Thebaid. As things worsened, efforts were made to conciliate the priesthoods as the main carriers of the national tradition. In 195 Ptolemy V was crowned in Egyptian ritual at the old capital of Memphis, and the priestly synod thanked him for remitting certain temple taxes. Peasants on the temple estates were not due for military service; priests did not need to travel yearly to Alexandria for the king's birthday. By the end of the 2nd century yet more privileges had been won; priestly land was almost free from taxation and its cultivation was not controlled by officials. The Hellenistic States had been for some time beset by political and economic problems they could not understand or overcome. As the impetus created by the Greek expansion died out, the control-systems tightened and made things worse. In Egypt a sharp decline began as early as Ptolemy IV, a weak debauchee, whose vices aided but did not cause the breakdown. The Hellenistic rulers made their difficulties a pretext for extracting more funds from the failing economy; the wars increased the problems and opened the way to the Romans, whose ruthless plundering in turn drove things downward. The loss of the Ptolemaic empire in Syria and elsewhere meant that cheap raw materials were not available in Egypt; the dwindling markets in Greece and the Aegean hit a system which like the Ptolemaic aimed at mass production for a world-market; and Rhodes, a rising maritime centre, was a strong competitor on the seas. The mercantilist structure was damaged; money deteriorated; confidence weakened. Now Greeks felt the pinch as well as Egyptians and were often drawn down to the same level. After Raphia the army ceased to be Greek as it had originally been; the settlement of soldiers on the land lost its Greek aspect and we find cleruchs making contracts in demotic. (It took the Romans to use the veterans as a sort of Greek middle class.) Tax revenues fell and an ever greater burden was laid on the small farmers and labouring population; the bureaucracy grew more strict as people could less bear its demands. The authorities tried to encourage the planting of waste lands, as a way of dealing with the problem of runaways from the villages, but without much effect. The extent to which official depradations grew is shown by the need to issue an edict in 118 that forbade arbitrary exactions of money, illegal billetings, the setting aside of the best land by officials for themselves when tenacies were arranged, their imposition of unpaid tasks, their selling debtors into slavery and their use of police arrests to enforce private debts. The currency grew more depreciated; gold and silver were short; prices rose. Like other Hellenistic rulers the Ptolemies had to resort to inflation; after 213 the silver coinage was largely replaced inside the country by copper money; and there was a heavy fall from the ratio set by Ptolemy IV (one drachma worth 60 copper pieces). Men complained of the rise in food costs. The brunt of the decline was borne by the natives; hence the increasing unrest. In the second half of the 2nd century there was general economic distress.

We get some glimpse then of the problems inherited by Cleopatra.[16]

From the outset there had been instituted a ruler-cult, with new priests to honour the king and his wife; and the conflicts in the royal family often found expression in attempts at official silences or blottings-out of opponents' names. Festivals were used for glorifying the rulers. Ptolemy II founded the Ptolemaia, four-yearly like the Olympics, which achieved a vast renown. At the third celebration, in 271–0 B.C., the procession took two days to pass through the streets; in front of the images of the old gods were carried the pictures of Saviour Ptolemy I and his Berenike, in whose honour the Games were established. There was a strong Dionysiac note in the whole festival, with stress on the god as a world-conqueror coming from India. The games included horse-racing, gymnastics, and field-sports, with tragedies and comedies in the theatres; a great sacrifice of 2,000 oxen provided the meat for the banquet. The Ptolemaia was held also outside Egypt, on a more modest scale; it was not tied to a particular spot like the ancient festivals. We hear of it at Miletos, Delos, Eresos and Methymna on Lesbos, Nesos; at Athens it was in high esteem. We must recall that for a while, during the Ptolemaic expansion, Egypt was struggling for command of the Aegean with the other Hellenistic kingdoms. The Ptolemies used the slogan Freedom and Independence for the Greeks; for example, when Rhodes was attacked by the Macedonian Demetrios, Ptolemy I gave aid with troops and grain, and the Rhodians responded with a hymn hailing him as Saviour. When pirates surprised Thasos, a Ptolemaic garrison was put into the acropolis. Ptolemaic influence reached even as far as the Crimea. These facts are important for our understanding of Cleopatra's hopes of regaining past Ptolemaic glories.

Some examples of papyri from her reign, or from the decades before it, will help to fill out the picture in a more concrete way. First some letters. The first, dated 95 B.C. is rather enigmatic; but it brings out some of the dangers and difficulties of the times. The man who 'did no harm' may be a *strategos* (local governor) whom the writer mentions in another letter as his protector.

Petosouchos son of Penebchounis to Peterharsemtheus and Paganis sons of Paras, and to Peterharsemtheus son of Psennesis, and to Horos son of Pates, greeting and good health.

I myself am well, and Esthautis and Patous and Almentis and Phibis and Psenosiris and Phapis and all our men. Do not grieve over the departed. They were expecting to be murdered [*phoneuthesthai*]. To us he did no harm, but on the contrary he has taken care of us. Write to me about anything you choose. We heard that mice had eaten up the crop. Do come to us and buy wheat here, or, if you prefer, at Diospolis [Thebes]. For the rest please do us a favour by watching over your own health. Horos and Petosiris are well. Goodbye.

Year 19, Pachon 8.[17]

A year or two before that Philoxenos, an official of fairly high rank, wrote asking his brother to do something to bring about the release of a man arrested for debt. A certain Demetrios, some other official, has written to tell him that the jailed man was under his protection. We see here an instance of the use of patronage, which led to much subservience, bribery, and corruption:

Philoxenos to Apollos his brother, greeting and good health.

As soon as you get this letter, go with Horos son of Kotys to see Hermias the village secretary about the man he's arrested, and to Chairemon the collector; and let him be released and not troubled by anyone. Demetrios has written to me about him, saying that he's under his protection and is his tenant. So I'm writing to you to give them instructions.[18]

Some letters dealing with the re-appointment of a man to the post of village secretary gives us details of the sort of exactions being carried out.

From Menches, village secretary of Kerkeosiris. On being appointed to the post of village secretary previously held by me I will pay at the village 50 *artabai* of wheat and 50 of pulse, namely 20 of lentils, 10 of bruised beans, 10 of peas, 6 of mixed seeds, 3 of mustard, 1 of parched pulse, total 50; total 100 *art.*

51st year, Pachon 6. And Dorion will pay 50 *art.* of wheat and 10 of pulse: namely 3 of bruished beans, 3 of peas, 3 of mixed seeds, 1 of mustard, total 10; total 60.[19]

The wheat that Menches promises may have been the payment he had to make to the king yearly for his office; but since the pulse and the payments made by Dorion are not normal, it is more likely that all the payments were special expenses or bribes to ensure that he was re-appointed. The articles would go to his official superiors in the village to gain their goodwill and their intervention with the *dioiketes*. It seems deliberate that no one is personally addressed; the document could not be used against any individual as proof of bribery, if it went astray. (An *artaba* was generally about 40 litres, but varied.) We have next the letter notifying that Menches has been appointed:

Asklepiades to Marres, greeting. Menches has been appointed village secretary of Kerkeosiris by the Dioketes on the understanding that he shall cultivate at his own expense 10 *arourai* [about 2,050 square metres] of the land in the neighbourhood of the village, which has been reported as unproductive, at a rent of 50 *art.* which is to pay yearly from 52nd year to the Crown in full—otherwise he is to measure out the deficiency from his private means. Give him the papers of his office and take care that the terms of his agreement are carried out. Year 51, Mesore 3.

Marres was the secretary of the *topos* (district, subdivision of the *nomos*); perhaps he was the man to whom Menches addressed the bribe-letter. We have also a receipt from Menches to Dorion for 100 *art.* of wheat and 61 *art.* made up of lentils, bruised beans, peas, mixed seeds, mustard, parched pulse; with a statement of further corn payments to be made from the next year onwards. From that next year we have two letters by Menches to men whom he calls his brothers, a term which may be a mere formality or the expression of an actual relationship. He tells Herodes that he has had a message from someone who has been at the office of the royal secretary 'about the detention of Aroteus the son of Petearphres' by that secretary in connection with 'the survey of the village and the measurements; and he has written to me to join them. I have asked him to wait for me till the 21st' (three days). And he writes to Ammonios to say that he has received the note from him; he asks to give the *periphora* (some sort of surveying instrument) to 'Dionysios for the survey, and tell him to join them at daybreak; for you know how busy I am and that I'm in attendance on the *strategos*. Tell Dionysios to wait till I've finished with this work on the 31st. I accept completely your views.'[20]

In 114 Menches wrote to Ptolemaios, probably the *strategos*:

On 16 Epeiph of Year 3 as I was inspecting, together with Horos the komarch [village headman] and Patanis and other elders of the cultivators, the embankment works near the village, we came along the drain . . . the banking-up of the surrounding dyke of the great god Soknebtynis, the lands near the village being situated between, and we found that certain persons in the employ of Philonautes son of Leon, one of the katoikic cavalry-soldiers at Berenikis Thesmorphorou had dug away part of the aforesaid drain, [undermining] the mounds of the surrounding dyke called that of Themistes for the length of 8 *schoinia*—and had piled the earth from it on to the mounds of the holding of the said Philonautes.

We immediately siezed one of the above-mentioned persons and sent a message to Polemon who performs the duties of epistates of the village, asking him to bring the offenders before you. . . . I send this report then so that you may, if you wish [give instructions], first of all for the mounds to be made secure . . . and that Philonautes and his agents . . . may appear before you and receive the punishment they deserve for their [act].[21]

This letter is only a rough draft, as is shown by many corrections and additions between the lines. It gives us a good idea of the sort of illegal actions, aimed at strengthening one landholder's dykes at the expense of someone else's, that the officials had to look out for. In another letter of the same year Menches writes to Horos (probably the royal secretary, not the komarch or village-head of that name) in reply to a letter about the appearance for trial of Heras accused of murder:

You wrote to me to give notice to Heras son of Petalos, inhabitant of the village, who is accused of murder and other offences, to appear in three days' time for the decision to be made about these charges, and you told me that till the matter was settled I was to drawn up a list of his property and arrange for it to be placed in bond. Also to send in a report stating the measurements, adjoining areas, and value in detail.

Accordingly I gave notice to the said Heras on the 14th of the current month at Ptolemais Euergetis that he was to appear for the decision on the aforesaid charges; and I report that he owns the 6th part of the Shrine of the Dioscures in the village, of which the adjacent areas are on the south and west the free space round the village, on the north and east a canal, of which the total value is one talant of copper. Goodbye.[22]

Private ownership of temples was common. In an ordinance of 118 we find the fifth part of shrines possessed by persons who supplied 30 days' work and cultivated the land (if any) belonging to the god.

We have three more letters from Menches to Horos in the same year. The first two are again rough drafts. In the first he describes a brawl:

On the 1st of the current month at about the 11th Hour a disturbance occurred in the village. On rushing out, we found a crowd of the villagers who'd come to the aid of Polemon, who's carrying out the duties of the village *epistates*. On inquiring, we were informed that Apollodoros and his son Maron had assaulted Polemon; that Apollodoros had escaped but Maron had been put into prison; and that the latter had appeared before Ptolemaios the king's cousin and *strategos* on the 1st. We thought it right to notify the matter for your information. Goodbye.[23]

The second (fragmentary) letter seems to describe the complaint made by the *epistates*; the third gives more details about offences by Apollodoros:

I reported to you in another letter on the 3rd of the current month the case of Polemon who's carrying on the duties of village *epistates*, now he was grossly insulted by Apollodoros and his son. These persons persisted in their violent behaviour on the . . . of the same month Mesore. They broke into the house of Petesouchos son of Polemon the *epistates* armed with a sword and . . . [carried off] 8 *dr*. of silver. Enclosed is the statement made by Petesouchos. I thought it right to report the matter for your information.

Horos has endorsed the letter. 'To whom it concerns: see that they are made to appear and receive suitable punishment.' Two further letters from Polemon to Menches announce the coming visit of the *epimeletes*, a financial official.

As it's decided the *epimeletes* is to proceed at daybreak, on the 15th to Berenikis and on the 16th to pass by the village on the way to Theognis, do your best to have all arrears owing from the neighbourhood in order, so as not to detain him and thus incur no little expense.

Since we are coming at dawn on the 29th, see that all debts due to you and the cultivators are in order on that day. You'll set out for Berenikis with me in connection with the matter on which you wrote to me and so that the report may not. . . .[24]

In a third letter Polemon, calling Menches brother, asks him to hurry on with collecting the taxes. At the top is a docket in another hand, consisting of a reference mark and a date: as often happens in official correspondence, the date is a day or two later than that of the letter

I got what you wrote to me; and as for the cultivators you said you were sending, I don't need them. Asklepiades has pressed matters on and has imposed, in addition to the proper amount, 1,000 *art.* of wheat more, besides money, so I'm anxious to make haste. As for the village secretaries you mention, they'll hardly go away till the 25th. You'll be right not to lessen the report in comparison with the first one, so we may make a good show, and for the rest hurry on with the collection of taxes. Take care of yourself so as to stay in good health. Goodbye.[25]

The officials had to help and warn one another or they would soon find themselves in trouble with their superiors.

In 113 Polemon wrote to say he was sending Arachthes to act as his substitute till he could come himself.

You'll do me a favour by personally introducing him and looking after them [? him]—and in regard to the additions to the revenue letting him do nothing without your assistance, and if accounts are demanded, consider that you have full powers till my arrival.

Next we have a letter of 112 in which Taos the village head and the elders address Menches in such ungrammatical diction that their meaning is hard to make out. What they seem to say is as follows.

On Phaophi 20, Apynchis met you about the matters on which we had a dispute concerning the land and for your sake I came to an agreement on most points accordingly we sent on the 21st for the seed but Kotys refused to pay it out referring the matter to the inspector whereon we have now sent Apynchis again tell us who is at fault . . . as for the inspector if he goes on opposing the payment of the seed send him to us under arrest.

We see that the headman had a superior position to that of the secretary. The latter, like all the other minor officials, had to be careful or he was liable to be assaulted or find himself in a feud. Marres wrote to Menches complaining about his conduct towards Melas, his *oikeios*, kinsman or dependant.

Melas my *oeikeios* has appealed to me about an alleged injury obliging him to complain to Demetrios son of Niboitas. I'm extremely annoyed that he should have got no special consideration from you on my account and therefore had to ask assistance from Demetrios. I consider you've acted badly in not having been careful to see he was independent of others owing to my superior rank. I'll therefore be glad if you'll even now endeavour more earnestly to correct your behaviour towards him and drop your present state of ignorance. If you have any grievance against him, apply together with him to me.[27]

Finally we have a document written on the back of a comprehensive survey of land at Kirkeosiris; it is a copy by Menches of an indictment of officials from various

villages of the three Divisions of the Nome by an unnamed person. Gaps and bad Greek make it hard to
follow; but we can see that the complaint is addressed to
some superior in the financial department and that the
accused were somehow concerned with the crops. Despite
its confusions it is worth citing as a testimony to the
complicated way in which problems of the bureaucracy
could develop, to the bedevilment of the ordinary folk
and small officials trying to do their job.

> . . . a village two stades distant from the metropolis in order
> to inspect this, still they didn't obey, supposing that the
> record would be made in the temple of Crocodilopolis
> without inspection. In order then to leave them in this matter
> also without excuse we obeyed the command and published a
> proclamation for an assembly at the Finance Office on Tubi 1,
> so that the business might be quickly completed at the
> proper time.
>
> Then, observing the danger that'd emerge from my attend-
> ing to the business in the matter of the reports on the
> irrigated land, and thinking their plans were being frustrated,
> they came to their senses. Supposing that they'd bring me to
> a dead stop at the beginning, they withdrew to the Herakleo-
> polite Nome. Through my giving information through the
> officials, they were with much trouble induced by the
> *strategoi* and *chrematistai* [a board of assize-judges] and others
> to return at the start of Mecheir, having been convicted. . . .
>
> About the 11th of the same month they came over to the
> Finance Office, and since on account of the prolonged atten-
> dance . . . there was a general expectation that the result would
> not agree with their return of the amount of crop, Theon, the
> official appointed for the survey of vineyards and gardens,
> delivered to me in the meantime [a report]; and sent concern-
> ing the state of affairs with him, being anxious in accordance
> with the memorial given by them . . . we provided suitable
> information about each and summoned . . .

And in this they probably meant, reckoning up together the amounts of what has been concealed on various occasions, to depart on the 13th after reporting the actual total quantity of crop, but neglecting to issue the lists of individual items, so that by this obstruction, plus their other acts of damage, they might bring about the dispersal of this revenue—the most opportune time for the produce's delivery having arrived.

From this statement may be seen their nefarious conduct on earlier occasions, and how much in contrast is their behaviour with the anxiety shown in your present letter as to this tax, that they should stay stationary at their posts. Most of them have been appointed without the *dioiketes'* cognizance; and some have wormed themselves into position of *oikonomos* [financial official], toparch, *sitologos* [corn-official], komarch, and other offices inconsistent with their work; others have transferred their duties to their sons, who are quite young men, and sometimes to other persons altogether; others are engaged in the duties of *topos*-secretary and control at least two village secretaries in each Division, and have handed over the posts of *epistatai*, into which they have crawled, to . . . or some of their brothers, contrary to the decrees . . . being brought to light because, careless of what is expedient, they do anything rather than the duties of a village secretary, and growing remiss . . .[28]

This correspondence of Menches gives us an excellent idea of what life was at village level, the level of the majority of the Egyptians, with its brawls, occasional violence, tedious supervision, and constant attempts to defraud the crushing government system or convert it into profit by various corrupt practices—while the cultivators struggled to carry on their productive labours, on which, in the last resort, the whole upper structure, including the court, depended.

The people in such a society were inevitably litigious;

and men needed every possible legal document for protection against the government, their neighbours, and everyone with whom they had dealings. Here is a contract, dated at the end of the Piper's reign (63–2 B.C.) in which three brothers renounce claims against a nephew who has borrowed from them:

In the reign of Ptolemy, the God New Dionysos Philopator Philadelphos, Year 19, and the rest of the formula as written at Alexandria, the — of the month Peritios or Choiach, at Oxyrhynchos in the Thebaid.

Pasion, Ptolemaios, and Apollonios, all three sons of Dionysios, Macedonians of the Katoikic Cavalry, acknowledge to the son their late deceased sister Berenike, Moschion son of . . ., Macedonian of the Katoikic Cavalry, all the parties being from the street of Cleopatra Aphrodite, that neither they nor anyone else on their behalf have or will have any ground of complaint or will proceed against Moschion or his agents concerning the loan of money at interest which, Moschion made from the mother of the three acknowledging parties and maternal grandmother of Moschion himself, Arsinoe daughter of Ptolemaios, who too has died, which loan has been otherwise specified by a contract drawn up through the Record Office in the aforesaid city in former times or concerning any other provision whatever of the above-mentioned contract of loan, because Moschion has for various reasons effected the renewal of the aforesaid money-agreement with Arsinoe under a pledge [?] on account of the above-stated kinship.

If any of us violates the contract or proceeds against Moschion, apart from the aggression being invalid, the aggressor or his representative shall in addition forfeit to Moschion, or any representative of Moschion against whom aggression is committed, a fine of 500 *drachmai* of silver, and to the State an equal amount, and nevertheless (this contract shall be valid) [names of six witnesses missing].[29]

We see how tenacious about money even close kinsmen were; the brothers were not letting Moschion go without paying, they merely admitted to some new arrangement being made with Arsinoe, his grandmother.

The document of 44, in which Ptolemaios (whether Ptolemaios XV or Caesarion) appears, is a typical land-lease, with all details specified:

In the Year 8 of Cleopatra and Ptolemaios Fatherloving Gods, and the rest of the formula as written at Alexandria, 27th of month Gorpiaios which=Epeiph, at Oxyrhynchos in the Thebaid.

Theon son of Theon, of the katoikic cavalry, has leased to Apollonios also called Harbichis, son of Apollonios also called Harbichis, Persian of the Epigone, both being of the street of Cleopatra Aphrodite, the holding of 30 *arourai* which belongs to him at Paimis, on condition that Apollonios shall sow half of it for Year 9 with wheat and cultivate the other half with aracus, at a rent for each *aroura* sown with wheat of 6 artabai of hard wheat, unmixed with barley, and for each sown with aracus likewise . . . art. of hard wheat, unmixed with barley. And Apollonios acknowledges that he has received from Theon the seed. . . .[30]

The squabbling went on all the while. In 34, the year when Antony held his great celebrations in Alexandria, two cultivators (apparently of Euhemereia in the Arsinoite Nome) complained of losses incurred through sheep.

To Eut . . . from Harneses son of . . . and Onnophris son of . . ., both cultivators in the services of Achillas, *Eklogistes*. On 9 Mesore of the 18th and 3rd Year, Hermiysis son of Psempnoutis let his sheep loose on the *knekos* which we have together with the chaff in the drying-place. They grazed away 15 *art.* of it and obliged us to present the petition so that you may force him to restore to us the aforesaid 15 *art.* of *knekos*, the rents suffer no loss, and he himself receive the penalties he deserves. Goodbye.[31]

Kneke or *knekos* meant pale-yellow, tawny; it was also the name for safflower, *carthamus tinctorius*. Harmiysis no doubt had to pay up; but he continued to be a careless shepherd, for soon after, between 33–30, as his Queen was declining in her fortunes, he had to meet other payments. We have a receipt of his:

Harnesis son of Sentheus and his sons Sentheus and Onnophris, all three inhabitants of Setrempaei, and Eubios son of Pnephoros, to Harmiysis son of Psempnoutis, herdsman of Euhemereia, greeting.

We have received from you the price of hay from the 17 sown *arourai* of revenue-land cultivated by us in the area of Setrempaei, which your sheep have grazed down, and we make no further claim against you. Didymos public scribe has written for them at their request because they are illiterate.

Preparations for the Final Struggle

When news of the Alexandrian Triumph reached Rome, Octavian wrote an angry letter reproaching Antony for his conduct. Antony's reply seems the letter that mockingly details Octavian's own amorous failings, already cited, but he also raised serious issues. He claimed his rights according to the Treaty of Brundisium to half the recruits levied in Italy and to allotments for his veterans. Where were his promised legions? He declared that only Octavian stood in the way of the republic's restoration. (This point, with Antony's name in place of Octavian's, was a stock argument on the other side.[1]) Octavian did not answer the genuine charges, but jeeringly suggested that Antony should find his veterans lands in conquered Parthia, and renewed the attacks on his enslavement by Cleopatra.

This reply reached Antony in Armenia in autumn 33. Once again he was being held up; only in November did Canidius bring his army to Ephesos. He felt that he should try to regularize things by a formal approach to the Senate

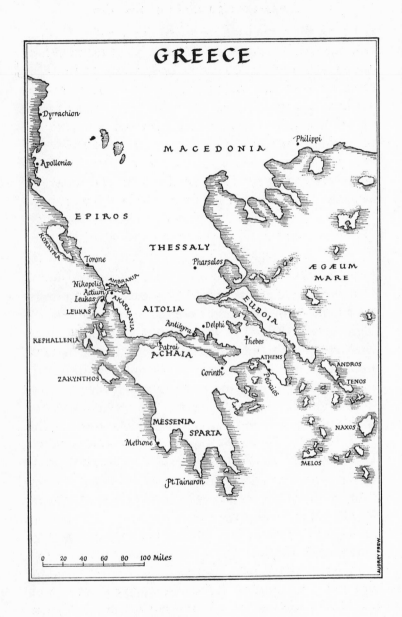

GREECE

MACEDONIA

Dyrrachion

Apollonia

Philippi

EPIROS

KORKYRA

Torone

THESSALY

Pharsalos

ÆGÆUM
MARE

Nikopolis
Actium
Leukas

AMBRAKIA

AKARNANIA

AITOLIA

EUBOIA

LEUKAS

Antikyra

Delphi

KEPHALLENIA

Patrai

Thebes

ACHAIA

ATHENS

ANDROS

Corinth

Peiraios

TENOS

ZAKYNTHOS

NAXOS

MESSENIA

SPARTA

Methone

MELOS

Pt.Tainaron

0   20   40   60   80   100 Miles

AUDREY FREW

at Rome. In a dispatch he asked for his Acts, which included the Donations, to be ratified, and expressed his readiness to lay down his powers if Octavian did likewise. From now on the war of vituperation was open and continuous. Cassius of Parma was among Antony's chief spokesmen, as he seems to have been earlier for Sextus: perhaps the squib about Octavian and the *lectisternium* was his work. Oppius and Messalla wrote on Octavian's side. In such exchanges the year 33 ended. With the last day of December the period of the Second Triumvirate expired Now was the crucial constitutional moment; and our sources are not helpful. Mainly pro-Octavian, they dodge the issue, since their favourite had a weak legal position. There were few precedents for the situation. The holders of such offices as the triumvirate could argue that the law had merely fixed a day up to which they could hold their powers, but it needed a formal act of abdication or a vote of termination by the granting body (the Roman People) to end their tenure. Antony kept the title; Octavian with his superior tactical position at Rome dropped it—though whether he gave up its powers is another matter. He was sacrosanct, he held Italy, he was to be consul in 31. He knew that any illegalities would be given restrospective legalisation as long as he won: as indeed happened in 29 and 28. If he lost, what did illegalities matter? So he writes in his *Res Gestae* simply that he held the triumvirate for 'ten consecutive years'.

Meanwhile Antony and Cleopatra had met at Ephesos, where the contingents of the client-kings were gathering from Syria, Asia Minor, Thrace. Of Roman troops in the east, there were nineteen legions (some 70,000 men) as his main force, with four as reserve and defence in Cyrene,

Altar dedicated by Ahenobarbus to Neptune. Relief of Marriage of
Neptune and Amphitrite.

and seven more in Egypt and Syria. Warships were being
busily built, though Cleopatra had 200 ships and a war-
chest said to hold 2,000 talants. Timber was scarce and
on Kos Antony's men felled even the sacred forest of
Asklepios. Cleopatra took charge of the docks at Berytos
near the Lebanon cedars. In the end some 800 ships were
perhaps available for various purposes, though by the
time of Action only 500 were massed in the fleet. Cleopatra supplied the provisions. Everywhere she went at
Antony's side, on horse or in litter, at banquets and at
councils; and already her intrusive presence in a war-
situation was offending and irritating Antony's Roman
supporters.

Cassius of Parma in his satirical verses was making
much of Octavian's mean descent. From the abuse of this
period no doubt came many of the traditions of his
family's disgraceful past: that his father was a moneychanger and usurer, even one of 'those who distributed
bribes and performed other tasks in the Campus'. Antony
jeered at his maternal stock, saying his great-grandfather
'had been of African birth and had conducted now a
perfumery shop and now a bakery at Aricia'. Cassius
twitted him for being the grandson of a baker and also of a

Continuation of the Relief of Marriage of Neptune and Amphitrite.

moneychanger: 'Your mother's meal came from a most vulgar bakery in Aricia; this was fashioned by a moneychanger of Nerulum with hands discoloured from changing coins.'[2] Suetonius cites these phrases as from a *Letter* (in prose), but has probably taken them from a work in iambic senarii.[3] The mocks at Octavian's father seem to go back to the first days after Caesar's murder; Antony had sneered at him as *argentarius*, meaning no doubt money-fingerer, money-man, rather than moneychanger in a precise sense.[4] And we are told that Octavian 'was charged with being excessively fond of fine furniture and Corinthian vessels as well as addicted to gambling. For, during the time of proscriptions [43 B.C.], this line was written on his statue: 'My father a silversmith, I deal in brass.' It was thought he put some persons on the list of proscribed only to get the Corinthian vessels they owned. And afterwards in the Sicilian War an epigram was made: 'Twice having lost a fleet in luckless fight, to win at last he gambles day and night.'[5]

Pseudo-Acron says that Cassius wrote satires 'of different kinds', and it is possible that all these verses were his—though there must have been many persons composing epigrams and lampoons of various kinds.[6] In deriding

Altar dedicated by Ahenobarbus. Lustration ceremony.

Antony, Octavian did not neglect even stylistic analysis, trying to show that Antony had an alien quality, inflated and Asiatic, with bombastic jingles; he himself prided himself on a sober style like Julius Caesar. One of Messala's polemics seems to deal with accusations that Antony let Cleopatra carry off works of art from many places to Alexandria. She may have done so, but a Roman leader was the last person to make such charges, in view of the vast lootings by Roman generals and others for a century and more. Cleopatra is said to have taken from Hera's temple on Samos the group of Zeus, Athena, Herakles by the bronze-caster Myron; from Roitaion on the Sigeian Promontory, a statue of Aias; from Pergamon paintings and 200,000 rolls (probably never removed).

With the opening of the year 32, however, Antony had an important constitutional point in his favour. The two consuls for the year, G. Sosius and Gn. Domitius, were his supporters. That they should be elected this year had been agreed on when he and Octavian were sharing out offices at the start of the triumvirate. His two adherents seem to have gone to Rome sometime before the end of 31; for Ahenobarbus appears to have at least now succeeded in founding a Temple to Neptune, or in recon-

Continuation of Lustration ceremony.

structing an earlier shrine. His coins show that he had
cherished such a project after his naval victory of 42
(gained on the same day as the first battle of Philippi); and
though he could not hope to celebrate a Triumph for a
defeat of the followers of the triumvirs, he used some
other pretext for paying his tribute to Neptune. Certainly
from his building work seems to come a frieze of the
lustration or purification of an armed force and another of
sea-deities taken as a Marriage of Neptune. (A lustration
could be part of the ceremony of closing a *lustrum*, which
followed the taking of the census; it was used also for
purifying the city after a prodigy or for sanctifying an area
that was to be used for a temple; an army was lustrated
before a campaign or an important battle, and sometimes
at the end of a campaign.) The sea-group, it has been
suggested, he picked up while governing Bithynia and
kept in hand for the work he had had so long in mind.
We know that Sosius brought with him a curious statue
of Apollo, carved in cedarwood, which he must have
collected while prefect of Syria and Cilicia. This statue he
dedicated in the Temple of Delphic Apollo, situated not
far north of the Temple of Marcellus. This was by far the
oldest shrine of Apollo in Rome, having been vowed in

439 B.C. by G. Julius, dedicated two years later, and restored in 350. We may conjecture that the religious work by the two consuls designate was aimed against Octavian. Sosius was drawing attention to the Delphic Apollo as far more important and ancient than the Palatine Apollo annexed by Octavian; and Ahenobarbus was making a claim to Neptune as against Octavian who had taken over the relationship of Sextus Pompey to that god. Their acts would then seem to have been concerted with Antony before they left for Rome.

Octavian had taken care to withdraw from Rome before the new year began; and at last Antony had a chance to make men in Rome listen to his case. Speeches in the Senate were one of the best ways of getting arguments through to the Italian *municipia*, to Antony's settled veterans, and others. Sosius, entering office on 1 January, made the statement; he was a better orator than Ahenobarbus. He praised Antony and attacked Octavian for his bad faith, but did not ask for confirmation of Antony's Acts, knowing well what antagonisms that would raise. He failed to put a motion against Octavian, as one of the latter's partisans, Nonius Balbus, a tribune of the *plebs*, vetoed any resolution. Octavian now decided that he had given the consuls enough time to show their hand. At the next session he appeared with an armed bodyguard of friends and soldiers. Launching a violent diatribe against Antony and his Donations, he complained of his and Sosius' behaviour, and offered to produce documentary proof of his charges at the next meeting. His show of force made any reply impossible; and he knew quite well that after it there would be no 'next meeting' of the Senate. The two consuls, considering that he had destroyed the constitution, fled with three to four hundred senators to Antony. That so many leading men, at this juncture, threw in their lot with Antony is remarkable; they made up about a third of the Senate. The fugitives joined Antony at Ephesos.

He was now able to make a good display of legality, with the two consuls and a large body of senators driven to appeal for his aid against an armed attempt to overawe the officers of the Republic. He had every right to declare war on Octavian as a usurper, on the lines of Pompey's declaration against Caesar after the latter had seized Rome: the legitimate government was wherever the consuls and the Senate were. He at once set about mobilizing for war on sea and land. Octavian's act had removed his qualms about fighting the Roman in command of Italy. And now at last Cleopatra was ready to contribute all she could, in men, ships, supplies, money. Antony called up all his client-kings, save Polemon and Herod, and exacted an oath of allegiance. Polemon had been given the task of guarding the Armenian frontier; Herod, who had come to Ephesos, was sent back by his enemy Cleopatra to deal with Malchos for withholding his rent. (He did after some trouble beat Malchos, but his work was nearly spoiled by Cleopatra's general in Koile Syria, who knew that she only wanted the pair to weaken each other. However in the long run she had done Herod a good turn, for the task she set him kept him away from Actium.) Cleopatra further got from Antony the important trade-town of Gaza; and Herod, before he left, is said to have advised Antony that his only way to victory lay over the dead body of his queen. Certainly the advice was sound enough; but whether Herod was indiscreet enough to speak out his thoughts is another matter.

From now on the contradictions in Antony's position became ever more evident and disastrous. As a Roman challenging Octavian he had some reason to think victory possible; as a Hellenistic ruler wedded to Cleopatra, he stirred up a maximum of resistance in the west. In the confused situation he might have made out a good juristic case against Octavian, which would have appealed to large numbers in the *municipia*, at Rome, and among the veterans—but only as long as he spoke securely as a Roman. By his continued association with Cleopatra he made all Octavian's accusations seem true, and put an intolerable burden on his own supporters. Some indeed like Canidius or Turullius were so closely connected with his career that they had little choice but to follow him, whatever they thought; but many others, like Ahenobarbus, were ready to stay at his side only as long as they felt him a fellow-Roman with understandable motives and aims that they could in some degree share. Others again, like Titius or Dellius, merely wanted to be on the winning side; and the more they saw of Cleopatra's dominance in the war councils, the more they felt that the time for desertion was at hand. Many men were painfully swayed between a genuine admiration for Antony and a conviction that by supporting him they were betraying Roman ideals in unforgivable ways. The more ardent adherents of Cleopatra and her opponents were in continual clash. At one moment Antony did tell her to go back to Egypt and let him fight out the war on his own. She refused. Canidius backed her, arguing that she paid and fed the army, manned the fleet, and had a better head than most men. His opponents said that she had bribed him. Ahenobarbus, who liked Antony and whose son was betrothed to Antony's elder daughter by Octavia, opposed Cleopatra's queenly arrogance with the haughty manners of a Roman noble and refused to address her except by name. Antony tried to make the best of both worlds by announcing that six months after victory he would lay down his powers. But who could credit any such statements while he could not send Cleopatra home?

At Ephesos he had sought to gain the support of athletes, musicians, actors, by making grants that enhanced their status. Such performers, if won over, could be relied on to sing his praises and do much to increase his popularity. Also, the patronage of artistic and athletic guilds suited his Dionysiac role. A copy of his rescript to the Koinon or Commonalty of the Hellenes in Asia has been found on the back of a medical papyrus:

Marcus Antonius, Imperator, Triumvir for the Restoration of the State, to the *Koinon* of the Hellenes in Asia, greeting.

On a previous occasion, when I gave audience in Ephesos to my friend the trainer [*aleiptes*], Marcus Antonius Artemidorus, together with Caropinos of Ephesos, eponymous priest of the Synod of World Victors in the Sacred Games and Garlanded Victors, he asked me to confirm the inviolability of the existing privileges of the Synod and to make these further valuable grants:

Exemption from military service, complete immunity from liturgies [public offices without payment, involving charges], freedom from billeting, and, for the duration of the festival, a truce and personal security, and the right to wear purple.

He asked me to agree to write to you at once, and I assented through my friendship for Artemidoros and my wish to do a favour to their eponymous priest for the honour and expansion of the Synod.

And now again, in audience with me, Artemidoros has asked for them to have permission to set up a bronze tablet and engrave on it the aforesaid grants. As I wish not to disappoint him in any request, I allowed him to set up the tablet as he urged.

Such is my letter to you on these matters.[7]

Athletes are not mentioned; but we may assume the Synod was composed in part, or mainly, of them; Artemidoros is himself a trainer of athletes.

Cleopatra was to some extent using festivals to take Antony's mind off the problems she created for him. When they moved their H.Q. to Samos, the whole body of Dionysiac Artists gathered on the island. 'While almost all the world around was filled with groans and lamentations, a single island for many days resounded with flutes and stringed instruments. Theatres were filled and choral bands competed. Every city also sent an ox for the general sacrifice and kings vied in entertainments and gifts. Everywhere men began asking: How will the winners celebrate their victories if the war-preparations are marked by such costly festivals? When the events were over, Antony gave the Dramatic Artists Priene as a place to live in, and sailed for Athens, where sports and theatres again took up his time. Cleopatra too, jealous of Octavia's honours there (for Octavia was a special favourite of the Athenians), sought by many splendid gifts to win the people's favour. So they voted her honours and sent a deputation to her house with the vote, among them Antony: for was he not a citizen of Athens?' Antony delivered the speech for the city. But to Rome, we are told by Plutarch, he sent men with orders to eject Octavia from his house. 'And she left it, taking with her all his children except the eldest son by Fulvia, who was with him; she was in tears of distress that she too would be regarded as one of the causes of the war. But the Romans pitied Antony, not her, and most of all those who had seen Cleopatra and knew she was not Octavia's superior in youth or beauty.' But can we imagine Octavian, in the midst of a war, allowing agents of Antony access to Rome and standing idle while they turned his sister out? Even if Antony had succumbed to pressure from Cleopatra and attempted such a stupid act, we cannot believe he would have succeeded in carrying it out. The plainest interpretation is that Antony did accept Cleopatra's argument that it was impossible for him to remain married to Octavia in the circumstances and that he sent her letters of divorce. Octavia then had no legal right to his house and would have accepted her brother's insistence that she should move out. The story of her ejection by agents of Antony would be a spontaneous response to the news of her removal or a version put about by Octavian's agents.[8]

Antony's adherents in Italy kept sending messages about the bad effects of his union with Cleopatra, but she was now in a strong enough position to turn the messengers out. Octavian, despite the flight of the consuls, had all the advantages that came from holding Rome. He summoned the remaining senators, read them a detailed defence of his own acts and position, and attacked those of Antony, especially the Donations. He contrasted his Illyrian successes with Antony's Parthian failure. But he was badly in need of money. The west was generally poorer than the east; and what Maecenas got in as contributions from the wealthy was not enough. A general tax was imposed: all freeborn landholders had to pay a quarter of their income, freedmen an eighth of their property if it was worth over 200,000 sesterces. The result was riots, arson, uprisings. Propaganda had no effect and Antony's partisans had an easy time in stirring up discontent. There were street fights at Rome of boys on opposite sides. Soldiers had to be used to restore order. But as Plutarch remarks, 'As long as the people were being plagued by the tax collectors, they were furious; after they'd paid, they quieted down'. If Antony had got rid of Cleopatra and invaded Italy in the summer of 32, he would have struck against an unprepared enemy. But he did nothing and Octavian was able to control the situation. Following the example of Pompey some thirty years before, he sent representatives to the more import-ant towns or *municipia*, with tales of Antony drugged and spelled by a foreign wanton, and urging them to pass votes of confidence in himself as the authentic leader of Rome and Italy. Slowly the movement gathered in strength. The oath was taken by *municipia* in the provinces of the west, Sicily, Sardinia, Africa, Gaul, Spain.

Desertions began from Antony's camp. Plancus and Titius went over to Octavian with useful information about his plans. Velleius, ardent supporter of Octavian, says that Plancus decided to go 'on being coldly regarded by Antony because of certain plain proofs of his dis-honesty. He later construed the victor's clemency as evidence of his own merit, alleging that Caesar [Octavian] had approved what he merely pardoned. Titius soon followed the example of this uncle of his. One day when

Plancus in the Senate charged Antony, the man he had so recently deserted and who was not present, charged him with many foul enormities, Coponius, who had been *praetor* [chief law-officer], a man of high character, observed with some humour, "Surely Antony did a great many things the day before you left him".[9] Plancus told Octavian that Antony's will had been deposited a short while before with the Vestal Virgins, and described its contents. Octavian realised, the tale goes, that here was the document he needed, since Sosius had omitted to read Antony's dispatches in his speech to the Senate. He demanded the will; the Vestals refused to give it up; Octavian siezed it by force and read it out to the Senate. We are told that the clauses included a declaration that Ptolemy Caesar was the true son of Caesar and Cleopatra; legacies to his children by Cleopatra; directions that he should be buried at her side in Alexandria. In the heated atmosphere the clause about his burial was taken to give further proof of his intention to remove the world-capital from Rome to Alexandria. The other clauses served perfectly to authenticate all that Octavian had been saying of Antony's views and aims.[10]

The more one considers this will, the odder it seems. What was the point in making a private will of this kind and sending it to Rome, where it would normally be opened only after his death? If Antony were defeated, the clauses could only serve for ribald denunciation; if he won, there was no need of the thing at all. In short, it served absolutely no purpose. Much of it seems to have been a political statement—for instance, the remarks about Caesarion and the Donations—but the only point in such a statement was in publicising it; not hiding it away in the temple of Vesta. The sole possible explanation of the document, if it were genuine, would be that Cleopatra wanted a formal declaration about the gifts and Caesarion; but what possible use could it be to her when lodged in the very place which could never by any stretch of imagination be thought of as accepting her and Caesarion? She knew that acceptance could be won only by Antony's military victory; and all her actions had been directed at bringing him to the point of war with Octavian.

On the other hand everything we know of the will shows it to have been exactly the sort of document that Octavian wanted at this juncture to complete his propaganda against Antony. That Antony should so opportunely have provided his enemy with all the proofs of his derelictions (from a Roman viewpoint), is something a little too good to be true. He was capable indeed, under pressure, of stupid actions that played into Octavian's hand, actions like the divorce of Octavia; but what argues against authenticity of his will is the pointless nature of the cited clauses. Quite possibly there was a will, and the clause about being buried in Alexandria may well have been in it; for that can be taken as a plea to Octavian, in the event of his triumph, to treat his body at least with mercy. But the other clauses do not carry conviction. It has been argued that the will must have existed, since the Vestal Virgins would have testified against Octavian if he had invented the whole thing. That contention carries no weight; for the Vestals were not likely to have contradicted the master of Rome if he told them to keep quiet. We may add that the story of Octavian only learning of the will through Plancus is another unconvincing detail. With his post of power at Rome he would certainly have heard through his agents and spies of any document lodged by Antony, even if the Vestals did not let him know, as they almost certainly would have done. Historians who assume that legal niceties and traditional respects were at all operative in Rome at this time have little sense of what such an epoch is in fact like. Another small point that suggests fabrication on Octavian's part is the statement in Nikolaos of Damas that Caesar's will rejected Caesarion. Such a statement was certainly an Octavian invention, directed against Antony; what more obvious than to charge him with championing Caesarion in his own will. Plutarch does not lay stress on the event. He says that Titius and Plancus told of the will, Octavian seized it, read it through himself, 'marked certain reprehensible passages; then assembled the Senate and read it aloud to them, though most of them were displeased to hear him do so. They thought it a strange and grievous thing for a man to be called to account while alive for what he wanted done after his death. Caesar laid most emphasis on the clause in the will relating to Antony's burial.'[11] Velleius Paterculus does not mention the will.

The abuse of Cleopatra grew yet stronger, together with the usual condemnation of Egyptians in general as beast-worshippers. Calvisius (whom Plutarch calls an *hetairos* or close personal friend or companion of Octavian) made a set of detailed charges against Antony: that he'd given Cleopatra the Pergamon libraries, that at banquet with many guests he'd stood up and rubbed her feet 'in compliance with some agreement and compact', that he'd let the Ephesians in his presence salute her as Lady [*kyria*], that often, seated on the tribunal and dispensing

349

justice to tetrarchs and kings, he received from her and read letters in tablets of onyx or crystal, and once when Furnius, 'a man of great worth and the ablest orator in Rome', was speaking, he sprang from the tribunal and left the trial on seeing her carried through the marketplace on a litter, 'and hanging on to her litter escorted her on her way'.[12] However, Plutarch adds, 'most of these charges were thought to be falsehoods'. Further charges declared that he used a golden chamberpot.

Meanwhile the Antonians at Rome went about defending him as well as they could, and sent one of their group, Geminius, to beg him not 'to let himself be voted out of office and proclaimed an enemy of Rome'. Geminius in Greece was watched suspiciously by Cleopatra, 'who' says Plutarch, 'thought he was acting in Octavia's interests'. He was treated mockingly and given low places at the table, but endured the insults, waiting for a chance to speak up. Once however at dinner he was bidden to tell the reasons for his coming. He answered that the rest of his communications needed a sober head, but one thing he could say, drunk or sober, and that was that all would be well if Cleopatra were packed off to Egypt. Antony was angry, but Cleopatra said calmly, 'You've done well, Geminius, to confess the truth without being put to the torture'.

So, a few days later, he went off for Rome again. Cleopatra's adherents drove away 'many of the other friends of Antony who could not bear their drunken tricks and scurrilities'. Among these were M. Silanus and the historian Dellius. Dellius declared that Glaukos the physician warned him of a plot against him by Cleopatra; for he had offended her at a meal by saying that while they drank sour wine, Sarmentus at Rome was drinking Falernian. 'Now Sarmentus was one of the boy-playthings of Octavian, the sort that Romans call *deliciae*', pretties, sweeties.

Octavian could now take the final steps. He got the Senate to vote for war against Cleopatra and the cancellation of the authority which 'Antony had surrendered to a woman'. He declared that Antony had been drugged and was no longer master of himself, and that the Romans were in fact at war with Mardion the eunuch and Potheinos, with Eiras, the tire-woman of Cleopatra, and Charmion, who were in charge of the main matters of government. Thus, cleverly, Antony was ignored as no longer a responsible agent, and the war became a war against a foreign country, Egypt, with its allies.

Octavian now had a strong legal position. Antony was deprived of his triumviral powers and of the right to be consul in 31. Octavian, as Ferial Priest, in front of the temple of Bellona, went through the formal proclamation of *bellum justum*. Marching into the Field of Mars, he hurled a spear dipped in fresh blood from the temple towards the east, the direction of the enemy. In 36 he had announced the end of the Civil Wars; by naming Cleopatra as the enemy, he saved himself from having to admit that those wars had not really been ended, as well as rallying all waverers in a sacred war, a national war, against a degenerate queen who wanted to destroy the whole Roman tradition. Between him and Antony there was merely *inimicitia*, a feud. The renunciation of *amicitia* was a customary Roman procedure, here lifted into an action of great significance because of the natures of the persons involved. *Amicitia*, friendship or good relationship, was a quality linked with the whole system of clientship and patronage, which was inherited by a son and which provided the main support and retinue of a politician. The network of patronage had grown more complex as the position of Rome grew in magnitude; non-Romans formed ties with members of the ruling class; communities and whole regions sought a patron who could forward their interests in the Senate, Assembly, or elsewhere. Ties between leading citizens were expressed by *amicitia*, oppositions by *inimicitia*. The triumvirs had been *amici*. But as the conflict between Octavian and Antony was now a personal one, an *inimicitia*, Antony's clients or *amici* could not be forced to fight against him. When the consuls fled in 32, Octavian said they had gone with his consent and others were free to follow them. He accepted Pollio's plea, 'My services to Antony are too great, his kindness to me too well known, for me to take part in your quarrel. So I shall keep out of it and be the prize of the victor'; and the people of Bononia, traditional clients of the Antonii, were not required to take the oath to Octavian. He later claimed, 'The whole of Italy of its own free will swore allegiance to me and demanded me as the leader in the war in which I was victorious at Actium'. (Note the periphrasis for the war.) The oath, it has been suggested, was similar to that later used by Gaius:

> I will be the personal enemy of those whom I know to be personal enemies of *Imperator Caesar Divi Filius*; and if anyone is threatening or shall threaten him or his safety, I will not desist from attacking him by land and sea with armed might in deadly war till he has paid the penalty. I will hold the safety of Imperator Caesar Divi Filius dearer than

myself or my children, and I will treat as enemies those who
entertain hostile opinions towards him.[13]

He does not claim that the provinces swore the oath of
their own free will; and he does not specify how 'Italy
chose him'. No doubt the Senate voted confidence in
him; but the vague phrase seems meant to cover the lack
of a precise role.

During the turn of 32–1 Antony with his fleet and army
wintered in Greece. Octavian gathered his forces at
Brundisium and Tarentum. All the while the propaganda
war grew fiercer. Much of what was then alleged has
affected historians up to the present day, especially the
picture of Antony as a drunken sot unable to leave
Cleopatra's arms. Certainly she had established something
of an ascendancy over him, in which sexual aspects
played their part; but at no point could the situation be
reduced to simple terms of drink, sex, and the rest of it.
Antony had slowly got himself into an untenable position.
Now he relied so much on Cleopatra for material aid that
he could not turn her out without wrecking his war
preparations and laying himself open to attacks from both
Octavian and the Parthians. He could only struggle ahead
on the unstable basis he had created for himself, hoping
somehow or other to light on a way of reconciling his
role as Roman general with that of Cleopatra's ally and
lover. She, clear-sighted as she was in many ways, seems
blind to the insoluble nature of the problem she had
brought upon him. All she could see was that the world
was in hopeless disorder and confusion, and that a strong
ruler was needed—a man with the qualities which Antony,
mated with her, was excellently suited to provide. Much

of his difficulties came from his god-masquing, and yet gradually the whole dynamic of his role in history had absorbed this masquing and become inseparable from it. Cut off as he was from Rome, his guising as Herakles-Dionysos had provided the basis for his close relationship with Isis-Cleopatra and given him the deep assurance of a tremendous force uttering itself through him—through his union with Cleopatra. And so his sense of purpose, powerfully maturing and in many ways achieving a genuine connection with the mass-needs of his world, was in the last resort reposing on an illusory pledge. For it was Octavian, acting less extravagantly and guided in many matters by Agrippa and by Livia, who had developed a god-role, that of Apollo, which worked out harmoniously with Roman traditional outlooks. Octavian had thus been able to develop an archaic backward-looking *pietas* or patriotism with Roman roots, while accommodating himself as far as was necessary to the mass demand for a saviour-god incarnated in the political leader.

If we look further at the propaganda created directly and indirectly by Cleopatra for the rousing of the eastern masses, we can better gauge the extent to which Antony was now involved in her dreamworld of myth, and to which that dreamworld both stimulated and fettered him.

Sibylline Prophecies

The main source for the ideas seething among the eastern peoples, certainly in part stirred up by Cleopatra's agents, lies in various passages from the *Sibylline Leaves*: strange prophetic verses that were widespread among the Greek-speaking peoples of the east and which were quite distinct from the official Sibylline pronouncements put out at Rome and controlled by the Board of Fifteen—though at certain points or moments the two series were liable to become entangled. It is indeed remarkable that the Sibyl, or Sibyls, had now gained so vast a reputation, without any normal forms of cult, that both the Roman ruling class and the oppressed craftsmen or farmers of the east appealed to the same source of revelation.

The verses that here concern us belong mainly to the last two centuries B.C. The earliest clear reference is to Antiochos Epiphanes; in later sections we find a reference to one of the triumvirs. Not that the writing or adaptation of the Sibylline utterances then cease; that went on for many more centuries, right into the Byzantine epoch, and up to the time of the Arab invasion.[1] For our purposes the most important section is one that seems definitely Greek in tone and inspiration, written about 33–32 B.C.

The wealth that Rome as tribute from Asia has taken away,
Asia shall thrice as much get back from Rome on a future day.
Insolent Rome shall be judged, Rome to the full shall pay.
How many Asian folk as slaves in Italy stay.
There yet shall toil in Asia twenty times as many
Italians, a host rejected, cast without a penny.

O Rome, luxurious Rome of gold, you Latin child,
Virgin drunken with lust in many beds you've run wild,
but you'll be married without due rites, a slave-slut of despair,
while still the Queen crops off your delicate head of hair
and uttering judgements will hurl you to earth from the sky,
then take up from the earth and set you again on high.

Because men cling to evil and paltry villainy,
to *Delos* she'll *deal loss. Samos* the *same* shall see.
Rome shall be forced to *roam*. Fulfilled each prophecy.
No word of ruined Smyrna. Judged and found-wanting her fate,
but the councils of the wicked and the wickedness of the great.

O serene peace shall journey to all the Asian land,
and Europe too shall be blessed, prosperous on every hand,
flourishing strong: of cold and hail alone there'll be a dearth.
O rich in cattle and all the beasts that move on the face of the
    earth.
O blessed shall be the man that lives in that wonderful time,
blessed the woman shall be.

True Order shall come to all from the starry heavens to men
and Justice shall be ours, and with Justice there must come then
sane Solidarity of men, the best thing life can give,
Love and Faith and Friendship for strangers, all that live.

And all Disorder and Envy, all Blame and Wrath shall flee,
no man shall then be poor, for gone is Necessity,
gone is the Murderlust, mad Hatred and bitter Strife,
and the Thieves that come in the night, and all the old Evil of
Life.[2]

The attempts to find Jewish elements are not successful.
The shearing of the hair is certainly not a reference to
Samson; rather we see the Greek notion that to cut off a
woman's hair was a sign of degradation: this is the main
theme of Menandros' comedy *The Shorn Woman*. The idea
of a revanche of Asia on Rome suggests the Mithridatic
war, with its massacre of all the Roman businessmen in
Asia; but such ideas must have sprung up passionately
and spontaneously at all phases of Rome's intrusion in
Asia Minor, Syria, and elsewhere. We know that prophecies of such a retort existed in powerful form in verses
called the *Oracles of Hystaspes* (a Persian mage), close in
style to the Sibyllines and composed probably in the last
century B.C.—that is, as an expression of the struggles
coming to a head in 32–1.[3] Justin in the second century
A.D. cites the work twice, and we learn that the Roman
authorities had forbidden its reading on pain of death.
The prohibition certainly goes back to the great burning
of books instituted by Augustus after becoming *pontifex
maximus*. The *Oracles* may have come into existence any
time between the Mithridatic war and Pompey's conquest
of Syria in 64; they belonged to the genre of apocryphal
visions, and we seem to have a fairly complete summary of
their contents in Lactanctius' *Divine Institutions*. He makes
the seer an ancient king of the Medes who prophesies the
stages of history leading to world-cataclysm and renewal;
and he says that similar doctrines were set out by the

Jewish prophets, the Sibyl, and Hermes Trismegistos. God, says Lactantius, created the world in six days and rested on the seventh; similarly there are six ages for the world (that is, 6,000 years in all), and at the end of the sixth the prince of demons will be let loose, Christ's reign will be established, and for a thousand years the world will repose from its labours in perfect justice and peace. Then the demon will escape from his prison to raise war against the righteous; but he'll be definitely conquered and at the end of the eighth age the world will be renewed, recreated for eternity. Lactantius thus gives a christianised version. We know from John Lydos that in fact Hystaspes defined his ages, not in terms of *Genesis*, but of the astrologic doctrine of the planets. However what matters for us here is that the first calamity announcing the world's end will be the destruction of the Roman Empire. 'The Roman Name, that rules the world, will vanish from the earth and dominion will return to Asia.' As long as Rome survives, the fearful convulsions of the last age will not be something to fear; but the day she falls, humanity will be near its death throes.

Here we touch a traditional aspect of Jewish and Christian apocalypse: that the Roman State will be the last State. But Lactantius adds the point, apparently from Hystaspes, that 'again the East will be master and the West will serve'. He tells us that the revelation of Rome's fate took in Hystaspes the form 'of an astonishing dream that a prophetic child [*puer*] interpreted'.[4] That other visions of this sort were current appears from various writings. Thus we meet in Hippolytos' *Antichrist*: 'He will gather all his forces from the rising of the Sun to the Setting, those that he will call and those that he will not call will march with him; the sea will be white with the sails of his ships and the plain will be black with his shields and his arms, and whoever stands up against him in war will fall under his sword.'⁵ Commodian used the same course in his *Carmen Apologeticum*, where he recounts the march of a King from the East against Rome; the first towns to fall before him are Tyre and Sidon. (Commodian used to be dated 4th century, or even early 5th, and set in North Africa; but it seems rather he is mid-3rd century and based in Palestine or a sect living there.)⁶ A Sibylline passage, also 3rd century, states:

> The Persians will take up arms, furious against the Ausonians.
> The Romans will flee. But then a Priest will come to them,
> truly Sun-sent, starting from Syria
> and with crafty blows he will change the situation.
> It's then there'll be a City of the Sun, and about it
> the Persians will have to meet the Phoenicians' heavy
>   threats.

There the hero from the east saves things for the Romans, but his advent is linked with the birth of the City of the Sun. This is a utopian idea, though perhaps connected with the actual Heliopolis in Syria. There was also a prophecy that went under the name of the Mad Praetor and seems to reach back as far as the first or second century B.C.⁷ It told how a great army came out of Asia from where the Sun rises, and how it enslaved Rome. To this series we must add the *Revelation* of St John. Though it does not mention the destructive forces as emanating from the East, its hatred of Rome and its joy in the thought of Rome's violent end is far more ferocious than anything in the other hostile prophecies:

And the heaven departed as a scroll when it is rolled together; and every mountain and island were moved out of their places.

And the kings of the earth, and the great men, and the rich men, and the chief captains, and the mighty men, and every bondsman, and every free man, hid themselves in the dens and in the rocks of the mountains;

And said to the mountains and rocks, Fall on us, and hide us from the face of him that sits on the throne, and from the wrath of the Lamb:

For the great day of his wrath is come; and who shall be able to stand? . . .

The merchants of these things, which were made rich by her, shall stand afar off for fear of her torment, weeping and wailing,

And saying, Alas, alas, that great city, that was clothed in fine linen, and purple, and scarlet, and decked with gold, and precious stones, and pearls!

For in one hour so great riches is come to nought. And every shipmaster, and all the company in ships, and sailors, and as many as trade by sea, stood afar off,

And cried when they saw the smoke of her burning, saying, What city is like unto this great city! . . .[8]

Revelation was composed under the early Empire, but it lineally carries on the note of the prophecies started off by Hystaspes and the Sibyl. And the rumour of those prophecies being revived by Cleopatra had much to do with the Roman fear of her. The guilt sense which they could not but feel, however they repressed it, at the vast lootings, exploitations, and oppressions by their generals, governors, and businessmen, found expressions in the scare at an uprising of the whole tormented east against them. Thus Virgil described, without any concern for historical accuracy, the forces led by Antony:

Opposing was Antony; with him aboard
were Egyptians and the whole strength of the East
even to far-off Bactria. On his side
was the Orient's wealth and all its varied arms;
victor he came from the Nations of the Dawn
and Redsea shores. Followed—alas, the shame—
by an Egyptian wife.[9]

The religious records noted the salvation of the Romans
from the threatening east, as we see from the *Fasti* of the
Arval Brothers and the Amiternan *Fasti*.[10]

If we look back at the Sibylline verses, we see that they
give a particular colouration to the general theme of
Rome's coming downfall, which shows clearly an
application of the schema of worldend-renewal to Antony
and Cleopatra. The avenging *despoina* can only be Cleopatra. Some critics have suggested that she might be Asia
personified. But two other prophecies in the Third Book
of the *Sibylline Leaves* place the end of the existing epoch
in Cleopatra's reign; and besides, Asia is separately
mentioned.[11] There could hardly be a direct reference to
Asia and an evocation of her as the *despoina* within a few
lines. Further, *homonoia*, community of mind or outlook,
solidarity of interest, was in Hellenistic times widely
thought of as the desirable result of a good ruler. We saw
how the King as Sun was viewed as the spreader in the
State of the *homonoia* of Universe; and inscriptions show
the kings or their representatives striving to create and
perpetuate *homonoia*.

All our information about the judicial commissions [in the
Hellenistic kingdoms] emphasises one point: they strove,
often unsuccessfully, to restore *homonoia*, concord, in the city.
Taken in bulk, the surviving dicast decrees are a paean in

praise of *homonoia*, that thing for which men longed but which they could not achieve . . . Every form of authority—kings, envoys, governors, generals of Laegues—was perpetually urging the people to live in concord; the most praised women of the time, a Phila or an Apollonis, were those who tried to promote it; even the gods intervened, and Apollo exhorts Iasos to *homonoia*. Homonoia herself was worshipped as a goddess at Iasos and Priene, and in Ptolemaic Thera Artemidoros set up an altar to her 'for the city'. She was one of the great conceptions of the Hellenistic age, but she remained a pious aspiration only. Not until Rome had crushed all internal feuds was concord achieved; then, in the Imperial period, cities freely celebrated Homonoia on their coinage, and she was frequently worshipped when all meaning in her worship had for Greeks passed away. [Tarn][12]

It had passed away because the crushing of the feuds was also the crushing of all freedom. The *homonoia* prophesied in the Sibylline verses was the exact opposite of Roman concord; and there, as in the inscriptions, it is a person who brings *homonoia* about. The person is Cleopatra. Some other details in the text further suit this identification. The *despoina* is to marry Rome off 'without due rites' and give her a mere slavewoman's ceremony. When we recall how Octavian was taunting Cleopatra as Antony's whore, we see here a retort on to proud Rome of the condition ascribed to Cleopatra. In calling Rome 'drunken' (*oinotheisa*) the poet produces a phrase unique in Greek, though that kind of metaphor was common enough among the Hebrew prophets. Jerusalem is drunken, all nations, Moab, Nineveh. 'Therefore hear this now, you afflicted and drunken, but not with wine,' says Isaiah of Jerusalem. But the metaphor does not prove the poet to have been a Jew; he may have read the

Septuagint in its Greek version, which must have been known fairly well to inquiring minds at Alexandria.[13] Or perhaps he has invented the phrase himself, wanting to retort back on Rome yet another accusation made against Cleopatra: that she was a drunkard. The word using for 'shearing' Rome is *kairei*, present tense. It may represent a prophetic present, but it stands out oddly among the futures and subjunctives. The poet may have in mind that Cleopatra has already shorn Rome of several important provinces or regions. (She had perhaps issued coins in Antioch, capital of Roman Syria.) So this part of the prophecy is already being actualised.

There is a likeness in the vision of the future with certain aspects of the Isis Aretologies, which go back to a *stēlē* of Memphis. Isis is hailed as the Queen (*despoina*) who abolishes murder and institutes a reign of love (*storgē*); she also makes the wrongdoer subject to his victim; she frees the captive and makes war cease; she has created law and made justice stronger than gold and silver.[14] (In the Aretologies those acts are part of the ideal or mythological past, which is being only imperfectly repeated in the present; they represent the standards of perfection created by Isis. In the prophecies and their accompanying social movements the attempt is made to recreate the ideal past in its totality, at a stable level.) The Queen of the Sibylline poem is thus close to Cleopatra in her Isis-guise. The golden age she inaugurates is primarily concerned with a fundamental change in human nature, though it is started off by a beneficent change in the outer world, by the ending of cold and hail, and by a general prosperity in the fields. We may note that the birds and creeping things share in the benefits, whereas in *Isaiah* they merely become harmless and in Virgil they perish. Indeed the high moral quality of the whole vision is remarkable; despite the fierce hate of Rome there is no wish for permanent revenge on Rome or Italy. They like the rest of the world will partake of the peace and happiness that is to come from the fall of empire.

The advent of the golden age, it appears, is to come about simply by that fall, which is to be the work of the *despoina*. There is no account here of destruction by fire, which in the Stoic scheme of world-renovation as in the Persian systems of saviour-advent is a necessary phase of complete death and renewal. Fire however plays its usual part in another Sibylline prophecy:

> And while Rome will be hesitating over
> the Conquest of Egypt, then the mighty Queen
> of the Immortal King will appear among men.
> And then the implacable Wrath of the Latin men.
> Three will subdue Rome with a pitiful fate.
> all men will perish in their private homes
> when a cataract of fire pours down from heaven.
> The Holy Lord, wielding the whole earth's sceptre,
> will come to rule for all the ages to come.[15]

Again, this statement has been called Jewish; but how the Queen then fits in, it is hard to see. Beliefs in a world-end by fire and in the emergence of a redeeming king were held by diverse groups under Persian mage-influence; and the reference to Egypt has nothing Jewish about it. The same considerations apply to another Sibylline prophecy:

> And then the whole wide world under a Woman's hand
> ruled and obeying everywhere shall stand,

and when the Widow shall queen the whole wide world
and into the sea divine have the gold and silver hurled
and into the water have hurled the bronzen swords of men
those creatures of a day, all the world's elements then
shall be widowed lorn and God who aloft in *aither* is found
around shall roll the heavens as a book is turned around.
And on earth divine and the sea the multitudinous sky
shall fall while cataracts the wild fire from on high,
ceaseless. The earth he'll burn, the sea he'll burn with his
  curse,
the days and the starry heavens and the whole universe
he'll break up into One, into Purity transmute.
The stars that laugh together as they bring us light shall be
  mute.
There'll be no more night or dawn, or the many darts of care,
no spring or summer or winter or autumn anywhere.
Then the Judgement of Mighty God shall come in the midst
of it all,
in the mighty age to be, when all these things befall.[16]

This passage follows what has been called the Beliar
Apocalypse; but in that section Beliar is destroyed by God
with fire, so here we must have a separate account of fire-
destruction, especially as Beliar's fall is to be followed by
the reign of the Messiah when all history ends.[17] The
Widow is clearly Cleopatra. Elsewhere in the *Leaves* are
passages that have been taken as the work of some learned
Alexandrian Jew who had studied Book II; here she is
thrice called Widow.[18] Efforts have been made to interpret
the widow as Rome; but the symbolism does not fit. Or
as the Woman of *Revelation*, but that is too late. The term
is best understood as referring to Cleopatra's odd position
as a sole queen, which breaks the normal Ptolemaic
custom of a wedded pair. There might even be a reference
to her as the Widow of Caesar. In that case the Mighty

King of the second prophecy cited above might be
Caesar become Divus rather than Supreme God. Cleopatra, in bringing Caesarion forward, may have stressed
her role as Caesar's widow; indeed that was the logical
interpretation of her position. We must also remember
that Cleopatra as widow of Caesar could become identified
with Isis the widow of Osiris, whom she sought with
lamentations—Caesarion thus in turn becoming the son
Horos who would revenge and justify his murdered
Father. In the speeches of the resurrection-mystery of
Osiris as inscribed on the walls at Dendera, Edfu, and
Philai we find the following:

[*Kheri Heb priest*] Where is he? where are you?
[*Woman*] I weep because he was forsaken. I invoke heaven
and I cry to the being in the Underworld. I clothed the naked
and dressed the divine body. The great ones lament you . . . .
[*Kheri Heb*] O Osiris, Khenti Amenti, rise up, raise yourself
and stand up in Netit. Your son Horos greets you with
life and happiness, you remaining among the gods, Osiris,
You hate sleep, you do not love darkness. To you it is
horrible to die. It is the thing abominated by your Ka. You
shall be justified, you shall be justified. Tua-Mut-f comes to
inspect you and he will hurl down your enemies on your left
side. . . .
[*Woman*] I have travelled through the land and traversed
Nunu and searched the stream. I lament with tears because
you were forsaken. . . .[19]

The scroll-image comes ultimately from *Isaiah*, but the
phrase may have been wellknown; it recurs in the passage
cited above from *Revelation*. Persian and Jewish ideas
indeed stress the fiery worldend, while the Greek concern
is rather with *homonoia*, the advent of true human unity.

In our first example we were told that Necessity, *Anangke*, was to flee; the term might merely repeat *peniē*, hardship, but more likely it refers to the sky-fate, read in the stars, which oppressed men with a burden of irrevocable destiny—the conviction of fatality coming largely from the heavy sense of social fetters and oppressions that seemed impossible of alleviation. Note in the Isis-Aretology of Kyme, 'I conquer Fate', and 'Fate hearkens to me'. In the *Golden Ass* Isis tells Lucius that if he is obedient to her commandments, 'know that I alone may prolong your days beyond the Time that your Fate has appointed'.[20]

In the vision of worldend under the Widow the casting of gold and silver into the sea has been taken to refer to Cleopatra's exactions in building up her fleet before Actium; and the passage attributed to the disgruntled Jews of Alexandria. But this analysis is wrong-headed. The reject of gold as money-power is an essential prelude to the golden age of peace; and the passage is Greek, not Jewish. However in Book XI Cleopatra does appear as the Widow in pejorative terms, and Book VIII has a passage that seems a conflation of two or three worldends. There are six sections. The stars fall down, new stars appear, with a comet, sign of war and calamity. Happy is the man who does not live under the reign of a Woman of Joy, but who lives when a Holy Child chains up the wicked, opens the abyss, and shelters mankind in a wooden dwelling—a sort of ark? With the descent of the Tenth Generation into Hades, the woman's power will reach its height; through her God will bring evil to its limit and she will have a royal robe and crown. Prodigies will accumulate, the sun turn livid, the stars leave the sky, tempests rage, the dead rise up, the lame run, the deaf hear, the dumb speak. There comes an Age of Gold with all things held in common. God's Judgement arrives.

The text is certainly confused. The stars fall twice, and there is no person or event to usher in the Age of Gold. It seems best to suppose two intercalations: one by a Jew, who opposes the Holy Babe (Messiah) to Cleopatra, and another by a Christian recalling *Matthew* xi 5 (*Luke* vii 22). If this is so, we may further conjecture that the Jew changed *kala* (fine or beautiful things) into *kaka* (evils) in the account of Cleopatra; for *kaka* contradicts the passage's tenor. We then get as the original text something like:

> All the confronting stars fall into the sea,
> many new stars arise in turn, and the star
> of radiance named by men the Comet, a sign
> of emerging troubles, of war and of disaster.
> But when the Tenth Generation goes down to Hades,
> there comes a Woman's great power. By her will God
> multiply fine things, when royal dignity
> and crown she takes. A whole year then will be
> prospering eternity.
> Common for all then is life, and all property.
> Earth will be free for all, unwalled, unfenced,
> and bringing forth more fruits than ever before
> it will yield springs of sweet wine, white milk,
>   and honey. . . .

The Comet here must be that taken to announce the deification of Caesar and the earth's last age, the advent of the Tenth Generation. The Golden Age is imaged in Dionysiac terms. An interesting suggestion is that, in the line about the Year, *epios* (gentle, favourable, prospering) should be amended to *nepios* and the phrase should be taken to mean 'the whole universe is still a cradle, is an infant's place or realm'. This reading may well be correct if the sentence has strayed out of a context dealing with the Holy Child. Herakleitos, centuries before, had declared in his enigmatic way, 'Time', *aion*, the word here used for age or eternity, 'is a Child moving counters in play; the Kingdom is a Child's'. *Basileia*, kingdom, reappears in the Messianic context of the Gospels as the Kingdom of God.

We may note that in such distracted times as the years following Caesar's death there was no lack of crazed or inspired persons ready to start disseminating rumours of worldend or of saviour-advents. Dion says that the news of the naval victory over Sextus Pompey was announced by one of the soldiers at Rome 'who had become possessed by some god on the very day of the victory'—he it was who laid his sword at the feet of Capitoline Jupiter to signify that the time of wars was over. (In such a gesture there is more than a mere foretelling aspect; the gesture also has a magical compelling force that ensures the success of the prophecy—or so it is felt.) Again, when in 38 the Hut of Romulus was burned: 'A statue of Virtue before one of the Gates fell on its face, and certain persons, inspired by the Mother of the Gods, declared the goddess was angry. So the Sibylline Books, consulted, were found to say the same thing, prescribing that the statue be taken to the sea and purified in the waters.' The goddess was taken far out into deep water and stayed there a long time. The Romans were scared 'and did not recover their spirits till four palmtrees sprang up round her temple and in the Forum'. Further, even comparatively unimportant persons appear as marked out by charismatic signs. Salvidienus Rufus, put to death by Octavian on suspicion of treason, 'was of most obscure origin, and once while he was tending his flocks a flame had issued from his head'.[21]

Prophets seem indeed to show up in genuine Roman circles, if we may identify the diviner and astrologer C. Fonteius Capito with a man who was a member of the learned Nigidian group (to which scholars like Varro and L. Tarutius Firmanus belonged). At the age of thirty-six he became a *pontifex*, perhaps at the time when Lepidus was made chief pontiff. He was an Antonian, as we saw earlier. Antony seems to have gained him another office, perhaps the tribunate, and Capito was in his retinue when he went east. In 37 he had some part in the temporary reconciliation of the two triumvirs; then he returned to Egypt and later went with Cleopatra to Syria. In 33 he became *consul suffectus* (substitute). His surviving fragments show him interested in divination and calendars. Perhaps following the expert on Etruscan antiquities, Tarquitius Priscus, he told how Tarchon first learned the lore of the *haruspices* from Tages, who rose out of the earth which he (Tarchon) was ploughing. A passage cited by John Lydos from his works runs:

The Moon [? Sun] in Capricorn. If it thunders in daytime, a tyrant will arise in lands from the Narrow [? Red] Sea to the Nile, but will fail in his enterprise. There will be a scarcity, especially in provisions. The Nile will subside, children will be at odds with their parents, and there will be trouble with the rulers in some districts. The Persians and the nations of western Europe will lead a careless life.

If it thunders at night, barbarian races will attack one

another, and those [or, foundations] of the Roman Peace will
be shaken because of some doctrines [or, decrees]; the
enemies will occupy some districts of the State for a short
period. Rulers will appear from the West and conduct public
affairs, in a lawless way. Most people will be unhappy, the
winter storms severe, and there will be shipwrecks and
perilous tossing of the sea.[22]

The tone of the writing suggests a date after the break
with Octavian. Note that the two enemies seem the
Persians (Parthians) and the nations of Western Europe
(Italy under Octavian).

Among the masses the hope of Rome's downfall and
the consequent establishment of a golden age went on
being asserted in Sibylline prophecies. In what seems a
Jewish declaration we are told that 'enemies will make
peace, for gold the cause of quarrels will be abolished'.

No longer will there be guileful gold and silver,
no settling of the earth, no slavery with its toils,
but one comradeship, one way for the kindly people,
all things in common and an equal life among men.
The evil on earth will be driven into the divine sea
and then coming near is the Harvest of Mankind.
A mighty fate will be ordained to complete these things.
No traveller then will have tales to tell of the sea
and the race of men will cease from its destruction
and then the Holy Race will wield the whole earth's sceptre
for all the Ages together with strong Fathers. . . .[23]

The Holy Race suggests the Jews, who at times were
called, or called themselves, the Pious (*Eusebees*) in the
Sibylline Leaves. But indeed any sectarian group, sure that
it held the secret of the universe and the right way of life,
might use the phrase. The Harvest of Mankind is a term

often used for the destruction of the human race (or of the Gentiles); after the Harvest comes a Vintage in which the grapes are cast into the great winepress of the Wrath of God. Here it seems to mean the end of all but the chosen people; but it comes oddly after the establishment of peace on all the earth and has perhaps been interpolated— if it belongs to this section, it should come just before the declaration about the Holy Race. The Fathers are the Patriarchs, certainly a Jewish touch.

A passage in Book VIII depicts the Sibyl prophesying the end of Rome, addressing her and saying that she has fulfilled her destiny, her number. *Romē* as numerals represents 948. If we take the traditional date of her foundation as 754 B.C., we are thus brought to 198 A.D. But some lines of Book XII state that Alexandria will supply Rome with corn for 948 years. Taking 332 B.C. as the date of Alexandria's foundation, we are brought to 617 A.D. when in fact Egypt was conquered by Chosroes the Persian. So the prophet must have been writing after that date, recalling an earlier prophecy that The Persians will never defeat the Romans while the Alexandrian corn export goes on. The importance attributed to Egypt and its corn supplies shows that many of the verses were composed in Alexandria.[24]

Rome appears as the Lion. Thus, after the Persian victory,

No more will the Lion stretch out his long spear against all men and bathe in the fourfooted suckling's blood.

The division of east and west then appears right till the end, and the Greek-speaking masses look to the east for a

Saviour. Only after that 'the two lordships of the earth shall be subject to one Lord'. Egypt continues to be seen as a source of plenty:

> There is a land bounteous in gifts of food to men
> a plainland bordered by the river Nile
> which cools with breezes [or guards over] all Libya and
> Aithiopia.

And once again the implacable hatred of the masses for the oppressive State is asserted:

> For then at last shall he bow his neck under the yoke
> of bondage, he who till then as suits his name
> was Head of freeborn men and was used to ply
> his council uncontrolled, a nightly theme of song.
> Such servitude shall the Wise King impose.[25]

We may also note Isis recurring in a mutilated Egyptian prophecy under the Empire, probably of the second century A.D., which is directed, at least in part against the Jews. 'Unhappy Egypt . . . men . . . sacred things [temples] . . . placed. So go against the Jews (?) . . . Your city become desolate . . . of horses [?stable] . . . shall be . . . lawless . . . and in place of property the lawbreakers . . . cast out of Egypt by the Wrath of Isis . . . they shall settle, a prophet shall have no office (?) . . . serve the divine . . . to the greatest.'[26]

The Wrath of Isis causing the expulsion of defiled people (Jews) from Egypt is mentioned in a passage from Chairemon's *History of Egypt* cited by Josephos. So we may assume that the Jews are here also those outcast. The period may be that of the anti-Jewish tumults at the time of Trajan; but the theme of the expulsion was an old one,

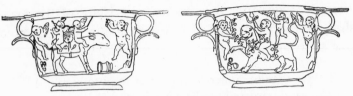

Reliefs on the Boscoreale cups with Dionysiac animal symbolism.

going back at least as far as Hekataios of Abdera and
continuing to Justinus and Tacitus.

Before we pass on we may note how animal symbolism,
sometimes via the stars, gets into the prophecies and also
into everyday propaganda. One Sibylline poem, *The
Battle of the Stars*, expresses the earthly wars by conflicts
among the zodiacal constellations. Orion and his Dog
join in, and at last heaven throws them all out; they fall
to earth and start off the final conflagration. In the
scrimmage we meet the New Bull fighting and killing
Capricorn. The New Bull must be the New Dionysos,
Antony, and Capricorn is Octavian, who took that sign
for his badge because of some connection with his
horoscope. We hear also of 'the Virgin charged with the
fate of the Twins in the Ram', who may be Cleopatra with
her twins; Alexander Helios might be linked with the
Ram, under which Alexander the Great is born in the
Romance (because of his link with ram-headed Ammon).

At Pompeii on a pilaster outside a brothel, between
Bacchus with panther on one side, and Mercury on the
other, we see an ithypallic Ass raping a Lion, for which
act he gets a crown from a palm-holding Victory. As
Antony was the Lion, we may take the Ass for Octavian—
recalling the victory-ass Nikon who gave him a good
omen before Actium. (It is perhaps only an odd coinci-

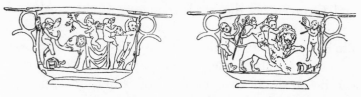

Reliefs on the Boscoreale cups with Dionysiac animal symbolism

dence that the Actium anniversary, 2 September, was close to the Egyptian Day of the Ass, since the first of the month Thoth was 30 August. This collocation has been suggested as the reason for the Egyptianising Caligula detesting the Actium anniversary; but his emotion had a more complex basis.) Elsewhere in the town we find a graffito *Taurus Octavianus Victoriae*: Bull Octavian linked with Victory. Similar imagery appears on silver cups from the treasure at Boscoreale not far away. One has a lion and elephant figured in it; a young drunken satyr rides the lion in orgiastic pose, while a young Love guides it; the elephant is ridden by two loves. The scenes have many Dionysiac elements, *e.g.* masks and a chest from which emerges the head of a serpent. The theme is perhaps Antony the Lion as the lover of Cleopatra. (The elephant might represent Africa; but it was also connected with Alexander and was an emblem of Ptolemaic power.) A second cup shows a pantheress ridden by a child Bacchos, over whom a Love holds a parasol; another Love leads the beast while a third holds her tail. The elements of the scene are again Dionysiac. On the other side of this cup however an ass brings in a note of discord, standing with neck outthrust and ears lowered, resisting the efforts of Loves to make him move. Here we seem to have the Dionysiac love-theme with Cleopatra as the pantheress and Octavian as the recalcitrant ass. If this analysis is correct, the cups must have been made in Alexandria in the last year or two before the city was taken; they were brought to Italy as Roman booty. But in any event there can be no doubt that this kind of political allegory was deeply imbedded in the art of the period. Augustan propaganda pervades the choice of theme in the mythological pictures on the Pompeian walls; and the dolphins and ships that appear profusely in the Pompeian Fourth Style have their Actium background.[27]

Astrological ideas were certainly entangled with the imagery of Antony as Lion fighting with Octavian as Ass-Bull. We can feel this aspect if we consider these lines from Seneca's play *Hercules Mad*:

> See where the fierce Lion,
> my earliest Labour, glitters up in the sky,
> flaming with wrath and threatening with his fangs.
> Surely he'll now devour some shining star,
> With jaws gaped wide and menacing he stands,
> breathing out fire and over his fiery throat
> tossing his mane. With one great leap he soon
> will overpass the fruitful autumn's stars
> and those that freezing winter lifts to view,
> and kill with furious lunge the vernal Bull.

And there seems little doubt indeed that Manilius, writing as an Augustan partisan, had Antony in mind when he wrote of the Lion constellation and went straight on, via a passage that reminds us of the Fourth Eclogue, to exalt Libra, the birth-sign of Octavian.

> If, at a child's birth, the voracious Lion
> raises his jaws above the water and gaping

climbs up the sky, that child will wrong his father,
will wrong his children whom he will not leave
aught of the wealth he heaps. He'll swallow it all.
His appetite, his deadly greed will swell
until, insatiate, he devours the whole.
Nothing he'll leave for his funeral, his tomb.
    Erigone, Virgin, who made pristine Justice
once reign, who left the world when it corrupted,
gives, at her rising, sovranty of power,
creates the giver of law and sacred right,
the chaste pure minister of holy shrines.
    When the Balance, sign of autumn, starts to rise
on the horizon, blessed the child who's born
under her beam's perfect equipoise.
He'll be the lord determining life or death,
he'll conquer lands, laws he'll impose, before him
kingdoms and towns will tremble; his will alone
will rule; and after earth remain for him
the judgements of heaven.[28]

Leo is there the omnivorous Lion-Antony of Octavian
propaganda, while Libra's child seems unmistakably
Octavian–Augustus. Erigone is the Virgo constellation,
which is identified with Astraea, Justice; Manilius is
thus making an astrological use of the Virgo of Virgil's
Eclogue while diverting the the whole of its glorifying
prophecy on to the Augustan line.[29] (Virgo appears as
Justice at the turning-point of a new creation in the
Dionysiaka of Nonnos.) The interpretations here are however complicated by uncertainties of Manilius' date; he
may well have begun under Augustus and continued
writing under Tiberius. It is suggested that Tiberius had
Libra as his constellation, and so the passage about the
Balance may refer to him rather than Augustus. But such
obscurities do not affect the general point of the Manilian

lines. The madly prodigal Lion gives way at the rise of Justice (the new dispensation), and the Augustan rule is firmly established. After the *princeps* has finished his term on earth, he ascends as a star to rule in heaven.[30]

But we can best end this series by looking again at Lactantius, who in his *Divine Institutes*, written or published under Constantine the Great, attempts a conflation of Christian ideas of worldend with those of Hystaspes and the Sibyls; we then see in him the convergence of all the prophetic traditions we have been tracing. In his picture are united the two strands: that of the Virgilian utopia, the Saturnian Earth, and that of the Sibylline redemption with its reversal of existing values. He concludes his last book with the account of worldend:

> First of all Egypt will pay the penalties of her foolish superstitions and will be covered with blood as with a river . . .
>
> [With the fall of Rome] the government will return to Asia and the East will again bear rule and the West be reduced to servitude. . . .[31]

Hystaspes is here his authority. In the next chapter he deals with the earth's devastation and its omens, twice citing the Sibyl:

> And that nothing may be wanting to the evils of men and the earth, the trumpet shall be heard from heaven, which the Sibyl foretells in this manner: 'The trumpet from heaven shall utter its wailing cry.' And all will tremble and quake at that mournful sound. . . .
>
> The world shall be disfigured and deserted: which is thus expressed in verses of the Sibyl: 'The world shall be emptied of beauty through men's destruction.'

He goes on to tell of the coming of the False Prophet (a

King from Syria), the hardships of the Righteous, and the Prophet's end. Again he cites Hystaspes, Hermes Trismegistus, and the Sibyls. One Sibyl stated:

> He also will come, seeking to break the City of the Blest;
> and a King will be sent against him from the gods
> who will slaughter all the great kings and chief men.
> Then another Judgment will come to men from the Immortal.

He cited the prophecy about the King from the Sun, which we have already considered. A third Sibyl has said:

> He'll do away with the intolerable yoke
> of slavery set on our necks and he'll do away
> with impious laws and with all violent chains.

Then, telling of Christ come to judgement, he cites the Sibyl again three times. A sword will fall from heaven. 'When he comes there'll be fire and dark in midst of the blackness of night.' And 'mortals will break to bits the images and all the wealth, and the works that the hands of the gods have made will be burned'. Next, on the Judgement, he cites the Sibyl three times. 'And the gaping earth will show Tartarean chaos, and all kings will come to the judgement of God.' 'Rolling along the heavens, I'll open the earth's caverns, and then I'll raise the dead and let go Fate and all the Sting of Death. . . .' In the chapter on the Resurrection he cites the Sibyl, and in that on a renewed world he has six citations. But this time he also cites at length Virgil's Fourth Eclogue. Here are two of the passages from the Sibyl, which closely accord with the Saturnian picture:

> Wolves on the mountains won't contend with the lambs
> and lynxes will crop grass beside the kids.

Boars will feed by the calves and all the flocks.
Serpents will sleep with babes orphaned of mothers . . .
And then God will give great joy to men,
for the earth and the trees and the numberless flocks
     of the earth
will yield to men the true fruit of the vine,
sweetness of honey, whiteness of milk, and corn
the best of all things for mortals. . . .

The sacred land of the pious will produce
all of these things: streams of honey from rocks
and from the fountains, and for all the just
the milk of ambrosia will be flowing. . . .

We have come back once more through the Sibyl, to the
milk and honey of the Dionysiac paradise. The hopes of
regeneration from above and from below, from the level
of state-power and from that of the rebellious masses,
have been given an illusory unity for the moment under
the Constantinean synthesis, with its accord of State and
Church.

Actium

As 31 came in, Octavian had his position strengthened;
he was consul. He should have shared the office with
Antony; but he now used his power to have M. Valerius
Corvinus set in the place of his denounced colleague. In
a few months, with spring coming on, he was ready to act.
And inevitably there was a crop of omens. 'Pisaurum, a
city colonised by Antony near the Adriatic, was swallowed
by a chasm in the earth. From one of Antony's marble
statues near Alba sweat oozed for many days, keeping on
though wiped off. In Patrai, during Antony's stay, the
Herakleion was destroyed by lightning; at Athens the
Dionysos in the Battle of the Giants was dislodged by
winds and carried down into the Theatre [of Dionysos].
Antony had linked himself with Herakles in lineage and
with Dionysos in mode of life; he was called the New
Dionysos. The same storm struck at Athens the colossal
figure of Eumenes and Attalos, on which his name had
been inscribed, and laid them low, only those two out of
many. Also, the admiral's-ship of Cleopatra, named

Antonios, was marked with a dire sign: swallows made their nest under its stern, but others attacked them, drove them out, and destroyed their nestlings.'[1] All omens against Antony, the product of Octavian's party. More impartiality appears in the tale of an artisan at Rome who trained two ravens, one to say, 'Hail Caesar victorious *imperator*', the other, 'Hail victorious *imperator* Antony'.

Antony had lost the initiative and never regained it. Not till the autumn of 32 had he moved from Athens to Patrai, Cleopatra with him, and there he struck coins' of her as Isis: another detail that Octavian could use to prove that the east was advancing on Italy. Antony tried in vain to assert himself in coins struck in the east which called him triumvir and consul for 31, with Victory holding out a garland on the reverse. About September 32 his troops had reached the coast of the Ionian Sea. Octavian left Maecenas in charge of Rome and Italy, with all disturbances sternly repressed; his naval squadrons guarded the shores of the western provinces; Cornelius Gallus, the poet who had celebrated Cytheris as Lycoris in his elegies, was sent to protect Africa. As soon as navigation opened, Octavian crossed to Greece with his fleet and transports. He carried with him a large number of senators, more than counterbalancing those with Antony; he may also have wanted to keep them under surveillance.

Antony's fleet, which had picked up more detachments at Kephallenia and Zakynthos, now held eight squadrons of the line (each 60 ships); one squadron was led by Cleopatra's flagship; and there were some five scoutships to each squadron. Over 500 ships in all, with 125,000 to 150,000 men as crews. He had set himself to outbuild

Octavian in size of ship. The largest ships had belts of squared ironbound timber to prevent ramming, powerful beaks, and heavy catapults mounted on deck-towers. (Agrippa meanwhile had armed his ships with boarding-grapnels shot from catapults.) On land Antony had nineteen legions, seven of the old army of Macedonia, and twelve, weakened, that had been in Media: 60,000 to 65,000 tough soldiers, with light-armed men, mostly Asian, perhaps 70,000 to 75,000 at most. Of cavalry he had about 12,000, the remnant of his own forces plus detachments from the client-kings. That Cleopatra could feed and supply such a large host shows her great resources. Of the other eleven legions, four were in Cyrenaica, the rest shared between Alexandria, Syria, and the Macedonian frontier.

There were some disturbances in the rear, which however he could not at the moment deal with. Sparta, where the ruler's father had been executed by him, joined Octavian, as did Lappa and Kydonia in Crete; Berytos revolted from Cleopatra during the winter. Further, Antony had a very extended line to defend and keep in contact with, a line running from Korkyra in the north, through Ambrakia, to Cyrene in the south. He also had long supply-lines. As his winter-H.Q. and as rallying-point, he had selected the Bay of Actium (Aktion) near Ambrakia. His host wintered on the line from Korkyra to Methone in Messenia, with the biggest section gathered on the Actium peninsula—the southern of two promontories flanking the narrow entry to the Ambrakian Gulf. He needed a long and wellguarded system to assure that the Egyptian supply-ships reached him, rounding Cape Tainaron and coming up round the Peloponnesos.

Stations stood at key-points, at Leukas and so on, with Methone as the most southern, commanded by Bogud (who had been driven from Mauretania by his brother Bocchos, acting for Octavian).

The Actium position was not a good one, open to attack from the sea and leaving free all the best land-routes to Macedonia and the east. No doubt Cleopatra chose it as the best site from which to cover Egypt. She knew well enough that Antony's heart was not in the war: he would not take the initiative but he would fight his hardest if attacked. And perhaps he himself wanted at all costs to get Octavian out of Italy, so that he left the Via Egnatia open and withdrew during the winter from Korkyra, allowing Octavian to get across to Dyrrhachion from south Italy. (Fighting in an invaded Italy, he would feel an eastern intruder; fighting in Greece, he would feel that once again, as at Pharsalos or Philippi, a civil war between Romans was in progress.) Perhaps he also considered that Octavian lacked money and supplies for a long war and would be driven to seek a battle decision under disadvantageous terms. But, even so, why did he make no effort to attack Octavian's ships during the crossing? He did not use his long-prepared fleet till too late. In so impetuous a commander as Antony, this behaviour suggests a mind confused by the camp-debates, unable to trust its own ardent impulses, and cut across by hesitations at the crucial moment of action. However, we may argue that he wanted the decisive battle to occur on land, where he would be incomparably more at ease than afloat. However all that may be, he allowed Octavian to land without any challenge. Turullius' coins show that Antony won some sort of engagement, since he was hailed *Imperator* for the fourth time. But our texts give no explanation.

If Antony was averse from using his fleet, Agrippa was not. Octavian had taken undefended Korkyra. Agrippa diverted Antony's attention by attacking Methone, where Bogud died, and at the same time put himself in a position to threaten the Egyptian supply-line. Octavian landed some 80,000 infantry at Torone in Epeiros without opposition and marched south to the bay where most of Antony's fleet lay. Cleopatra tried to belittle the movement with a joke: 'What does it matter if Octavian is sitting in the Ladle (*toryne*)?' As a *toryne* was used for stirring things that boiled, she was suggesting that he would fall into the seething pot.[2]

Octavian indeed tried a combined land-and-sea attack, and found that it was not easy to force Antony's position. The entrance to the Gulf, not more than half a mile across, was guarded by towers with heavy artillery along the shores, and his ships could not get in. Antony hurried up with his land-forces and pitched his main camp on the southern of the two promontories near the temple of Apollo Aktios.

Octavian, it has been argued, had over 400 ships, mostly the heavy kind with which he had beaten Sextus, but apparently only the usual number of light fast scouts, Liburnians (so called after the pirates of Liburnia in Illyricum). He could have swollen his fleet much more, but Agrippa had evidently decided that 400 were enough. The question of the respective sizes of the fleets, however, is difficult to settle. Plutarch says that at the outbreak of war Antony had not less than 500 ships; Octavian (cited by Plutarch) claims that he captured 300 enemy ships—

and this detail, given after the account of the battle, seems
to mean the total then taken, not the total for the war. But
Florus says Antony had less than 200 ships in the fight,
and Orosius gives him 170; Dion cites no figures but
implies that Antony's fleet was the bigger. (Orosius'
number has been explained as omitting Cleopatra's
squadron, which would bring his account up to the same
level as that of Florus.) It has further been pointed out
that Antony had detachments at Leukas and Patrai as well
as at strongpoints guarding his line of communication
with Egypt. And he had already lost some ships: Livy
speaks of a naval encounter before Actium and Velleius
says there were two such clashes. Also Antony, burned
some of his ships before sailing out, through lack of
rowers (say Plutarch and Dion).

To buttress the case that he had some 400 ships in the
battle, it is held that Orosius was citing figures for the
right wing, which he mistook for the whole fleet. A
dubious argument; the right wing never functioned, as
far as we know, as a separate unit before the battle.
Orosius, or rather his source, did not forget to add up the
two divisions of Octavian's fleet: that stationed at
Tarentum under Agrippa and that under Octavian at
Brundisium—divisions which in fact did at first operate
separately—and thus gave the total number as 230
rostratae and 30 without *rostra* (curved prow-ends or
beaks). Probably the same source underlay Plutarch's
figure of 250. Florus says that Octavian had 400 ships, and
seems correct. There remains however a good way of
checking the numbers: the amount of soldiers taken
aboard. Plutarch says Antony put in 20,000 legionaries
and 2,000 archers: a force appropriate for some 170 ships.

386

Octavian, who on the whole had smaller ships, embarked eight legions and five praetorian cohorts, perhaps 37,000 men, presumably some light-armed troops as well. It seems certain then that Octavian had a much larger fleet in the battle.[3]

A contemporary relief in grey marble, found in the temple of Fortuna at Praeneste, shows the prow of a battleship, perhaps a four-decker. On the prow stands a castle (a tower used as artillery-platform); an officer in body-cuirass and a marine have climbed out for attack; other marines crowd the deck. The ship is certainly Libyan; for the big land-crocodile, carved on the prow, is emblem of that land—thus a crocodile appears on coins of Canidius who commanded Antony's land-army; and the snake-encircled trident of one of the marines is also a Libyan ensign. The slab is a corner-block, part of a large frieze; its style is rather heavy, but attempts to depict many postures that involve foreshortenings. Perhaps the relief was a translation into stone of the triumphal paintings carried in procession and displayed afterwards, no doubt in some public place. Our crocodile-ship was the sort of thing that would have been on show at the Actium Triumph.

But to return to the campaign. By the time Antony got his army on to the peninsula, Octavian had fortified his position and built long walls to link it with the roadstead of Komaros, while Agrippa had taken the isle of Leukas and destroyed the squadron there. Now Octavian could blockade the Gulf, as far as galleys could blockade, and prevent the cornships getting in. Agrippa proceeded to worsen Antony's position by taking Patrai and Corinth; Antony was cut off from the Peloponnesos and his large host began to feel the pinch. He made a sortie with his fleet. The dynast Tarkondimotos was killed. This fact has been taken to show that he was grudging legionaries to the ships, hoping to force a land-battle and win it.

Next he crossed from Actium and camped right in front of Octavian; his infantry he shipped up the Gulf while his cavalry rode round it. He was hoping to reverse the situation and cut off Octavian's water-supply—his one weak point. But Octavian refused to be lured into a pitched battle; he said that he wanted to spare Roman blood. In fact he was afraid of such a confrontation, but felt sure that he could wear Antony down. Antony's attack failed. His cavalry, forming the northern or outer wing of his encircling forces, let him down; two dynasts, Rhoimetalkes of Thrace and Deiotaros of Paphlagonia, went over to Octavian. To the former, who abused Antony, Octavian coldly replied, 'I like treason, but I don't like traitors'. Antony tried to mass more cavalry and led the second assault in person. This time his man Amyntas went over to the enemy with 2,000 first-rate Galatian horsemen. The dynasts may well have been suspicious of the claims that a victorious Cleopatra would make, but most likely they were mainly moved by the recognition that Antony, with his divided councils, was doomed to lose. Antony realised that he was frustrated on land and returned to Actium. Now he was again blockaded. On the flat swampy ground his cooped-up men suffered from fever and malaria as well as from hunger. Press gangs might bring in more rowers, but nothing could alleviate the condition of the troops. Plutarch here gives us one of those rare anecdotes which shows us vividly the common man caught up in the turmoil of great events. Many

Greek cities were hard hit by lack of food on account of Antony's requisitions:

'They were in a miserable plight and had been stripped of money, slaves, and beasts-of-burden. Anyhow, my great-grandfather Nikarchos used to tell how all his fellow-citizens were forced to carry on their shoulders a stipulated measure of wheat down to the sea at Antikyra and how the pace was quickened by the whip. They had got one load down in this way, the second was already measured out, when word was brought of Antony's defeat. This was the salvation of the city; for at once his stewards and soldiers decamped, and the citizens divided the grain among themselves.'[4]

But even the expedient of bringing food on men's backs over the Aitolian mountain-tracks was threatened when Octavian sent a detachment eastwards. Desertions increased. Antony tried to deter his followers from escaping by harsh treatment of runaways caught. He had a senator Postumius and an Arab prince, Iamblichos of Emesa, executed, but only made things worse. Ahenobarbus, ill, slipped off to die in peace, infuriated with Cleopatra. Dellius followed. Antony was upset by the loss of his friend Ahenobarbus and tried to joke the matter away by saying that he'd been longing to see his mistress Nais at Rome; and he generously, despite Cleopatra's protests, sent his baggage and attendants after him. Plutarch says that Ahenobarbus, 'as if repenting when his lack of faith and his treachery had become known, straightway died'.[5]

There was general distrust. But the tale that Antony was afraid of being poisoned by Cleopatra and had his food and drink tasted, is certainly Octavian propaganda. It went on: Cleopatra threw some flowers from a garland

round her head into his wine, then as he was about to
drink, she stopped him. Calling for a condemned criminal,
she gave him the wine. The man dropped dead. Cleopatra
pointed out how easily she could murder Antony, despite
the precautions, if she wanted to.

The blockade went on for four months. Antony knew
that he must somehow break out or be slowly annihilated.
At the end of August 31 a council was held. Canidius
wanted to abandon the ships, retire into Macedonia, gain
reinforcements from Dacia and the east, and then force
Octavian into open battle. This plan must have appealed
to Antony, though he would have disliked the heavy blow
that a retreat would inflict on his prestige. Anyhow he
ended by supporting Cleopatra's insistence that the fleet,
to which she had contributed so much, must be used—
even if the landforces had to withdraw. A rallying-point
in Macedonia was not the sort of thing she would like;
she preferred a battle by sea, and then, if necessary, a
breakthrough back to Egypt, where fresh plans could be
prepared. Octavian learned of the decision from deserters.

Perhaps if a decisive use of the fleet had been attempted
earlier, Cleopatra's reliance on a sea-battle might have had
better results but even then only if she and Antony had
had an admiral as experienced and resourceful as Agrippa.
She was right however in her contention that to abandon
the fleet would be to give Octavian free access to the east
and to Egypt; he would then have complete control of the
seas. A largescale breakthrough would at least prevent
that. Through losses and desertions the fleet needed to
take on considerable bodies of legionaries to make up the
fighting sections of the crews. Canidius did not like the
depletion of his landforces, but Antony sided with

Cleopatra. Dion mentions at this point the omens of the swallows and the statues, adding that 'milk and blood together had dripped from beeswax'. He says that the omens scared Cleopatra, whose fears infected Antony; hence a decision to flee under pretence of staging a sea-battle.[6] This story is rank propaganda, as is Plutarch's picture of Antony broken by her mixture of cowardice and treachery. The exchange of vituperations seems still to have been going on. If we may trust Pliny, Octavian issued an attack that hurt Antony so much, 'shortly before the battle of Actium he vomited that *volumen*' (roll, book), his reply.[7]

No doubt the sort of things that Octavian wrote were those which Dion puts into his mouth as a speech before the battle of Actium. The whole stress is laid on Cleopatra. Shall the Romans who have conquered the world 'be despised and trodden underfoot by an Egyptian woman?' and so on. The enemy are Egyptians who 'worship reptiles and beasts as gods, who embalm their own bodies to give them the semblance of immortality', and, worst of all 'are slaves to a woman and not to a man'. As for Antony, who would not weep to see him, 'the man twice consul, often imperator, to whom was committed with me the management of public affairs—now that he has left all his ancestral habits of life, has emulated all alien or barbarian customs, pays no honour to us or the laws or his fathers' gods, but gives homage to that creature as if she were some Isis or Selene, calling her children Helios and Selene, and finally taking for himself the title of Osiris or Dionysos, and, on top of all that, making gifts of whole islands and parts of continents as though he were master of the whole earth and the whole sea'.[8] He says that he has

Naval battle of Actian type from Pompeian wall-painting.

not declared war because of the insult to Octavia by Antony's preference of the Egyptian Woman; and he has tried to treat Antony differently than Cleopatra, hoping that a Roman citizen might come to his senses. But Antony 'is heedless or mad or bewitched by that accursed woman, and so he pays no heed to our generosity or kindness, but as that woman's slave he undertakes the war and its self-chosen dangers on her behalf and against us and his country'. Antony then is to be treated as an Egyptian himself, a mere gymnasiarch, a cymbal-player at Kanopos, become hopelessly effeminate—as was proved by his failure against Parthia.

Plutarch says that a slave-deserter told Octavian how Antony went up and down between the long walls connecting camp and sea. So a party of soldiers was sent to lie in ambush, but they acted too soon and grabbed the man in front of Antony, while Antony escaped by running off.[9] The time was now nearing for the fleet to sail out. Antony had all the Egyptian ships but sixty burned, keeping the biggest and best of those 'with ten banks of oars'. A centurion, scarred from many battles fought for Antony, burst out as his master passed: '*Imperator*, why do you distrust these wounds and put your hopes in

Naval battle of Actian type from Pompeian wall-painting.

wretched logs of wood? Let Egyptians and Phoenicians fight by sea, but give us land where we're used to stand and conquer or die.' Antony could not trust his voice; he merely encouraged the man by a gesture and a look, and went on.

At last the time came to man the ships and take to sea. The account of ancient historians, long followed by modern ones, was generally that Antony continued the sea-battle till he was demoralised by the treachery or cowardice of Cleopatra; he then abandoned the battle, deserted his men, and followed her. But Dion sets out consistently that the plan was to breakthrough and retreat; and this interpretation makes the best sense of the facts we have. There is no sign that Antony has two plans: to fight on till he won, if possible, but in the event of a bad setback to break through and sail off for Egypt.[10] Up to the time of the battle Agrippa's fleet had all along demonstrated its superiority; and Antony's refusal to be drawn earlier into a naval battle is best explained, not by irresolution, but by a realistic recognition of the extreme likelihood of himself being worsted. His fleet was not large or strong enough. He had known this months before, and he would not have changed his mind when he had to face Agrippa's ships with his own forces much weakened. He had already been beaten at sea in two or three minor engagements; he had remained shut up in the Gulf without the least attempt to hamper or stop Agrippa's movements and his important captures of Methone, Patrai, Leukas, and apparently Corinth. Velleius stresses this point by saying that the capture of Leukas was done 'in the mouth and eyes of the Antonian fleet'. To support the thesis that Antony now seriously meant to engage in battle, we must believe that he relied on Agrippa making some signal error—a very remote possibility—or that he had devised some brilliant tactic by which he hoped to outwit the enemy. It has been suggested for example that he aimed at outflanking their left by a movement towards his own right, and at thus driving them down the wind and away from the camp.

In summer a morning wind usually blew in from the sea; about noon it shifted to northwest and blew with some force. The idea is that Antony, coming out with Octavian's fleet to seaward of him, meant to use this wind change to turn the enemy left; if he managed to break or disperse the ships there, he'd be able to starve out their camp in his turn. But we may note that in the earlier phase of this manœuvre he'd have to rely on oars to move his heavier ships, which could hardly be very mobile, especially as he was short of rowers. Also, by putting Cleopatra's squadron behind his centre, he hampered any effort to swing in from the north: that is, he began by shortening his line. It is hardly convincing to say that her ships were put at the rear to prevent desertions—and yet, as the action started, they would have had to sail in between the centre and right so as to fill the gap caused by the movement rightwards (northwards), since it would be just at that moment that desertions would be most likely to occur—and when there would have been nothing to stop the left and centre from turning tail. We may add that this tactic would have been very risky in itself, as the enemy, with faster ships coming in with the wind behind, might easily have driven into the gap and cut Antony from Cleopatra.

Relief from Praeneste with Cyrenaic ship at Battle of Actium.

The argument that Antony meant a proper battle indeed depends on the claim that after Cleopatra moved into line the centre and the left did in fact withdraw and return to harbour. The only evidence for such a thing happening lies in Horace's Ninth Epode. This opens with the cry: 'What shall I drink in joy for Caesar's Victory' at the house

of Maecenas (to whom the poem is addressed). It recalls
the rejoicings when Sextus Pompey, 'Neptune's Son,
driven from the straits, went fleeing', with his burnt-out
ships abandoned. 'Friend of false slaves, he'd threatened
Rome with bonds that from their hands he'd loosened.'
The poet then slips from Sextus to Antony: a clever
transition, for he thus equates Sextus, the leader of runaway slaves and pirates, with Antony, the leader of aliens
and un-Roman forces, and also couples the two sea-
victories.

> A Roman Soldier—posterity won't believe—
> sold as slave to a woman
> has carried stakes and arms, and has stooped to serve
> a herd of wrinkled eunuchs.
> Amid the standards of war the Sun looks down
> upon the shame of an awning.

We recall the Arretine vessels with Antony-Herakles
under a parasol. Horace goes on with an abrupt transition
from the episode of the deserting Galatian horsemen to
that of Antony's defeat at Actium:

> Then two thousand Gauls wheeled their loud steeds to us
> and sang in chorus *Caesar*,
> and the sterns of hostile ships rowed backwards to the left
> now lie hidden in the harbour.

He raises the triumph cry, *Io Triumphe*, praises Octavian,
and returns to Antony in headlong flight on the high seas:

> By land and sea the defeated now changes his cloak
> from purple into mourning.
> And gales, not his wish, bear him away to Crete
> that hundred-cities island,

or he sails for the Syrtes that the southwinds vex
or wherever the wild waves take him.
Bring cups of a larger size to me, my boy,
wine of Chios or Lesbos.
Mix for us Caecuban to put an end
to all this vomiting sickness.
My care, my fear for Caesar's future I'm glad
to drown in releasing wine.

Where is Horace as he writes: in Rome or with the fleet? He addresses Maecenas who had been left in charge of Italy and speaks of drinking in his house; but he may be referring to the future. Also we cannot be sure if Maecenas is with him or not. It is possible that Maecenas may have considered that everything was quiet on the homefront, and have come to join Octavian; but unless he was coming to discuss some urgent matter, that seems unlikely. Various troubles did crop up at Rome, for instance a plot by the son of Lepidus. Horace may have come with a letter or message from Maecenas to Octavian, and have arrived just before the battle. He certainly seems to be on the spot; and one interpretation of the Epode is as an excited poem written directly after the battle, before it was known what had happened to Antony. (Octavian had excused Horace from active service, but he still might have come as a message-carrier.)[11]

The argument that the poem refers to some earlier engagement is based on the point that after Actium the episode of the Galatian cavalry would be too trivial for mention. But that contention is weak. Horace is using the Galatian desertion as the crucial moment of Antony's defeat on land, of his failure to break Octavian with his army; he moves on to Actium as the corresponding defeat on water. But is he making a yet closer equation of the two episodes, saying that the crews deserted Antony as the horsemen did? This is an attractive suggestion, but a close consideration of the verses does not substantiate it. If Horace had wanted to bring out this point, he would surely have phrased his appositions differently, drawing a clearer parallel. A phrase that seems definitely to suggest that Horace is on board a ship is *fluentem nauseam* near the end; the meaning is not sure, but it does seem to refer to sea-sickness. If so, Horace had somehow turned up at Actium. In any event, we have here a poem written very soon after the event. Horace is describing what he has seen or what has been stated in dispatches sent to Rome immediately after it had become clear that Antony was defeated. Antony has lost; most of his ships have gone crippled or cowed back into harbour, and Antony himself has vanished into the distance.

The crux however is the term *sinistrorsum*, 'to the left'. The usual picture drawn of Antony's dispositions shows his centre stationed in front of the Gulf, with Cleopatra's squadron behind it. He had abandoned his camp on the north side of the strait, though no doubt he still kept connection with it. Otherwise that region was handed over to the enemy. The left then was to the south of the entrance. The centre and left, if returning to harbour, would move to the rear and to the right respectively. But Horace writes of ships 'rowed backwards to the left'. He is viewing the scene (whether directly or via dispatches) from the angle of Octavian's fleet; and from that angle the retreating ships, whether making for the Gulf or trying to draw off further south, went *sinistrorsum*.

Antony's aim, it seems sure, was to get away with as

many ships as possible, wreaking some damage on Octavian's fleet if he could do so without getting too embroiled. He drew his ships up in a strong defensive position near the entry to the Gulf, in close order, possibly in crescent formation, with the tip of each wing resting on the shore; Cleopatra's squadron stood in reserve to deal with the enemy if they broke through at any point. Plutarch records the instruction given to the steersman: 'To receive the attacks of the enemy as if their ships were lying quietly at anchor, and to maintain their position in the Gulf's mouth, which was narrow and difficult.'[12] These orders prove that the fleet was in some such position as we have suggested. Cleopatra's squadron was behind, mainly no doubt because it carried the army treasure: it was therefore important that its ships should not be captured or sunk. In this packed position any attack by Octavian could easily be repelled, and then the west or northwest wind could be used for the retreat. But Octavian—or, more likely Agrippa—was too shrewd; he refused to attack. Dion says that Octavian told his men, 'They are making this sally, not to fight a naval battle but to secure a retreat'. Agrippa then dissuaded Octavian from his first plan. ('He planned to let them sail by and then attack them in the rear as they fled.')[13] By simply doing nothing, while impeding Antony's movements, Octavian forced him to join in battle against his will. He had decided not to encumber his ships with masts and sails: that is, to base his tactics on holding Antony's fleet. When Antony stayed as he was in his defensive line, he did not come in to attack, as Antony expected him to do. Thus in the end Antony was forced to move from his line and to engage with Octavian's larger and more mobile fleet. Plutarch seems to suggest that the left wing moved without orders: an unlikely thing. Antony could not stay indefinitely where he was. He had either to give up his whole plan and return ignominiously to his beleaguered camp, or to sail out against Octavian. The latter lured him yet further out by drawing his line back, then extending it, so that he threatened to turn both Antony's flanks. Antony was in an increasingly untenable position. If he became too entangled in battle, he was liable to meet a heavy defeat and lose his chance of escape to Egypt with the remnant of the treasure. Dion implies that Cleopatra demoralised him by retreating too soon. But it is more than improbable that she lost her nerve and acted prematurely; at such an important moment she would have acted inflexibly according to plan. Antony seems to have given the signal for her retreat; she at once hoisted sail and got her squadron away. In her reserve position she was clear of any opposition. As the battle-line was now widely stretched out, she may well have found no difficulty in sailing through gaps. Antony then tried to follow her. But he could not extricate his flagship. He therefore boarded the first ship of the line that was free, a quinquireme, and sailed away after Cleopatra with any other ships of his squadron that could avoid the enemy. (A quinquireme was not a fast ship; it was slower than a trireme. So the charge that he changed into a fast ship to abandon his fleet and rush after Cleopatra falls down.)[14]

How many ships thus escaped we do not know; probably only a few. The extending and flanking movement of Octavian's right wing made retreat difficult for ships that were already engaged in battle. However they could do one thing: they could back into the Gulf. And this is the movement that Horace describes. Some must have been sunk or fired or captured by boarding parties. Plutarch, probably citing the *Memoirs* of Augustus, says that not more than 5,000 men were killed; we cannot check his figures. By the time that Antony got away, the afternoon was waning and the cleaning-up process must have lasted well into dusk; for we are told that Octavian stayed on board his ship all night. No doubt he wanted to leave no chance for the ships in the Gulf to slip out. This fact alone seems to give the lie to the theory of desertion; for he would not have felt such a need of vigilant action if the squadrons had deserted Antony.[15]

Two myths emerged from the battle. One was the accusation of Cleopatra's treachery, which was clearly baseless. Thus Plutarch: 'As Agrippa was extending the left wing with a view to encircling the enemy, Publicola was forced to advance against him and was separated from the centre, which fell into confusion and engaged with Arruntius [commander of Octavian's centre]. Then, though the sea-fight was still undecided and equally favourable to either side, suddenly Cleopatra's sixty ships were seen hoisting their sails for flight and making off through the midst of the combatants. For they'd been posted in the rear of the vessels which they threw into confusion as they plunged through. The enemy looked on in amazement as they saw them take advantage of the wind and make for the Peloponnesos. And now Antony exposed to all the world that he was swayed by the senti-ments, not of a commander or of a brave man, not even by his own safety, but, as someone in playful wit has said a lover's soul inhabits someone else's body, he was dragged along by the woman as if he had become incorporate with her and must go where she did. For no sooner did he see her ship sailing off than he forgot everything else, betrayed and ran away from those fighting and dying in his cause, got into a five-oared galley where Alexas the Syrian and Scellius were his only companions, and hurried after the woman who had already ruined him and was to make his ruin yet more complete.'[16]

The other myth was that Octavian had won a great seabattle instead of merely foiling in part an attempt to retreat. For this purpose it was necessary to suggest, as Dion does, that Octavian was fighting against heavy odds or that he won by using a number of light waspish Liburnians which played havoc with Antony's big warships.[17] Antony's fleet would have had its share of these light boats, which, after their introduction into Aegean warfare by King Philip in 201 B.C., had become a normal part of every fleet. One reason for stressing the role of the Liburnians seems to have been the fact that Octavian, perhaps for reasons of personal safety, was on one of them. Appian tells us, 'he himself embarked on a Liburnian, in which he sailed round the whole fleet, exhorting them to have courage. Then he lowered the general's ensign, as is usual in times of extreme danger.'[18]

The fight took place near the waters where later was fought the Battle of Lepanto.

Plutarch gives us a moving account of Antony in the moment of retreat. When he came up to Cleopatra's ship and was taken aboard, he avoided her; he did not see her nor she him. He went forward alone to the prow and sat there in silence, holding his head in his hands. At this moment Liburnians were seen coming up in pursuit. (Another detail which stresses that Antony had made no quick getaway.) Antony ordered the ship to be turned to face the pursuers and thus kept them off, except for one ship under Eurykles, a Spartan. The latter attacked vigorously and was seen on his deck brandishing a spear as if he wanted to throw it at Antony. So Antony stood up in the prow and called, 'Who is this pursuing Antony?'

Eurykles shouted back. 'I am Eurykles the son of Lachares, whom the Tyche [Fortune] of Caesar enables to avenge his father.' Antony had executed Lachares on a charge of robbery.

However Eurykles missed Antony's ship and hit the second admiral's ship; for there were two of them. His bronze beak swung the ship round sideways and he captured her as well as another ship in which was stowed the costly equipment for household use. 'When Eurykles was gone, Antony threw himself down again in the same posture and didn't stir. He spent three days alone at the prow, angry at Cleopatra or else ashamed to face her. Then he put in at Tainaron. Here Cleopatra's women at first managed to get them to speak to one another, then persuaded them to eat and sleep together.'[19] The morning after the battle Octavian took over the surrendered squadrons. He burnt the larger part of these, according to custom, and kept the beaks to decorate the monument raised where his camp stood. The surviving ships he finally stationed in a squadron at Forum Julii (Fréjus), one of the posts of the imperial fleet; the crews he transferred to his own ships. The ten ships that he dedicated to Actian Apollo each represented a type of warship, from the small Liburnians to the huge *dekteres*. The ships that sailed to Forum Julii, presumably in the autumn of 31, represented the foundation of the imperial navy; and Octavian had no doubt such a project in mind when he spared them.[20] Canidius tried to escape with the army; but though he staved off surrender for seven days, he was only negotiating terms during that time. The situation was hopeless; in the end he fled to Antony in Egypt.

Octavius was hailed *imperator* for the sixth time; and it was considered just that Cicero's son read to the Senate the dispatch announcing Antony's defeat. Some Antonians were put to death; others, including Sosius, were spared. Antony's legions were broken up and their corn distributed to hungry Greece. Veterans from both armies were sent back to Italy or scattered to various regions. Octavian wanted no mutinies. Agrippa returned to Rome to help Maecenas, while Octavian went to Athens, where he was initiated into the Mysteries, and then to Samos. But even with Agrippa at hand the veterans in Italy grew unruly, considering that they'd been cheated of booty. Agrippa sent word to Octavian, who crossed the Adriatic despite the risky weather. The latter distributed among the veterans what money he could get hold of, and took lands from communities that had favoured Antony, some of the expropriated land-holders being settled at Dyrrhachion and Phillipi. He also took land from other townships, which became military colonies. But his main way of appeasing the discontented was to dangle before them the treasure of Egypt that was soon to be his. Let them be patient and he'd meet all demands. He knew that he must gain Cleopatra's treasure or come up against considerable trouble. In the spring of 30 he went back to Asia via Corinth and Rhodes, meaning to attack Egypt by land through Syria.

The poets give us some idea of the bogey that had been summoned up of Cleopatra the whore-witch with her eastern hordes. We have already seen the lines in which Virgil depicted Antony come victorious from the Nations of the Dawn. That passage is prefaced by a contrasting account of Octavian.

> Augustus led the Italians into battle,
> with Senate and People, Homegods and Mighty Gods,
> high on the poop, his brows emitted twin beams,
> his Father's Star opened on his head.[21]

An account of Cleopatra with her monstrous gods such as barking Anubis follows. These gods fight with Neptune, Venus, Minerva, Mars; and Actian Apollo bends his bow, terrifying all the Egyptians, Arabs, and Sabaeans. Cleopatra sails wildly off, 'pale with the pallor of impending death, as she sped on the waves before the northwest gale'. The River Nile before her opens his full robe and invites the conquered into the bosom of his blue waters. From this account we could not know that there was a single Roman in the army of Antony.

Propertius in the elegy where he introduced both Semiramis and Omphale went on to attack Cleopatra. She

> as the price from her lascivious husband demanded
> the Walls of Rome and the subjected Senate.
> Vile Alexandria, land of treacherous craft,
> and Memphis bloodied often by our disasters
> where the sands stripped Pompey of his three triumphs—
> no day will ever cleanse your shame, O Rome . . .

The harlot queen of incestuous Canopus
(the sole blot on the line of Philip) dared
to set up barking Anubis against our Jove
and force our Tiber to bear the threats of Nile,
silence the Roman trumpet with jingling sistrum,
follow Liburnian beaks with pole-driven barges,
spread foul mosquito-nets on the Tarpeian Rock,
and lay down laws amid Marian arms and statues.[22]

In another poem he again celebrates the battle. Stress is laid on Apollo. 'Rome conquers as Phoebus promised. The Woman pays the penalty, the conquered Queen flees over Ionian waves. But Father Caesar looks down in admiration from the Idalian Star: I am a god, he cries, and here's the proof that he's indeed my blood.' Actian Apollo gains his monument because 'one arrow from his bow defeats ten ships'. Then 'victorious Apollo calls for the lyre and puts his arms away for the dance of peace'.[23]

Servius repeats the tradition in prose. 'And it's a fact that in Antony's army were all the barbarians.' True, several client-kings were in his army, because they had to obey his call; but, as we saw, some of the most important deserted him and did much to help Octavian's cause. The eastern masses were on Antony's side, but they could do little to affect the issue. We may add that the Getae were among his partisans, and Canidius, advising a land-policy, wanted him to wait for the aid promised by their king Dikomes.[24] Virgil has this fact in mind when he says that he who knows the country-gods is happy, unconcerned with the purple of kings, the strife of brothers, or 'the Dacian descending from oath-bonded Danube'. Horace in a satire writes:

A chilling rumour spreads through the streets from the
   Rostra:
Whoever I meet, inquires, 'Good Sir, have you heard—
of course you have, you're nearer the gods—the tale
about the Dacians?' 'Nothing at all,' I answer.
'You always mock.' 'May the gods treat me badly
If I know a thing.' 'Will Caesar give the soldiers
the Italian lands he promised, or the Sicilian?'
I swear that I know nothing. They gape at me,
such a remarkable creature of deep secrets.[25]

Antony in turn accused Octavian of promising his
daughter Julia to Kotison the Getic king and asking the
hand of the king's daughter for himself. Probably both
sides were wooing the Getae. We have already seen how
Antony made overtures to the Medes with the offer of
marrying Iotape to his son.

But in all this there was nothing new. For long the
barbarians (all races not Roman or Greek) had been drawn
in as part of the extending conflicts. Dion laments,
'Pompey and Caesar were both fatally led into the same
acts to attain their ends; they could not do so without
making war on fellow-countrymen and without arming
barbarians against their fatherland'.[26] Pompey mobilised
the kings and peoples of the east against Caesar, who
stressed this act in his *Civil War*; the Caesarians did not
allow their enemies to forget it; Antony referred to it in
his speech after Caesar's death.[27] Pompey had tried to
gloss over his behaviour by referring to the kings as if
they were normal clients of his.[28] But Dion draws
attention to the way he used against Rome the foreigners
he had conquered; Cicero admits it; Virgil discreetly
mentions it.[29] Cicero was furious at Caesar for using

Gauls, whom the Romans had long looked on as their fiercest foes; the very thought of it made him consider flight. Seneca accused Catilina of wanting to use these aliens. Dion says the Pompeians were afraid to return after their defeat because 'the greater part of their army was composed of barbarians'. Pompey had large native contingents at Pharsalos; Dion comments, 'All the soldiers of the conquered nations fought ardently, using for the Romans' enslavement the vigour previously used in defending their own freedom'. But that is mere rhetoric, and he goes on to picture the Romans cutting one another's throats as they conjure up their misfortune and their homeland's disaster, while the barbarians fight with stubborn rage. All far from the facts. Pompey indeed thought of calling on the deadly foe, the Parthians, as we learn from a letter Cicero wrote while governing Cilicia; Dion shrinks from the facts; but Justin admits, 'The Parthians were on the Pompeian side'. Even some Pompeians felt the whole thing a scandal.[30]

Pompeians in flight went to the Illyrians or used Spaniards to commit atrocities on the Caesarians. Soliciting aid from Juba, they sank to the role of simply aiding a foreign monarch against Rome. Caesarians denounced the servility of Scipio before the king (who ordered him to put off his purple clothes) and his cruelty to prisoners—and this was a descendant of the once-great foe of Rome, Jugurtha, whom the Pompeians were servilely aiding and to whom Scipio promised 'all that the Romans possessed in Africa'. Only circumstances had saved Pompey from bringing in the Parthians, but other generals of the senatorial right did it easily enough, for instance Caecilius Bassus in 46, who also allied himself with the Arabs. How opportunist were the attitudes may be seen in Cicero, who early in 43 was horrified at the thought that Antony might use Gauls and Germans, but who in July was delighted that the murderer of Caesar, D. Brutus, could count on 'the fullest and most faithful aid of the Gauls'.[31] The triumvirs officially accused Brutus and Cassius of enlisting the aid of 'irreconcilable enemies of Rome and of her empire', and in fact two of their generals did turn to the Parthians. At Philippi native contingents were strong in the army of Brutus and Cassius, while the opposing camp also had its non-Romans.[32] We have seen how Labienus, one of the republican party, did not hesitate to lead Parthians, and call himself *Imperator Parthicus*. He was defeated; but Sextus Pompey, on fleeing eastward, dreamed of heading a Parthian host. He sent envoys 'secretly to the princes of Thrace and Pontos, intending, if he failed to get what he wanted from Antony, to take flight through Pontos to Armenia; he also sent to the Parthians, hoping that, for the rest of their war with Antony, they'd be eager to take him as general, because he was a Roman and above all because he was the son of Pompey the Great'.[33]

We see then how hypocritical was the attempt to build up a picture of Antony putting himself at the head of eastern forces to overrun Rome. Indeed, through his association with Cleopatra, he can be described as the only one who acted in this respect in a principled way; the accusations would have done much better for Pompey, Brutus, Cassius, Sextus Pompey, and the many Pompeian or Republican leaders who had no hesitation in turning to any enemy of Rome when their personal or class position was threatened. In the case of Antony and that of Caesar the action was principled because it was linked with an outlook that had broken from the narrow Roman positions and, one way or another, realised that the non-Roman peoples had their rights and must be given their places in whatever imperial system was arrived at. The success of Octavian ensured that these rights would be admitted as slowly and partially as the circumstances permitted.

Last Days

The series of setbacks, checkmates, divided impulses, and defeats of 31 had left Antony a broken man. He knew now that he had no chance against Octavian, and he lost all taste for the conflict. His mind must have gone round in the bitter circle of his errors, misjudgements, and ill chances, seeking for the central point of failure. Not so Cleopatra. She meant to fight till the end and never admit defeat. She sailed into Alexandria with victory-garlanded ships, amid triumphal songs, and her head was unbowed. She thus had a few hours in which to take strong measures, execute all whom she suspected of possible treason, and assess her resources. Antony had sailed for Cyrene, only to find that his legions there had gone over to Gallus. After being prevented in a suicide attempt, he turned for Egypt. He and Cleopatra had in fact one year of life ahead.

Cleopatra set herself to think of some new scheme for repairing their fortunes. A naval war was now out of the question; but they held Egypt and could use it as base.

There was still unrest in Spain: why not sail there along the African coast, seize the silver mines, and lead the hill tribes in revolt, as Sertorious had? Or why not sail down the Red Sea to the elephant-country and found a new realm somewhere in the Indian Sea? She decided on the southern venture, which would keep her in regions of ancient Pharaonic and Ptolemaic influence. As the canal connecting the Nile with the top of the Red Sea, built by Ptolemy II, was out of order or too small for warships, she had some ships hauled over the isthmus to Heroon-opolis.[1] But her old enemy Malchos took advantage of her distressed state to strike and burn the ships. He is said to have been instigated by the Roman governor of Syria, who had now deserted Antony, but he was not likely to need any urging. Herod too had turned to Octavian. Cleopatra executed Artavasdes of Armenia, to secure the Median alliance, hoping for help from that quarter; she sent the severed head to the Median king.

But, whatever her plans, she needed Antony's co-operation; she had once for all thrown in her lot with his. And he was useless. He had cut himself away from all society, in a house he had built 'in the sea at Pharos, by throwing a mole out into the water'. Here he played the role of the misanthrope Timon of Athens.[2] Canidius brought him news of the loss of the landforces and of Herod's defection; but he was too deep in despair to be moved by such details. However, after a while he became suddenly bored with his lonely Timonion. He went to join Cleopatra in the palace, resumed the round of dinners and drinking-bouts, distributed gifts once more, and inscribed in the lists of *epheboi* (youths) Caesarion—Plutarch simply calls him 'the son of Cleopatra and

Caesar'. And he gave his own son Antyllus the *toga virilis* of manhood. The celebrations in honour of the two lads lasted many days. He and Cleopatra dissolved the society of Inimitable Livers and formed another, 'not at all inferior to the first in delicate ways, in luxury [*tryphe*] and extravagant outlay, which they called the Society of Partners in Death [*Synapothanoumenoi*]. For their friends enrolled themselves as ready to die together, and passed the time delightfully in a succession of dinners.' The change of name must have been Antony's work. He made no effort to collect his remaining legions and hold the strong line of the Nile; he no longer believed that he could command the loyalty of men. Only one body stayed true, and they, of all men, were the gladiators training at Kyzikos to fight in the games after his victory. They started off for Egypt; but Didius, governor of Syria, held them up, and later Messalla destroyed them.

The question of suicide must have been discussed, though we need not credit the tale of Plutarch about Cleopatra's trial of various venoms on condemned prisoners, till she found that the bite of the asp induced a sleepy torpor and lassitude without a spasm or groan, a gentle sweat on the face with a slow dimming of the faculties. The author of a poem *De Bello Actiaco*, of which fragments survive from the charred papyrus-rolls of Herculaneum, goes further and makes her test out the death-modes on criminals in the middle of the Alexandrian marketplace, describing in minute sensational detail the death agonies.[3] In fact the rulers of eastern lands had long been acquainted with poisons and their effects. Attalos III of Pergamnon had had his garden of poisonous plants which were tried out on criminals; in Alexandria the first

Ptolemies permitted vivisection for scientific purposes. Cleopatra could learn all she wanted to know about ways of killing herself from her physician Olympos. Galen states that he had witnessed the execution of Alexandrian criminals by the application of a cobra to the chest: this was considered the most humane way of killing.[3] We can be sure that Cleopatra had long since been satisfied as to what was the best way to die, if she needed to kill herself; but it would have been queenly dignity, not painless process, that she considered. Having settled the matter, she would have given all her thoughts to the problem of staying alive and of ensuring the survival of her dynasty, if not of herself. Antony was the one who would have abandoned himself to death-meditations; for suicide as a way out for the desperately pressed had become a Roman tradition.

As Antony had given up any serious thought of military resistance, Cleopatra put her mind to what possibility there still was of diplomatic negotiations or bargainings about her treasure. Other client-kings, after aiding Antony, had made their submission and been reinstated. She was in a special position and could not expect easy treatment, but she still hoped to achieve something for her children. So, when the Egyptians offered to rise and fight for her, she forbade them, saying that she would not inflict vain sufferings on her people. How and through whom the offer was made, we do not know. The leading citizens of Alexandria could hardly speak for the people of the *chora*; perhaps the high priests gathered in council.

All the while Octavian was steadily advancing from Syria towards the Egyptian border. Antony is said to have sent envoys to him, asking to be allowed to live as a private citizen in Athens, then offering to kill himself if it would help Cleopatra. Octavian did not deign to answer. Cleopatra was building a mausoleum next to the temple of Isis. No doubt to enhance the importance of her son Caesarion, she staged an impressive ceremony to celebrate his coming of age; he was about 16 if born in 47, 13 if born in 44. But what she did was to ensure his death at the hands of the remorseless Octavian; for now he was legally a responsible agent capable of claiming his birthright. Antyllus also, we saw, was dressed in the toga of a Roman adult.[4]

Contemporary sources such as the poets Horace and Virgil, or the historian Livy (whose version however we have only in epitomes), do not refer to any treacheries on her part; but later writers like Plutarch and Dion are full of tales about her double-dealing—tales that are certainly part of the Augustan propaganda against her after her death. She sent to Octavian asking the realm of Egypt for her children. The only trustworthy envoy that she and Antony could find was Euphronios, their children's teacher. Alexas of Laodicea, who had more influence with Antony (says Plutarch) than any other Greek, had been sent to keep Herod from going over, but had himself betrayed Antony. Then, relying on Herod, he came into Octavian's presence, was at once imprisoned, carried in fetters to his home town, and executed.[5] To Euphronios Octavian said that Cleopatra would receive all reasonable treatment if she put Antony to death or cast him out. He also sent along with him a freedman of his, Thyrsus, 'a man of no mean parts, suited for persuasively carrying messages from a young general to a woman haughty and astonishingly proud in matters of beauty. He had longer interviews that the others. Suspicion was stirred in Antony, who seized him and sent him back with a written statement. Thyrsus by his insolent and arrogant airs had irritated him at a time when misfortunes made him very touchy. "If you don't like it," he added, "you have my own freedman Hipparchos. Hang him up and give him a flogging. Then we'll be quits." After that Cleopatra tried to dissipate his causes for suspicion and complaint by paying extravagant court to him. Her own birthday she kept modestly, in a way befitting her circumstances, but his she celebrated with an excess of all sorts of splendour and cost: those asked to dinner came home and went home rich. Meanwhile Caesar was called home by Agrippa, who kept writing from Rome that affairs there much needed his presence.'[6] The Hipparchos mentioned was son of Antony's steward Theophilos who had been at Corinth at the time of Actium; he was the first of Antony's freedmen to go over to Octavian.

As Octavian neared, Cleopatra sent him her sceptre and diadem, asking him to crown one of her sons. Officially he ordered her to disarm; secretly he assured her that she had nothing to fear. At all costs he wanted to stop her taking some drastic step such as killing herself and burning up her treasure; and she in turn, with her insight in such matters, must have played on his fears. But he knew just how much and how little reassurance to give: enough to keep her hopefully alive without anything definite that she could use against him. It was to his advantage to separate her as much as possible from Antony, who might do anything in his desperate despair. A feint of bribery was made from Alexandria, perhaps aimed at making Octavian all the more anxious to gain the treasure and to accept compromises. Antyllus, who had been engaged to Octavia's daughter, was sent with a large sum of money; Octavian took the money and sent the lad back with no answer. Cleopatra had all her treasure of gold, silver, pearls, emeralds, ivory, ebony, cinnamon, carried into the incomplete mausoleum; tow and pitch were set all round. According to Dion, Octavian had gone so far as to pretend in messages to Cleopatra that he loved her; but that is unlikely.[7]

Gallus now took Paraitonion, the key to the approach from the west. Antony had meant to go to Syria to rescue the gladiators; but on the news about Gallus he turned the other way, 'hoping to win over the troops without a struggle, if possible, as they had campaigned with him and were fairly well disposed; but otherwise to subdue them by force', since he had with him a large body of footmen and ships. But when he neared the ramparts, Gallus ordered all the trumpeters to sound. So he could not address the men. Then he failed in an attempt to storm the place and suffered a reverse with his ships as well. Gallus let them sail into the harbour, then, by means of machines, drew up chains that had been sunk under water. 'Encompassing the ships from all sides, the land, the houses, the sea, he burned some and sank others.'[8]

Pelousion fell to Octavian, who had been helped in his advance from Syria by Herod. Plutarch and Dion suggest that Cleopatra was betraying Antony, that the commander at Pelousion, Seleukos, surrendered with her connivance, and that she secretly prevented the Alexandrians from making a sortie, while ostensibly exhorting them to fight. Plutarch adds that, though herself an accomplice, she allowed Antony to put to death the wife and children of

Seleukos. Such an act is uncharacteristic of Antony, though he may have now acted cruelly in his blind rage; on the other hand, as the charges about Cleopatra's treachery are certainly untrue, she may have been the one infuriated against Seleukos. Octavian himself claimed to have stormed Pelousion.[9]

As his last hours came, the old fighting spirit reawoke in Antony. Because he now knew he was doomed, he could fight his hardest; because success was impossible, he was troubled with no afterthoughts, no pressure of insoluble problems. Octavian had encamped east of the city near the Hippodrome. In a brilliant cavalry action Antony routed the advanced horse.

He returned jubilant to embrace Cleopatra in his war-gear and presented to her one of his soldiers who had distinguished himself by his bravery. She gave the man a golden breastplate and a helmet. That night he deserted to Caesar. The prisoners whom Antony had taken refused to join him, preferring death. He challenged Octavian to a duel. Octavian coldly replied that Antony was not short of ways to die. Antony shot missiles with leaflets tied to the shafts into the enemy camp, promising big rewards to deserters. Octavian showed his contempt by reading the leaflets out and announcing that in a few days victory would procure them all Antony's wealth. The use of leaflets and pamphlets was typical of these wars. At Philippi, 'as Brutus was reluctant to join battle, they managed somehow to throw pamphlets into his camp, urging the soldiers to embrace their cause and making certain promises—or else to come to blows if they had the least bit of strength'. During the Parthian invasion of Syria, 'Saxa fled because he feared his associates would take up the cause of Labienus, who was trying to lure them away by pamphlets, which he kept shooting into Saxa's camp'.[10]

On the night of Antony's brief triumph, he feasted with his friends, determined to launch next day a big attack by sea and land. He bade the slaves pour for him lavishly as it was uncertain whether they'd repeat such services on the morrow or be attending other masters while he himself lay dead, a mummy and a nothing. His friends wept. He declared that he wouldn't lead them out to battle, as what he sought was honourable death rather than safety and victory. That night, the tale went, a sound was heard in the city, a sound not of man. 'When the city was quiet and depressed through fear and expectation of what was coming, suddenly certain harmonious noises from all sorts of instruments were heard, and the shouting of a throng, together with cries of Bacchic revelry and satyric leapings, as if a troop of revellers were making a great tumult as they passed out of the city; their course seemed to lie through the middle of the city towards the outer gate opposite the enemy. At the gate the tumult became loudest and then fell away. Those who sought the meaning of the sign concluded that the god to whom Antony was always most likened and to whom he attached himself, was now deserting him.'[11] An Octavian tale? But it could have been invented only after his death, when the victor needed no more such propaganda. More likely it represented a genuine bit of folk-mythology born among the Alexandrians.[12] Men asked: How could Antony, in whom the god had been incarnated, come down in disaster and death? The answer was: At the last moment the god left him and he became a mere man again. We may compare the tale about the end of the emperor Domitian. 'And it seemed to him that Minerva, whose statue he had in his bedroom, cast away her arms and on a chariot drawn by black horses was falling into a chasm.'[13]

Cleopatra had shut herself in the mausoleum with her two girls. Charmion had a Greek name, connected with *charme*, joy; Eiras may have been a Negress if her name was connected with *eiros*, wool, thus meaning Woolhead—but the derivation is unsure. Eiras may be short for Eirene, Peace, as Lucas for Lucanus.[14] When Antony drew up his forces, the cavalry and Cleopatra's ships (apparently merchantmen for the most part) went over to Octavian; but he and the infantry fought for a while. Then he returned in misery to the city, 'crying out', says Plutarch, 'that he had been betrayed by Cleopatra to those with whom he waged war for her sake'. It was at this point, Plutarch adds, that she, 'fearing his wrath and madness, fled for refuge into her tomb and let fall the dropdoors, which were made strong with bolts and bars'. (It is more likely that she retired there as soon as the battle began; for in the confused situation of Antony's return with curses on his lips she would not have much time to learn of his words and hide herself.) Messengers now came up to tell Antony that she was dead. That was, the final blow. He unfastened his breastplate, laid it down, and cried, 'O Cleopatra, I am not grieved to lose you, for I'll join you at once. I'm only grieved that an imperator like myself has been found inferior to a woman in courage.' He called on a slave named Eros, whom he had long before made promise to kill him if the need arose. But Eros, holding his sword as if he meant to strike his master, turned it on himself. Antony said, 'Well done,

Eros, you were not able to do it yourself, but you teach me what I must do'. He then ran himself through the belly and dropped on a couch. But the blood stopped flowing after he lay down. He revived and begged the bystanders to finish him off. They ran off as he lay writhing and crying out. Then at last Diomedes the secretary came from Cleopatra with orders to bring him to her in the tomb. Learning that she was alive, Antony eagerly bade his servants raise him up and he was carried in their arms to the tomb's doors. Cleopatra refused to open, but appeared at a window and let down ropes and cords. She and her two women drew Antony up. 'Never, as those who present tell us, was there a more pitiful sight. Smeared with blood and struggling with death, he was drawn up, stretching out his hands to her while he was dangling in the air. For the task wasn't an easy one for women. Cleopatra, with clinging hands and strained face, could hardly pull up the rope, while those below called out encouragements and shared her anguish. And when at last she got him up and laid him down, she tore her clothes over him, beat and scratched her breasts with her hands, wiped off some of his blood on her face, and called him lord and husband and *imperator*. She almost forgot her own miseries in pity for his. But Antony stopped her lamentings and asked for a drink of wine; he was thirsty or hoped it would hasten his end. After drinking he advised her to consult her own safety, if she could do so without disgrace, and among all Caesar's companions to put most trust in Proculeius, and not to mourn him for his final reverses, but to count him happy for the good things that had been his, for he had become the most illustrious of men, had won the greatest power, and now had not been ignobly conquered, a Roman by a Roman.'

Did Cleopatra give orders that Antony should be told of her death, or was a mistake made in the confused situation with all its criss-crossing rumours of disaster? We do not know. It is the one genuinely equivocal detail in her behaviour. There is however no hint in her later dealings with Octavian that she claimed responsibility for Antony's death; and in the circumstances such a claim would have strengthened her position. The story that in his blind despair Antony accused her of betrayal may well be true; in that dark last moment he must have felt strongly that his devotion to her had ensured his downfall. Also, the sight of her ships deserting must have filled him with a sense of ubiquitous treachery; and Cleopatra, informed of his outcry, may have thought discretion the best plan for the moment, without considering the effects that a report of her death would have. If we accept Plutarch's account, which seems based on the narrative of an eye-witness (probably Olympos), Antony did not really believe that Cleopatra had betrayed him; otherwise his change of mood after the news of her death could hardly have come about. We may well imagine him caught in a skein of shifting despairs, disillusions, anguishes. In a sense, the report of Cleopatra's death was a blessing, since it restored him simply to his love and trust, and thus enabled him to die in dignity. Not that she could have meant it that way.

No sooner was Antony dead than Proculeius came. For while Antony was being carried to the mausoleum, one of his bodyguard, Derketaios, took up his sword, hid it, and slipped off. Running to Octavian, he told him of

Antony's death; and Octavian retired to his tent and wept. (No doubt he made a show of grief on the principle that he must act as Caesar was said to have done at the news of Pompey's death.) Now that Antony was removed, what he truly felt was relief and a guilty wish to justify himself. He read over to friends some letters that he had exchanged with Antony, and argued that he had always striven for reconciliation against the latter's overbearing and arrogant temper. But his mind was on the treasure. He sent Proculeius again with instructions that everything possible must be done to capture Cleopatra alive. 'He was fearful about the treasures in her funeral pyre and thought it would add much to his triumph's glory if she were led in the procession.' She refused to open and conversed with Proculeius through a groundfloor door which remained bolted and barred. She kept on asking that her children might have her kingdom, while Proculeius kept on putting her off with amiable advice to trust Octavian.

Proculeius had a good look at the mausoleum. Gallus was sent to hold Cleopatra in talk at the door while Proculeius set up a ladder and got in through the window where Antony's body had been taken in. Then he went down with two attendants and came up behind Cleopatra. One of the women cried out, 'Poor Cleopatra, you're taken alive'. Cleopatra turned round, saw Proculeius, and tried to stab herself. 'For she had at her girdle a dagger like those robbers wear.' Proculeius ran up, threw his arms about her, and said: 'Cleopatra, you're wronging both Caesar and yourself by trying to rob him of a chance to show great kindness and by setting on the gentlest of generals the stigma of a ruthless lack of faith.' He took her dagger and shook out her clothes to make sure she wasn't

hiding a poison. A freedman Epaphroditus was then sent
to keep strict watch, while agreeing to any concession
that made things more comfortable for her. When the
news reached Rome, the standard rate of interest dropped
from 12 per cent to 4 per cent, and Octavian was later able
to satisfy all the claims of the army and the veterans,
paying for all the land he took, though prices had
doubled. So great was the captured treasure that he could
still, after carrying out many public works, distribute a
large surplus as bonuses to the populace.[15]

Alexandria has been continually lived in; the old city
is almost quite lost; but we can get an idea of the mausoleum from the reliefs on some lamps.[16] We are looking in
from the sea at a bay surrounded by dense constructions;
in front are arcades bearing a mole with a gate or triumphal arch at one end. On the same side are rocks, and,
facing the mole, large buildings with two high doors and
a portico in front. Behind is a square tower with pyramidal
roof; a building that reminds us of the Hellenistic horned
altars of Egypt, in which the raised angles are higher than
the centre. In the background rise the impressive contours
of other buildings dominated by a sort of *tholos* (rotunda).

That is the scene on one lamp; analogous views occur
on others. What we see is certainly the port of Alexandria.
The mole is the Heptastadion linking mainland and the
Pharos island; the arch on the left is the entry into the
further harbour—a typical engineering and architectural
solution of the period. An arch-entry would have existed
at either end. We are perhaps standing on the island and
looking over. Tritons appear on the arch-relief, and we
know that they played an important part in the lighthouse-
decorations. Between Heptastadion and Cape Lochias

(out of sight on the left) lay the Royal Quarter, which is what confronts us: its nekropolis preceded in the foreground by gates and porticoes. How are we to define the three monuments behind? The first, on the right, rises above the others on a base of stone-blocks, its upper portion showing the conic form of the *tholos*. This must be the Tomb of Alexander. 'Though the dead Ptolemies and their shameful line,' writes Lucan, 'are hid by pyramids and mausolea too good for them.' In our relief the Tomb stands behind the central building. Nearer the shore, east of the Tomb, is an edifice with square tower—two windows in the upper part. Its roof recalls an altar-crown; and it was perhaps the Tomb of Cleopatra, completed by Octavian who gave it the altarform of the second half of the first century B.C.

Between these two buildings is a square structure, which looks like a tower with roof of double pitch underlined by a broad cornice at the base of the frontal triangle. Under the pediment, in the upper part, are two squared windows. The walls are made of rectangular blocks, of which the outlines appear on our lamp-design. This must be the first Tomb of Alexander, which was turned into the temple of his cult.

The lamp's miniature relief seems based on an art-work, probably a painting, by some master working soon after 30 B.C. Perhaps he was the Ludius whom Pliny mentions. The lampform itself dates from the early first century A.D., and the lamp may have been one of those used to light up houses in memory of one of the celebrations in honour of Augustus, his burial or some later commemoration.

A sarcophagus-relief at Ostia is carved in a style later than the third century A.D.: the items are selected and related in a rather schematic way. It shows three boats in a harbour, with Loves playing instruments or fishing; the buildings ashore are bisected by a column; the lighthouse stands on the extreme right. The column we may take as that which in medieval times was called Pompey's, but which in fact was set up in 296 in honour of Diocletian's magnanimity. On the left three arcades crowned by two tritons seem to represent the Heptastadion: one boat has an oar in an opening, suggesting that it has just come through. Next is a round tower with two oblong windows under the conical roof topped by a sort of globe. This is the Soma of Alexander. Another building, with a double-slope roof, stands at its side; the upper story has two oblong windows under the pediment, while two horizontal windows open in the side-wall; the lower part of the structure is formed of arcades. This seems the first Tomb of Alexander. At the left end of the scene a big palmtree gives a picturesque touch. The view differs from that on the lamps; we are looking from the west across to the island and the mole, with part of the royal nekropolis shown. Cleopatra's Mausoleum is omitted as no longer of interest or has been destroyed. There was much destruction, it seems, during the riots under Aurelian in 275 and under Diocletian in 296. So it was not merely rhetoric when John Chrysostom cried, 'Where then is the Tomb of Alexander? Show it to me'.[17]

Cleopatra had asked Octavian for permission to bury Antony with royal honours, and he agreed. He himself had entered the city on 1 August. He gave his right hand to the philosopher Areios and talked with him. Then he went into the gymnasion and ascended the tribunal erected for him. The people, scared, prostrated themselves, but he told them to rise. He forgave them, he said, because of Alexander their founder, the great size and beauty of their city, and his wish to please Areios. He further pardoned several individuals at the request of Areios (who became, or already had been, his instructor in philosophy). 'Among these was Philostratos, a man more competent in speaking extempore than any sophist who ever lived; but he improperly represented himself as belonging to the School of the Academy. So Caesar refused to hear his entreaties. But Philostratos, in a dark robe and with a long white beard, when trailing behind Areios, always declaring this one verse: A wise man, if he's wise, will save a wise man. When Caesar heard of this, he pardoned him, to free Areios from odium rather than Philostratos from fear.'[18] We have already met Philostratos as a close acquaintance of Cleopatra; and it was this relationship, not any question of his being or not being an Academic, that moved Octavian against him. Krinagoras wrote an epigram on his end:

> O Philostratos, unhappy for all your riches,
> where are the sceptres, the intercourse with princes
> on which your days depended? Ah, will your tomb
> stand out by the Nile in the region of . . . .
> Aliens have shared the fruit of your toil, and, harried,
> in sandy Ostrakine your corpse will be buried.[19]

Ostrakine was somewhere between Egypt and Palestine; and the 'aliens' were the Romans.

After Antony's funeral, Cleopatra returned to the palace in a state of anxious uncertainty. Octavian executed only four men: Turullius and Cassius of Parma, whom he could not forgive for his satires; the senator who had managed the textile mills; and Canidius, Antony's faithful lieutenant. He also killed the two boys, Antyllus and Caesarion. Antyllus was betrayed by his tutor Theodoros; and when his head was cut off by soldiers, the tutor took away a precious stone from round the lad's neck and sewed it into his own girdle. Convicted despite his denials, he was crucified. Cleopatra's children by Antony were kept under guard but treated well. Caesarion, sent by his mother with much treasure for India via Ethiopia, was betrayed by his tutor like Antyllus. The man, Rhodon, persuaded him to go back with a story that Octavian was promising him Egypt. Plutarch says that while Octavian was deliberating, Areios said, 'It's not a good thing to have too many Caesars', adapting a line of Homer. So Caesarion was killed. But that happened after Cleopatra's own death.[20]

Meanwhile she was tormented by fears for her children and the prospect of walking in Octavian's Triumph. She kept repeating, 'I'll never go in his Triumph'. Her lacerated breast was inflamed. Fevered, she took no food and tried to starve herself to death, aided by her physician Olympos. Octavian stopped her with the threat of making her children suffer. He was torn between the wish to show her at Rome and the wish to get rid of so difficult a captive. He wanted her to die, but in a way that did not reflect on himself.

At last, feeling that he had kept her long enough in miserable expectation, he visited her on 8 August. We meet two versions of the meeting: one more realistic, the other constructed so as to contrast her with Octavia, as Octavian with Antony. She is depicted as a siren in calculated dishevelled charms, trying to turn her mourn-

ing to amorous account, surrounded by busts of Julius
Caesar, and carrying in her bosom letters written in his
own hand. With languishing glances she read passages out
and whispered her admiration of Octavian. 'In this man,
Caesar, you too are alive for me—but if I have you as
well.' Octavian stared at the floor in prudent chastity. At
last she clung vainly sobbing to his knees. He told her
calmly that she had no need to despair, nothing amiss
would happen to her. Florus comments, 'The chastity of
the Princeps was too much for her'. The same motive
pervades Dion's account. No doubt the story was a
rhetorical version of what Octavian himself recounted in
his *Memoirs*.

Plutarch gives a more sober narrative. Cleopatra was
lying on a mean palletbed, dressed only in her tunic, but
sprang up as he entered and cast herself at his feet.

Her hair and face were in terrible disarray, her voice tremu-
lous, her eyes sunken. Many marks of the cruel blows on her
bosom could be seen. In all, her body seemed no better off
than her spirit. Still, her famous charm and the boldness of
her beauty were not wholly extinguished; though she was in
such a sad plight, they shone out from within and showed
themselves in the play of her features.

After Caesar bade her lie down and took a seat near her,
she began a sort of justification of her course, ascribing it to
necessity (*ananke*) and fear of Antony. But as Caesar disputed
each point and refuted her, she quickly changed her tone and
tried to move his pity by prayers, like someone who above all
clung to life. Finally she gave him a list of all her treasures;
and when Seleukos, one of her stewards, definitely proved
that she was stealing and hiding some things away, she
leaped up, gripped him by the hair, and showered blows on
his face.

Caesar stopped her with a smile, and she said, 'But isn't it a monstrous thing, Caesar, that when you've deigned to come and speak to me despite my miserable condition, my slaves denounce me for putting aside some woman's adornments. Not for myself indeed, unhappy woman that I am, but as trifling gifts for Octavia and your Livia—in the hope that their intercession will make you merciful and gentler.'

He was pleased with this speech, now convinced that she wanted to live. So he told her that he left these matters for her to manage, and that in all other ways he'd give her more splendid treatment than she could possibly expect. Then he went away, supposing that he'd deceived her, but in fact himself the more deceived.

The truth was that he knew exactly what he was doing. If he had wanted to keep her alive, he would have guarded her properly with Roman soldiers and wardens. Instead he left her among her own servants, with only his freedman in charge. The latter knew what his master wanted; and if things went wrong he could always be disowned and executed, as Antigonos I disowned the women used to murder an earlier Cleopatra. A freedman was expendable, while a high-ranking Roman officer could not be treated as a tool with impunity. We may assume that at the interview Octavian had removed her last reason for living by letting her know that he meant to annex Egypt; she would then be sure that he'd make her walk chained in his Triumph. But even so he wanted to ensure that she would kill herself. So he used one of his friends Cornelius Dolabella, next day, 9 August (16 Mesore), to make certain that the point had got home.

Plutarch describes Dolabella as acting out of 'a certain tenderness' for Cleopatra. But clearly none of Octavian's friends would have dared to go on his own initiative and tell her that she was to be shipped off with her children within three days. After the interview she begged Octavian for permission to pour libations on Antony's tomb. The request was granted. She had herself carried to the tomb, where, amid her women, she embraced the urn and cried to the dead man (according to Plutarch); 'Dear Antony, I buried you only recently with hands still free. Now I pour libations for you as a captive—so carefully guarded that I cannot with blows or tears disfigure this body of mine, which is a slave's body, closely watched so that it may grace the Triumph over you. Don't look for any other honours or libations. These are the last from Cleopatra the captive. In life nothing could part us, but in death we're likely to change places. You the Roman lie buried here, while I, a luckless woman, lie in Italy and get only that much of your land as my portion. But if indeed there is any might or power in that land's gods—for the gods of this have betrayed us—don't abandon your wife while she lives, don't allow a Triumph to be celebrated over yourself in me, but hide and bury me here with you. For out of all my countless ills not one is so great or dreadful as the short time I've lived apart from you.' This speech has all the signs of a rhetorical exercise. However, what is certain is that after Dolabella's visit she determined to kill herself. She knew now she had nothing to hope from the victor, and perhaps she believed that Caesarion had got away. She killed herself.

No one knew for sure what happened, except perhaps Olympos, and he does not seem to have spoken out. Plutarch says that after kissing the urn, she took a bath, then reclined at table and ate a sumptuous meal. A countryman came in with a basket. When the guards asked what he had, he lifted the cover of leaves and showed figs of a great size and beauty. He gave them some, so they felt no mistrust and let him in. After her meal, Cleopatra took up a sealed tablet, on which she had already written, and sent it to Octavian, dismissing everyone except her two most trusted girls. Octavian opened the tablet and found that it contained a prayer to be buried with Antony. He at once sent messengers, who went off at a run. They found the guards unaware that anything untoward had happened, but on entering the room they saw Cleopatra lying dead on a golden couch, dressed in her royal robes. Of her two girls, Eiras was dying at her feet, while Charmion, tottering and heavy-headed, was trying to arrange the diadem on the queen's brow. Somebody cried in anger, 'A fine deed, this, Charmion'.

'Indeed, most fine,' she replied, 'and right for the descendant of so many kings.' She said no more, but fell at the side of the couch.

Plutarch goes on to state that an asp was said to have been brought in with the figs. Cleopatra had meant to let the asp fasten itself on her without her awareness; but she took away some figs and saw it. 'There it is, you see.' She bared her arm and held it out. Others said the asp was kept in a water-jar; Cleopatra stirred it up with a golden distaff and it sprang at her arm. Others again said she carried poison in a hollow comb which she hid in her hair. No spot or sign of poison was found on her body; no reptile was seen in the chamber—though traces were said to have been noted near the sea, on to which the windows of the chamber looked out. Some persons said two slight indistinct punctures were seen on Cleopatra's arm. 'And thus Caesar also seems to have believed; for in

his Triumph an image of Cleopatra with the asp clinging
to her arm was carried in the procession.' But Plutarch
cautiously adds, 'The truth of the matter no one knows'.
Dion mentions the slight pricks on the arm. Some, he
says, spoke of an asp brought in a water-jar or amid
flowers; others, of poison on a hair-pin with which she
scratched her arm.[21] A passage in Propertius suggests that
the poet had seen the picture carried at the Triumph.

> I saw your arms the holy asps had stung,
> the deathsleep on its secret courses stealing.

It has been suggested in modern times that the asp-death
was a deliberate act of apotheosis, in which Cleopatra
carried out her goddess-masquing to the bitter end. The
asp was the uraeus, the emblem of the Pharoahs, which
rose proudly menacing on the royal diadem—crushing
the ruler's foes and putting him under the protection of
his divine Father the Sungod, Re. Plutarch says that
Cleopatra chose an end 'befitting the successor of so many
kings'. In its origin the uraeus was the embodiment of
Wedjoyet, goddess of Buto, and it seems to become a royal
sumbol through the idea of the king as Horos (early
identified with Re); this interpretation is better than
linking Wedjoyet's snake with the one playing a part in the
cult and myth of Isis. At times in Hellenistic sculpture
from Egypt Isis appears as a snake herself, probably
through identification with the snake-goddess Renutet
or Thermouthis. Two serpents in a shrine, on a limestone
relief of about 150 B.C., seem to be Isis and Osiris, here
symbolising Upper and Lower Egypt; a marble figure of
Isis in Greek dress shows her holding a cobra in her right
hand; silver armbands from Naukratis represent Isis and

Sarapis with human heads and snake-bodies. (It has been argued that Isis got her snake-attributes through the Greeks who identified her with Demeter; but to see only Demeter-Isis in the snake-aspects is far too narrow, even though it was mostly outside Egypt, and especially in her Roman cult, that Isis was linked with serpents.) As for apotheosis, Josephos says that Egyptians considered death by asp or crocodile to lead to a state of blessedness and godhead; but we have no earlier or Egyptian reference to this belief. We must also recall that Cleopatra was already a goddess; as queen she was a goddess, daughter of Re; she had been hailed as Nea Isis and worshipped as Aphrodite. However she died, her death united her with Re.[22]

It has also been argued that two asps, not one, were used, and the reason lay in the double uraneus as a royal symbol common in iconography. The first use of the double form was probably connected with the winged disk of the Sun, already closely linked with the royal person; but in the New Kingdom the form at times appears on the royal diadem instead of a single cobra, and, common under the Ethiopian kings, it persisted into the Ptolemaic era. The double cobra could be described as a weapon, *e.g.* by which Horos of Behdet terrifies his foes; Osiris is called its lord; Wedjoyet-of-the-two-Cobra-goddesses is the Great Mother of Horos. Queens and princes are depicted with long wigs and often with vulture-headgear as well; we see a Ramesside princess with two cobras in front of her wig (without the vultures), the whole topped by a circlet of cobras with disks on their heads. A relief at Hathor's Dendera temple shows Cleopatra as Hathor-Isis; beneath the symbols of these goddesses she has the vulture-headgear topped by a circlet of cobras, but without the uraeus, single or double, in front. (It is argued however that the figure is simply Isis and that Cleopatra stands behind the king on the far left, with a single uraeus; but however we allot the identifications, the main point holds.) When she appeared in royal guise—*basiliskos*, as Plutarch puts it—she probably wore a crown with double cobra in front.

Double uraeus are mentioned in pyramid texts and there identified with the eyes of the king, who is probably Horos. Duplication here, as in so many Egyptian matters, was linked with the notion of the Two Lands forming a single State. The doubling process is seen with both cobra and vulture goddesses, the latter being assimilated in form to the first pair.

We have seen that Propertius speaks of asps, not asp. Florus gives us a romantic version. 'Dressed in her best clothes, as she was used to dress, she set herself by her dear Antony in a coffin filled with rich perfumes, and, applying snakes to her veins, died a death resembling sleep.' Virgil in the *Aeneid* writes, 'She as yet had no thought of the pair of asps that fate was holding in store for her.' On the other hand, Dion and Plutarch mention only one asp.[23]

The probability then is that Cleopatra did die by asp-bite and that she had a general feeling that such a death suited an Egyptian monarch, especially one who had been the New Isis. Her death was a royal death as contrasted with the servile fate that Octavian was preparing for her. But we need not attribute to her any precise or formal idea of apotheosis. How her two girls died, we do not know. Even if only one cobra was used, there would most likely have been enough venom left for them; but they may well have felt that the cobra was for their mistress alone and that some lesser way, perhaps by poison, should be their choice.[24] A painting in a catacomb on the old Appian Way (on the Via Dino Compagni) has been taken to represent Cleopatra in her death, but there is probably no reference to her.[25] A nimbused and half-draped woman reclines against a basket in a garden of scarlet flowers, while a small snake writhes by her; the scene is probably one of pagan apotheosis in paradise, with the snake as an emblem of the dead.

Plutarch says that Antony's statues were broken, but Cleopatra's left. One of her friends, Archelaos, paid Octavian 2,000 talants to save them. In B.C. 28 however Octavian had his revenge on the cult of Isis. 'He did not allow the Egyptian rites to be celebrated inside the pomerium' at Rome.[26] In Egypt Cleopatra's memory long remained. Two generations later the Alexandrian grammarian Apion was championing her memory; and her cult as Neotera seems to have been still celebrated in the third century. She was called Neotera or Younger on coins of Berytos and Cyrenaica; a gem shows Isis-Tyche reclining on a couch: 'Great is She the Younger the Unconquered.'[27] Another gem, of brown and dark green jasper, has a bust of Sarapis with an encircling inscription, 'Great is the Name of the Lord Sarapis', and on the reverse, 'Great Tyche [Fortune] of the Unconquered Neotera'. Neotera here is clearly Isis, and the question is whether she is further Isis-Cleopatra. At Dendera an inscription dedicates certain repairs to a Neotera who seems to be (Hathor) Aphrodite and who has been taken as Plotina wife of Trajan, but who also may be Cleopatra. A return

of temple property from Oxyrhynchos of A.D. 213–17
mentions a sanctuary of Neotera.[28] And a papyrus of the
3rd century seems to show that the cult of Cleopatra
Aphrodite continued till the reign of Alexander Severus.

Isis is called Nea in an uncertain locality (perhaps
Patmos), and we find Hera as Nea, but in connection with
the age-groups of her worshippers. Neotera however
seems an epithet that does not belong to any Greek or
Egyptian goddesses, except Kore (the Maiden, Perse-
phone); its best interpretation seems to be that it was first
used for a royal person identified with Isis or Hathor,
though after some time the identification became so
complete that the historical character faded out inside
the deity.[29]

Cleopatra's fame grew so great in legend that many
great works of the past, the palace, the pharos, the
heptastadion, the canal bringing water to Alexandria,
were all attributed to her. We have seen how her name
lived on in alchemic tradition. In the 7th century the
Koptic bishop John of Nikiou declared that none of
the kings before her did such great deeds as she did;
he praised her as 'the most illustrious and wise of
women'. She was 'great in herself and in her achievements, in courage and strength'. Her name thus seems
to have helped to foster Egyptian nationalism under the
Romans.

But to return to her reputation in Roman literature:
Horace wrote an ode after the news of her death reached
Rome, which, despite many touches of the vituperative
tradition, somehow comes out as a tribute to the great
power of her personality and the impact it had made on
the whole of her world.

Now is the time to drink, with feet released
to beat the earth, and gratefully to spread,
   my friend, with Salian feast
   each god's reclining-bed.
Till now we dared not raid the ancestral rack
for Caecuban. A Queen had planned in hate
   to smash the Capitol and sack
   the conquered Roman State.
She and her plotting gang, diseased and vile,
went mad with heady dreams of baseless pride:
   drunk with their luck were they awhile,
   but soon the frenzy died
when not a single ship of hers escaped.
Though Mareotic juices dazed her head,
   back to true terrors she was raped
   by Caesar when she fled
from Italy. He followed hard the scent
as men chase hares on Thessaly's snowy plains
   or hawks a fluttering dove. He meant
   to load with captive chains
the fatal creature. But more bravely she
turned to her death, no woman's part she bore,
   the swordblades did not make her flee
   to find some hidden shore.
Seeing her ruined court with placid eyes,
she grasped the asps and did not feel the pains,
   wishing the venom to surprise
   and brim at once her veins;
for brooding arrogance had nerved her thought.
She grudged in triumph-shackles to be seen,
   by the Liburnian galleys brought
   to slavery, a queen.[30]

After reigning twenty-two years, she had died at the age of thirty-nine.

The Romans had feared and hated no foreign ruler so much, apart from Hannibal. A further tribute to her appears in the deep imprint she has left on Virgil's *Aenid*. That does not mean we must look into that poem for any sustained allegory or for definite identifications— Aeneas as Octavian, Dido as Cleopatra—of the protagonists in the great conflict, let alone of lesser characters. What we can validly look for are deep and strong emotional links between the epic's theme and the experiences of fear and release which Virgil and hosts of other Italians, siding with Octavian, had felt in the events leading up to Actium. Virgil seems to have begun his epic in 29, when those events were still fresh in his mind. When he worked out the long episode of Dido and Aeneas as prelude to the struggle to found Rome, he could not but have deep in his thoughts the fatal attraction, as he would see it, of Cleopatra for Antony, and the resistance shown by Octavian. In Aeneas he to some extent fused the two reactions. Aenas is powerfully drawn by Dido's charms, but at the last moment does not succumb. He listens to a higher call and turns away.

Both Dido and Cleopatra are queens in Africa, of great beauty and attractive powers; each in youth is driven from her homeland by a brother and finds refuge elsewhere; each, in seeking to bewitch a hero from afar, has recourse to splendid shows of luxury and regal gold. Dido amuses herself with hunts, to beguile Aeneas, to the scandal of public opinion, as Cleopatra in similar ways beguiled Antony. Each queen in the end fails and commits suicide, hiding her resolve till the end. Aeneas and Octavian are both accused of having hard hearts; they struggle to repress their emotion. Dido wants to establish her throne with a fixed successor; Cleopatra hoped to base her throne firmly, first on Caesar, then on Antony.

Juno wishes to place the new capital in Africa, as Antony and Cleopatra were suspected of wanting to shift the world-centre from Rome to Alexandria. There are naturally differences. Dido shows great devotion to her dead husband—though even this has its echo in Cleopatra's attitude to Julius Caesar.

When we consider what Virgil and the Roman world had just gone through, to see these analogies as accidental or superficial, is to show a total inability to grasp how poetry is written. For his purposes, Virgil has to separate out Cleopatra as a vile monster-worshipping menace and to clothe Dido with the romantic Hellenistic colours created by poets like Apollonios of Rhodes in his picture of Medeia. But all that cannot disguise the profound effect that Cleopatra has had on his mind, and the way in which the tensions of the great epoch through which he had just lived reappear in his epic.[31] While he was writing, Carthage was being restored as a Roman colony, despite the old curse on her stones. Even at the time of the curse, the *devotio*, there had been some disquiet at the destruction. In 1916 on the slopes of the Bursa an altar was found with reliefs on four sides: one was of Aeneas carrying his father and leading the young Ascanius. It seems clear that the *Aeneid* was used to defend the restoration and support the action of the *gens Augusta*.[32]

Aftermath

Dion tells us that the speech in which Octavian pardoned the Alexandrians was delivered in Greek—though Suetonius says that 'he never could speak the Greek tongue readily, nor ever ventured to compose in it. If there were occasion for him to express his sentiments in that language, he always stated what he had to say in Latin and gave it to another to translate.'[1] He must have felt that it would be a bad thing to address the impressionable Alexandrians in Latin. After the speech he had a look at the mummied body of Alexander and touched it, breaking off by accident a piece of the nose. But he declined a view of the Ptolemies despite the eagerness of the Alexandrians to show them. 'I wished to see a king, not corpses.' After all his attacks on the Egyptians as beast-worshippers, it is not surprising that he refused to enter the presence of Apis, remarking that he was accustomed to worship gods, not cattle.

Before Cleopatra's tomb statues of her two handmaids were set up in praise of their fidelity-to-death. The three younger children, who had been less politically involved than Caesarion, were handed over to Octavia, who brought them up. The little Sun and Moon walked in Octavian's Triumph, and after that nothing more is heard of the boys. If they survived, they were kept in obscurity— though legend made one of them Zenobia's ancestor. But Selene married Juba II of Mauretania and built up a little Alexandria on the Moroccan coast. Dion says that Octavian as a favour 'made a present' of her two brothers to Selene: that is, sent them to live in Morocco. Juba had had a good Greek education and he gained a name as a voluminous compiler in Greek of books of secondhand erudition; he reigned as king from 25 till about the start of the first century A.D. He had been on campaigns with Octavian and was clearly trusted as a harmless character. Dion adds, 'To his nieces, the daughters whom Octavia had had by Antony and had reared, he assigned money from their father's estate. He also ordered Antony's freedmen to hand over at once to Illus, son of Antony and Fulvia, all that by law they'd have been required to bequeath to him at their death.' Drusilla wedded Antonius Felix, the governor of Judaea in the story of St Paul. The son of Selene and Juba fell a victim in 40 the emperor Gaius, who was angered at his wearing a purple mantle more conspicuous than his own in the amphitheatre at Rome, exiled him, then had him murdered on the highway.[2]

Antony's memory was damned by senatorial decree; his name was erased from inscriptions and coins; his statues were overthrown. It was forbidden to link the names Marcus and Antonius, says Plutarch; Dion merely states that relatives of his were not allowed to use the name Marcus. Inscriptions show the name Marcus Antonius was common among soldiers and freedmen; we find among its owners a *faber* (smith), gladiators, a *stator Augusti* (orderly), a quaestor's scribe, an *eques*, and a man who held all the offices of his hometown. It was probably slower in reappearing at senatorial level.

A village in Lydia continued to honour Antony's memory; a tribe with his name remained at Prusias on the Hypios, and perhaps at Ephesos. Otherwise he left little traces in the east except that Polemon, who married his granddaughter, called their eldest son, future priestking of Olba, Marcus Antonius Polemon, and their daughter, who married Kotys of Thrace, Antonia Tryphaina. But we must not forget that from Antony and Octavia descended the emperors Gaius and Nero, so that his strain triumphed over that of Octavian on the imperial throne after all.

There were many Actian monuments. Octavian ascribed his success to Actian Apollo, whose temple was enlarged; and the local Actian festival was made five-yearly, equal in honour to the Olympian—as once the Alexandrian Ptolemeia had been. It was to Apollo that Octavian reared his ten-ship trophy.

The day before the seafight near Socilym as he was walking on the shore a fish leaped out of the sea and laid itself at his feet [as a sign of sea-homage]. At Actium, while on his way to the fleet before the battle he was met by an ass with a fellow driving it. The man was named Eutychos [Fortunate] and the beast, Nichon [Victorious]. After the victory he erected a brazen statue to each, in a temple built on the site of his camp.[3]

Near the camp-site he founded Nikopolis, Victory-town, into which he synoicised most of the cities of Akarnia and Epeiros, including Pyrrhos' capitol, Ambrakia, now fallen to village-level. The people had to move to the new city, whether they liked it or not. Coins show him posing as the counterpart of the Antigonids who had beaten the Ptolemies: Demetrios who worsted Ptolemy I and especially Antigonos Gonatas, who killed Rome's enemy Pyrrhos and humbled Ptolemy II at Kos. The coins which show Neptune with his foot on a globe recall those of Demetrios with Poseidon—even if their symbolism also glances back at Sextus. Nikopolis was a copy of Demetrios' synoicism of all Magnesia into Demetrias. We may note too the coins showing a ship's prow that bears the Victory of Samothrace: a statue set up by Antigonos Gonatas to commemorate Kos. The ten-ship trophy had been as near as he could get to Gonatas' dedication of his flagship Isthmia to Apollo; at Actium he, Octavian, had had no flagship. By associating himself with imagery of Demetrios and Gonatas he was seeking to make Actium out as a great sea-battle.

From Egypt he travelled back through Syria into Asia Minor, restoring to the cities many artworks taken by Antony. He had already made some new dispositions of the client-kings; now he made more—though the total effect of his changes was slight. The Donations were cancelled; Cyprus and Cyrene once more became Roman provinces. Two petty dynasts were executed, not as Antonians, but as mere murderers: Adiatorix for massacring Romans, Alexandros of Emesa for inciting Antony to kill his brother, Iamblichos. The tyrant Straton, removed from Amisos, was not Antony's man. In Asia

Minor most of the dynasts had changed sides in time. Deiotaros of Paphlagonia and Rhoimetalkes of Thrace kept their realms; Kleon, who had been a brigand leader of Mysia, became priestking of Zeus Abrettenios in Aiolis; the priestking of Komana Pontika, though Caesar's man, had his post given to Adiatorix's son or to Medeus, who had revolted against Antony in Mysia. Tarkondimotos, fallen fighting for Antony, had been succeeded by his son, whom Octavian dethroned. Till 20 Amanos was treated as part of Cilicia; then the old line was reinstated. Of Antony's three most important kings, all did well. Amyntas had his territory enlarged with lands that had been given to Cleopatra; he also got Derbe and Laranda from a local tyrant; Archelaos too had his realm widened; Polemon managed to keep Pontos, he lost Armenia Minor but gained the right to expand on his northeast.

Octavian gave freedom to the Cretan towns which had declared for him; on the mainland he founded Nikopolis and rewarded Sparta by increasing its territory and setting it over the Actian Games.[4] In Syria the Phoenician cities regained their freedom, Berytos being specially favoured. In Judaea, Hyrkanos, returning from Parthia, was killed by Herod for fear that Octavian might make him king. Herod, who had stood by Antony till Actium, now boldly took off his diadem and laid it at Octavian's feet without excuses. He had been true, he said, to his benefactor Antony; if Octavian tried him, he'd find him as true. Octavian restored the diadem with his own hand; he also restored the balsam-gardens and added all Palestine except Askalon, together with Cleopatra's Galatian bodyguard. Nikolaos of Damas, who had been tutor of Cleopatra's children, joined Herod and served him well. Beyond the Euphrates, Octavian made no attempt to interfere. He did nothing about the massacre of Romans by Artaxes of Armenia; he merely held his brothers as hostages. When in 30 the pretender Tiridates fled to Syria, he allowed him asylum but not aid, and received the envoys of Phraates amiably. The Median king, Antony's friend, he treated well, returned his daughter Iotape, and gave him Armenia Minor as a trusty frontier-warden. On the whole then the settlement in the east followed Antony's lines and was a tribute to his good sense.[5]

What of Egypt? In this relation Tacitus speaks of an *Instituta Augusti*. Straight after Cleopatra's death, on 1 Thoth, Octavian seems to have taken charge of the country, which in due course was to be proclaimed a Roman province but in effect remained his direct property in a way that no other province did.[6] At once he forbade entry to senators. The legal code, the *Gnomon*, which we meet later, seems certainly to include an Augustan basis. We do not know just when the fifteen-year census-cycle began; the first documents date from 19–20 A.D., suggesting that the system was instituted in 5–6 A.D. and B.C. 10–9. The *epikrisis* or verification of titles, brought in to maintain the separation of classes, preserves in some later examples a scrutiny of ancestors going back as far as a list established in A.D. 4–5. In short it seems that Octavian at once set Egypt in a special category, but took several years to work out in detail just what this entailed. Essentially he stepped into Cleopatra's Ptolemaic shoes; he appointed a prefect as a sort of viceregent, something quite unlike the officials taking over the administration of other provinces. Continuity is shown by the way in which the *Gnomon* speaks of the *prostagmata* of kings; these are the laws of the Ptolemies. The ruler of Rome had to take the place of the Pharoahs, as the Ptolemies had; without the rites which the king or his representative alone could carry out, the Nileflood, it was thought, could not occur.[7]

On Octavian's obelisk at Rome (B.C. 10) he declared that Egypt was 'reduced into the power of the Roman People,' and the same statement appears in his *Res Gestae*. But clearly the place was not a normal province; no Roman magistrates were there, no official deriving his nomination from the People. When the provinces were divided into those administered by the Princeps and those by the Senate, Egypt was not mentioned at all. It coexisted as the private domain of the prince, administered by a man he appointed. Who then dealt with the taxes and revenues? The Ptolemaic *dioiketes* was gone. Plutarch preserves the name Eros of the freedman who ran things awhile for his master and was then crucified for misdemeanours. Yet Octavian, now Augustus, kept the *idiologos* who had grown up under the Ptolemies and whom Strabon described in the early days of the empire: 'his business is to inquire into property for which there is no claimant and which of right falls to Caesar'. He and the governor (who has 'the rank of a king') are accompanied by 'Caesar's freedmen and stewards, who are entrusted with affairs of more or less importance'. Of the native town-magistrates, he adds, 'the first is the law-expounder, clad in scarlet; he has the care of providing what is necessary for the town and receives the customary honours of the country; the second is the record-writer; the third is the chief judge; the fourth is the commander of the night-guard'.[8] The old royal land was now, though

447

not consistently, called public land: which did not mean a clear assimilation to the *ager publicus* of the empire: that itself ended by being confused with the emperor's lands. No doubt it was out of the royal lands that Antony made up the big estates which seem to have passed, through Antonia Minor, to Germanicus and Claudius. We hear of an *ousia Louriana*, held by M. Lurius, who commanded the right wing of the fleet at Actium.

Because of Octavian's control of the Egyptian revenues, he was able to come four times to the aid of the public treasury, transferring 150,000,000 sesterces, and to declare that he 'had made distributions of grain and money from his own granary and patrimony, sometimes to 100,000 persons sometimes tó many more'—as well as handing over 170,000,000 sesterces when the military treasury was founded, to provide money for soldiers who had served twenty years or more. The prefect of Egypt was only a procurator or steward of the prince. This trick of giving public authority to a private procurator had come up among the many abuses of power in the later Republic. The big usurers (Pompey, Brutus, and the like), who exploited the towns and client-kingships, gave their stewards the official title of prefects. Thus, private debts, owed to great men, became public debts; and we meet such largescale gangster-exploits as the restoration of the Piper by a Roman army in the interests of businessmen and usurers. We can estimate what the provincials suffered from the men of the Roman senatorial class when we read what Cicero found out about Brutus while governing his province, Cilicia, in 50. Scaptius, an associate of Brutus, claimed to be a prefect and Cicero correctly disallowed the claim. Then Cicero, who had fixed the interest rate at 12 per cent 'with the approval of the most miserly money-lenders', found that Scaptius was demanding 48 per cent from debtors of Brutus in Cyprus, and that he had used his powers as 'prefect' in the previous year to besiege the senate of the town of Salamis in their own council-room till five councillors died of starvation. The Salaminians begged Cicero to let them deposit their own money in a temple, but he refused, though he knew how badly he was acting. 'What will happen if Paullus, brother-in-law of Brutus, comes here?' We understand how such usurers as Brutus felt the need to kill Caesar.[9]

But Augustus' procurator-prefect in Egypt needed to have *imperium*, so that he might own authority over all Romans in Egypt. We are not sure if this power was granted by a law or a constitution of Augustus. The latter's behaviour throughout was dictated by fear: fear of the eastern masses and fear of a senator setting up as a rival if he wielded Egypt's resources. He gave up founding colonies in the east; he isolated Egypt with its own money, calendar, census-system; he forbade entry to senators, and to the richer *equites*, says Tacitus. Egyptians could not leave their country without authorisation; they needed a passport. Pliny noted with surprise that Egyptians were not classed as *peregrini* among other non-Romans. They were forbidden to form any kind of political organisation; they could not even establish *municipia*. The aim was to hold them fast in village-communities. In the *metropoleis* of the Nomes a simple council of administrators, with the gymnasiarch especially prominent, took the place of municipal councils. Here again Augustus carried on with late Ptolemaic developments. Not even Alexandria, a great city, was allowed its own council or senate. (It seems to have lost its senate in the late Ptolemaic period; but the question is highly controversial.) Alexandrians however held a superior status. The Greeks in general were denied direct privileges and were submitted even to capitation in an attenuated form. Greek however remained the official language, and this fact help to carry on the Hellenisation of the culture. Romans in Egypt were the only favoured section; and strong efforts were made to keep them intact, separate.[10]

Augustus further introduced two important principles: compulsion in the performance of public functions and collective responsibility—for taxes, for the maintenance of the water-system, and so on. He wanted to get rid of the tax-farmers whom the Ptolemies had failed to keep under effective control; and for the same reason he dropped the system of monopolies. He preferred to treat directly with corporations (except for mines and quarries). A crisis in the Augustan system arrived under Nero, which need not concern us here. Whatever changes came in, the sharply-cut lines of the original settlement continued to make Egypt different from the rest of the empire. It is relevant however to ask here to what extent the system developed in Egypt, with its many Hellenistic survivals, affected the empire as a whole. There can be no doubt that over the years the influence was considerable, though we cannot trace it in detail. It has been well said, 'It was in Egypt that was worked out the regime of the future'. Egyptian religious influences were strong; a bureaucratic system invaded the whole empire with the advent of the great freedmen of Claudius. No doubt something like this would have happened anyhow, as the result of the inner needs of the empire; but the existence of advanced bureaucratic models in Egypt could not but hasten the process and determine many of its lines of growth. As resilience died out of the empire, it took on more and more the shape of an Hellenistic monarchy. In this sense, the ideas of Antony and Cleopatra belonged to the future rather than to the past.[11]

More of that in a moment. Now let us glance at the ways in which Octavian consolidated his religious position as the expression of his political position. Actium, we saw, finalised his claim on Apollo as patron; he himself became in some sort Apollo, though he never made the kind of assertions that Antony and Cleopatra made. A monument at Cyrene records the eponymous priests of Apollo from A.D. 102 to about 107; each name is still dated by the year of the Actian Era. Ovid ends the first book of his *Fasti* with the announcement of universal peace:

> Come, Peace, neat tresses wreathed with Actian laurels,
> let your gentle presence abide in the whole world . . .
> May the world near and far dread Aeneas' sons;
> if any land doesn't fear Rome, let it love instead.[12]

But Octavian wanted a closer link in religion with everyday life than the cult of Apollo could bring him. In 30 a decree ordered that a libation should be made to him at the beginning of meals.[13] He thus was linked with the household cult of the Lares, and we find the imperial cult itself emerging in the Lares Augusti, when the *vici*, districts, got their Lares in the reform about B.C. 7.[14] The Roman *equites* of their own accord celebrated his birthday for two days together; and all ranks of people, for years,

Gemma Augustea (in Vienna), sardonyx. Augustus seated with helmeted Roma; sceptre and eagle under throne; he holds augural staff, left foot on a shield (the *clipeus aureus* in the Curia Julia?). A woman (? Oikoumene, the civilised world) holds over him a *corona civica*. Above is the Capricorn Sign. Terra Mater and perhaps Oceanus on one side; a warrior descending from Triumphal Chariot on the other (Tiberius in A.D. 12, with Germanicus by the horses; or the German campaign of 7 B.C. in which Gaius Caesar took part). Below soldiers erect trophy, with captives on right. The cameos may have been presents to foreign princes.

in performance of a vow, threw pieces of money into the Curtain Lake (an enclosure in the Forum) as an offering for his welfare. Also on 1 January they presented for his acceptance (though he was absent) New-Year gifts on the Capitol; with the proceeds he bought costly images of the gods to be set up in various streets, *e.g.* that of Apollo Sandalarius, Jupiter Tragoedus, and others.[15] Livia, we may note, became in Egypt Pronuba like Juno, a patroness of marriage; and this title had a long history, leading on to Marcus Aurelius and the younger Faustina with the same role. On coins Faustina was associated with Fecunditas, Fortuna Muliebris, Laetitia (Joy); and the opening of a marriage contract of A.D. 170 from Egypt invokes her and her husband.[16]

Octavian dedicated the Palatine Shrine of Apollo on 9 October 28; and there in a *templum*, part of the portico, not aedicular in form, the Senate used to meet. The *Tabula Hebana* tells us that Tiberius also set there portraits of Germanicus Caesar and his father the elder Drusus: 'Over the capitals of the columns of that roof by which the statue of Apollo is covered.' So it seems that the god's statue was not inside the temple.[17] Probably the canopy had one of its sides supported by consoles set in the wall against which the statue stood, so that only two columns were at the side standing out from the wall.[18] We have an account of the place by Propertius. He deals first with the portico. 'Then I saw Phoebus in marble more comely than life.' He goes on to mention an altar with oxen carved by Myron around it. 'From between the porticoes the temple rose.' Two sun-chariots stood on the acroterion; and there were ivory-covered doors. 'Lastly the Pythian god between mother and sister.' From this account it seems the god was twice represented. The three statues finally mentioned are logically inside the temple; and Pliny mentions in the shrine (*delubrum*), an Apollo by Skopas, a Latona by Kephistodotos, and a Diana by Timotheos.[19] The images of Germanicus and Drusus were set up because of their claim to be called orators; it was in that character that Augustus was himself shown there—probably the work of Tiberius, but on Augustus' own instructions. The images were not in the Library, the traditional place for images of writers ever since Asinius Pollio founded the first public library of Rome in the Atrium of Liberty.

Terra Mater panel from the *Ara Pacis*.

It was usual to depict only the dead, but Pollio made an exception for Varro. Soon after the temple of Apollo was finished, Augustus built the Porticus Octaviae, which was provided with a library after the death of Marcellus in B.C. 23. Normally the portraits in libraries were *imagines clipeatae*, set in shields, and we know that those in the Palatine temple were such. There was another image of Apollo in the library attached to the temple of Augustus. We do not hear of any identifications of the Apollos with Augustus except that Servius and pseudo-Acron speak of a statue of Augustus as Apollo in the library.[20] In building the Apollo temple and settling in it the Sibylline Books

Panel from *Ara Pacis* with the Imperial Family. The man in profile with the military cloak has often been taken as Nero Drusus (then commander in Germany); if so the women in front of him is Antonia Minor and the child holding her hand is young Germanicus. In the next group the young man may be Domitius Ahenobarbus with his wife Antonia Maior and their two children, a boy holding on to Drusus' cloak while an elder girl smiles down at him. This girl has her hair drawn back in a small bun and has a necklet with crescent pendant.

Augustus was removing the anomaly that so great a god as Apollo had had no new temple in Rome for centuries; but he was also championing Apollo as the god of his own dispensation. From early times a certain rivalry of Apollo and Diana as a divine pair with the Capitoline triad can be traced. The handing over of the Sibylline Books to the safe hands of Apollo was linked with burning of the heretical prophecies.[21]

After Actium the temple of Janus was closed (in 29) for the first time. In 28 a laureate head of Octavian appeared on a tetradrachm of the east with the legend giving his name as *Imp. Caesar divi f. consul* for the fourth time and proclaiming him *Vindex* (Vindicator) of Roman Liberty.[22] Cicero in his *Philippics* had called Peace a Tranquil Liberty; Augustus restored the temple of Jupiter Libertas or Liber on the Aventine, and in Egypt was called Zeus Eleutherios, Liberator. On the reverse of the coin cited above is a woman with caduceus, Pax; behind her is a snake with the mystic *cista*. A similar *pax*-coin of Pella, Macedonia, appeared in 25. After the Calabrian war the temple of Janus was closed for the second time, and probably about this period Virgil wrote his prophecy of eternal peace in the first book of the *Aeneid*.[23] The connection of peace with a ruler can be traced back to Alexander, Demetrios Poliorketes at Athens (B.C. 291–0), Pompey at Mytilene (62), and Caesar near the end of his life. We must recall also the early Roman use of the theme *Pax Deorum*: a pact with the gods gained by prayers, sacrifices, *lectisternia*, votive offerings. The peace here gained was not a pact or peace between equals; by submission to the gods men got rid of all sorts of troubles, diseases, famines, wars. The gods could thus be seen as active peace-makers. Their power was now in the hands of the emperor, and by total submission to him peace might be won.[24]

The term war had become equivalent in these years to civil war; so peace was civil peace or *concordia*.[25] Peace reverted to its meaning of a pact; of the nineteen uses of the term in Caesar's *Civil War* seventeen are linked with the idea of negotiations. Cicero, Brutus, Cassius insisted on no 'peace of servitude'. Cicero, we saw, stressed the aspect of liberty and condemned the 'insidious condition of peace'. Sallust uses the same vocabulary. In 43 Cicero several times referred to a 'war called peace'. Plutarch says the massacre at Rome by Marius' slaves, in 87, made the Romans 'look on the evils of war as a Golden Age'.[26] The same kind of idiom was carried on by writers of the first century A.D. thus Manilius denounced the Wars of Peace, the *funera* of Peace, the Various Slaughters of Peace.[27] In Calpurnius freedom from war becomes the Golden Age.[28]

So we see that from B.C. 63 (the Conspiracy of Catilina, which announces the irretrievable inner crisis of Roman society) peace has attached to it terms like *Tranquillitas, Quies, Otium, Concordia*. *Otium* has a special significance for Cicero, representing inner or domestic calm and leisure. (*Otia dia*, divine leisures, is a pastoral term in Lucretius, reflecting the happiness of a golden age.)[29] Cicero was the great propounder of these ideas; for him war and sedition had become synonymous. Most important was his fusion of the ideas of *pax* and *concordia*: peace proceeds from the assent of everyone—the readiness of the middle and lower orders to accept the rule of the *optimates*.[30] By a simple extension we reach the view that *pax-concordia* can only be reached by everyone accepting the role of the single ruler. Cicero or Antony tells the Senate that they must maintain Caesar's Acts—for which he has been murdered—for the sake of *concordia*; such a plea wakes strong emotions, the fear of further seditions and conflicts, the hopes of a stable situation in which past gains can be held and extended.[31] Peace comes to mean both inner and outer concord. In the whole of Caesar's *Civil War* we do not once meet the word *concordia*, doubtless because he had no illusions about premature or false attempts at stable balances. Lucan later has *pax* forty-three times and *concordia* only five times, because for him *pax* has come to mean wholly an inner peace. *Concordia* thus came to take over much of the colouration of the Hellenistic *homonoia*; and it had the same complex of meanings according to the social level of the person using it. *Concordia* for Cicero was the agreement of all classes to accept a constitution dominated by the very rich landlords, with the middle class or *equites* allotted an honourable position above the masses; *homonoia* for a Hellenistic king meant all his subjects accepting his unifying rule; for the Sibylline poet it meant the elimination of all class differences and of money-power; for Augustus *concordia* meant the Ciceronian scheme developed under his own unchallenged personal rule.[32]

In B.C. 45 there had been a scheme to build a temple to a New Homonoia (Dion's term) as a counterblast to that of Concordia built by the extreme reactionary Opimius in 121 to celebrate the murder of G. Gracchus and the victory of the *optimates*. When Augustus accepted the calling of the eighth month of the year after his new name, Pythagoreans at least saw it as a consecration of *homonoia*, the number of which was eight. It was in August 28 that he officially and finally ended the civil wars.[33]

One important monument by which Augustus tried to annex the ideas and imagery of golden-age prosperity was his Altar of Peace. 'When I returned from Gaul and Spain after successfully settling the affairs of those provinces, in the consular year of Tib. Nero and P. Quintilius [B.C. 13], the Senate voted that an Altar of Augustan *Pax* should be consecrated for my return in the Field of Mars and ordered that magistrates, priests, and vestal virgins should bring a yearly sacrifice to it.'[34] The site was an enclosure in the Campus Martius west of the Via Flaminia.

Terra Mater from a Phaethon sarcophagus (Villa Borghesi).

The Altar was ceremoniously dedicated on 30 January 9 B.C.[35] The section that concerns us is the panel showing Terra Mater with two children, a lamb and cow at her feet. (The woman is surely Terra Mater rather than *Saturnia Tellus*—though we might indeed describe her as the Blessed Italy of Virgil expanded to become a world-symbol.) Terra appears also on the breastplate of Augustus, on the Prima Porta monument, where she has a cymbal at her feet, showing a link with Cybele; and the same link is stressed on a patera from Parabiago.[36] The two nestling infants are the *karpoi*, the fruits of the earth, emblems of her fertility. A late poet, John of Gaza, tells how she brought them forth at a birth. One twin stretched out hands 'to catch the rain that sprouts the thirsty plants', but the other, close to his mother, kissed her. This conceit appears on a sarcophagus of Phaethon and a mosaic from Sassoferrato.[37] The children play around, help to carry the horn-of-plenty, tug at Terra's drapes to bare her breasts; the motive of suckling is rare, but certainly existed. As well as at Prima Porta, the Terra-motive appears on three breastplates of Augustus, two of which represent him as conqueror of East and West, as the Prima Porta statue does; he is the beneficient master of the universe.[38] On an Augustan monument, the temple of the Dioscures at Naples, Terra Mater appears on the pediment, facing Oceanus; on the *Gemma Augustea* she has risen from the reclining to the seated posture and leans on the emperor's throne. Of her two children, one is a little boy with two long cornstalks, who rests an arm on her knee; the other, more a babe, peeps over her shoulder; at her back are gathered a group of cosmic deities. On the Parabiago patera the rebirth is represented by the marriage of Cybele with reborn Attis.

This sort of imagery continued under the empire. Thus, on a coin of Severus and Caracalla we see the ritual of Terra Mater as carried out at the Secular Games of A.D. 204. The mystique of the Fourth Eclogue provided an essential part of the imperial ideology; but it has dropped the classless *homonoia* of the Sibylline version. It had its value as an ideal, but it remained little more than a dream, a halo used to gild the harsh realities of imperial rule. At best it helped to stimulate the humane impulses of the more well-intentioned rulers. For the masses the divine babe had become the Christchild suckled by Mary instead of Cleopatra and rejected by the world, not raised aloft on a golden throne. The divine child returned to the world of nature, but to the beasts in the lowly Bethlehem stables, not those in a Dionysiac world of milk and honey. He was heralded by his own star, not by the Julian Star; and his star brought, not Roman generals, but shepherds to his side. True, it later was said to have brought mages or kings. The heralding star of the shepherds was purely Mithraic in origin, just as the Bethlehem rockcut stable seems to have been a Mithraic cave of rebirth. But all these points of contact with the Eclogue and with other legendary moments of the period we have examined are merely examples of the way in which Christianity sprang from, and gathered together, the manifold hopes of death-birth and redemption which agitated the last century B.C.

There is one more Augustan ritual we must notice if we are to complete our series. In B.C. 17 Augustus felt sufficiently secure in his power, and considered that his laws aimed at re-establishing strict morals, especially in marriage, had been effective enough, for him to declare a return to the ancient Roman ways, a turning-point of regeneration. (He had made an attempt at moral reforms after Actium; but in face of protests and opposition he withdrew his law; and in 22 he gave up the project of Secular Games. Now, returning from the east in 17, he made a second effort to stage the Games and carried them through.) Horace composed the Hymn extolling the definitive return of peace, prosperity, and ancient morals. Not that even now things went easily. The Senate was unfriendly; the public demonstrated; Augustus wore a cuirass under his toga to be safe from daggers. He punished the Senate by making them listen while he read out the whole of a speech which a Metellus had once delivered in a vain attempt to stop the falling birthrate.[39]

As the name shows, the Games were meant to express the successful transition from a dangerous period into the establishment of a new *Saeculum* or Age. Their management was under the Fifteen Men who had charge of the Sibylline Books, together with the antiquarian Ateius Capito. They began on the night of 31 May and lasted three days and three nights. On the first night came sacrifices to the Moirai, Fates; on the second to the Ilithyiai, Birth-goddesses; on the third to Terra Mater. The first day (1 June) was sacred to Jupiter Capitolinus; the second to Juno Queen; the third to Apollo and Diana. Augustus alone offered prayers and sacrifices at night, but by day Agrippa helped him. An inscription tells us that Horace's Ode was sung on the third day—apparently at the temple of Apollo on the Palatine 'and in the same way on the Capitol'.[40] (Mommsen thought this meant it was sung in procession from the Palatine to the Capitol.) The chorus consisted of the usual number of 27 girls and 27 boys. The Ode opens by calling on Phoebus and Diana, asks Sol to maintain Rome's pre-eminence, Ilithyia to look after the offspring. The Fates are to give good fortune equal to that of the past, Earth is to grant bounteous harvest. If, by the aid of Apollo and Diana, Aeneas came to Italy, let the land now prosper with goodness and happiness, and Caesar's prayers be granted—he has conquered all lands and restored all virtues. The Hymn ends with the claim that Apollo and Diana hear, all the gods lend their ears.

A poor conclusion after the vast hopes inaugurated by the Star (Comet) coming to announce Caesar with the Evangel for all men, after the Blessed Earth of the Eclogue, after the Redeemed World of the Sibyllines.[41]

The Secular Games had originally been dedicated to Dis and Proserpine of the Underworld; but these deities are here dropped out and the whole system is dominated by Apollo and Diana (Octavius-Augustus and Livia). We may argue that the latter pair are the heavenly counterpart of the underworld-pair; Servius identifies Apollo and Diana in heaven with Liber and Ceres on earth and Dis and Proserpine below. But Apollo, god of healing and light, was also a destroyer, and we find in Italy he had chthonic rites. Apollo Soranus, originally Pater Soranus, was worshipped on Mt Soracte, and he was a chthonic power comparable with Dis. Vejovis, worshipped by the Julian *gens* at Bovillae, was also chthonic, with destructive powers, and often linked with Apollo. Augustus, looking for divine sanctions, had the idea of appearing as Vejovis, god of the Julian clan when he died; Tiberius dedicated a statue of him at Bovillae. Also *divus* Augustus bears the attributes of both Jupiter (the thunderbolt) and Sol-Apollo (radiate crown and star) which seem taken from the Vejovis-cult.[42] There may indeed be connection between the Golden Bough of underworld-guidance and the boughs carried by the boys and girls in the processional chorus for Apollo and Diana—*ramus aureus* and *ramus laureus*. The Sibyl played an important part in the Apollo-aspects according to Macrobius. The diviner Marcius and the Sibylline Books ordered the inauguration of the Apollinine Games. During the first celebration the city was attacked, but a cloud of arrows was launched from the sky on the enemy. Macrobius also states that the Games were begun on the evidence of the decemvir Cornelius Rufus—and he adds, with fanciful etymology, that Rufus was thus surnamed Sibylla, from which came the name Sylla or Sulla by corruption. Rufus wanted the Games to ensure victory in the first Carthaginian War; the Senate ordered the consultation of the Sibylline Books and learned from them how to institute and carry out the ceremony.[43]

We may note too that the Star turns up again. M. Sanquinius, moneyer of Augustus at Rome in 17, struck coins with a young laureate head, with the Sidus Julium above. The head has been taken as that of a rejuvenated Julius Caesar; the comet of 17 was seen as his Star returning. But the head must be rather Augustus in whom Caesar is reincarnated. If a resurrection-motive is intended, as it well may be, the stress is on the new form of the hero-god. Augustus had no wish to revive thoughts of Caesar except in so far as they glorified himself. Caesar was the man of the Civil War; Augustus was the man breaking through into a new dispensation, the *pius Aeneas*—or perhaps rather Iulus, son of Aeneas, who founded the Julian *gens*. There may however be a side-glance at the two sons of Julia and Agrippa, one born 20, the other 17, who were both adopted by Augustus this year.

As for the Augustan system itself we need not trace its evolution in any detail. Constitutionally it was based on the edict ending the triumviral period. Astutely, however, Octavian linked the return of *Libertas*, not with the restoration of the Republic, but with the ending of Civil War, thanks to *Concordia*, the bond linking Peace and Liberty. Thus in 28–7 he announced the return to the traditional State while in fact busily inaugurating and consolidating a new régime.[44] He drew on the linguistic system of Cicero, that arch-opportunist and equivocator, who was an expert in smothering a situation of conflict and oppression in fine phrases—as long as the *optimates* were on top. He had a delicate job to carry out. The Senate now had many leading men who had come over to his side not long before Actium, when Antony's link with Cleopatra had turned them against him. Their antecedents were Republican or Antonian—not that they had any attachment to Republican ideals, but wanted the Republic as a system giving their class freedom to plunder and oppress. Octavian had to devise measures that would keep his own role intact without too far antagonising these men. He had not merely to cover up a corrupt system in high-sounding Ciceronian terms, but also to say one thing while doing quite another in a massive way. He had to talk about a return to old forms, while depriving those forms of any meaning, and yet he had to satisfy his suspicious and hardheaded senatorial audience. He had toyed with the idea of being the New Romulus in 36 with his installation on the Palatine near the Hut of Romulus; in 28 he had the idea of building a mausoleum on the Field of Mars on the model of ancient Italic tumuli; his absolutism in 30–27 drew on the prestige of the king-founder and leant on the tradition that Romulus was both legislator and warrior (though commonly the legislative aspect had been taken on by the second king Numa).[45] From Agrippa he gained the concept of an abdication which held fast to all the realities of supreme power. In 28 came the return to the yearly election of two consuls, who however lacked all the essential powers of the pre-50 consuls. Octavian could move from the role of Conservator of Old Rome to that of Founder of the New Rome as Augustus. Consecrated by this semi-divine title, he was in effect above the laws which he seems to have restored; above them, he controlled them. As Augustus he need not fear or grudge the salutation of *Imperator* to his generals.[46]

The *cognomen* Augustus was conferred on him by the Senate in January 27. He now had lost all his original names, but had achieved a set of three names which revealed plainly how he had arrived at his position: *Imperator Caesar Augustus*. The *nomen* Caesar he had used to make himself out as Caesar's political heir; the *praenomen* Imperator expressed the military power on which he had risen; the *cognomen* suggested his status above the law. Augustus was a word used of gods and their sanctuaries, of auguries or a fountain. The three-name system was however used only in official documents. In other matters all sorts of jugglings were possible. Vitruvius, an old officer, dedicated his book on Architecture, soon after 27, to Imperator Caesar. Imperator Augustus was rarely used—no doubt the collocation of two such powerful names was felt too much without the human Caesar to link them. So Caesar Augustus became the common form, with Augustus Caesar to stress the moral or religious aspects of his role—Augustus there becoming a sort of *praenomen*. Also, Imperator suggested too strongly the days of civil war; after Actium it was less used. But new titles, 'Highpriest, Endowed with Tribunician Power, Father of the Country', came up to provide further variations.

No one was now in a position to point out the complete contradiction between the *restitutio in integrum* (the return to some essential but not defined *Romanitas*) and the actual situation of supreme power wielded by an unchallengeable individual. The *auctoritas* or authority once owned by the Senate now belonged to Augustus; it was a power extending over all citizens and was distinct

The sides of the altar showing Augustus as augur (figure 10): a Victory and Trophy; two Lares Augusti.

from the *potestas* exercised over his magisterial colleagues. He became Princeps of the Senate, ostensibly its chief or chairman, but in fact its master. (The populace had hailed him as *princeps* on his return from Actium.) He was First Citizen, an honorary title not without a military colouration. But his propaganda modestly stressed, not the aspect of civil and military power, but the notion of primacy in morals and excellence. Such a term suited him, new, vague, and yet precise enough in warning others not to trespass on his unique position. A harmless and spontaneous tribute to his services, it acted as a cloak for his absolutism in which so much depended on not forcing any clear definition of his supremacy. For the moment his role was also hidden under a ten-yearly delegation of powers. Gradually, step by step, the imperial autocracy was gathered firmly around his person, with a minimum of open or declared ruptures with tradition.[47] Thus Augustus was able to achieve what Caesar had failed to do with his blunt and careless disregard of forms, or Antony with his rich and cloudy vision of a Dionysiac leadership.

We have noted that it was Antony's lineage that triumphed, rather than that of Augustus in Gaius (Caligula) and Nero. Gaius deserves a few words for the odd way in which he seems to have attempted to intrude an Antonian system into the Augustan constitution. Antony's daughter, Antonia Minor, had married Drusus Claudius Nero and borne Germanicus, who married Vipsania Agrippina and begot Gaius. Gaius, emperor from 37 A.D. to 41, reintroduced the Isiac cult into Rome; he built the great temple of Isis Campensis on the Field of Mars. Oddly, however, we have no record in any of the sources (Seneca, Suetonius, Dion, Josephos, Philon) of a devotion on his part to Isis. One might argue that his devotion was omitted, since the denigratory tradition preferred him as a sheer madman; but this suggestion could hardly apply to Philon with his full account of an embassy to Rome. Still, the facts are consistent: his eastern policy in favour of vassal royalties, his night-extravagances, his marriage with his sister Drusilla, the ceremonies he carried out after the death of his sister-wife and the birth of the little Drusilla, his divine pretensions linked with a daily ritual, his sacred marriage with the Moon, the generous amnesty and tax remissions after his accession. He had passed his early years with his grandmother, who must have told him much of Antony. Iconographically, we see him as a child with the Horoslock of hair; Drusilla as Isis-Aphrodite in the temple of the Esqueline Venus; his three sisters all supplied with attributes of Isis; and a posthumous portrait of the elder Agrippina in Egyptian technique and with Isiac elements, *e.g.* the ringlets falling to the shoulders.[48] Further, his strongly pro-Antonian attitudes appear in his refusal to say or believe that Agrippa was his grandfather. He hated the man who had commanded the Roman fleet at Actium; he held that battle a disaster to the Roman People and forbade its commemoration. He also hated Agrippa for his anti-Isiac role. It was perhaps a mere accident of wilful despotism that when, after Drusilla's death, he chose Lollia Paulina, wife of the governor of the Balkans, he was acting in a style attributed by the Pyramid Texts to the Egyptian king, who took wives from husbands at his will—and that here the husband, bringing his wife to Rome and giving her in marriage 'like a father', was using the procedure of *engyesis*, of contract between the lord *kyrios*, of a young woman and the man she was marrying, as practised in Egypt. There seems however an Isiac motive in some of his appointments, *e.g.* of Gn. Sentius Saturninus, Paulina's nephew, a famous adherent of Isis, who had caused an amorous scandal leading to anti-Isiac legislation in A.D. 19. An obelisk (now in St Peter's Place in Rome) was cut and inscribed in Egypt before being sent to Italy in his reign. And perhaps his murder of young Ptolemaios of Mauretania, grandson of Cleopatra Selene, was motivated by a deeper jealousy than the tale of the purple garment allows for. Juba II had installed at his capital, Caesarea, a lighthouse which in plan imitated the pharos of Alexandria and was connected with a sanctuary looking over the sea—surely dedicated to Isis

Coin showing Juba II of Mauretania and his wife Cleopatra Selene. Coin of the son who was murdered by Caligula.

Pelagia. Gaius may well have considered the Moroccan branch of the Antonian family a rival for the favours of Isis.[49] A not-very-tactful epigram by Krinagoras had suggested that they might one day unite North Africa; he was celebrating the marriage of Juba and Cleopatra Selene:

> Great bordering regions of the world that stand
> cut from black Ethiopians by the Nile—
> your marriage makes you sovrans of each land,
> Egypt and Libya mated in your smile.
> Ah, may the children of these two again
> yet on both lands own an unshaken reign.

The picture of Gaius as an Isiac seeking an Antonian reversal of Augustan positions can only be pieced together by inference, but it certainly explains his behaviour as nothing else can. Similar elements in Nero's career may ultimately go back to the same sort of revolt against the Augustan system, though not based on so definite an Isiac and Ptolemaic outlook as that of Gaius seems to have been. We may here note one of his positions. He saw himself as a sun-god. In 65 he received the Armenian Tiridates, a Mazdean, in a setting of gold; investing him, he seems to have acted the role of the god Mithras, the Fate and Fortune of the King. Not only was the whole setting golden; it was covered by a *velarium* or awning embroidered with stars (to stress the cosmic imagery), on top of which he was represented as a solar charioteer; he called the event the Day of Gold. He built his Golden House, not merely as a residence for a sun-king, but as a magical act transforming his world into a Golden Age, a theme developed for him by the poet Calpurnius Siculus. The collossal statue with his head at the threshold seems an imitation of the Helios of Rhodes. Thus what was a world-vision embracing all men in Virgil became a personal religious concept of transformation for Nero— though doubtless his solar benevolence was meant to bless all men in turn.[50]

But the actions of Gaius and Nero could only appear as aberrations inside the Augustan world. How, however, we may ask would things have worked out if Antony and Cleopatra had after all won? Like all 'ifs' in history, the question does not admit of a plain answer. In fact Antony had no chance of winning after he became identified with the east. It has been well said:

In Italy society was in fact being formed, completing the process of Romanising itself there where regional traditions

471

and non-Latin speech had put up the longest resistance (in Campania, for example), at the moment when the Principate was established, and it was in certain respects the decisive balance giving Octavius victory over Antony. The Empire, at its birth, repaid it with a certain gratitude. Augustus restored to it, amid and above the provinces, the prerogatives and actual privileges that the radically audacious plans of Caesar had threatened.[51]

With Italy and its manpower thus behind him, Octavian was assured of victory. Still, we can make some general points about the world that Antony and Cleopatra, if successful, would have brought about. There would have been nothing like Octavian's caution, which, while it raises charges of hypocrisy and craft, did have the virtue of preserving, as intact as the situation permitted, certain important and valuable Roman ideas and procedures— political forms and their tradition—even if under the principate and empire the forms grew ever more hollow, ever more in flat contradiction with the world that professed or exploited them.

The concept of the rule of law, for instance; even the notion of *Libertas* itself and of the virtue of republican institutions continued its uncertain existence, emptied of content and twisted into various accommodation with absolutism. If Antony and Cleopatra had won, a Hellenistic type of kingship of some sort or another would have been imposed at once. We should have had something not unlike what did eventually come about in the 4th century A.D. But there would have been a great difference between the world of (triumphant) Antony and Cleopatra and that of Constantine the Great. Constantine's system arrived at a quite different historical level, when the full possibilities of the Augustan world had been worked out. The Constantinean level was the result of that working-out of the complex contradictions and positive energies of the Roman world of B.C. 30; and so, if history had been short-circuited and a 4th-century State imposed on a 1st-century situation, a great deal would have been lost. We are compelled to make this judgement, even if there is much in the dream of Antony and Cleopatra that attracts us, and much in the skilful politics of Octavian-Augustus that repels us. In that conflict between the dream-potentialities and the actual possibilities of the situation lies the tragic nature of what happened. Stirred by the Plutarchian narrative, Shakespeare, however ignorant of the full bearings of the events, was able to penetrate to the essence of the conflict and to produce a play which is true in its value-judgements of the epoch.

And we must not forget that the last word was not altogether said in the political sphere. There were deep reactions and responses in the depths of society, which also needed some centuries to work themselves out. The religious agitations and aspirations of our period, baffled of a valid expression in the existing world, turned away from the State and its protagonists. The result was Christianity. Whatever other elements one sees in that creed, the actual crystallisation of its hopes in the period following the conflicts we have traced was determined by those conflicts, their forms of expression, the world-end fears and the desperate search for salvation which struggled at their heart. The fusion of mystery-cult and State-religion could no longer hold the loyalty of the masses. The failure of the State-cults, which in the revolutionary epoch were transformed into saviour-cults

centred on some politician (from Sulla and Marius to
Caesar, Antony, and Octavian) and hoping to bring about
the millenium of peace and plenty, inevitably begot a new
kind of saviour-cult, one which claimed an historical basis
like the politician-heroes, but which was absolutely
opposed to the State. The forms of opposition were
determined by the forms in which acceptance of the State
was expressed, especially sacrifice to the emperor living
or dead; and as the early Christians could not conceive
any other sort of State than that which they knew, and
as they believed the advent which would institute a
new sort of life to be imminent, they poured all their
fierce resistance to the World (the *status quo*) into their
rejection of the imperial cult and its associated pagan
cults which sanctified and upheld the emperor and his
social system. There is then a very definite sense in which
Caesar, hailed in the east as the Bringer of the Evangel,
Antony with his promise of a liberating Golden Age, and
Cleopatra with the divine babe at her breast, were the
forerunners of Christ and Mary. But what with them still
seemed possible as an act from above, from the State,
became a demand from below, totally rejecting the rent
and compromised State. Lactantius seems the first
Christian who declared in writing that Virgil was the
prophet of Christ; and in a way in which he did not understand he was right in his statement.[52] And Eusebios made
this odd computation of the year of Christ's birth, linking
it with the death of Antony and Cleopatra:

> It was the forty-second year of Augustus' reign, but the
> twenty-eighth after the subjugation of Egypt and the death
> of Antony and Cleopatra, which terminated the dynasty of

the Ptolemies, when, according to prophetic prediction, Our
Lord and Saviour Jesus Christ was born in Bethlehem of
Judaea; the year when the census was taken and Quirinius
was governor of Syria [i.e. 3 B.C.].[53]

The struggle of Antony and Cleopatra with Octavian-
Augustus had not been a passing event; it expressed both
a permanent tension between east and west in the Roman
world, which Augustus tried to lessen, and a permanent
tension between the rulers and the ruled. The years which
saw the political triumph of Christianity saw also the
fissure between the east and the west of the empire
asserting itself.

Because of the important part it played at a great
moment of human development, the drama of Antony and
Cleopatra has an unceasing appeal and interest; the problem of values which it raises has an undying significance.
Once again we must look to Shakespeare's play for the
magnificent evocation of those values. A critic, after
citing his sonnet, 'If my dear love were but the child of
state', goes on to comment:

In the dissociation of genuine love from the accidents of rank
and status ('state') and the transitory glories of the milieu
of court politics, in its rejection of human relationships based
on short-run expedience and calculation (based in the image
drawn from estate-management), in the assertion of the
constancy of genuine relationships, it is in fact an epitome of
the play. Especially it is relevant to the play in its view of love
as being, not merely *opposed* to 'policy', but in truth *wiser* and
more *aware* of its own long-term interest than the politic
Machiavellian. In the metaphoric brilliance of the vision of
love that 'all alone stands hugely *politic*' is contained the
audacious realism of *Antony and Cleopatra*.[54]

The immediate tragic aspect of the story of Antony and Cleopatra lies in the fact that Antony's relationship to Cleopatra has stimulated and created his Dionysiac vision of politics (as compared with the politic Machiavellianism of Octavian-Augustus), but at the same time it destroys his possibility of success in action. A deeper tragic aspect lies in the opposition of values that the above quotation implies. The wider vision of love goes down before the short-term calculations, yet is undefeated in the longer perspective. Cleopatra with the babe Horos-Caesarion at her breast is hopelessly defeated, but out of the disaster emerges Mary with the babe Christ at her breast. The political calculation triumphs, and yet mankind remains somehow still convinced that it is love that 'all alone stands hugely politic'.

Appendices

1. *Note on Sources*

Many primary sources are lost; but on the whole we have much valuable contemporary materials of the kind not usually extant for ancient history, above all Cicero's Letters and Speeches, and Caesar's *Commentaries*, with the Continuations, whether by A. Hirtius or not. Hirtius certainly meant to work up the *Commentaries* with supplements of his own into a continuous account from the start of the Gallic Wars to Caesar's death. He probably did not live long enough to do all this, but he wrote at least the 8th Book of the *Gallic War* and perhaps the *Alexandrian War*, though some persons thought this by Oppius or someone else. Who wrote the *Spanish War* we do not know; but it was a participant.

Sallust on Catilina deals with some of the preconditions of our period. He certainly did not write the *Invective on M. Tullius* (Cicero), and probably he did not write the two pamphlets under his name, a speech and a letter supposed to be addressed to Caesar. The latter is certainly spurious. We further have the *Res Gestae* by Augustus.

477

Then there are the poets, especially Virgil and Horace, but often valuable sidelights are given by Ovid, Tibullus, Propertius. Much of the voluminous writing has gone, *e.g.* Q. Dellius on Antony's Parthian Campaign; works by Agrippa, Messalla, Pollio, etc., as well as the numerous vituperative works of which we have fragments.

Of the extant historians, Vellius Paterculus derives largely from Livy (lost for this period except in epitomes or writers known to cite him) and Augustus. His work was published about A.D. 30; it follows the official line: Lana. Nikolaos of Damas is lost except for passages. Florus in the next decade carried on the Augustan version with Antony as 'firebrand and tornado of the age', a drunkard who fell into the hands of a *monstrum*. Seneca tried to take a more balanced view: 'A great man of notable ability was turned to alien ways and unroman vices by his love of drink and his equal passion for Cleopatra.' A little later came Suetonius with his varied collection of information; he used Augustus' *Memoirs*, but also drew to a certain extent on the opposing tradition. By this time Gaius and Nero had been on the throne; the Julio-Claudian line had died out; and it was possible to use more of the Antonian positions or at least to question the picture of an immaculate Augustus. Some elements of the attacks on the latter find their way into Seneca, Tacitus, Plutarch, and affected later narratives in slight degrees.

Appian of Alexandria wrote on the Civil Wars about A.D. 160; but we only have his account up to B.C. 35. He used both Livy and some of the Antonian tradition. Dion Cassius, a Greek Senator of the early 3rd century, gave us mainly the Augustan version. In him, as in

Appian, despite some information that tells against Augustus, the tone is dominatingly official.

Plutarch, writing in the earlier 2nd century, used diverse material. Though he carried on much of the Augustan interpretation, he drew on writers like Dellius, Pollio, and especially the physician Olympos. Hence the variety of his perspective, which makes his account in its general bearings so much richer and fuller than any of the others. (He mentions Dellius in ch. lix, and also used him in the *Life of Crassus*: Adcock 59. In that *Life* he also mentions Fenestella (v, 4), who wrote in the early part of the Augustus' principate.) See Garzetti for *Life of Caesar*; also H. Strasburger.

There was in existence, we may also note, a certain anti-Roman tradition, represented in a way by Pompeius Trogus (Trogus is Gaulish), whose father served under Caesar as a sort of confidential secretary. His *History* in 44 Books excluded Rome and dealt with world-events from the time of Ninus of Assyria to the absorption of other nations, apart from Parthia, into the Roman Empire. We have his work only in some fragments and an epitome by M. Junianus Justinus of uncertain date.

To this tradition belonged Timagenes (perhaps the influence behind Trogus). Augustus expelled him from his court. In return he dropped Augustus out of his history. He recognised not only the inner weakness of the Roman republic, but also the strength of anti-Roman feeling in the east, where Parthia was the champion of Hellenism. See Bowersock 125 f., 109 f. (For Dionysios of Halikarnassos, see Marin and Hill, but also Bowersock 110 and 131.)

It is probable that his break with Augustus came about

around the year 23 when Livy was writing his Book ix
which (chs. 17–9) breaks off from its theme of early
Roman history to indulge in a violent diatribe against
Alexander the Great and his men as poor creatures
compared with the Romans and their generals. Behind
this outburst there seems an effort to depreciate the
Parthians (*i.e.* the sort of eastern peoples with whom
Alexander had to fight): 'But, as frequently repeated by
the most frivolous of the Greeks, who are fond of exalting
the reputation, even of the Parthians, at the expense of the
Roman Name, the danger was that the Roman People
would not be able to bear up against the splendour of
Alexander's Name, who in my opinion was not known
even by common fame!' He is praising the Augustan
Pax.

Our ignorance about these 'frivolous Greeks' shows
how little we know of unofficial or unorthodox accounts.

Nikolaos of Damas, friend of Herod and Augustus,
represented the pro-Roman line among the Greeks. He
wrote a universal history and a life of Augustus. Of the
latter excerpts survive (made for Constantinos Porphyrogenitos of Byzantion); it was clearly an unreliable eulogy.
He also wrote a life of Herod, mentioned by Josephos as
defending or ignoring his cruelties.

It is hard to find an ancient historian with a philosophy
of history. Writers like Thucydides or Polybios were rare.
Plutarch's aim was moral. 'Using history as a mirror I try
by whatever means I can to improve my own life and to
model it by the standard of all that is best in those whose
lives I write.' However the vital element in his work
appears in his next sentence. 'As a result I feel as though
I were conversing and indeed living with them; by means

of history I receive each one of them in turn, welcome and entertain them as guests and consider their stature and their qualities, and select for their actions the most authoritative and the best with a view to getting to know them.' (*Timol. pr.*, cf. *Alex.* 1).

However, like most ancient historians, he mostly sees only the more trivial or egoistic impulses or motives: Caesar is simply driven by ambition, and so on. The good men are normally those who strive to maintain the *status quo*. Dion and the others are the same. Appian makes Antony say: 'There was no way to gain our ends openly by arms, we had necessarily to have recourse to the laws' (iii 5, 36). Plutarch's value is that he realises the value of the casual or everyday action or word for its revelatory effect (Barrow 53); but like the others, if he wants to express something that went deeper than the egoistic drive or the virtuous quest for balance, he has to invoke a divine intervention (Barrow 65).

Dion is the same. He has almost nothing of significance to say of the movements he describes. The Caesarian revolution is in the last resort caused by a god; the murderers are killed off through *to dikaion* and *to daimonion* (xlviii 1, 1). Appian says, 'The god thus shook the most powerful mistress of so many nations and of land and sea; and so brought about, after a long stretch of time, the present well-ordered condition' (iv 3, 16). Individual or local events are also explained as the result of a divine force. Cicero acted 'not because of some underlying hostility [to Antony], it seems, but at the instigation of a *daimonion* goading the Republic to revolution (*metabolē*) and meditating destruction to Cicero' (iii 8, 61—the action is falsely attributed to Cicero, but the point is unchanged).

At a naval engagement in the Adriatic on the same day as Philippi: 'The wind suddenly failed and the rest drifted about in a dead calm on the sea, delivered by one of the gods into the enemies' hands' (iv 15, 115).

2. *More on Moral Abuse*

Vituperation had a long history in Rome. It involved a habit of drawing a larger-than-life picture of an enemy, inflating him into a monstrous incarnation of evil, and thus somehow turning him into an object which at all costs must be destroyed by all right-thinking men. Cicero's speeches against Catilina are good examples of these vast slanderous exercises in impassioned rhetoric, fed at most with a modicum of historical fact or distortion of fact, and given their force by a ferocity of fear and hate.

There was thus a tendency to personalise political or social issues, building up ideal figures or bogeys. The argument, after Caesar crossed the Rubicon and defeated the Senatorial Party, tended to gather round the character of Cato, glorified or mocked. Cicero again, in his *Philippics* against Antony, built up a monstrous figure of the man who dared to challenge the *status quo*, the *concordia* of the exploiters.

In these exercises the terms are usually ethical; and one of the problems in dealing with our period lies in the way one analyses the terms for their hidden social or political meaning. Thus, when Sallust, Cicero, Seneca, dilate on the decay of morals and denounce *Avarice*, they are not primarily attacking the corrupt practices of their class. Avarice for them means the attack on property by some confiscatory process, legal or otherwise. The Avaricious are not the middle-class usurers and the upper-class looters, but the impoverished who want to change the *status-quo*.

Thus Sallust says of Catalina, 'He was covetous of other men's property and prodigal of his own' (v 4), and of the youth of the period, 'They grew at once rapacious and prodigal, undervalued what was their own, and coveted what was another's, set at nought modesty and continence, lost all distinction between sacred and profane, and cast off all consideration and self-restraint'. There we see the definition of a revolutionary by the men of property.

To call a man bold (*audax*) and accuse him of *audacia* was to see him as a rebellious overthrower of conventions and sanctions. Antony was the typical *audax* in conservative eyes. Words similarly charged with great emotive force were *furor*, *temeritas*, *libido*, *licentia*, *levitas*, and *gravitas*, *constantia*: fury, rashness, lust, license, frivolity, for the radicals, and gravity, constancy (in upholding the *status quo*), for the conservatives.

(Antony as *audax*: Weische, Wistrand, Helleggouarc'h. For *populares*: Meier *Real. Enc.* (P.W.); Rubeling. Haffter on traditions of Roman popular poetry and Menippean satire, to which Caesar's Anti-Cato belonged; Seneca's *Apocolocyntosis*, the title as a political calembour of *crassus-carbo* type. For *Dignitas*, Wegehaupt.)

3. *Augustan Dating Systems in Egypt*

Octavian's personal treatment of Egypt appears in the dating system he used in B.C. 30. Documents give his regnal years in the normal Egyptian way, but there was also another system side by side with the first. Both systems reckoned from the Egyptian newyear-day of 30: 1 Thoth: 29 August.

Once again records at the Boucheion help. A Bull, born in 53, died on 21 Pharmenoth (16 April) in Year 1 of Octavian (29 B.C.). The hieroglyphic text opens: 'Year 1 Phamenoth 21 of Caesar the Mighty One, beloved of Osiris Bouchis, Great God. Lord of the House of Atum.' The Caesar is Octavian. Thrice the same Egyptian word *mhti* (power) appears in connection with the date after the name Caesar (which is enclosed in a royal cartouche). In one case, from Hermonthis, the words after Caesar are a parenthesis: 'He is powerful' but in two from the Year 21 of Octavian the name is followed by 'of the power which he wields'. This term corresponds to the Greek *kratesis* (conquest). In one example, after the name Caesar, and outside the cartouche, is an Egyptian term that represents *Divi Filius*, Son of the God (Wilcken (3)).

Several documents used the term *kratesis*, thus referring to a Conquest Era. We also meet attempts to find an Egyptian equivalent.

The regnal dates could not have been used before the priestly hierarchy recognised Octavian as pharoah with all the relevant titles and honours, including divinity, which had become customary. Significantly the Hermonthis inscription does not put Caesar in a cartouche. The priests were merely accepting Octavian as conqueror— not as legitimate ruler. Yet in a monument set up only one day before the Bull's death, at Philai, by the prefect Cornelius Gallus (with a trilinguial inscription) the name Caesar is in a cartouche and he is 'his Majesty the Horos the Handsome Youth . . . Caesar whom we pray may live for ever'.

Why the difference? The Philai monument gives the explanation. It records that, shortly before, Gallus had suppressed a revolt in the Thebaid in fifteen days and captured five towns. Hermonthis is not mentioned; but its site, fourteen miles or so south of Thebes, on the left bank, and the prominence of Thebes in the cult of Bouchis, leaves no doubt that it was involved in the revolt. The angry priests had deliberately omitted the cartouche.

Octavian had certainly lost no time in making himself master of the Egyptian system. He began his rule from 1 Thoth: which became the date from which his regnal years were calculated. Before he left Egypt he had installed Psenemon as Prophet of Caesar in Memphis (Gauthier v 4; Blumenthal (3) 317; Wilcken (3) 142). A papyrus from Oxyrhynchos (1453) refers both to Cleopatra's last year and Octavian's first:

'Copy of an Oath. We, Thonis also called Patoiphis son of Thonis and Herakleides son of Totoes, both lamp-lighters of the temple of Sarapis, the Most Great God, and of the Isis-shrine there, and Paapis son of Thonis and Petosiris son of the aforesaid Patoiphis, both lamplighters of the temple of Thoeris, the Most Great Goddess, at Oxyrhynchos, all four swear by Caesar, God and Son of a God, to Heliodoros son of Heliodoros and to Heliodoros son of Ptolemaios, overseers of the temples in the Oxyrhynchite and Kynopolite Nomes:

'We will superintend the lamps of the above-named temples, as aforesaid, and will supply the proper oil for the daily lamps burning in the temples signified from

Thoth 1 to Mesore [?intercalary day] 5 of the present
Year 1 of Caesar . . . in accordance with what was
supplied up to the 22nd which was the 7th Year [of
Cleopatra]; and we the aforesaid are mutually sureties and
all our property is security for the performance of the
duties herein written.'

All this goes to show that Octavian took at once the
decision to rule alone in Egypt; he had no doubt arrived
at it long before in discussions with Agrippa.

For the Senate the new system in Egypt was that of
the Conquest; for Octavian it was that of himself as the
New Horos. He who had so viciously attacked Antony
as an Egyptianiser was now doing the same thing himself—at least within the confines of Egypt. His Sphinx
seal was not Egyptian. (JRS 1955 193; Dion li 3,
6–7, who mentions also his cipher that used 'for the
appropriate letter in a word the letter next in order after
it'.)

However as time went on, the distinction between the
two eras was forgotten. From the years 36 and 38 we have
documents in which both datings are used by the same
person on a single page (BGU 174; *Hermes* xxx 151; Fay.
89; Wilcken (3) 140 n. 16). Hieroglyphic texts from the
years 21 and 41 show a cartouche round Caesar and a
kratesis dating. So the Egyptians themselves forgot what
it was all about. However the *kratesis* era ended with
Augustus: on coins as in documents.

The evidence from the early dates is of importance
incidentally in showing how the Egyptians opposed
Octavian.

Appendices

4. The Smiling Baby

The motive of the smiling baby so strongly affected commentators on the Fourth Eclogue that they associated it with the poet himself. We are told by the Donatus-Suetonius Life, drawn in part from reliable sources near the poet, that Virgil's mother dreamed of giving birth to a laurel bough. Then, as babe, the poet never cried and had a sweet expression foreshadowing his destiny, while a poplar branch, planted at his place of birth, grew rapidly up and was honoured as Virgil's Tree. (For parallels: D. R. Stuart—but we may note the somewhat similar tales about Octavian.)

Another fantasy, common in connection with poets, told of a swarm of bees attending him as a babe and nourishing him with honey. (This is in Focas, lines 28 ff.) Virgil, familiar with bees, used works by Aristotle, Varro, and others for the technical aspects of bee-keeping in the *Georgics*; but Suetonius says that his father was a potter (figulus) who increased his wealth by buying forests and keeping bees. (M. Geer, TAPA 1926 lvii 107–15 for a non-Suetonian basis.)

These texts help us to interpret the difficult end of the Eclogue. We must not read 'those on whom their parents have not smiled', but 'those who have not smiled on their parents'—thus supporting the text in Quintilian's *Inst. Orat.* ix 3, 8; Stuart 222 f.; Duckworth in CW li 1957–8 125 f.; P. Maas, *Textual Criticism* 1958 36 f.; Duckworth (1). Focas not only brings up the smiling infancy but directly connects it with the eclogue (lines 23–7):

The Earth supplied flowers, and, greening with spring's
 own gift,
put underneath the boy a grassy support.

See, further, for the smile of Zoraster at birth (known to
Pliny, vii 16); Bidez-Cumont i 24 f. and Gagé (13).

5. *Saturnian Earth*

The extent to which Virgil is haunted by dreams of the
Golden Age prevents us from seeing the Fourth Eclogue
as a work unrelated to his main lines of thought. What is
strange in it is the peculiar moment and intensity of the
application. In the *Georgics* (i 121–46) he uses the Golden
Age to explain the origin of Work. He is here close to
Hesiod, but instead of that poet's scheme of decline we
find something like the Lucretian vision of progress from
barbarism (Ryberg 119 ff.). In another place (ii 458–542),
in praising the life of the farmers, he assigns characteristics
to Italy which are of the Golden-Age type: absence of
savage beasts, serpents, poison herbs. And he calls Italy
Saturnian Tellus or Earth. Then he appeals to the Muses to
teach him the ways of the Cosmos and turns to a picture
of the idyllic life of the farmer free from the power
struggle and the war threat. This is not the primitive
Golden Age, but rather what is named the Age of Jove
(in *Georgics* i) where men have developed various arts.

We may compare his ideas with those of Aratos (*Phain.*
90–115) where we are told that men of the Golden Age
tilled the soil but did not sail the seas or know overseas-
trade; Justice dwelt among men, dispensing to all the

fruits of their toil (Ryberg 126). There is also perhaps the influence of Varro, who, in his book on farming, called Italian farmers the surviving stock of Saturn (iii 1, 4). Virgil himself turns from his account of the countryfolk to a direct comparison with early Saturnian days (532–4, 538).

All these ideas are expanded in the *Aeneid*, *e.g.* in Evander's account of the early history of Italy (viii 314–27), of the age of peace that darkened into the madness of war and property-lust. In the epic the vision of the Roman past is also one of the future. Saturn's reign of peace is to be realised afresh in the Golden Age established by the New Romulus (explicitly stated in vi 792–4). But in fact the idea and the image pervade the whole *Aeneid*. Latinus is the true early type who passes on the Saturnian heritage; he describes his people in Golden-Age terms, and so does the messenger from Diomedes (vii 202–4, xi 252 f.). Latinus is a key figure merging the Saturnian and the Roman.

The first book of the *Aeneid* (286–96) expresses the poet's belief in the advent of a new cycle, not just a repetition of the past, but a new expansion on a higher level. He somehow managed to believe that the imperial stabilisation, plus peace and justice, is going to bring about the new start, The last six books show the working-out; they depict what is in fact a civil war between men whom the gods meant to be friendly. Latinus and Aeneas can only regret and resist; they prefigure Augustus.

We may note that in a sense the *Aeneid* shows a reversal of the history-pattern, reflecting the *Iliad* in mirror-fashion. The Trojan War is repeated with the Trojans as winners (W. S. Anderson: 2). There is irony in that the idea of the redeeming union of Antony and Octavian, ratified and expressed by the Son that Octavia was to bear, became in time the idea of Octavian-Augustus alone in himself the saviour.

In the *Aeneid* the epithet Saturnian is especially the property of the goddess Juno. It is used of her especially when she is in direct defence of the old order and the native traditions. In the final judgement on reconciliation made by Jupiter, the indigenous Latins (whose family derives from Saturn vii 45–9), while defeated, are to keep their name, tongue, political and racial identity; then Juno (no longer Saturnian, since the old order is doomed) willingly accepts the new dispensation. (L. A. Mackay.)

Notes

In dealing with familiar names like Cleopatra, Pompey, Marc Antony, Plutarch, Pliny, I have used the forms that everyone knows, whether they represent Anglicised forms of the Latin or Latinised forms of the Greek. However, with Greek names that are in any event unfamiliar to the general reader, I have permitted myself a more exact transliteration.

Cleopatra and the World of her Youth

1. Bevan 354 f.; 346. Preis.-Spieg. *Prinz Joachim Ostr.* no. 1. Bevan sums up: 'On the suppositions, all doubtful, (1) that the mother of Ptol. Auletes was a pure Greek (2) that his wife Tryphaina was his whole sister (3) that Cleo. was the daughter of T., the proportion of elements in Cleo.'s blood would be—Greek 32; Macedonian 27; Persian 5.' Two Cleopatras: note however that Cleopatra II had two daughters by Ptol. Philometor, both Cleopatras, one C. Thea.

2. Suet. *Jul.* liv 3; Diod. i 83.

3. Annexation of Cyprus: Badian (3); Oost; Olshausen. The testament was by Ptol. Alex. I (not II).

4. *Ad Q. frat.* ii 3.

5. *Klio* x 1910 55; OGI 190; Bevan 369 f. and 337; OGI 194. Ptolemais: Plaumann 35. Recent study by Hutmacher: bringing out the way these viceroys of Upper Egypt got a dominant position as central Ptol. power weakened; and citing the eight inscrs. about the family. See 43–5 for Ma'at and the ruler's responsibility; 54–8, *agathos daimon*; 64–7, *soter*. Date: H. thinks 39, pp. 28 f.

6. Perdrizet; Caesar BC iii 108; Plout. *Pomp.* 77.

7. OGI 256; Plout. *Brut.* 33. Doubling: G. May. Poetry: Il. vi 132; Orph. hymn liv 1. Childhood of Bacchos: R. Turcan (1); F. Simon (1). *Sammelb.* 1568, 2 (2nd *c.* B.C.). Ptolemies: Kornemann (2) 67–83; Kern RE sv *Dionysos* V 1040; BL i 328 and sv Index *Dionysos*; Athenaios v 196a–202a; Cerfaux, etc. Mithridates: Bevan 344 f.

8. CIG 4926. Dancer: P. Tebt. 208 (1st *c.* B.C.).

9. Bevan 347 f.; Brugsch, *Dict.* 1879 and *Thes.* 1883–91. The Egyptian coronation of Ptol. X did not take place till March 76, and then, oddly, not at Memphis but at Alexandria. Otto ii 302 n. takes the king to be Ptol. XIII, but wrongly.

10. Bevan 277–80; Wilcken *Archiv* vi 372 and *Grundz.* 7.

11. Yoyotte; Skeat (6); Meulenaere 2 and 22. For an earlier ex. of an Egyptian as Kinsman, Bevan 281.

Caesar in Alexandria

1. Strab. xvii 1, 8 ff.; Plin. NH v 21, 62; Diod. xvii 52; Plout. *Alex.* 26. Préaux (3); Tarbell, CP i 283.

2. Other quarters doubtful: Philon, *in Flacc.* 973a and 757; Jos. BJ ii 8; Diod. xvii 59; Steph. Byz. sv *Alexandreia*, etc.

3. *De arch.* v 11, 2; Souid. sv *Exedra*.

4. Préauxa (3), quarter of cemeteries, etc.; Breccia, de Zogher, etc.

5. See J L (1) and (2).

6. BC iii 110. Papyrus: CJP no. 140; Aug., Strab. xvii 819 cf. CJP 139, Jewish drinking club at Apollinopolis Magna; 138 (Ryl. 590), Jewish assn. of Cleo's reign: CE 1953 158 and Taubenschlag (2).

7. *Ad Fam.* viii 4, end; Samuel (1).

8. May: BGU 1829; OGI 190 and BGU 1826.

9. OGI 741: the Egyptian expression of what the Will tried to do in Roman legal terms.

10. BGU 1827.

11. Samuel; Skeat (4) Otto-Benston, etc., for details and refs. Heinen agrees with Samuel that Cleo. hid her father's death and claimed to be coregent with him for a while.

12. Tarn (7).

13. Skeat (3) 39; (2) 40 f.

14. PSI 1098.

15. BGU viii.

16. Berol. inv. 16277: E. Visser, *Symb. von Oven* 1946 116–21; E. P. Wegener, *Mnemosyne* xiii (ser. 3) 1947 302–16.

17. Skeat (4).

18. Wegener for Cleo T.; Skeat for Ptol. XIII.

19. Ptol. XIV: Skeat (1) 102.

20. P. Fay. 151; Skeat (1) 103; poss. BGU 1839.

21. BC iii 103.

Notes

22. SB 1754: almost certainly deals with produce of Year 3.

23. SB 1730. Volkmann (1) 60 takes as referring to a famine. There may have been shortages; if at the same time there was a state of war, the situation would be sharpened.

24. W. Kunkel (1); re-edited BGU viii; Wilcken (4).

25. For Queen before King, cf. OGI no. 167 (Cleo. III and Ptol. Philom. Soter).

26. NH v 58: *prodigium*.

27. Von Stauffenberg 119 f.

28. BC iii 108; Heinen; Badian (1) 258. Pompey was not a blunt man of action forced into a political position; rather, a crafty contriver watching out for his own and grasping, and, with all his prevarications, careful not to get isolated or go too far: Sherwin White (1).

29. Not sure how many ships: BC iii 106. Legions: 6th, come from Thessaly; 27th brought from Rhodes by gov. of Achaia, Q. Rufius Calenus.

30. BC iii 106. Cleo. and Caesar: Dion xlii 34 f. does not have the carpet story; she just slipped in.

31. Caesar's birth: Carcopino (5), prob. 12–3 July 101.

32. *Ant.* 27.

33. End of *Civil War* iii.

34. Bouché-L. ii 199; Birt thinks the Library destroyed in 46 (in I. v. Mueller, *Handb.* 339).

35. BC iii 107.

36. BA i 1, 9 and 26 f.; Dion xlii 40; I call the author Hirtius for convenience. CAH ix 676 f.; see BG viii (by H.) praef.; Suet. *Jul.* lvi.

37. BA i 24; Heinen 122 ff.

38. Dion xlii 42 f.; Heinen.

39. BA 26–31; Jos. BJ i 187–92 and AJ xiv 128–36; Dion xlii 41–3. Sijpersteijn for source-analyses and refs.

40. Dion. xlii 43; see Sijpersteijn on the two battles. Onias: Tcherikowa 275 ff.; *Not. Dig.*, xxv, calls Castra Judaeorum.

41. Suet. *Jul.* lxxvi 3. Perhaps Rufio not Rufinus: Münzer, RE 1a 1198. Pompey had previously made much use of freedmen: Syme 76.

42. Heinen 142–58, refuting Lord, JRS 1938 19 f.

43. For dead in the Nile: JL (2) and (3).

44. He may now have ceded Cyprus to Cleo.; it was still Ptolemaic at time of his death.

Cleopatra

Cleopatra and Caesar

1. *Rev. Egyptologique* vii 168; Meiklejohn. Also Balsdon (1). Chalkis: H. Seyrig, *Syria* xxvii 1950 43.

2. Volkmann 76 f. Caesar: Petrie.

3. Bevan 292 citing Otto; P. Reinach 9, 10, 14-6, 20. Note demotic marriage doc. from Deir el Ballas, Choiak 30 Year 19=Feb. 5, 186 B.C. (Ptol. V). 'Demetria, daughter of Phileinos bearing the Victory-trophy before Berenike the Beneficient, Philinna, d. of Ptolemaios, bearing the Golden Basket before Arsinoe Brotherloving, Eirene, d. of Ptolemaios, being Priestess of Arsinoe Fatherloving, and the Priest of Ptol. Soter who is in Psoi in the Nome of Thebes.'

4. W. Spiegelberg; H. Gauthier (2); Bevan 388-92.

5. Dion xliii 27, 3.

6. *Jul.* lii.

7. *Ib.* xlix-l.

8. Toynbee.

9. *Jul.* xlv. See Dion xliii 43 for fuller account of Sulla's remark and of Caesar's relation to Venus.

10. Balsdon (1). Volkmann thinks 47 date of C.'s birth. Note that Dion says the dedication of the Cleo. statue was by Augustus (li 22, 3), but seems impossible. In general, also Balsdon (2).

Cicero, *Pro Marcello*, on Caesar's *Clementia* bringing him near divinity. *Theoi synnaoi*: Nock (4). For personification of the Triumphator: Ehlers.

11. P. Oxy. 1628 and 1629. In 1628 the rulers are Fatherlovers and Philadelphoi.

12. Caesar's titles: Dictator for 4th time and at end of 45, Consul for ten years; early 44 dictator for life (d. was term in several Italian states for chief magistrate; at Rome he was chosen at time of severe crisis with absolute power for 6 months; *Dict. IIII*, etc., Carson pl. iii, 1; *Dict. perpetuus* by Lupercal 15 Feb., Cicero *Phil.* ii 34, 87). Also given permanently the *praefectura morum*, controlling entry into Senate (given him for 3 years in 46); also his decrees made binding and magistrates on taking office swore not to upset them. All this was done rather *ad hoc*, no clear system: Dion xliii 45, 1; Suet. *Jul.* lxxvi 1; Dion xliv 6, 1; App. ii 106.

13. Balsdon (7) 206; Hor. *carm.* ii 15; Virg. *georg.* iv 146; Mart. iii 58, 3; Quint. viii 3, 8; Plin. xii 6-13. Topiary: JL (2) chs. 12 and 16.

Notes

14. Ivy: Plin. *ep.* v 6; Cic. *ad Q.* iii 1, 2; creepers, Plin. *ep.* i 17; v 6. Cryptoporticus still seen on Palatine and Hadrian's villa.

15. Balsdon (7) 195; Grimal. 121–3. Agrippa's Gardens, *ib.* 193–6. Suet. *Jul.* xxxix (mentioning Codeta Minor after the Campus, but not necessarily placing it there). In Tacitus we get readings of *trans* and *cis*; but Augustus' own statement is definite, Dion lv 10 places the lake in the Circus Flaminius. R.G. shows that Aug. created a new lake (Caesar's had been dug nearly half a century before); but both lakes may have been within the *Horti*.

16. Cic. *de leg. agr.* v 16; Marcell. *dig.* i 16, 87; Paul. ex Fest. 58, 4, cf. 38, 17, Mueller.

Modern fashion is to underrate the relations of Caesar and Cleo., following Carcopino (1), cf. Syme (1) 275.

Calendar: Balsdon (1) ch. 2. Sosigenes is called a Peripatetic; his date is unclear. Simplikios connects him with Aristotle's *de caelo.* Plin. NH ii 8; xviii 25; Fabric. *Bibl. Gr.* iv 34.

17. C. Meier.

18. Meier on difference made at Rome with its aristocratic constitution between public and private interests, the opposition of *partium sensus* and *necessitudo.*

19. Meier 31–7; R. E. Smith (1) 31–3. During civil troubles, rival gens sometimes had their men swear or renew oath. Men transferring allegiance were usually sworn in to the new commander. For distinction of military oath and oath of fidelity: Von Premerstein 73 ff. Patronal ties strong, but could weaken or fail, e.g. Picenum, Pompeius' stronghold, saw its towns open gates to Caesar: BC i 15 f. Also communities could have more than one patron. In general, Brunt (2).

20. Brunt (3) and Watson; Smith 44 f.

21. Again difference under Flavians; men who were mostly leaders in their *municipia*, but drawn from a widening circle of provincial towns as well as Italian: Levy (6).

22. Brunt (2).

23. *De offic.* ii 21 and 73. E. Gabba (1) denies continuity; but it was there despite the confused and changing patterns. For concentration of distress in the veterans: Gabba 215 ff.; Tibiletti; Scullard; App. i 27.

24. There were some 300 towns, with landowners as the curial class, plus some rich freedmen; below then, the smaller owners or yeomanry, tenants and day-labourers.

25. *Cat.* ii 20.

26. App. v 17.

27. Caesar BC iii 91 and 99. See Rambaud for propaganda in Caesar, but much of his argument seems to me unfair and incorrect.

28. *Ib.* i 71 f.

29. *De imp. Gn. Pomp.* 13; 37–8; *Pis.* 86; 91. Caesar. BC i 21; B. Afr. 54.

30. *Dig.* xix 2, 15, 2; 2, 13, 7; Dion. xlvii 14, 3 f.

31. Dion xlviii 9.

32. *E.g.* Cic. *ad Att.* i 18, 6; by 59 the law still not implemented In 63 Rullus' bill was defeated, etc.

33. Fredericksen. Also Crook (2).

34. *Ib.* 133 ff.

35. *Pro Sest.* 132; schol. Bob. *ad loc.* Estates: Plout. *Pomp.* vi, 1; Vell. Pat. ii 29, 1; Caesar BC i 15, 4; M. Gelzer (3); Syme (1) 28. Caesar BC i 17, 4; i 34, 2. Cato: Plut. *Cat. min.* xx 2, cf. *Cicero* vii, 2.

36. Wirszubski (2); Cic. *ad fam.* iv, 14, 1.

37. Vatinius: *ad Att.* ii 24, 3

38. Suet. *Jul.* lxxx.

39. Plut. *Caes.* lvi 7–9; Dion xliii 42, 1. No note in Cicero's letter of resentment at the Triumph.

40. *Ad Fam.* vii 30: to Manius Curius.

41. Epicurean Fadius Gallus wrote a eulogy; *ad fam.* vii 24, 2; Momigliano JRS 1941 152. The cult persisted, *e.g.* bust found at Volubilis in Morocco, R. Theuvenot, *mon. Piot* xliii 1949 71–5.

42. *Phil.* ii 11. Conspirators: says 60, Nikolaos 80, Appian lists 15, we can make up 20 names.

43. *Ad att.* xiii 9, 2; 10, 3; 11, 2; 16, 2; 22, 4. Plut. *ant.* xiii 3; Cic. *ad Brut.* 1 17, 6; *de off.* iii 83 cf. 19.

44. *Phil.* ii 11.

45. *Municipia*: M. Cary; Jones (4); Rudolph.

Caesar's Murder

1. Dion xliii 14, 6. Quirinus: Dion xliv 6 2; xliii 45, 2 f.

2. *Ad Att.* xii 45 and xiii 28. Cicero is meditating a letter to Caesar, cf. Dion xliii 45, 3. Appian draws directly on parallel of Caesar and Romulus, ii 114, 276; not so Dion. Hal. AR ii 56 and 63. See also Cic. *de rep.* ii 20; Liv. i 16, 5–8, etc.

3. *Phil.* ii 110; xiii 41 and 47; Warde Fowler (1) 117–20; opposing view Taylor (1) 67 ff. We cannot appeal with Meyer 513 n 7 to ILS

6343 as this is no proof C. consecrated officially Jan. 42. Dion xliii 45, 2 for his statue with that of Victory at Games after Munda; Caesar was absent and the statue may have merely been meant to rep. him, though the practice then became common at other games. Dion xliv 11, 2; App. ii 109; Plut. *Caes.* lxi 3. Two statues on Rostra were ordered in 44, Dion xliv 4, 4f.

4. Vell. Pat. ii 24.

5. Dion xliii 43, 3. Cassius, though Epicurean, had borne before him, shortly ere Philippi, the statue of his Victory.

6. Dion xliv 5, 2; Schelling 314; Jal (3).

7. App. ii 106 and see n. 1 above. Carson pl. iii 9.

8. All given in fuller details in Carson; the four moneyers worked in pairs. *Desultor* was a bareback rider who had a pair of horses reined together; he vaulted from one to other—perhaps at end of each round in the Circus. Cicero says a *d.* stood lower in esteem than a fourhorse-chariot driver; Varro says the horse that served him differed in points and training from a good chariot-horse. Men of highest rank acted as J.C.'s *desultores* at Games of 46 (Suet. xxxix). This kind of racing went back to 169, and its reps. on coins of later date seem to record ancestral victories in such contests. Records of the Secular Games of 17 and of the Arval Brotners give a picture of both this bareback riding and chariot-racing; but *d.* did not leave mark like the driver; no inscriptions of *desultores*: Balsdon (7) 323 and 435 n. 403.

9. Nik. Dam. xx 69 (xxii 76 says C. later let them return to Rome); Liv. *epit.* 116; V.P. ii 68, 4; Plut. lxi 8; Meyer 527 n. 2—contrast BC i 7, 2 f. Other episodes, Suet. *Jul.* lxxix 1.

10. *Ad Att.* xiii 7, 15 Marsh 61.

11. Date unsure: Meyer 526 n. 2, Cic. *de div.* i 119 and Val. Max. viii 11, 2. Cicero's nephew may have been among the Lupercals. In general, Plin. xxxvii 186; Dion xliv 11, 2; Cic. *Phil.* ii 34, 85 and *de div.* i 52, 119.

12. Kraft is a modern exponent of idea that Ant. wanted endanger C.

13. It is suggested (Grant (5) 259), 'it may have been a gesture that misfired; he may have wished to display himself as a patron receiving his clients, and perhaps this was the sort of extra-constitutional, emotional basis that the future monarchy might have been intended to possess. As client, every senator had enrolled himself, rather more than metaphorically, in Caesar's bodyguard. He was also formally invested with the inviolability possessed by tribunes.'

14. Raubitschek for refs. Also Toynbee and Raubitscheck HN xxxiv 18.

15. Dion xli 61, 4.

16. Dion xliii 43, 3. Divine honours: Heinen (2); G. Herzog-Hauser, RE suppl. iv 817–20; Wickert; Steildle. 60–7. Note grandson Gaius Caesar hailed Neos Ares in Athens: Judeich (2) 99 n. 9; IG ii (2nd) 3250; M. and E. Levensohn. The monument with inscr. (IG ii (2nd) 3222) seems linked with J.C.'s brief visit to Athens, autumn 47, when he made big donation for building what is now called the Roman agora; it is suggested the large base once held colossal statue of J.C. and the dowel-hole still there once held the end of the spear.

17. Tonybee 8; Chamoux. Toynbee 4 says the Mytilene statue is prob. of Augustan date.

18. Bowra for refs. Also Latte 312 ff.; Habicht, *Att. Mitt.* lxxii 1957 243, 250 (Antioch on Maiandros); Bowersock 115 f., 118; Taylor (1) 270 ff. For early Anatolian cult of Roma: Larsen (2)—appeal for protection of the State; only Smyrna mentions a temple.

19. *Phil.* xii 14 f.

20. *Ad Att.* viii 7 and ix 9, 2. In general, Weinstock.

21. Plut. *Alex. fort.* i 9; Windisch, *Z. f. NT Wiss.* xxiv 1925 251 ff. Note Cic. *pro Marc.* xxxiii (B.C. 46) and close relation to Horace CS 57 ff. and V.P. ii 126, 2: Fraenkel 376 ff.; Petr. 124, 249 ff.; Claud. *in Ruf.* i 51 ff.

22. Lepore.

23. Béranger 31 ff. and 282 f.; Henderson JRS 1954 125; Carson 49.

24. Dobesch 32 n. 52; Carson (1).

25. Carson 52; Numa, *ib.* pl. iii 15.

26. Dion xliv 15, 3; Suet. *Jul.* lxxix 4; Cic. *de div.* ii 110 f.; App. xiii 44, 1 has no connection. Meyer 528 f. accepts the tale. But see M. Levi (3).

27. *Jul.* lii, cf. Cicero's blind abuse, *Phil.* ii 28.

28. Cinna: Dion xlvi 49, 2; Val. Max. ix 9, 1; RE viii 225 f. (no. 11).

29. *Ad Att.* xv 15; xiii 52.

30. Cic. *pro Marc.* 25; Suet. *Jul.* lxxxi 1, 2; *Phil.* i 38.

31. *Phil.* ii 14 and 29; *pro Deiot.* 15–22. Cassius: *Phil.* ii 26; Holmes iii 210 n. 6 rejects; Meyer 536 believes. Probably untrue. Dangers: *Pro Marc*, 21–3; Suet. *Jul.* lxxv 5. Knife: *Phil.* ii 74. Trebonius: *Phil.*

Notes

ii 34; xiii 22; *ad fam.* x 28, 1 and xi 28, cf. *Att.* xiv 14 1 f. Syme (1) 99 n. 4.

32. *Ad Att.* xiv 8. Pelops: Plut. *Cic.* xxv: Cicero writes to him about some honour the Byzantines propose to bestow. For Sextus Clodius: *ad Att.* xiv 19.

33. *Ib.* xiv 20.

34. *Ib.* xv 1.

35. *Ib.* xv 4.

36. BC iii 34 f.; *Phil.* xiii 16. Petreios was Thessalian epithet of Poseidon as rock-cleaver, Pind. *Pyth.* iv 426 and schol. Artemidoros of Knidos was son of Theopompos and a friend of J.C.: Strab. xiv 656. He was a rhetorician who taught Greek at Rome; he warned J.C. against the plot: Plut. *Caes.* lxv; Zosimos i 491 (Paris ed.). For Theopompus: Bowersock, 9, 114.

Cleopatra and Caesarion

1. *Chemistry*, Oct. 1965; *Nature* 13 Jan. 1968 (217, 160); Gilfillan, *Mankind Quarterly* v 131 (Jan.-March 1965); J.L. *The Ancient World.*

2. Bevan 348.

3. Meiklejohn; Balsdon (1) and (2); Carcopino (1) 35 ff.

4. Dion xlix 10; Plut. *Ant.* liv 4.

5. Carcopino (3) 141 ff.

6. Moret 68–70; CIG 4717. Coins: BMC *Ptol.* p. lxxxiii, pl. xxx 6. Svoronos (2) 380, pl. lxii 26 (dating 46).

7. Suet. *Aug.* vi.

8. Dion lv 1, 1.

9. Suet. *Jul.* lxxxiii. Will: Crook (1) for refs. Also CR lxviii 1954 152 f; Charlesworth (4).

10. Dion xliii 34, 3; xliv 5, 3.

11. *Dig.* i 7, 25.

12. *Dig.* xxxvi 1, 65, 10; Suet. *Tib.* vi 3.

13. App. iii 49.

14. App. ii 389, correct this time.

15. Tac. *Ann.* i 14; Suet. *Aug.* ci.

16. Nik. Dam., FGH xviii 55 (Jac.).

17. Suet. *Jul.* lii; Plin. xii 2, 6; Tac. *Ann.* xii 60. For Matius, Cic. *ad fam.* xi 28, etc.

18. Nik. xx 68.

19. Dion. xlvii 31.

20. Oxy. 1629.

21. Dion xliii 27; App. v 91.

22. Jos. AJ xv 4, 1; Porph. in Euseb. *Chron.* (Schöne) i 168–70. Death at Rome, Mahaffy 463 and Bouché-L. ii 227; after return, Stahr 56.

23. News late: Hohmann 50 ff.

24. See intro. Oxy. 1629.

25. Coin: Poole, Cat. 122; *Stēlai*, Strach (1) 212.

26. Lefebvre ASAE 1908 241 (undated).

27. OGI 194; Oxy. 1635; PSI 549; Lefebvre, *Mél. H.*; P. Cairo dem. 31232 (prob. 12th rather than 16th year), see Oxy. vol. xii p. 170. Oxy. 1635: see vol. xiv p. 39 for katoikic cessions.

28. Sen. NQ iv.

29. Volkmann 91; Souida sv *Diosk.* (confused with D. a follower of Herophilos: Galen, *Gloss. Hipp.* proem).

30. Lefebvre, M. H. 103 ff.; Bevan 371 f. *Stephanoi*: Tebt. vol. i pp. 223 f. and no 746 1. 24. *Epigraphai*: tax, PSI v 510, 11. Assessment: Oxy. 1145, 8 (2nd *c.* A.D.). Defaulters: Tebt. 61 (a) 9 ff. *Stephanoi* not to the king; Fay. 14 and Grenf. i 41; cf. Tebt. 95, 8.

31. Tebt. 5, 57–61.

32. *Phil.* ii 38.

33. *Ad Att.* xv 11.

34. Botermann.

35. Oct. temporarily held Africa for Lep.—to be handed over if Lep. found satisfactory; we may assume Lep. also to get back the 7 legions he had lent the other two.

Marcus Antonius

1. Cic. *Phil.* ii 2; xiii 10; *ad Att.* xvi 11.

2. Hor. *Sat.* i 2, 55; 10, 77 (Schol. Cruq.); Serv. *ad Verg ecl.* x 1; Cic. *Phil.* ii 24; *ad Att.* x 10, 16; *ad Fam.* ix 26; Plut. *Ant.* ix; Plin. viii 16. For Vol. Eut., Cic. *ad Fam.* ix 26; *Phil.* ii 24 and xiii 2 f.; *ad Att.* xv 8; Nep. Att. 9, 10, 12; Hor. *Ep.* i 18, 31.

3. Balsdon (7) 51; CIL iv 7698b; Hor. *carm.* iii 6, 21–33; Plin. xiv 141. Aristippos, head of Cyrenaic School, who held pleasure the highest good.

4. *Ad. Fam.* vii 32 (from Cilicia in ? 51), and 33 (July 46, from Tusculum ?).

5. *Phil.* ii 58 and 61 f.

6. Plut. QR lxxxi; Plin. viii 21; Plut. *Ant.* ix.

7. *Sat.* i 2, 44–7; the dwarf may belong to a later phase, with Cleopatra. Cf. *Sat.* i 5 with buffoons at villa. *Nani*: Suet. *Tib.* lxi; Prop. iv (v) 8, 41; Juv. *Sat.* viii 32; Lamprid. *Alex. Sev.* xxxiv. For Oct., Suet. *Aug.* lxxxiii; he however showed at some Games a youth of good family, Lucius, not quite 2 feet high, weighing 17 lbs., with a stentorian voice: *ib.* xliii.

8. Grueber iii 48b and 398 no. 60.

9. Arnim. *Stoic. Vet. Fr.* i 499; Athen. 693 ef.; cf. Orphic terns, Rapp, *Helios.* Roscher 2024. Tarn (2) 149; Macrob. *Sat.*

10. Cic. *de Rep.* vi 17, 17.

11. Grueber i 525 no. 4044, about 46 B.C.; pp. 578, 585, sun only refs. to ancient history of Sabines. Alföldi (2) 374 thinks it already refers to new era.

12. Tarn (2) 149.

13. *Sib.* xi 290, etc.; Grueber ii 395 n. For Lion and Sun, see my *Origins of Alchemy,* index; Cramer, index *Leo,* etc.

14. *Phil.* ii 30 f. for Ant.; *Pro Caelio* for Clodia. Cicero says nothing of rumours of Caesar's death.

15. *Ant.* xxiv.

16. Scott (1) 24; Dion xlix 32, 3; App. v 7 (calling Arch. Sisina). L. Craven 29 ff.; W. Gwatkin 7 n. 5 says Arch. had not yet proved his ability; but Ant. may still have realised it. Suet. does not mention Glaphyra.

Antony and Cleopatra

1. *Carm.* ii 3; Sen. *Suas.* i; Vell. P. ii 84.

2. *Ant.* xxv.

3. Athen. iv 147 f.

4. Müller-Graupa in RE sv *Museion,* iv 810 ff.

5. Philostr. *Lives Soph.* 48b. For earlier links with Juba: Plut. *Cat. Min.* lvii. Ant. gave her the Pergamene Lib., but doubtful if books were moved. Newman (2) 33 for 'the one blot on Philip's line'.

6. Cited Bernard Shaw, *Caesar and Cleo.* with note by G. Murray. Also seems a *Geponika* or work on farming attributed.

7. Full refs. in my *Origins of Alchemy; JHS* 1930 116.

8. App. v 1, 11.

9. *Ant.* xxviii–ix.

10. Tarn (2) 48 f.;—Lewy, *Sobria Ebrietas* (1929).

11. Suet. *Aug.* lxix.

12. App. v 3, 18.

13. Dion xlviii 48, 5: after defeating Oct. in 38.

14. App. v 2, 15; Suet. *Aug.* xiv; App. v 2, 16. Nonius was the centurion. For Fulvia on coins: Balsdon (8) 49; Gardthausen (2) 92; RE vii 284; BMC Rep. i 570, 575 and pl. lvi, 1 and 10; Vessberg 248 and pl. xiii, 7 and 8.

15. Plut. *Ant.* xxx 2; App. v 19; v 66. Manius; App. v 3, 22.

16. Lucius took a prob. sincere republican stand.

17. *Aug.* xv.

18. Scott (1) 27 f.; Dion xlviii 14, 3–5; Sen. *de Clem.* i 11. 1; App. v 48 f.; VP ii 74, 4; Gardthausen (2) iii, 3, 208 f. and Haddas 79 accept the story.

19. App. v 24; v 29; v 45.

20. Mart. xi 20; Malcovati p. xii n. 3. There would be no point in Martial's use of the epigram to defend his own downright language if it were not by Oct.

21. App. v 6, 52. Also iii 51 and 32; v 52 and 63. Another problem was the invasion by Parthini of Macedonia, where Ant.'s general Censorinus was in charge.

22. Dion lii 36; lvi 43; Zonoras 544b; Zos. i 6; Suet. *Claud.* iv; Strab. xiv 674; Louk. *Makrob.* xxi; Cic. *ad Fam.* iii 7; xvi 14; Porph. *in Categ.* 21a; Simplik. *Categ.* 15b; Stob. *Sen.* 33; Plut. *Poliork.* xvii; Athen. xii 519; DL iii 3; v 36, etc. Nestor: Strab. xiv 674 f.

23. Dion xlv 7, 1 (44 B.C.).

24. Grueber ii 495; Caesar, i 529, 546; globe, 523, 543, 551; Alföldi (2) for blessing he will give to men, 374; Grueber sees an emblem of power. Dion xliii 14, 6; 21, 2. Later Pax type: Mattingly (1) 290 n., 302, 304 n. Sun: G. i 582 no. 4276.

Antony and the Return to Cleopatra

1. Scott (1) 28.

2. Dion xlviii 31, 5.

3. Dion xlviii 37. Almost all exiles now free to return; men like Gn. Calpurnius Piso Frugi, Tib. Claudius Nero, L. Arruntius, M. Julius Silvanus, the younger Cicero.

4. Plut. *Ant.* xxxii.

5. *Ib.* xxxiii.

6. Dion xlviii 44.

Notes

7. *Aug.* lxviii.

8. *Ib.* lxix; diminutives of Tertia, Terentia, Rufa. Dion lxxi; Scott (1) 40.

9. Tac. *Ann.* i 10.

10. Suet. *Aug.* lxix. Dion xlviii 54 twists the episode, says Ant. came all the way from Syria 'to spy upon Oct.'s actions'.

11. Plut. *Dem.* ii; Dion xlviii 39 (4 million sest.) and Sen. *Saus.* i 6 (1,000 tal.). Note Elegabal demanding dowry for marriage of images of Caelestis and the Sun: Herodian v 6, 5; Dion lxxx 12, 1 f.

12. Coins: Tib., Mattingly pl. xxiv 6, personified cornucopia (twin sons of Drusus and Livilla), cf. statue in E. Pottier, *Cornucopia*, Darem.-Sag. fig. 1966. Crossed cornucopiae with capricorn heads (sign of Aug.) on two altars, *Röm. Mitt.* xlii 1927 163 and 176, pl. xx-xxi; for such, Lenmann-Hartleben. Child: J. Kromayer, *Hermes* xxix 561 f.; App. v 278; Dion xlviii 31, 4 cannot stand. For rulers linked with Dionysos: Antigonos Monophthalmos, Herodian *ab excessu divi Marci* i 3, 3; his son Demetrios Poliorketes, Scott (4); Mithridates Eupator, Cic. *pro Flacco* 60 and P. Riewald 319; Antiochos VI, Riewald 318; Antiochos XII, ib. 319. For Attalids and Ptols., von Prott; Blumental (3) 317; Schubart (2 and 3); Kaerst ii 237, 341. In general, Cerfaux.

13. Plut. *Ant.* xxxiii. 'He left at home the insignia of command and went out with the wands (*rhabdoi*) of a gymnasiarch, in a Greek robe and white shoes, and he'd take the young contestants by the neck and part them.' Gymnasiarch has been translated 'minister of education', which has some of the meaning, though not exactly.

14. Amyntas had Pisidia and Phrygia-towards-Pisidia. Polemon, centred on Ikonion, had Cilicia Tracheia, wild country once part of R. prov. of Cilicia.

15. Aphrodisias got freedom and tax-immunity; the grant has the most-favoured-nation acluse in simple form (app. its first appearance). He also raised fleet to 5 squadrons of the line, partly by incorporating Ahenobarbus' ships; with stations at Kephallenia and Zakynthos good for watching Sicily; the detachments were under Proculeius and C. Sosius who struck coins with naval symbolism.

16. Plut. *Ant.* xxxiv Paus. i 28, 4: near the cave esp. connected with Apollo (who there seduced Kreousa); was the oracle Delphic? See J. Harrison, *Proleg.* 303 fig. 181, Herakles on Corinthian alabastron.

Aisch. *Eum.* 736, Athena, 'I praise the Man in all things save for marriage'.

Ventidius as new man: Syme (1) 199–201; note the non-Latin end of family-name.

17. Ward-Perkins for the fusion of Romano-Greek, Parthian, and ancient Mesopotamian traditions in the borderlands. Parthians: Oltramare, etc.

Virgil's Fourth Eclogue

1. The literature is vast. Here for the moment we may refer to Norden, Weber, Boll, Carcopino, Jeanmaire, Fowler, Slater, Hermann ch. v, Tarn, Corssen, R. Waltz, Perret (2).

2. J. L. *Short History Culture* 242 f.

3. *Sat.* xlv.

4. J.L. *ib.* 226.

5. *Isaiah* lx 20–2. See Royds, who however thinks V. drew on the Jewish scriptures.

6. Ages: again a large theme. Note however Hor. *Ep.* xvi end; Lucret. iii 12; v 950; Ovid *Met.* i 89 ff., putting silver before bronze.

Great Year: Plato *Polit.* 269c; Rose CQ xviii 1924 113 ff., etc., Cic. *de nat.* ii 51 f.; Serv. *ad Aen.* iii 284.

7. Tarn (2) 147 f.

8. Carm. i 2, 25–32

9. Rose, *Handbook* 138 f. Hellespontine and Phrygian seem to be the Marpessian again; also she of Sardis, etc. The tale of Apollo and the Cumaean Sibyl is late and seems partly based on legend of Kassandra: for Ovid, Rose 143 f. In gen., Bouché-L. ii 133 ff.; Buchholtz in Roscher sv. Herakleides Pontos was first to recognise more than one Sibyl.

10. Tale of 9 Books offered to Tarquinius Superbus by the S.; he refused to buy; she burned 3 and asked same price for the 6; he refused; she burned 3 more and still asked the same price; he bought the 3. Oracles of Sibyl of this period: Dion xlvii 18, 6; xlviii 43, 5, etc. For a late oracle of the Tiburtine S., *The Oracle of Baalbek*, P.J. Alexander, 1967. 'And there will arise another King from Heliopolis (City of the Sun) and he will wage war against the King from the East and kill him.' He gives tax-exemptions and plenty; then comes the Ruler of Perdition, followed by the Son of God. During the last war 'the land of Egypt will burn 12 cubits deep'.

Notes

11. *Ann.* vi 12; Rzach (4).

12. *Georg.* ii 458–74, note use of *fundere* as in Eclogue.

13 *Sat.* 124.

14.. *De L.L.* vi 11; Plautus, *Truc.* 22; 'Chrysippus' is wrong. See also Censorinus xvii 13; Livo. vii 3, 4; Nilsson (1).

15. CIL i pp. 430, 434.

16. L. R. Taylor (6); Nilsson; Gardthausen (2) i 1006–8.

17. *Levit.* xxv.

18. Plut. *Sulla* vii; Serv. *ad Aen.* viii 56 and ix 46.

19. Alföldi (2).

20. *Ad ecl.* iv 4; Rzach (4) 114 ff. Tarquitius Priscus: Macrob. *Sat.* iii 7; Serv. *ad ecl.* iv 43; Festus p. 274 (Müller); Heurgeon; Lachmann *Grom. Vet.* i 350; Grenier 16 ff., 22, 77; Weinstock (4).

Arruns: Piotrowicz (2); Latte (2); Zancan; App. i 36; cf. Liv. xxix 10, 5 (Sibyl). John Lydos: Piganiol (5); Bezold and Boll, *Hémérologies* 1939 and *Sitz. heidelb. Ak. Wiss, ph.-hist. Kl.* 1911 fasc. 7; Kroll in RE xxxiii 208 f. Cic. *de har. resp.* xix and x; John L. describes the text as by Nig. after Tages. For Coptic Gnostic text from Nag' Hammadi: Goedicke and A. Boehlig and P. Labib, *Kopt.-Gnost. Apok. aus Codex V von N.H.* 1963 107 (Wiss. Z. d. M.-Luther-Univ. Halle-Witt.).

21. J. L. (2) 334 f.

22. Acanthus: *Georg.* ii 119; *Ecl.* iii 45 (on drinking cup); *Georg.* iv 123; *Aen.* i 649. Honey: Virgil and Bees. B. G. Whitfield, *Gr. and Rome* iii (Oct. 1956) 99–117.

23. First triumvirate formed in Metellus' consulship; in calling the *amicitiae* of the leading men *graves* Horace is implicating Oct. as well as Ant.

24. Norden (2).

25. D'Anto (1) 266.

26. Norden; Mattingly (2) 14.

27. Syme (2) 45; Mattingly (2) also for further points, esp. the later versions of the Eclogue's imagery; also Waltz 14–20.

28. Mattingly (3) 165.

29. Serv. *ad ecl.* iv 1. Name of Gallus prob. referred to Pollio's command in Gaul 41–40: Syme (1) 46. Pollio in *Ecl.* viii: Syme (3) 47 f. Waltz thinks the ecl. refers to child of Pollio.

30. Jachmann thinks ref. to child of Oct.; Carcopino (4) 159 and (7) 229. Marcellus: Tarn 153 f.; Faider; Kroll (2); Hermann (3) 21, follows Dion, 157 n. 6; see him also in (5) using Serv. *ad Aen.* vi 861; Schol. Bern. (Carcopino 159, citing Garrod and Boll); D'Anto (1).

Latter 267 for legal aspects; Perozzi in *Studi Simoncelli* (1916) 234. Rose, R. *Lit.* 242, thinks the child is by Scribonia; but the marriage was not till 39.

For Tityrus as Eros, see Grizart, who claims rightly there is no basis in Bayet (2) 276, André (2) 20, and Liegle (2) 222. He sees Moeris of *Ecl.* ix, where Virgil does appear, as Menalcas. For the dispossession: Vanderlinden.

31. Carcopino (4).

32. Norden 153.

33. Weinreich 298; Carcopino (4) 124–33; Tarn (6) 151.

34. S. Sudhaus, *Rh. Mus.* lvi 1901 38–42; Nilsson 1710.

35. Epode vii. Burck's app. to Heinze's ed. of Epodes 646 f.; Fraenkel 47 f.; Newman 24. For Hor. and Maecenas: Noirfalise.

36. As does Duckworth (1) 117.

37. Slater; Fowler (2) 126; Garrod 150. Hermann denies likeness. Voll. 17 n. 1 takes Slater to see the child as Alex. Helios; Herman (1) 92 as Marcellus—cf. RA 1931 47. Achilles as model of Aeneas; xx L. A. Mackay. For attempt at a formal division of the eclogue, see J. Préaux in *Conferences de la Soc. d'Et. lat. de Brux.* 1963–4 and 1964–5 (ed. G. Cambier) 123–43. The poem has 3 intro. verses, 4 at end; between are 8 sets of 7, each set with complete sense; the 28 lines staring with puer, 18–45, are the core, promising the age of gold. Application to the 63 lines of the rule of the golden number brings out at line 39 the word *tellus*. The eclogue expresses the hope of the peasants and Romans in general to see Oct. the benevolent lawgiver, who in the 1st ecl., assures Tityrus the enjoyment of his land, as the re-establisher of liberty, justice, peace. The allegories of earth, plenty, *fides* and peace are found extended on the coins of the epoch; and the investigation of the eclogue's astrologic terms confirms this analysis; *puer* is just an allegory of the great hope. Unfortunately this kind of attitude to Oct. is quite unhistorical for the years 30–1.

38. Tarn (4) 153.

39. Prop. iii 18. Servius says M. 'fell into his disease in 16th year and died in 18th', but Propertius is contemporary. Note also App. v 8, 73: M. betrothed in 39.

40. Dion xlviii 31, 4; App. and Plut. say nothing. J. Kromacher (3) 561 f.; D'Anto 264.

41. Carcopino thinks the *puer* already born, but admits the Ecl. does not explicitly say so.

42. Tac. *Ann.* i 10, 2; Dion xlvii 31; App. v 64 and 66 reflects

stress put on Pollio. V.P. and Liv. *epit.* lay no emphasis on the occasion.

43. Theok. xxiv 31.

44. Pompey as Alexander: W. S. Anderson; Treves. The rise of Parthia revived the idea of west versus east.

45. Tarn (6) at end; Mattingly (3) 164. Gallus: Anderson CQ xxvii 1933 36–45, 73; Norden, *Berl. Sitz.* 1934 627 ff.

46. *Georg.* i 24 ff.; *Aen* vi 789–94.

47. Dion xlix 15, 2. Note Pax in action, setting fire to heap of arms with torch, first on coins of Galba and Vespasian. Diana-Lucina: Macr. *Sat.* vii 16, 27; Catullus' hymn to Diana.

48. Weinstock 47.

49. For a too-ingenious effort to link the ecl. with Sextus' blockades; the judge Palaemon (=Portunus, god of harbours), Galatea as Sextus, Amaryllis as Ant., Menalcas as Virgil, Damoetas as the poet Aemilius Macer: see Savage. Damoetas says, 'Tell me, and you'll be my great Apollo where heaven's circuit extends no more than three ells'. But this is not addressed to Palaemon. For time V. passed from Pollio to Maecenas: JRS 1964 248. Does *ecl.* v allude to J.C.'s deification? the star of ix to J.C. or to Oct. himself as Oct. thought: Plin. ii 25, 93 f.; H. Wagenwoort.

Choice of Aeneas to displace Ulysses: Galinsky (1).

50. Latte 279. Sulla also looked to Venus as shown by cognomen Felix Epaphroditus: JRS 1961 209; Balsdon (6) 3. Sulla's *Ludi Victoriae* lead on to *Ludi Vict. Caesaris*, though we must also recall Marius' Games of Honour and Virtue.

51. Dion xlviii 16, 1.

52. Dion xlvii 18 f. In 208 *Ludi Ap.* were set for 13 July; but by 42 the whole period from 6 to 13 were allotted. Caesar's birthday on 12. 'Previous day' here means 'day before the *Ludi*,' *i.e.* 5.

53. Dion xlviii 52.

54. Dion. xlix 15.

55. Suet. *Aug.* xciv: with other tales of his birth, including a Dionysiac one that links him with Alex. and Juppiter; with rising sun. Tale of Caesar and palm, *ib.*, *cf.* trees of xcii; eagle xcvi-vii; fish (rivalry with Sextus) xcvi; relations to Juppiter xci. Laurels and Regia: Julius Obseq. 19; Liv. *epit.* Oxy. 127–9; FE Brown, *Mem. Am. Ac. Rome* xii 1935 72. The great fire of 50 also prob. affected Regia. Gn. Domitius Calvinus celebrated triumph 36, spent most of coronary gold on rebuilding Regia.

56. Hermann (2) 491 f., and (3).

Ovid and Augustan worship of Apollo (*Met.* xv 622 ff.): Holle-mann.

Cleopatra Again

1. Capito had been with Maecenas to Ant. from Oct. in 37; he stayed with Ant. and was prob. the *consul suffectus* in 33 with Manius Acilius. A coin of his (showing Ant. and Cleo.) calls him propraetor and gives him praenomen Gaius. Hor. *Sat.* i 5, 32; Plut. *Ant.* xxxvi.

2. Plut. xxxvi. Selene, a Ptolemaic name, gets a new significance through the brother Helios. Sun and Moon kept time of cosmos; Isis was their mistress: 'I arranged the course of sun and moon,' Kyme 14, Ios 11. The names perhaps makes them *kosmokratores.* An inscription from Baalbek, the Sun-city, shows Sun and Moon as associated and supporters of Victory, but this is prob. 1st c. A.D. There seems a clear setting-up of the twins against the Parthian King 'Brother of Sun and Moon'. Macr. *Sat.* i 19 that Sun and Moon represent Daimon and Tyche. D. and T. are also the Fravashi and Hvareno of the Parthian King: Cumont CRAI 1930 216–20. So it seems Ant. and Cleo. take over divine attributes of the King as prelude to conquest. When they walked in the Triumph at Rome they were simply called Sol and Luna, Euseb. ii 140 (Schoene); Zonaras x 31 (531): perhaps from Livy via Dion.

3. Jos. JA xiv 447.

4. Koile Syria of Herod's letter, not the Chalkis of Lysanias, which was in valley between Lebanon and Anti-Lebanon; Jos. takes it as Kanatha in Transjordanian region on slopes NW of Mt of Hauran (85 km. SE of Damas). Thus, not the Chalkis and the *topoi* about it of Porphyry: Dobiaš.

5. Dion xlix 32 4 f. displaces territorial gifts: Tarn (6) 145.

6. Ant. xxxvi.

7. Budge 204 f.; Hiller de Gaestringen, IG xii fasc. v pt. 1 (1903), etc., Cleopatra as Isis: Plut. *Ant.* liv 9; Dion xlix 40; von Sallet 52; Vandebeek 75; Tarn (6) 139. See later for her as Neotera. Arsinoe II as Isis, SB 601–2; OGI 31 (Strack, *Mitt. Ath.* xix 234 ff.); Cleo. III had a priest as *Isis Megalē Mētēr Theōn*: P. Dem. Leid. 185 (*Rev. Egypt.* i 1880 91; Spiegelberg ZAS 1899 38; Otto i 158. In gen. Cerfaux.

8. See earlier ch. 9; Corssen; K. Sethe, *Gott. Nach.* 1920 30; Nock, AfR 1933.

Notes

For Helios in Egypt: Hoffmann; Helios Sarapis under Ptols., Weber, *Drei Untersuch. z. äg.-gr. Relig*; Helios-Hermanubis, Weber, *Die äg.-gr. Terrakotten* 139; Helios-Souchos, *ib.* 141 f., 169. Sol is shown in chariot over a crocodile (Egypt) on contorniates of Theodosius, Alföldi (3) 105 no. 20.

9. *Sib.* iii 652 f.; Tarn (6) 146; Norden 55.

10. Roberts (1) 272.

11. Reitzenstein for argument that there are Jewish and Persian elements. For Egyptian national prophecies, J.L. (3) 179 ff.

12. Struve sees only Ptol. III, his campaigns, a famine, calendar-reform of his reign; but the City of the Persians is not Persepolis, but Antioch: Tarn (13) 11. Also Nilsson, *Gesch. Gr. Rel.* ii 106; Nock. F. Altheim and Bidez-Cumont uncritically accept Reitzenstein.

13. Natural order: J. L. (3) 205. The term girdle-wearers seems to apply to Persians. See discussion in intro. Oxy. 2332, with further refs.

14. Pap. Anastasi iv 10, 1 ff.; Erman, *Anc. Eg. Lit.* 309 where Blackman takes just as bad weather.

15. Bevan 240 f.; Wilcken (5) 544 ff.; Syria as traditional foe, Oxy. 2332 intro.

16. Oxy. 2332 intro.

17. Ps.-Plut. *de proverb. Alex.* no. 21 (Crusius); *Souda*; Meyer, ZAS xlvi 1910 135 f.; Weill, *La fin du moyen emp. ég.* 116, 622; Ailian NA xii 3; Manethos fr. 54 (232 ff.); Synkellos 138, 140; Euseb. Armenian version 104. The demotic version of the tale: Krall (2) 3–11.

18. Oxy. 2332 intro. Norden notes parallels of theme and style with Sibylline oracles (suppressed hexameter rhythms).

19. Also Kanopos and Ombi. Seems little or no link with vision of 4th *Ecl.*; see Oxy. intro. as to *phyllorosei*.

20. OGI no. 83.

21. Proklos on Plato's *Tim.* 21E; Norden 30. Proklos i 30D; Plut. *Mor.* 354C.

22. Aigina: R. Harder, *Abh. Berl.* 1943 xiv 9 n. 7; Nilsson ii 496; Nock JRS 1957 121.

23. Tarn does not decide if similar coins of Ptol. V are copies or if Arsinoe III was also Isis.

24. Diod. ii 59, 7.

25. AJ i 3, 106.

26. *Malachi* iv 2; Dolger 83–99; Nock (5) 71 f.; Tarn (6) 148.

27. Budge 190; moongod 238, etc.

28. Goodenough 82, 85, and 97.
29. Baynes (1) with many refs.

The Parthian War

1. JA xv 3.
2. There is an impossible tale of envoys to Ekbatana; Dion xlix 27 says that at the siege he decimated his army; this seems unlikely; Plut. xxxix 7.
3. V.P. ii 82.
4. *Ant.* xlii–l. *Testudo*: Dion xlix 3. The herb was said to make men desperately turn stones over, finally vomit and die.
5. Antony's legions: Tarn (2) 98. Xenophon in his retreat had lost nearly as high a percent, but had not had to face Parthian arrows.

Deepening Divisions

1. App. v 77 and 80; Hadas 104 f.
2. R.G. xxv.
3. This analysis of names largely based on Syme (2) with its comprehensive material. Agrippa refused Triumph after Gaul, though Imperator appears in ILS 8897 Ephesos and in original ded. at Nemausus, CRAI 1919 332. His nomen (Sen. *controv.* ii 4, 13) emerges with females and freedmen: Syme 185 f.
4. Syme 185 f. for more examples. *Praenomina* lose importance save with *nobiles*: Syme 186 f. and (4).
5. Dilke (2). Achilles-Magnus and Domitian: Sauter 96–102. Oriental: Cic. *de imp. Pomp.* xxiv.
6. No contemporary author or coin attest Imperator Caesar: McFayden 11 f.; Premerstein (1); Alföldi 28 ff.; Kraft (1). But a general by retaining Imp. after his name gave it an effect like *cognomen*, and a *cog.* could be transferred and used as *praenomen*. Pompey with his three Triumphs had several years during which he was Imp., and the title thus had a tendency to cling. For Caesar's negligence of imperatorial salutation: Syme 178 f.; not in his official nomenclature in *Fasti Consulares*. See further Alföldi (1) 1 ff.; Kraft 7 ff.; Kraay.
7. Combès. The first general saluted as Imp. was Scipio Africanus: the act was that of heterogeneous troops, Roman and Latin, looking rather to the man than the fatherland: Combès 65 f., 71. The

initiative came from the soldiers; sanctioned by Senate it became title to a Triumph. J.C. did put it at head of his titulature: Combès 127. After Vespasian it became the very title of the ruler.

In Greek, *Imp.* is *Autokrator*, which can render the Roman titles of magistracy.

8. Dion xlix 33. He goes on, 'As for Ant., he grew more than ever a slave to the passion and witchery of Cleopatra'. Drumann's idea that he heard in Egypt is impossible. Cf. Bouché-L. ii 268 and n. 1; Craven 82; Staehlin 762.

9. *Ant.* lii.

10. *Comp. Demet. and Ant.* iii; cf. previous account of Demet. as Dionysos; Volkmann 139; Oxé. Cf. tales of Alex. and Roxana, Perikles and Aspasia, etc.

11. Prop. iii 11, 17–20.

12. *Fasti* ii 327–30. Note parasol both feminine and Dionysiac: a sky (cosmic) emblem. See J.L. (2) 332 f., 335–46. R. Turcan shows (Ovid *Fasti* ii 329) relation of transvestism of H. and Omphale to sacra of Bacchus: REL xxxvii 1959 195 ff.; MEFR lxxiv 1962 601 ff.; H. Brandenburg, *Stud. z. Mitra* 1966 is wrong.

13. V.P. ii 82 and 83.

14. Strab. xi 2, 18 (499); xii 3, 29 (556); xii 3, 37 (559 f.); xiii 3, 29, 31, 37; xiv 1, 42. For Titius: Taylor (7).

15. It seems that now Cleo. was tidying up and expanding the system she had worked out at the time of the first gifts. The tale of the betrayal of Artavasdes may be an Octavian invention to counter the charge that Oct. was instigating Artavasdes. Later, early 33, Ant. in response to an urgent message, went to Median frontier and saw the king there, who feared a Parthian attack. The king restored his share of the Roman Eagles; and probably Ant., who took Iotape back with him as hostage, gave him temporary aid; for the legions were not withdrawn from Armenia till autumn. But the Mede in fact secured himself for a while by alliance with Tiridates (who had perhaps been a general of Phraates in the war with Ant., and who may even have been Monoases). The situation is unclear. A revolt early 31 or late 32 expelled Phraates, who returned in 30 with the aid of 'Skythians' (prob. the Sakaraukai), and Tiridates, not an Arsakid, could not hold out. He and the Median king fled to Syria (now held by Oct.).

16. I omit the question how far chthonic elements were or were not central in the early Osiris.

17. *Ant.* liv for the way it was taken. For previous effort (and

failure) of T. Albucius to triumph outside Rome: Cic. *de. prov. cons.*
vii 15; *in Pis.* xxxviii 92.

18. Cyrenaica: had been bequeathed to Rome in 96 by last king;
Senate accepted his estates, left cities independent; but flare-up of
class war in 75 made them take over as province. Sallust *hist.* ii fr.
43; P. Romanelli *La Cirenaica Romana* 1941 ch. 3; A. H. M. Jones (2)
360 f. An organised group of R. businessmen there since 67 (prob.
earlier) who, prob. including the publicani dealing with the large
tracts of ager publicus, wanted no disorders. Pompey there:
Reynolds 102 f. Also E. Rosenbaum, *Cat. of Cyr. Portrait Sculpture*
1960 no. 11; Romanelli 49.

19. In Plut. xxxvi 2, Cleo. is sole beneficiary; in 54, 4 (cf. Dion
xlix 41) the children as well. Meiklejohn 191 f.

20. *Ad Aen.* viii 696. It is argued that the gifts were not made in
block; in 37-6 Ant. made Cleo. content with Ituraian kingdom with
capital Chalkis, ejecting the ruler on pretext he had betrayed the
Romans. For the rest she prob. got only Damas. Then Ant. yielded
to her desire for Judaea and Arabia to extent of giving Koile Syria,
soon after adding Jericho area, part of Malchos' land, and Phoenician
coast. Then he confirmed all her holdings near end 34. Indeed maybe
he granted demands gradually; but it is hard to be sure from sources
(Plut., Dion, Jos., Porph. in Euseb., coins). But gradual expansion
seems likely. First over Syria (at least central and S. parts, long
debated by Ptols. and Seleukids); then dissensions at Jerusalem, 35,
gave excuse for more demands. Hence Herod called in, spring 34.
She insisted on balsam lands and part of Nabataian realm plus coast
minus free towns. However, on this basis hard to explain how Malchos got in arrears. See Meiklejohn on Dobiaš and Kromayer's 5th
objection. See these writers plus Schürer, Gardthausen, Tarn.

21. OGI 196. For era: Fraser (1) with refs.

22. Scott (1) 44 n. 1.

23. This by Agrippa, 33: Dion xlix 43. For Oct.'s building, R.G.
xix-xxi; App. 2-3. For the maze-dance see Jackson Knight (2),
with the relation to the Sibyl or cave-guarding Earthmother. This
connection could hardly have been known at all to Agrippa, etc.!

24. Fetials: Rose, *Prim. Cult. in Italy* 222 f. and 45.

25. Caesar BC iii 105; cf. Oct. and palm-tree.

26. *De Div.* ii 54, 112. For whole of this section, Jal (3) with refs.
and more material.

27. Macrob. *Sat.* i 12, 35.

28. Note Oct.'s reward to Messalla. Perusia: Suet. *Aug.* xcvi. Cic.

Phil. xiii 10, 12. Combès 388, 402–5, for use of augurship to increase religious force of army leader; not so sure Sulla, Cicero, etc., attributed a political value to it. (But it seems clear they did to its use.) Still, in end the religious force of it weakened, *e.g.* from 27, when Oct. is called augur the term has rather a general and mystic value than a precise ref. to the *disciplina*. (But then the civil wars were over.)

29. R.G. xxv 3.

30. Civil wars made much use of *charismata*, gods, priesthoods: Picard (4) 236; Grimal (1); Bayet (1) 502.

Cleopatra's Egypt

1. Laberius: Suet. *Aug.* xliii on Augustus engaging *equites* to act on stage or fight gladiators, till a senatorial decree forbade it. Plin. ix 58 (117–22); he adds that Fenestella said pearls came into common use at Rome after Alexandria fell, but small cheap ones first came in about the time of Sulla—this, says Pliny, was an error as large pearls were known at the time of the Jugurthan wars. Macrob. *Sat.* ii 13. For pearls, Gagé (11) 36.

2. Hor. *Sat.* ii 3, 239; Val. Max. ix 1, 2p; Suet. *Calig.* xxxvii; Volkmann 151; Balsdon (8) 263 f.

3. OGI 195; Fraser (1); SB 8777 i.

4. Plat. *Phaid.* 81b; festival, Xenophon *Hellenika* v 4, 4; vagina, Louk. *Nigr.* xvi; temple, Zen. *ib.* v 4, 58; GDI 5075, 70 (Crete); statue, Plut. *Thes.* xxi and P. Petrie iii p. 113. Decree; Tebt 6 (i p. 64, n. to 1.29), cf. P. Par. 34, 6; and Strab. xvi 745 and viii 378; Philostr. *epist.* 60 (23); also P. Grenf. ii 41 and *Fay. Towns* pp. 149 ff.

5. Athen. vi 234d–235f, citing many authorities. The *parasitos* might himself sacrifice, *e.g.* at Acharnai to Apollo.

6. De Visscher (2) with refs. and much more material.

7. Martial xi 43; Stat. *Silv.* iv 6.

8. For the open-air festival and improvised pergola leading to constructions: de Visscher 101 ff.; relation to ciborium; columns of Herakles, etc. We have seen how Dionysos and Herakles became supreme types of heroes, conquerors, turning into gods; Osiris and Alexander were drawn into the H. line. At Rome H. became symbol, model, guarantee of the Universal Conqueror. The idea appears already late in 2nd c. when Q. Fabius Maximus Aemilianus, defeating Averni, built temple of H. at confluence of Isère and Rhône. In following century H. became emblem of Rome and its ruler,

conqueror of Cacus, founder of the Great Altar, the beneficient
Conditor. Caesar wrote *Praises of H.*—'some things pass under his
name, said to have been composed in his youth, such as the *Praises
of H.,* a tragedy *Oedipus,* and a coll. of Apothegms; all of which
Augustus forbade to be published, in a brief plain letter to Pompeius
Maior whom he employed to arrange libraries' Suet. *Jul.* lvi. Later
the poets took H. from Ant. and linked him with Aug. who was said
to have gone beyond both H. and Bacchus. (H. Schnepf; Diod. v 21,
2; Bianchi, *Rend. Lincei* xviii 1963 110, etc.—in general, Harmand
(2); Gagé REA xliii 1940 432; Gruppe *Herakles* RE Suppl. iii 1918
998, etc.)

    Ant. as H.: App. iii 16, 60; 19, 72; Plut. *Ant.* iv, xxiv, xxxvi, lx.

    9. Suet. *Aug.* lxx.

    10. Liv. v 13; Dionys. xii 9 (ordered by Sibylline Books); Liv. xx
1 and 10. The 4th ex. was in time of pestilence after consulting of S.
Books. Liv. vii 2 and 27; viii 25. There seems a constant, perhaps
daily, *lect.* to certain deities: Liv xxxvi 1; xlii 30; linked with
supplicatio iii 63. No connection with Epulum Jovis. Note R.G. ix 2,
'All the citizens, individually and on behalf of their towns, have
unanimously and continuously offered prayers at all the pulvinaria
for my health'.

    11. Mart. xi 15, 1.

    12. Carcopino (7); App. v 77; Rice Holmes 108 (1); Suet. *Aug.*
lxix 1; Dion. xlviii 44, 3, cf. 44, 5.

    13. Suet. *Claud.* i 1.

    14. *Ant.* xxiv.

    15. Oros. vi 19.

    16. H. I. Bell; Tarn and Griffith, Préaux, Bouché-L., Einaudi.

    17. Grenf. ii 36.

    18. Tebt. 34, about 100 B.C.

    19. Tebt. 9–11 (119–8).

    20. *Ib.* 12.

    21. *Ib.* 13.

    22. *Ib.* 14; see Tebt. Pap. i p. 41 note on 1.65.

    23. Tebt. 15–6.

    24. *Ib.* 17–8, *Epimeletes*: *Arch. Pap.* ii 83; P. Amh. ii 337. He is
some sort of 'manager', but the term was used variously in the
Greek world.

    25. *Ib.* 19; ref. mark seems short for *elabon* (I received it).

    26. *Ib.* 20. Note *ib.* 21 (B.C. 115), letter from Polemon (prob.
epistates of Kerkeosiris) to another official of same name. 'I've

written to the collector Artemidoros to stop work at Kerkeosiris till he proceeds to the city, and that Aristippos will come to an understanding with him. So don't run away from anyone, for at present you have no produce. If he gives you trouble, go up with him.'
27. *Ib.* 22 (119 or 114 B.C.); phylakes and crops: Tebt. 27 and note on 5, 1. 159.
28. *Ib.* 24 (117). Whom to? See P. Tebt. i p. 95. Cf. 27 dated 113.
29. Oxy. 1644. More examples: lease of cleruchic land, Oxy. 1628 (73 B.C.); sale of house, BGU 998 (101); loan of wheat, Tebt. 110 (92 or 59); transport of corn, Tebt. 92 (late 2nd c.); cession of katoikic land, Oxy. 1635 (44–37); BGU 1761, restitution of profits (51–50); summons, SB 7610 (Aug. 51); Ryl. 590; JJP vi 1952 299; CE lv 1953 158 (burial guild).
30. Oxy. 1629. No need here to go into status of Persians of Epigone.
31. Ryl. 69 and 73; wild *Knekos* liked by goats, Theophr. HP iv 4, 5; name for goats, Theok. iii 5.

Preparations for the Final Struggle

1. Suet. *Jul.* lii 2; Scott (1) 38.
2. Suet *Aug.* iii 1; iv 2, etc. For list, Scott (1) 12 f. Cic. *Phil.* iii 6, 15–7. For Thurinus: Blanchet 134–42; Deonna 35 n. 6 tries to link with Etruscan Mercury (vainly); Scott (3) 26; Kalinka 42.
3. Kalinka 44.
4. Scott (1) 14–6. For wealth of the father, Nikolaos *Life* 2 and V.P. ii 59, 2.
5. Suet. *Aug.* lxx: *Pater argentarius ego Corinthiacus.* For Ant.'s abuse of Cicero: Scott (1) 17; Cicero on Oct. *ib.* 16 f. Ant. on Cicero: Piotrowicz; note Tac. *Ann.* iv 34, 8, speech invented for Cremutius Cordus. Also Pollio, *Contra Maledicta Antonii*, and speech of Messalla *Contra Antonii Litteras*; attack on Domitius, Suet. *Nero* iii 2. See further Charlesworth (2); and Sen. *de clem.* i 9 ff. for tale that Oct. stabbed Hirtius in back and poisoned Pansa (Glyco his agent), but see ad Brut. i 6, 2; also ps.-Cic. *Epistula ad Octavianum.*
6. Weichert 36 ff.; Howard; Kalinka 45–8; Scott (1) 15 f.; ps. Acron on Hor. *Ep.* i 32. Kalinka thinks all the poems from a single original; unlikely. Oct. on style: Suet. *Aug.* lxxxvi.
   The reliefs of Domit. Ahen. were kept from 17th c. in Palazzo Santa Croce, next to site of San Salvatore where a temple of Neptune

was found. Earlier possible dates are 118 or 115 B.C. See Ryberg (2) 27–34; Nash i figs 831–5; Castagnoli 181–96. Domitius: Munzer (2) V.P. ii 68 and 84; Suet. *Nero* iii; Vessberg (2) 150–2; Broughton ii 332, 353, 365; Shipley ix 43 f.; App. v 50, 63, 75; Plut. *Ant.* xxxix and lxiii; Dion xlviii 54, 4; coins, Grueber ii 487 (an altar to Neptune early as 206 B.C.; Platner-A. 'Neptune'; Bithynia, Fürtwangler 43.

Sosius: Broughton ii under C. Sosius; Shipley 9–60; von Damaszewski *Abhandl.* 232; Liv. xxvii 37. The temple much venerated; Cic. *ad Q.* ii 3, 3; Liv. xxxiv 43; xxxvii 58; xxxix 4; xli 17. Many important assemblies of Senate here and processions of Juno Regina began from it.

For the *lustratio* as connected with the census, not a victory: Ogilvie 37.

7. J.L. (2) 155 f.; for link with Herakles 157–9.

8. *Ant.* lvii; Ptol. tradition was to favour Athens. Divorce of Octavia in May or June.

9. V.P. ii 83.

10. Crook for discussion; Levi (5) points out the document is a political manifesto not a will; CR lxviii 1954 152 f.; Charlesworth (4); Syme (1) 282 f.

11. *Ant.* lviii.

12. *Ant.* lviii-lix. C. Furnius, Caesarian, took part in Perusian war on Antonian side; one of officers negotiating peace, made his own side suspicious (App. v 30, 41; Dion xlviii 13, 14); prefect of Asia Minor in 35, took Sextus P. captive (App. v 137–42); after Actium. was reconciled to Oct. and much favoured. From *De Oratoribus* xxi he seems a speaker with meagre and obsolete diction.

13. *R.G.* xxv 2. Oath: Volkmann 173.

In general for religious propaganda of Ant. and Cleo.: Jeanmaire (1); Tondriau (3) and (7); Immisch; Heinen (2). It is not sure if the 2nd Triumvirate ended 1 Jan. 31 or 32: see Grenade, ch. i and Brunt (1) 236–7.

Sibylline Prophecies

1. First Book in present form not later than 3rd c. A.D.: Rzach, RE sv *Sib. Orakel*, 2 *Reihe* ii 2118–69 and *Wiener Stud.* 1912 xxxiv 114–22; Bousset *Die Relig. d. Judentums* (3te Auflage 1926) 38. See further Fuchs (2) 30–6.

2. Tarn (6); Geffcken.

Notes

3. Cumont (1) 71; Bidez-Cumont. i 215 ff., etc.; H. Fuchs (2) 8 f., 31 ff.; K. Latte (1); Windisch 52, etc.

4. Cumont (1) 72.

5. *De Antichr.* 15 and 54; Cumont 72 n.

6. Commod. 903; Ephraem *sermo ii de antichristo* 12 (Lamy, *Sancti Ephrem hymni et sermones* iii 210). Date: Grégoire; Gagé (11) 294.

7. Phlegon *Mir.* 32. For oracle under Tiberius: Dion lvii 18, 5. Sibyllines: xiii 151 ff.; discussion, Gagé (11) 285 ff. Note coins with *Oriens Aug(usti)*: Emperor supported by Sun and himself the Rising Sun: Turcan (2) 15–8 and (3).

8. *Rev.* vi 14–7 and xviii 15–8.

9. *Aen.* near end viii.

10. CIL i (2nd ed.) p. 214; p. 244 under 1 August; *Fasti Fratrum Arvalium*, p. 214.

11. Taken as ref. to Mithridatic war: Geffcken (2) 8 ff.; Norden 637; Lanchester in Charles (1) ii 372; Weber 59 n. 1 sees no historical application.

12. Tarn (11) 90 f., with refs. (Messalina as Homonoia in sanctuary of Halasarna at Kos?—Veyne 54.) Also Diod, ii 58, 1; Poehlmann i 404–6; G. Cardinali in Beloch, *Saggi* 269.

13. Taken as Jewish: Geffcken, Norden, Weber, Pincherle (pp. xvi ff.). *Septuagint* had long been available in Alexandria, going back to Ptol. I who at Gaza beat Demetrios Poliorketes and brought back among other 'Syrians' a Jewish highpriest Ezechias (Jos., citing Hekataios, who says Ez. explained about his people, 'for he had all their habitations and policy down in writing'). This has been doubted but a coin from Beth-Zur had names of Onias and Ezekias (Jehohanan and Hezekiah). So it is possible that, in time of Ptol. I and highpriest Onias I, Ez. interested Hekataios and perhaps Demetrios of Phaleros in translation of the Bible; the Jews would be pleased to gain authority for their religion with hope for a charter for politeuma or citizen-body of Alex. Jews. Ez. was *dioiketes* or finance-minister of Onias; what was brought from Jerusalem was no doubt the authentic rolls, not a group of translators (as in the legend). The account of the translation attributed to Aristaios was prob. written under Titus, linked with the *Epistle to Barnabas* which sought to refute the Jewish stress on the Law. Onias represented the legitimate lines of Pharisees ousted by the Seleukids; he fled to Egypt and was let build a small copy of Jerusalem Temple on site of an old deserted temple of Bast at Leontopolis on east arm of Nile. Worship went on till Vespasian closed it; its existence gave

a special character to the Jews in Egypt. Bevan 299 and 306 f.; M. O. R. Sellers, *Citadel of Beth Zur* 1933 73 ff.; Loeb Jos. vii 6 n. 8; A. Olmstead *J. Am. Or. Soc.* lvi 1936 244; H. St Thackeray, *Letter of Aristaeus* 1928, intro. p. xv; L. Herrmann (4); Jos. *Contra Ap.* i 187.

14. Kyme, lines 35, 48, 16, 4, 13; Andros 105, 158; Ios 13, etc. H. Frankels reading 1. 158 Andros, GGA 1930 128; Nock (3).

15. *Sib.* iii 46–54.

16. Tarn (6).

17. Bousset (1) 289 and 322; Rzach RE A ii 2, 2131.

18. *Sib.* xi 245–60, 272–314, esp. lines 254, 277, 290.

19. Budge 506 f.; H. Junker *Die Stundenwachen*, etc., in *Denks. d. Ak. Wien, p.-h. Kl.* 1910.

20. *Isaiah* xxxiv 4 (20), cf. Paul on stars, etc. *Golden Ass* xi 6. Also the whole problem of fatalistic astrology. The following section is based on Jeanmarie (3) *Sib.* iii 75–96; xi 290 (cf. 279); viii 190–212. Also Jeanmaire (1) and (2). Geffcken takes the Widow as Rome.

Herakleitos, fr. 52 Diels; 24 Wheelwright. This image is attributed in varying forms to H. by Clement, Proklos, Loukian. Plutarch (*On E at Delphoi* 393E) does not mention H. but speaks of 'the poet's fancied child playing a game among the sand that is heaped together and then scattered by him'. The counters of the game of chance here become the particles of a Demokritean universe.

21. Dion. xlix 15; xlviii 43 (Magna Mater temple on Palatine). xlviii 33, 2.

22. Plut. *Ant.* xxxvi 1; CIL i (2nd ed.) *Fasti Venusini* 66; Cramer 67; Weinstock (3) identifies the Capito and Fonteius of John Lydos (Wachsmuth, 88, 13 ff.).

23. *Sib.* xiv 284–361; 348. Harvest, *e.g. Matt.* xiii 24–30; 37–43.

24. *Sib.* viii 148 ff.; xii 46–9; xiii 38–45.

25. W. Scott (1) and (2) esp. (2) 158 f., 226 f.

26. CPJ iii 520; see Oxy. xxii 89 n. 4; CE xi 1936 525 n. 3; Manteuffel, *Mél. Maspero* ii 1934 123; *Archiv.* x 25.

Wrath of Isis: Jos. *Contra Ap.* i 289 Schwyzer, *Chairemon* 1932 F1 p. 26=Jac. FGH iii C 618, F1). Expulsion: Diod. xl 3, 1; Jos. *Contra Ap.* i 86, 88, 94; Diod. xxxiv 1, 2; Aly, *Strabon von Amaseia* 1957 199 ff.; Justin xxxvi 2, 12; Tac. *Hist.* v 3. Wrath of Egyptian Gods; Nock, *Conversion* 280.

27. See J.L. (2) 182–91 for fuller account and refs. Types of some of the cups may go back to the 3rd c. B.C.: T. B. L. Webster, *Hellenistic Poetry and Art* (1964) 298 f. But this would not preclude

topical adaptations. For cups illustrated (Triumph, etc.): **Strong (2)** 82–4, 101; Villefosse *Mon. Piot* v 1899 141–8; Brendel RM xlv 1930 209 f.; Ryberg (2) 141 f. For an oratory of Dionysos-Osiris at Pompeii: Le Corsu.

Day of the Ass: Gagé (11) 54.

For Capricorn, see Gagé (12): it is not clear how Capricorn was brought into Augustus' horoscope; the Scorpion played a similar part for Tiberius. For Alexander the Great see further *Bull. Fac. Lett. Strasb.* Dec. 1954: geniture half-way between Fishes and Aquarius.

28. Manil. iv 534 ff. Taurus was astrol. house of Venus and so of the Julian *gens*. Lion with star on Alexandrian coin as zodiacal sign: Anson, *Num. Gr.* p. vi pl. ii (1916) no. 137, cf. Bull, 141 and Archer 139.

29. Erigone as Virgo: Hyg. *fab.* 130; 254; Virg. *georg.* i 33 (Servius); Ovid *met.* iv 25. Astraea: Mart. Cap. ii 174. Virgo as Justice at turning-point of a new creation: Nonnos, *Dionys.* vi 248 f.

30. Housman (1) and his edition; Smygly. For Capricorn: Manil. ii 507–9; Germanicus, *phaen.* 558–60; Suet. *aug.* xciv 12; Coins; Hor. *carm.* i 12, 50; Bouché-L. 374 (*Astrol.*). But Suet. *aug.* v, says Oct. was born 63, etc. If so, Libra was in his horoscope. Smygly suggests an earlier notion of Moon as dominant (Cic. *de div.* ii 91 and 98; Man. iv 773; Solin. i 18); so perhaps Libra was occupied by the Moon, cf. Manil. ii 507–9, contrasted with iv 547–52. When Manil. wrote iv 243–55, 568–70, 257 ff., Aug. was dead and he links Capricorn with miners, smiths, clothiers, sailors, young men spending vigour on women. For Libra and Tiberius: Housman (1) 112.

31. Lact. end of 7th Bk. of *Div. Institutes*. He also cites the Sibyl for Rome becoming a *Rhymē* or road; the mountains of Syria are named as those sinking. Some of the cited verses are only known from this text; for others see *Sib.* iii 65 and 741; vi 40; iii 787 and 619.

Actium

1. *Ant.* lx. Dionysos: one of group of figures at S. wall of Akropolis dedicated by Attalos I of Pergamon: Paus. i 25, 2, with Fraser's notes. Cf. iv 1–2 and xxiv 3.

2. Others say more, *e.g.* Volkmann (600). Legions at Actium: Tarn (7). For enrolling Italians from Caesar's colonies in east, cf. App. v 570 (Sextus P. and Italians at Lampsakos); Tarn thinks Ant.

had about 75,000, not 100,000 (*Ant.* lxi) and client-kings did not bring 35,000 foot.

3. Richardson: whose account of the battle I mainly follow. For relief: W. Amelung, *Katalog d. Skulpt.* ii 65–72, pl. 5; H. S. Jones, *Comp. to Rom. Hist.* 1912 264 (ships at Actium); R. Heidenreich RM li 1936 337 ff., fig. i; Hanfmann 104 fig. 100.

4. *Ant.* lxviii 4 f.

5. *Ib.* lxiii 2 f.

6. Dion l 15, 1–3.

7. Plin. xiv 22; Scott (2) 138 f.; Riewald 320.

8. Dion l 24–30.

9. *Ant.* lxiii and lxix; Dion l 15 and 23.

10. Richardson 157.

11. Porphyr. on *Ep.* i 7; Tarn (4) 176.

12. *Ant.* lxv 3.

13. Dion l 25, 3 and 31, 2; for V. P. Woodman (1) on ii 85 2–5 and 57, 1; Solid construction: Dion xlix 1, 2; 1, 19, 3; App. v 106; Flor. ii 21; Tarn (4) 191 n. 8; Kromayer (1) and (2); Ferrabino; Tarn (4 and 5); Richardson; M. A. Levi; Starr 7 f.; Casson 108 and 213 f.

14. Tarn (4) 193; Liv. xxviii 30, 5.

15. Cf. Agrippa at Mylae and his failure to carry out intentions after battle: App. v 108, 445 f.

16. *Ant.* lxvi.

17. Cf. Vegetius iv 33. In part the misunderstanding of later writers who used *liburna* as synonym for *navis*, e.g. echoes of Hor. in Prudentius *Contra Symm.* ii 530 f.; Starr 10. Lines from Horace also helped: *epod.* i 1–4; Plut. *Ant.* lxv.

18. Tarn (4) 193; App. v 111.

19. *Ant.* lxvii 1–5.

20. Starr 11 f.

21. *Aen.* viii end.

22. Prop. iii 11 (12).

23. *Ib.* iv 6; *Fasti* already cited.

24. *Ant.* lxiii.

25. *Georg.* ii 497; Hor. *Sat.* ii 6, 53, also *Carm.* iii 6, 13 f.

26. Dion xli 54.

27. Caesar BC iii 3–5; Dion xliv 44, 2.

28. *Ad Fam.* ix 92; Lucan ii 632.

29. Dion xli 13, 3; Cic. *ad Att.* viii 11, 2 (Feb. 49); ix 10, 3 (3 March); *Aen.* vi 831.

30. Dion xli 8, 6; Cic. *ad Att.* viii 11, 4. Pharsalos: Caesar BC iii 3 ff.; App. ii 49, 202 ff.; Lucan vii 526 f.; Dion xli 59, 4 and 2, 5; Justin lii 4, 6; Lucan viii 323 f., cf. 309 f. and 412–5; App. ii 83, 350.

31. *Bell. Alex.* xliv 1; Val. Max. ix 2, 4; Lucan viii 287 f.; *Bell. Afr.* lvii 5; *Bell. Civ.* ii 44, 2; Hor. *Carm.* ii 1, 25–8; Dion xlii 9, 3; xliii 4, 6; Cic. *ad Att.* xi 6, 2; *ad Fam.* vii 3, 3; *pro Lig.*; Quintil. x, 11, 1, 80. Tyrell and Purser on *Ad Fam* xi 1a (v p. 244); *Att.* xiv 9, 3; Dion xlvii 27, 3.

Phil. v 2, 5; xiii 37, cf. vii 1, 3; *ad Brut.* i 10, 2; App. iv 8, 33; 63, 271; 133, 558. Dion xlvii 30, 3; Levi (4) i 168 ff., etc. P. Jal (2).

32. See further Jal.

33. App. v 133, 544; Dion xlix 18, 1.

Last Days

1. Perhaps neglected as the overland route had come to be the one normally used: see BIFAO xvii 1920 103–7, etc.

2. *Ant.* 71.

3. Volkmann 193.

4. Boys of 14 commonly enrolled in epheboi in Egypt, or even earlier: Jouguet, *Vie municipale* 150; Antyllus may have been about 14—but this proves little about Caesarion. It is possible that Oct. himself stressed Ant.'s championship of Caesarion (Meiklejohn 193; Dion l 1, 5 cf. 3, 5), but it seems rather that Ant. had some success with the opposing of the boy to Oct. in the two years before Actium: Charlesworth (2) 176 on Suet., *Jul.* lii.

5. *Ant.* lxxii, adding that Timagenes introduced Alexas to Ant. while still at Rome, and that he had been Cleo.'s agent in working Ant. up against Oct.

6. *Ant.* lxxiii; Dion li 9, 5 for different time. Plut. says Hipparchos had great influence with Ant., lxvii. Plut. says (lxvii) that in his flight after Actium Ant. meant to cross from Tainaron to Africa, tried to get his friends to take rich presents, they refused and he comforted and sent them away, then he 'wrote to Theophilos his steward in Corinth that he should keep the men in safe hiding till they could make their peace' with Oct. This T. the father of H.

7. Dion li 8, 6 f.

8. *Ib.* 9, 1–4.

9. *Ib.* 9, 6; *Ant.* lxxiv, 1.

10. Dion xlvii 48, 1; xlviii 25, 3 f. Terms are *charkoma* and *biblia*.

11. *Ant.* lxxv.

12. Rose (1); Scott (2).

13. Dion lxvii 16; Suet. *Dom.* xv 3. For the special relation: J. Janssen, *Suet. Tranq. Vita Dom.* (1919) 74; and G. R. Gephart, same title, 1922 97 n. 12.

14. Bevan 381; Pape, *Gr. Eigenname.*

15. In all this following *Ant.* lxxvi-vii.

16. Bernhard. Lucan viii 694; x 19. Tomb: Suet. *Aug.* xviii; Plin. xxxv 1161. Relief: Picard BCH lxxvi 1952 92, fig. 14; T. Thiersch; Perdrizet REA i 4 (1899) 261–72.

17. John Chrysos. x 625 (Montfaucon); Bernhard 138 ff. John had never been to Alex. but had defended those persecuted by its patriarch Theophilos.

18. *Ant.* lxxx; Dion li 16; Julian *epist.* li; Strab. xiv 670; Suet. *Aug.* lxxxix; Themist. *Orat.* v p. 63d; viii 108b; x 130b; xiii 173c, Petav.; *Quint.* ii 15, 36; iii 1, 16 etc.

19. *Pal. Anth.* vii 645, see also Krinagoras vii 633; vi 161 (Marcellus); ix 284.

20. *Ant.* lxxxi; *Iliad* ii 204.

21. Dion li 14; tale of Pselloi also, certainly untrue. He says Pselloi have no females in their tribe; they can suck out poison of any reptile, etc. Dion also has a eunuch: 'he had of his own accord delivered himself up to the serpents at the very time of Cleo.'s arrest, and after being bitten by them had leaped into a coffin already prepared'.

22. *Ant.* lxxxv; see JEA 1965 210.

23. Flor. iv 11, 11; and note the pairs of double snakes in the *Aeneid*: viii 697; 289; ii 203 f.; vii 450—see discussion by Griffith.

24. Temple of Edjo, Delta-type, rebuilt in Ptol. times: *Antiquity* 1969 no. 170 108–10.

25. Ferrua; Toynbee in JRS 1962 257.

26. Dion li 19; liii 2 (28 B.C.); popularity CAH x 35–8.

27. Bonner (1) 322 f. no. 398, with refs. Second gem, in Southesk Coll. K7 pl. 11.

28. Bonner (1); CIG 4716c; Oxy. 1449; Wilcken *Chrest.* 115; HTR xli 1948 213–5; *BM Quart.* xi 33 f., etc., Isis as Conqueror: Bonner D216.

29. For Venus and the Antonine Empresses: Aymard.

30. *Fatale monstrum*: Verdière.

31. Pease 23 ff., with refs. and discussion.

Notes

32. Dion lii 43, 1; Pease 28 f.; Dessau *Hermes* 1914 xlix 508–11; Hermann (7). *Pius Aeneas* cannot have been conceived without a thought of Oct. with his stress on *Divi Filius*. For reliefs: Ryberg (2) pl. xxvii; CAH plates iv 134.

Aftermath

1. Dion li 16, 4; Suet. *Aug.* lxxxix; *ib.* xciii, his attitude to foreign cults; commends his grandson for not paying devotions at Jerusalem.

2. Dion li 15, 6; *Ant.* lxxxvii; Strab. xvii 828. Also App. ii 101; Plut. *Caes.* lv. His trouble with Gaetulians: Dion liii 26; lv 28; Strab. xvii 828, 831. Caesarea (Iol): Strab. xvii 831; Eutrop. vii 10. Divine honours after death: Lactant. *de fals. rel.* i 11; Min. Fel. xxiii. Honours, Athens, Paus. i 17, 2; Gades, Avienus v 275; ? New Carthage, *Mém. Ac. Inscr.* xxxviii 104. Plin. oft cites, cf. Plut. *Sestor.* ix; Athen.; Avienus v 279. He wrote History of Africa, the Assyrians, History of Arabia, *Romaikē Historia*, a comparison of customs of Greeks and Romans, *Theatrikē Historia* (seems on all matters connected with stage), what seems a history of painting, two small treatises of botanical or medical nature (one on *euphorbia*, a plant he found on Mt Atlas), a grammatical work; an epigram on a bad actor in Athenaios (viii 343). Jos. AJ xvii 13, 4 says he married Glaphyra, daughter of Cappadocian king, after Cleo.'s death, but this seems wrong.

3. Suet. *Aug.* xcvi.

4. Also made Eurykles tyrant, imitating Ant. who set up a city-tyrant Boethos in Tarsos.

5. Following Tarn (1) and (2).

6. Piganiol (1); Stein (2) 80–119 esp. 92; Arrian *Anab.* iii 5; Milne (2) 1.

7. Jouguet, *Rev. Egyptol.* 1919 57, etc., J.L. (1) 59 f., 324 f.

8. Strab. xiii 797. G. Cornelius Gallus, from Forum Julii, father may have been Gallic notable; he invented the Roman elegy, developing from Catullus, may have served as equestrian officer on staff of Pollio 41–40; gave up verse for political career; prob. went east with Ant. after Pact of Brundisium; later turns up on Oct.'s side. Became first Prefect of Egypt and met disaster through Oct.'s jealousy. He and men like Salvidienus Rufus show rise of equestrian *praefecti* in civil wars (Syme 355 f.). Octavian disowned him and

broke off *amicitia*; Gallus committed suicide. Rumours that he erected statues to self and cut boastful inscription on the Pyramids. Certainly he set up inscriptions: CIL 8995. Oct. sanctimoniously praised *pietas* of Senate for ruining Gallus, Suet. lxvi 2. Gallus and obelisk incr. dated 30: G. Guadagno, *Opuscula Romana* vi 1968 21–6. He probably knew Virgil well through Pollio, but we saw above no reason to believe the Servian statement that extensive praises of him in *Georgics* iv were cut out at orders of Oct.

9. J.L. (5) 187–9; Cassius too was extremely rapacious. Aug. chose his men from assured friends, his praetorian prefects, men of letters like Balbillus or Vestinus; even a freedman turns up under Tiberius: Dion lviii 19, 6—Stein takes him as vice-prefect. *Imperium*: *Dig.* i 17, 1; *Aeg.* ix 1928 296; Tac. *Ann.* xii 60; *Dig.* xi 2, 21.

10. Piganiol 197. Alexandria: Bell JRS 1946 130; Fraser *ib.* 1949 54; Bell JEA 1949 167; Arangio-Ruiz (1) 59, etc., *Rev. Phil.* 1927 362; *Berl. Sitz.* 1928 424; *Rev. Int. Droits de l'Ant.* iv 1950 7.

11. Préaux (1). Even in Egypt the Roman system, with its search for entities responsible for fiscal failures, separates town from country and marks out towns by privileges and charges; so a movement towards urbanisation. Towns grow slowly round sanctuaries like Hermopolis; cities of a more lay character like Antinoe or Oxyrhynchos gain in 2nd c. a growth impetus. But they stayed separate from the land around, cut off from peasant immigration. Even after the Constitution of Caracalla the Egyptians could not rise to higher offices. Dion says of the Augustan settlement, 'of the system then imposed', which prevented Egyptians from becoming senators, 'most of the details are rigorously preserved at the present time'. At Rome they could only be mages, doctors, entertainers, while a Syrian of Emesa, a Bedouin of Hauran, could become emperor.

12. J. Reynolds JRS 1959 96 f. *Fasti* i 711 f., 717 f.

13. Dion li 19, 7; Hor. *Carm.* iv 5, 34.

14. JRS 1961 211; Latte 307, 4, etc.

15. Suet. *Aug.* lvii.

16. Latte 322; Wilcken (8). Faustina: Aymard 192; Oxy. 905.

17. Dion liii 1, 3; CIL I (2nd ed.) p. 249; *Inscr. Hal.* xiii 1, 31 (p. 329); see Last, JRS 1953 27–9.

18. If the canopy was carried by columns at each corner, two of them were so near the wall that images put on the entablature at these points would have been inconspicuous and impossible to see both at once.

Notes

19. Prop. ii 31; Plin. xxxvi 25, 24, 32. *Delubrum* is not used by him for precincts.

20. Weinstock (2) for refs. also for chairs in theatre and *Ludi*, links with Mars and Fortuna. As he took over Neptune from Sextus, he took Hercules (from Pompeius and Ant.) when in 20 he fixed his Triumph on the day after the festival, 12 Aug., of Hercules Invictus: Grimal (2) 54. Suet. *Aug.* lii, on his melting down all the silver statues of himself and using the metal for tripods which he consecrated to the Palatine Apollo.

21. Mattingly (3); Wissowa 296. Burning of books: Tale of Timagenes on disagreement with Aug. tossing his *Acta Caesaris* into fire; Sen. *de ira* iii 23, 6; Sen. *Controv.* x 5, 22: astonishment at Aug.'s forbearance 'in as much as Timagenes had done violence to his *Praises* and his *Acta'*. Loukian on Alex. of Abouniteisho and burning copy of Epikouros' *Kyriai Doxai* in market place on fire of figwood (ritual timber): Macrob. *Sat.* iii 20, 2 f.; cf. Virg. *8th ecl.*, Theok. *2nd Idyll*, Catullus threatening to burn poems, etc. The fire is more than just a destroying medium; it has a ritual purifying effect.

22. Weinstock (1), with more coins.

23. *Ibid.*

24. *Ibid*; and Instinsky (2): *Securitas* won by Aug. in *Pax R.* emerges later as a personification, under Nero, etc.

25. Jal (7).

26. Cf. wordplay in Cicero and Florus. *Condicio*: *Phil.* xiii 1, 1. Plut. *Sert.* v, cf. Dion xlv 11, 1.

27. Jal 214.

28. Jal 216.

29. *Ibid.*, cf. André. *Otia dia*: Lucretius v 1387; vi 92 f. Jelenko 66 f.; Boyancé 92; André 7 f. For *Pax-Auctoritas* and *res rep. restituta*: Wirszubski (3) ch. iv.

30. *De doma sua* vi 15.

31. Jal 219.

32. New Homonoia: Dion xliv 4, 4; Jal 226. Opimius: App. i 26; Plut. *G. Grac.* xvii; Aug. *Civ. Dei* iii 25. Cicero, as advocate of the worst traditions of senatorial rule, lamented the fate of Opimius: *pro Planco* 28; *Brut.* 34; *in Pis.* 38; *pro Sest.* 67; Schol. Bob. *ib.*, p. 311 Orelli.

33. Jal 227; role of temple of Concordia 226; Calenus 226. And Dion xlvi 28, 3. Correspondences: Lucan iv 189–91.

34. R.G. xii; see Tib. i 10, 45 ff.; Ovid *Fasti* i 717 ff.

35. Hanfmann 105–7 with refs.; Toynbee; CAH plates iv 112–21,

esp. 120 for *Terra Mater* and refs. See Schwartz for idea that the T.M. figure is Opsor Ceres (who got altars, 10 Aug. 7 B.C.). For link of Ara with Aeneas, Toynbee (2) 156.

36. Strong (1) 116.

37. *Ib.* 117; in the Renascence it was copied and passed into iconography of Venus.

38. *Ib.* 118.

39. Prop. ii 7; Liv. *praef.* 9. And Suet. *Aug.* lxxxix 2; Liv. 59.

40. He transferred the festival of Honos and Virtus to the end of May in 17, as he connected these deities with the L.S.: Heinze, note to Hor. CS 57.

41. Galinsky (1) for some of the problems. The not convincing theory that it was all done to win over the hellenising aristocracy: R. Gelsomino *Maia* x 1958 154. Zos. ii 5 cites Sib. verses: 'But when the greatest length of life comes to men travelling in the style of a hundred and twenty years, remember O Roman, take good care not to forget it, remember all these things. . . .' For use of anniversaries: Grant (1) *e.g.* Ara Pacis on 49th birthday of Livia; Tiberius ded. a statue of Div. Aug. on 49th anniversary of his own assumption of *toga virilis*; temple of Concordia in Arce was vowed in 150th year (218 B.C.) of traditional foundation—date of first temple of Concord. Same with colonies: Colonia Copia at Thurii founded 250 years after Greek foundation there; J.C. planned new Carthage 100 years after destruction of old city; Severan issues linked with 250 years after foundation-plan: *Indulgentia Augg in Carth*. See Grant 3 f., 10, 120.

42. Hirschfeld (*Kl. Schr.* 438 ff.) conjectures Aug. first fixed L.S. for 23; postponed through death of Marcellus in midsummer. But the games were trad. given at end of May, so this is not correct. But possible he had intended 22; structure of *Aen.* vi suggests: lament for M. followed by promise of Golden Age. This would also help to explain the ban on the ref. to the gods of death. Mattingly (3) 162 f. Hirschfeld's strong point is that Domitian celebrated the Games in A.D. 88, using Aug.'s computation (Suet. *Dom.* iv); this points to 23–2, not to 17. For Sib. poems and events leading up to 17 B.C., see Gagé (2) 542–55.

43. Macrov. *Sat.* i 11.

44. *Aen.* ii 682 ff.; Chevallier.

45. Sattler. Note that when Aug. reorganised the *cursus*, the patricians were given the advantage; they could move straight from quaestorship to praetorship: Mommsen, *Staat.* i 554 f.; Badian (4) 88.

Notes

For treason in early empire: R. S. Rogers JRS 1959 90–4; C. W. Chilton 1955 73–81. Romulus: App. 13, 94, etc.; Gagé (3).

46. Syme (2) 182–4; Liv. i 19, 3; coins BMC *Roman Empire* i 17 ff., 51 ff. We might say that bedrock was reached in 19 B.C., when he finally consolidated his position, perhaps uniting both consular and censorial powers: Sattler. Still, he was too shrewd to attempt a closed shop in the Senate. For *Concilium Principis*: Crook (3). Censorial power: Astin. Foreign Policy, H. D. Meyer; Brunt in JRS 1963 170–6 arguing for a defensive policy. Eastern policy: Bowersock; T. Liebermann-Frankfort *Lat.* xxv 1966 172–4. Despite all the scare-propaganda of the years leading to Actium, Augustus knew he must in some degrees integrate the Greek East in the empire. For Nikopolis as a Greek city: Bowersock 93 f. For opposition among the Greeks, ch. viii.

Picard (3) tries to argue that Aug. had a Pythagorean phase as a retort to Ant. as Dionysos, 59; this phase ended in 26 B.C. with exile of Pythag. Anaxilas and dedication of the *clipeus virtutis*, a return to Stoicism. This is dubious: JRS 1967 249. *Virtus* at Rome not exclusively Stoic; and note the prominence of *Clementia* on the *clipeus*.

47. See for ex., Syme (1) ch. xxxii–iii, the Doom of the *Nobiles*, and Pax and Princeps. For the fate of *Libertas*; Wirszubski. For Tiberius and name Augustus: Gagé (11) 85.

48. Koeberlein (1) and JRS 1964 203. Agrippa: Dion liii 2, 4; App. liv 6, 6. See also Gagé (11) 57 f.; also 103 f. on his feeling for oriental royalty.

49. *Ib.* 29 on his two brothers as Dioscures. Pharos: J. Lassus. Egyptian marriage: J. Nietzoll, *Die Ehe in Eg. z. ptol-röm. Zeit* 1903 30; in general J.L. (1) ch. 2. Krinagoras: AP ix 235, cf. vii 633—vi 161 is on marcellus; ix 284 on J.C.'s colonisation of Corinth (ironical).

50. JRS 1964 203; Willrich, *Klio* iii 1903 21 f. See Gagé (11) 111–4, citing L'Orange and Cumont (*Riv. di Filol.* 1933 145–54). Picard however sees a Dionysiac symbolism. Further for Caligula: R. Merkelbach *Isisfeste* 1963.

51. Gagé (9) 37 f.

52. Waltz 14 ff.

53. *E.H.* i 5.

54. D. Nandy in *Shakespeare in a Changing World* ed. A. Kettle (1964) 194.

Bibliography

Alföldi, A. (1) *Studien über Caesars Monarchie* 1952–3 (2) *Hermes* lxv 369–84 (3) *Die Kontorniaten.*
Altevogt, H., *Labor Improbus, Orbis Antiquus* (Heft 8, 1952).
Anderson, J. G. C., JHS xxx 1910 181–91.
Anderson, W. S. (1) *Pompey* 1963 (2) TAPA 1957 20 f.
André, J. (1) *Recherches sur l'Otium romain* 1962 (2) *La Vie et l'Oeuvre d'Asin. Pollio* 1949.
Andrieu, J., *César, La Guerre d'Alex.* 1954.
Anto, V. d' (1) *Lat.* xxiii 1964 258–70 (2) *Ann. d. Fac. Lett. Napoli* vii 1957 117 ff.
Arangio-Ruiz, V., *Nuova Antol.* (May 1947).
Astin, A. E., *Lat.* xxii 1963 226–39.
Aymard, J., *Mél. Ec. Rome* li 1934 178–96.

Badian, E. (1) JRS 1968 208 f. (2) 1967 246 (3) 1965 110–21 (4) 1959 81–9.
Bahrfeld, M.v. (1) JId'AN xii 1910 (2) *Die röm. Göldprägnung während d. Rep. u. unter Aug.* 1923.
Baldwin, B., JEA 1964 181 f.
Balsdon, J. P. V. D. (1) CR lxxiv 68 (2) *Hist.* vii 80–94 (3) JRS xxix 87 ff. (4) 1955 161–4 (5) G. & R. 1957 19–28 (6) 1951 (7) *Life and Leisure in Anc. Rome* 1969 (8) *Roman Women* 1962.

Balty, J., *Lat.* xxii 1963 565 f.

Barwick, K., *Caesar's Bellum Civile* 1951.

Bayet, J. (1) *Bull. cl. lettres Acad. Belg.* 1955 (*Sacerdoces rom.*) (2) REL 1928 276.

Baynes, N. H., *Mél. Bidez* 1934 13–8.

Becher, I., *Das Bild der Kleo. in der griech. u. latein. Lit.* 1966.

Becker, C., *Hermes* lxxxiii 1955 341–9.

Bell, H. I., *Egypt from Alex. the Gt. to the Arab Conquest* 1948.

Béranger, J., *Recherches sur l'aspect idiologique du Principat* 1953.

Bergener, A., *Die führende Senatorenschicht im frühen Prinzipät* 1965.

Bernhard, M. L. (*Topographie d'Alex.*), RA xlvii 1956 129–56.

Bickel, E., *Rh. Mus.* xcvii 1954 218–21.

Bidez (with Cumont) *Les Mages hellénisés.*

Bingen, J., CE nos. 77–8 174–6.

Birt, T. (1) in I. von Müller, *Handbuch* 329 (2) *Frauen d. Antike* 1932 142–99.

Blanchet, A., CRAI 1919 134–42.

Blumenthal, F. (1) *Wiener St.* xxxv 1913 113–30, 267–88 (2) xxxvi 1915 84–103 (3) *Archiv f. Pap.* v 1913.

Boer, W. den, *Mnemosyne* viii 1955 137.

Boll, F., *Mem. Acad. Sc. dell'Ist. di Bologna* v–vii 1920–3 18–22.

Bonner, C. (1) *Stud. in Magic Amulets* (2) HTR xli 1948 213–15 (with Nock).

Botermann, H., *Die Soldaten u. d. rom. Rep. in d. Zeit von Caesars Tod* 1968.

Bouché-Leclerq (1) *Hist. des Lagides* 1903–6 (2) *L'Astrologie grecque* 1899.

Bousset, W., *Die Religion d. Judentums.*

Bowersock, G. W. (1) *Aug. and Greek World* 1965 (2) JRS 1960 112–8.

Bowra, C. M., JRS 1957 21–8.

Boyancé, REA 1947 92.

Breccia, E., *Alexandria ad Aeg.* 1914.

Brett, A. G., *Am. J. of Arch.* xli 1937 452–63.

Broughton, *Magistrates of R. Rep.*

Brunt, P. A. (1) JRS 1961 236–8 (2) 1962 69–86 (3) PBSR xviii 1950 50 ff.

Bruscher, C., *Caesar u. sein Glück* 1958.

Buchheim, H., *Die Orientpolitik d. Trium. M. Ant.* 1960.

Budge, *From Fetish to God.*

Buren, A. W. van, JRS iii 1913 134 ff.

Bureth, P., *Les titulaires imp.*

Buttrey, T. V. (1) *Stud. in Coinage of M.A.* 1953 (2) *Am. Num. Soc. Mus. Notes* vi 1954 95–109 (Neotera).

Campbell, A. Y., CR lii 1938 55 f.

Carcopino (1) *Annales Gand.*; 1937 37 ff. (2) *Passion et Politique chez les Césars* (3) *Points de vue sur l'imp. rom.* 1934 (4) *Virgile et le mystère de la IVe Eglogue* 1930 (4) *Mél. Bidez* 35–69 (6) RA 1913 i 255–70 (7) *Rev. Hist.* 1929 iii 225–8 (8) *Sylla ou la monarchie manquée* 1931 (9) *César* (4th ed.) 1950.

Carney, T. F., *Procs. African Class. Assn.* v 1962 31–42.

Carson, R. A. G., *G. & R.* iv 1 (1957) 46–53.

Cary, M., JRS 1937 48–53.

Castagnoli, *Arti Figurative* i 1945.

Cerfaux, L., with J. Tondriau, *Le Culte des Souverains* 1957.

Chamoux, *Mon. Piot* xlvii 1953 131–47.

Charbonneaux, J., *L'Art au siècle d'Aug.*

Charles, R. H., *Apoc. and Pseudoepigraph. of OT.*

Charlesworth, M. P. (1) *Camb. Hist. J.* ii 1926 9 (2) CQ xxvii 1963 172–7 (3) *Virtues of a Rom. Emp.* 1937 (4) *Procs. Camb. Philol. Soc.* cli-cliii 1932 6 f.

Chevallier, R., *Lat.* xxi 1962 542–54.

Chilver, G. E. F., *G. & R.* 1957 71–7.

Colin, J., *Lat.* xiii 1954 394–415.

Collins, J. H., *Historia* iv 1955 445–65.

Combès, R. *Imperator* 1966.

Conway, with Mayor, in Fowler (2).

Corssen, P., *Philol.* lxxxi 1926 38–40.

Corte, M. delle, *Cleo., M.A. e Ottav. nelle allegorie . . . Boscoreale* 1951.

Cramer, P. H., *Astrology in R. Law* 1934.

Cleopatra

Craven, L., *Ant.'s oriental policies* (Univ. of Missouri St. iii no. 2 1920 29 ff.).
Crook, J. (1) JRS 1957 36–8 (2) *Lat.* 1967 363–76 (3) JRS 1955 252–4.
Cumont, F. (1) RHR ciii 1931 (2) *Mém. Délégation en Perse* xx 1928.
Cuntz, O., *Jahreshefte* xxv 1929 70 ff.
Curtius, L., *Mitt. deut. AI röm. Abt.*, xlviii 1933 182–92.

Dalzell, A., *Phoenix* x 1956 151–62.
Delayen, G., *Cleopatra* 1934.
Dessau, H. (1) *Hermes* xlvi 1911 613 ff. (2) xli 1906 142 ff.
Dilke (1) *G. & R.* 1957 78 ff. (2) *Lat.* xxii 1963 498–503.
Dobesch, G., *Caesars Apotheosis zu Lebzeiten* 1966.
Dobiaš, J., *Mél. Bidez* 287–314.
Doblhofer, E., *Gnomon* xl 1968 616–18.
Dolger, F. J., *Die Sonne d. Gerechtigkeit u. d. Schwarze* 1918.
Duckworth, C. E. (1) TAPA lxxxix 1958 1–8 (2) lxxxvi 1956 286–90 (3) CW li 1958 125.

Einaudi, *Greatness and Decline of Planned Econ. in Hellenistic World* 1950.
Erkell, *Augustus, Felicitas, Fortuna.*

Faider, P., *Rev. belge de phil. et d'hist.* ix 1930 787 ff.
Ferrabino, A., *Riv. di fil. cl.* xxi 1931 173–99.
Ferrara, J., *Poematis latini rel. ex. vol. Herculan.* 1908.
Ferrero, G., *Grandezza e decadenza*, etc.
Ferrua, A., *Le Pitture della Nuova Catacombe di Via Latina* 1960.
Fontaneau, R., *Bull. Assn. G. Budé* iv 1954 3, 41–59.
Fontenrose, J. E., TAPA lxx 1939 439–55.
Forni, G., *Reclutamento delle legioni* 1953.
Fowler, W. Warde (1) *Roman Ideas of Deity* (2) *Virgil's Messianic Eclogue* 1907.
Fraenkel, E., *Horace* 1957.
Fraser, P. M. (1) JRS 1957 71–3 (2) JEA 1960 96 no. 13.
Frederiksen, M. W., JRS 1966 128–41.

532

Bibliography

Frisch, H., *Cicero's Fight for the Republic* 1946.

Fuchs, H. (1) *Aug. u. d. ant. Friedensgedanke* 1926 (*Neue Philol. Untersuch.* 3 185 ff.) (2) *Der geistige Widerstand gegen Rom* 1938.

Fuhrmann, MdI ii 1949.

Fürtwangler, *Intermezzi*.

Gabba, E. (1) *Athen.* xxix 1951 (2) *Par. d. Pass.* xiii 1950 66 ff. (3) *Appiano e la Storia d. Guerre civili* 1956.

Gagé, J. (1) *Congr. int. de num.* (Paris 6–11 July 1953) ii 1957 219–27 (2) *Apollo rom.* 1955 (3) *Mél Ec. Rome* 1930 159–62 (4) RH 1936 (5) M.E.R. 1931 75 ff., 94–8 (6) RH clxxi 1933 1–43 (7) *Recherches sur les Jeux Seculaires* 1934 (8) REL ix 1931 290–308 (9) *Les Classes sociales dans l'emp. rom.* 1964 (10) M.E.R. 1936 37–100 (11) *Basiléia* 1968. (12) *Rev. ét. ital.* 1962 25–62 (13) *Rev. de Hist.* (Sao Paulo) no. 17, 1954.

Galinsky, G. K. (1) *Lat.* 1969 1–18 (2) 1967 619–33.

Gall, H. von, *Basileia tou Theou*.

Gardthausen, V. (1) *NJf. kl. Alt.* xxxix 1917 158–69 (2) *Aug. u. seine Zeit* 1891–1904.

Garrod (1) CR xxii 1908 150 (2) in Fowler (2).

Garzetti, A., *Plut. Vita Caesaris* 1954.

Gauthier, H. (1) *Livre des Rois* (2) CRAI xix 1923 376 ff.

Gelzer, M. (1) *Caesar Politician and Statesman* 1968 (2) *Die Nobilität d. röm. Republik* 1912 (3) *Cicero u. Caesar* 1968 (4) *Kl. Schr.* 1962 i 95–7.

Glauning, A. E., *Die Anhängerschaft d. Ant. u. d. Oct.* 1936.

Goodenough, E. R., *The Political Philosophy of Hellenistic Kingship* (Yale Cl. Stud. 1 1928) 55–102.

Goosens, B., *Mél. Bidez* 415–49.

Gorlitz, W., *Kleopatra* 1936.

Graindor, P., *La guerre d'Alex.*

Grant, M. (1) R. *Anniversary Issues* 1950 (2) in Coleman-Norton *Stud. in R. Econ. and Soc. Hist.* 1951 106 (2) *Archaeol.* vii 1954 47 (4) *From Imp. to Auctoritas* 1946 (5) *J. Caesar* 1969.

Grégoire, H., in *Les Persécutions dans l'emp. rom.* (Mém. Ac. roy. Brux., Lettres xlvi, 1) 1951.

Grenade, P., *Essai sur les origines du principat* 1961.

Grenier, *Les religions etrusque et rom.*

Griffith, J. G. (1) JEA 1961 113–8 (2) 1965 209–11.

Grimal, M. P. (1) REL 1957 190 (2) REA 1951 53 f. (3) *Jardins rom.*

Grizart, F. A., *Les E. C.* xxxiv 1966 115–42.

Grueber, H. A., *Coins of the R. Rep. in BM* 1910.

Guarino, R.G. *divi Aug.* 1968.

Gundel, W. (1) *Gnomon* 1928 449 f. (2) in Boll and Bezold, *Sternglaube u. Sterndeutung* (3rd ed.) 1926 (3) *Philol.* lxxxi 1926.

Gunzel, F. K., *HB d. Math. u. tech. Chronologie* ii 1911.

Gwatkin, W., *Univ. of Missouri Stud.* v (no. 4) 1930.

Hadas, M., *Sextus Pompeius* 1930.

Haffter, H., *Röm. Politik u. röm. Politiker* 1967.

Hahn, E. A. (1) TAPA 1944 206–12, 216 f. (2) AJP lxxvii 1956 290.

Hammond, M. (1) *The Aug. Principate* 1933 (2) *City-State and World-State in Gr. and R. polit. theory until Aug.* 1951.

Hanfmann, G. M., *Roman Art* 1964.

Hanslik, R., *Serta philol. Aenipontana* 1962 335–42.

Hardy, E. G., *The Mon. Ancyranum* 1923.

Harmand, J., *L'Armée et le soldat à Rome . . .* 1967 (2) *Lat.* 1967 956–86.

Heinen, H. (1) *Rom. u Aeg. von 51 bis 47 v.Chr.* 1966 (2) *Klio* xi 1911 129–37.

Hellegouarc'h, J. (1) *Lat.* xxiii 1964 669–84 (2) *Le vocab. latin des relations et des partis polit. sous la Rep.* 1963.

Hermann, E., *Philol. Woch* li 1931 1100–2.

Herrmann, L. (1) *Les Masques et les Visages dans les Bucol. de V.* 1930 (2) *Mél. Bidez* 487–94 (3) REL 1932 (4) *Lat.* xxv 1966 58–77 (5) RA xxxiii 1931 46–68 (6) REL 1937 308–15 (7) *Mus. Belge* xxx 1926 234–7.

Heurgon, J. (1) JRS 1959 41–5 (2) *St. Etr.* xxiv 1955–6 102 ff.

Hill, G. F., *Hist. R. Coins* 1909.

Hill, H., JRS 1961 88 ff.

Bibliography

Hoffmann, H., *J. Am. Res. Centre in Eg.* ii 1963 117–24.

Hohmann, *Chronolog. d. Papyrusurk.*

Hollemann, *Lat.* 1969 42 ff.

Holmes, T. R. (1) *Architect of R. Emp.* 1928, 1931 (2) *The Rom. Rep.*

Houssaye, H., *Aspasie, Cléopatre, Théodora* 1890 47–218.

Howard, *Harv. St. in Class. Phil.* x 1899 24 f.

Hutmacher, R., *Das Ehrendekrit f.d. Strat. Kallimachos* 1965.

Immisch, O., in *Aus. Roms Zeitwende* 13–21.

Instinsky, H. V. (1) *Stud. D. M. Robinson* ii 1953 975–9 (2) *Sicherheit d. röm. Kaisertums* 1952.

Jachmann, G., *Ann. d.Sc. norm. d.Pisa* 1952 xxi 13–62.

Jal, P. (1) *Bull. Assn. Budé* 1961 iv 470–501 (2) *Lat.* xxi 1962 8–48 (3) AC xxx 1961 395–44 (4) *La Guerre civile à Rome* 1963 (5) REL xl 1962 170–200 (6) *Les Et. Class.* xxx 1962 257–67 (7) REL 1961 xxxix 210–31.

Jeanmaire, H. (1) RA xix 1924 241–61 (2) *Le Messianisme de V.* 1930.

Jelenko, G., *Komposition d. Kulturgesch. d. Lucret.* 1936.

Johnson, A. C., *Egypt and R.E.* 1951.

Jones, A. H. M. (1) *Studies in R. Govt. and Law* 1960 (2) *Cities of Eastern R. Provs.* 1937 (3) JRS 1955 9–21 (4) 1936 268–71.

Jong, L. L. Tels de, *Sur quelques divinités rom. de la naissance et de la prophétie* 1960.

Jouguet, P. (1) *L'Eg. ptol.* 1933 (2) *La Vie municipale.*

Judeich, W. (1) *Caesar im Orient* (2) *Topog. v. Athen* (2nd ed.).

Kaehler, H., *Die Augustusstatue von Primaporta* 1959.

Kaerst, *Gesch.d. Hellenismus* (2nd ed.) 1926.

Kahrstedt, U., *Klio* x 1910 275–8.

Kalinka, E., *Sitz. Ak. Wiss. Wien,* p-h. Kl. cxcvii 1922.

Khan Istvan, *Vestnik drev. ist.* ciii 1968 (1) 72–86.

Kloesel, H., *Libertas* 1935.

Knapowskim, R., *Die Staatsrechnungen d. röm. Rep.* 49–5 v.Chr. 1967.

Cleopatra

Knight, D. W. (1) *Lat.* 1969 878–83 (2) 1968 157–64.

Knight, W. F. Jackson (1) *Poetic Inspiration: an approach to V.* 1946 (2) *Cumaean Gates* 1936.

Köberlein, E., *Caligula u.d. aegypt. Kulte* 1962.

Koch, C., *Gestirnverehrung im alten Italien* 1933.

Kolbe, W., *Von d. Rep. zur monarchie* 1931.

Kornemann, E., *Jahrb. f. cl. Phil.* Suppl. xxii 1896 557 ff.

Kraay, C. M., *Num. Chron.* (6th) xiv 1955 18 ff.

Kraft, K. (1) *J.f. Num. u. Geldgesch.* iii–iv 1952–3 7 ff. (2) *Der goldene Kranz Caesars* 1955 (3) *Hermes* xcvii 1967 496–9.

Krall, J. (1) *Wien. Stud.* v 1993 313 ff. (2) *Festgaben f. Büdinger* 1898.

Kramer, H., *Quid valent homonoia in litteris Gr.* 1915.

Kromayer, J. (1) *Hermes* xxxiii 1898 13–70 (2) xxxiv 1899 1–54 (3) xxix 1894 576 ff. (4) NJ xvii 1914 145 ff. (5) *Hermes* lxviii 1933 361–83 (6) *Ant. Schlacht.* iv 1931 662–71.

Kugler, F. X., *Sibyllin. Sternkampf u. Phaethon* 1927.

Kunkel, W., *Archiv* viii 212–5.

Kurfess, A., *Philol.* xci 1936 415–20.

Lana, I., *Vell. Patercolo e della propaganda* 1952.

Larsen, J. A. O. (1) *Representative Govt. in Gr. and R. History* 1955 (2) *Mél. Piganiol* 1966 1635–44.

Lassus, J., CRAI 1959 215–25.

Last, H., JRS 1953 27–9.

Latte, K. (2) *Röm. Religionsgesch.* 1960 (2) *Philol.* lxxxvii 1932 270.

Le Corsu, F., RA 1967 239–54.

Lefebvre, G., *Mél. Holleaux* 1913 103–13.

Legley, M., *Lat.* xxii 1963 346–8.

Lehmann-Hartleben, K., MDAI xlii 1927 165–6.

Lenger, M. T., CE xxv 1950 324–7.

Lepore, E., *Il Princeps Ciceriano* 1954.

Lepsius, C. R., *Denkmaker.*

Levensohn, M. and E., *Hesperia* xvi 1947 68 f.

Levi, M. A. (1) *Athenaeum* x 1932 3–21 (2) *Par. d. Pass.* ix fasc. 37 1954 293–5 (3) *Ann.d. Ist. sup. di mag. del Piemonte* vii 1934

Bibliography

1–10 (4) *Ottaviano Cappoporte* 2933 (5) xx *C. Suet. Tranq. Divus Aug.* 1951 (6) *Il Tempo di Augusto* 1951.

Liebmann-Frankfort, T., *Rev. Int. des Droits de l'Ant.* xiii 1966 73–94.

Liegle, J. (1) JDAI lvi 1941 91–119 (2) *Hermes* lxxviii 222.

Lindsay, Jack (1) *Daily Life in Roman Egypt* 1963 (2) *Leisure and Pleasure in R.E.* 1965 (3) *Men and Gods on the Roman Nile* 1968 (4) *Origins of Alchemy* 1969 (5) *M. Antony* 1936 (6) *The Anc. World* 1968.

Lord, L. E., JRS xxviii 1938 19–40.

McCarthy, C. P., xxvi 1931 362–73.

McCown, C. C., HTR xviii 1925.

McDonald, A. H., JRS 1955 176–8.

McFayden, D., *The History of the Title Imp. under the R.E.* 1920.

Mackay, C. A., TAPA 1957 11–6.

Macurdy, G. H., *Hellenistic Queens* 1932.

Magdalain, A., *Recherches sur l'Imp.* 1968.

Mahaffy (1) *Hist. of Eg. under Ptol. Dyn.* 1914 (2) JEA ii 1–4.

Malcovati, *Caesaris Aug. op. frag.* 1928.

Mamroth, A., *Berl. Num. Zeit.* i 1949–52 161–5.

Mansuelli, G. A., *Il mon. Aug. del 27 A.C.* 1960.

Marcien, L., *Les Et. Cl.* 1956 330–48.

Marin, D., *Studi in On. di Calderini* 1956; 157 ff.

Marsh, F. B., *The Found. of the R.E.* 1927.

Marshall, A. J., JRS 1968 103–9.

Mattingly, H. (1) *Coins of R.E. in BM* (2) JWCI x 1947 14–9 (3) CR xlviii 1934 161–5 (4) *Num. Chron.* 1933 182 ff.

May, G., *Mél. Gerardin* 1907 399–412.

Méautis, *Arch. Eph.* i 1937 27–9.

Mederer, E., *Die Alexanderlegenden* 1936.

Meier, C., *Respublica Amissa* 1966.

Meiklejohn, K. W., JRS xxiv 1934 191–5.

Meulenaere, *Riv. st. or.* xxxiv 1959.

Meyer, E. (1) *Caesars Monarchie* 1922 (2) *Pompeius* (2nd ed.) 1919.

Miller, E., *Study of Cassius Dio* 1964.

Milne, J. G. (1) JEA i 1914 99 (2) JRS xvii 1927 1 ff. (3) JEA xiv 1928 229.

Mommsen, T. (1) *Provs. of R. Emp.* 1909 (2) *Röm. Forsch.* ii 153–220.

Mond, R., and Mayers, *Bucheum* ii 1934.

Moret, *Du Caractère relig.* 1904.

Moretti, L. *Aeg.* xxxviii 1958 203–9.

Munzer, F. (1) *Röm. Adelsparteien u. Adelsfamilien* 1920 (2) RE *Domitius* no. 23.

Nash, E., *Pictorial Dict. of Anc. Rome* 1961–2.

Newell, E. T., *Coinage of Demetrios Poliorcetes* 1927.

Newmann, J. K. (1) *Cult of Vates in Aug. Poetry* 1967 (2) *Aug. and the New Poetry* 1967.

Nilsson, RE (2nd) ii 1698 f.

Nissen, H., *Hist. Zeit.* cxv 1916 473–95.

Nock, A. D. (1) *Syllabus of Gifford Lectures* (Aberdeen) 1939 (2) JHS xlviii 1928 21–43 (3) JEA xvii 1931 120 (4) *Harv. St. Class. Phil.* xli 1930 (5) in A. E. J. Rawlinson, *Essays on Trinity and Incarnation*.

Noirfalise, A., *Et. Class.* xviii 289–303.

Noldeke, *Z.d. deut. morgenländ. Gesell.* 2885 349.

Norden, E. (1) *N.J. Kl.-Alt.* xxxi 1913 656 ff. (2) *Die Geburt des Kindes* 1924.

Nörr, D., *Imperium u. Polis in d. hohen Prinzipatszeit* 1966.

Ogilvie, R. M., JRS 1961 31–9.

Olshausen, E., *Rom. u. Aug. von 116 bis 51 v Chr.* 1963.

Oltramare, A., REL 1938 xvi 121–38.

Oost, CP 1955 98.

Ooteghem, J. van, *Pompée le Grand bâtisseur d'empire* 1954.

Pack, R. A., *Cat. Lit. Texts from GR Eg.* 1952.

Parker, R. A., *J. of Am. Res. Centre in Eg.* ii 113–6.

Parsons, E. A., *The Alex. Lib.* 1952.

Passerini, A., *St. Fil. Class.* xi 1934 35 f.

Pease, A. S., *P. Virg. Maro Aen. Lib. IV* 1935.

Bibliography

Peck, W., *Der Isishymnus* 1930.

Perdrizet, P., ASAE ix 2908 243–5.

Perret, J. (1) *Horace* 1959 (2) *Virgile, l'homme et l'oeuvre.*

Picard, C. (1) *Honn. P. Oikonomos* 1954 1–8 (2) *Mél. O. Navarre* 1935 317–37 (3) *Aug. and Nero* 1936 (4) *Les Trophées rom.* 1957.

Piganiol, A. (1) *Mus. Helv.* x 1953 193–202 (2) REA xlii 1940 285–92 (3) *La Conquête romaine* 1927 (4) *Hist. Rom.* iv 2, *l'emp. chrét.* 1947 (5) *Studies in R. Econ. & Soc. Hist. in Lon. A. C. Johnson,* ed. P. R. Coleman-Norton 1951 79–87.

Pighi, G. B., *De lud. saec. libri sex* 1965 (2nd ed.).

Pincherle, A., *Gli oracoli sibyl. giudaici* 1922.

Piotrowicz, L. (1) *Charist. Casimiro de Morawski,* etc., 1922 221–30 (2) *Klio* xxiii 1930 336 ff.

Platner-Ashby, *Topog. Dict.*

Plaumann, *Ptolemais in Oberäg.* 1910.

Poehlmann. *Gesch. d. sozialen. Frage,* etc. (3rd ed., F. Oertel).

Poulsen, V., *Claud. Prinzen, Stud. z. Ikonog.* 1960.

Preaux, C. (1) *Mus. Helvet.* x 1953 203–21 (2) *L'Econ. roy. des Lagides* 1939 (3) CE xliii 1965 176–87.

Premerstein, A. von (1) *Bayer. Ak. d. Wiss. p.-h. Abt.* NF xv 1937 45–50 (2) *Vom Werden u Wesen d. Principats* 1937 (3).

Prott, von, *Ath. Mitt.* xxvii 1902 161–88.

Radet, G. (1) *Alexandre le Grand* 1933 (2) 2nd ed. 1950 (3) *J. Savants* 1935 145–52.

Rambaud, M. (1) *L'art de la déformation hist. dans les Comm. de César* 1953 (2) *Cicéron et l'hist. rom.*

Raubitschek, A. E. (1) TAPA lxxvii 1946 146–50 (2) JRS 1954 65–75.

Rebuffat, R., *M.Ec. Rome* 1961 161–228.

Reinhold, M., *M. Agrippa* 1933.

Reitzenstein, r (1) with Schaeder, *Stud. z. ant. Synkretismus aus Iran u. Griechland* 1925 (2) *Nach. Gött.* 1904 309 ff.

Remy, E., *Trois Philippiques de Cicéron* 1941 ii 245 ff.

Renard, M., *Etudes horat.* vii 1937 189–99.

Res Gestae Aug., J. Gagé; P. A. Brunt and J. M. Moore.

Reynolds, J., JRS 1962 99–103.

Richardson, G. W., JRS xxvii 1937 153–64.

Riewald, P., *De imperatorum Rom. cum certis Dis et comp. et aequatione.*

Roberts, C. H., *Mus. Helvet.* x 1953 264–79.

Rose, H. J. (1) *Ann. arch. anthrop.* xx 1924 25–30 (2) CQ xviii 1924 116 (3) *Handbook* R. *Lit.* 1936 (4) *Eclogues of V.* 1942.

Rossi, R. F., M. *Antonio* 1959.

Rostovtzeff (1) SEHRE 1957 (2) *Hist. of Anc. World: Rome* 1960

Royds, T. F., *Virgil and Isaiah* 1918.

Rübeling, *Untersuch. zu dem. Pop.* 1958.

Rudolph, H., *Stadt u. Staat in röm. Italien.*

Ryberg, I. S. (1) TAPA 1958 112–31 (2) *Rites of R. State Religion* 1955.

Rzach, A. (1) *Chresmoi Sibylliakoi* 1891 (2) *Mél. Nicole* (3) RE Aii 2, 2131.

Saller, A. von, (with Regling), *Die ant. Munzen* 1922.

Samuel, A. E. (1) CE xl 376–400 (2) *Ptol. Chronol.* 1962 (3) *Et. de Pap.* ix 1964 73–9.

Sands, P. C., *Client Princes of Rome under Rep.* 1908.

Sattler, P., *Aug. und d. Senat* 1960.

Sautier, F., *Der rom. Kaiserkult bei Martial u. Statius* 1934.

Savage, J. J. H., TAPA 1958 142–58.

Sbordone, F., *Riv. indo-gr.-it.* xiv 1930 1–20.

Schaper, C., *Virgilis Gedichte.*

Schilling, R., *La Vénus romaine* 1954.

Schlag, U., *Regnum in Senatu* 187.

Schmitthenner, W. (1) *Historia* vii 1958 189–236 (2) *Oct. u. das Testament Caesars* 1952 (3) *Hist. Zeit.* cxl 1960 12 ff.

Schnepf, H., *Gymnasium* lxvi 1959 250–68.

Schubart, W. (1) with D. Schafer, *Aeg. Urk. aus den staat. Mus. zu Berl.: Griech. Urk.* viii 1933 (2) *Amtliche Berichte aus den kgl. Kunstsamml.* xxxviii 1916–7 189–97 (3) SB 1927 no. 7266.

Schürer, E., *Gesch. d. jüd. Volkes* i 1901.

Schwartz, J., *Rev. Philol.* 1945.

Bibliography

Schweicher, G., *Schicksal u. Glück in d. Werken Sallusts u. Caesars* 1963.

Scott, K. (1) *Mem. Am. Ac. Rome.* xi 1933 (2) CP xxiv 1929 133–41 (3) *Hermes* lxiii 1928 (4) AJP xlix 1928 222 ff.

Scott, W. (1) CQ x 1916 7–16 (2) ix 144–66, 207–28.

Scullard, H. H., JRS 1 1960 62 ff.

Sherwin-White, A. N. (1) JRS 1956 1–9 (2) G. & R. iv 1957.

Shipley, F. W., *Mem. Am. Ac. Rome* ix 7–60.

Shuckburgh, E. S., *Augustus* 1903.

Siber, H., *Das Führeramt d. Aug.*

Sijpersteijn, P. J., *Lat.* xxiv 122–7.

Simon, E. (1) *Röm. Mitt.* lxix 1962 136 ff. (2) *Arch. Anz.* 1952 126 ff.

Sinko, T., *Rosprawy Ak. Umiejetnosci, widzial fil.* xxi 1903 268–75.

Skeat, T. C. (1) JEA 1962 100–5 (2) *The Reigns of the Ptols.* 1954 (3) *Mizraim* vi 1937 (4) JEA xlvi 1960 91–4 (5) JRS xliii 1953 98–100 (6) *Mizraim* ii 1936 30–5.

Skutsch, F., *Aus Vergils Frühzeit* 1901.

Slater, D. A., CR xxvi 1912 114.

Smith, R. E. (1) *Service in the Post-Marian Army* 1958 (2) CQ vii 1957 82 ff.

Snell, B., *Hermes* lxxiii 1938 237–42.

Spiegelberg, W., *Sitz. d. bayer. Ak. d. Wiss.* 1925 ii 1–6.

Stadelmann, H., *Kleopatra* 1925.

Stähelin, F. (1) RE xi 1 (1921) 550–81 (2) *ib.* 784–5.

Stahr, A. (1) *Kleopatra* 1864 (2) 1879.

Starr, C. G., *Rom. Imp. Navy* 1960.

Stauffenberg, von, *Die röm. Kaisergesch. bei Malalas* 1931.

Stauffer, E. (1) *Jerusalem u. Rom im Zeitalter J.C.* 1957 (2) *Christ. u. d. Cäseren* 1948 (3) *Christ and the Caesars* 1955.

Steidle, W., *Suet. u. d. ant. Biographie.*

Stein, A. (1) *Die Präfekten von Aeg.* 1950 (2) *Untersuch z. Gesch. u.Verwaltung Aeg.* 1915.

Stein, P., *Die Senatssitz. d. Ciceron. Zeit.* 1930.

Stoffel, E., *Hist. de J. César, Guerre Civile.*

Strack, M. L. (1) *Die Dyn. d. Ptol.* 1897 (2) *Hist. Zeit.* cxv 1916 489.

Strasburger, H., *Concordia Ordinum* 1931.
Strong, E. (1) *Apotheosis* 1915 (2) *Scult. rom.*
Struve, *Racc. Lumbroso* 1925.
Stuart, D. R., CP xvi 1921 224 f.
Svoronos (1) *Ta nomismata tou Kratous ton Ptol.* (2) *Die Munzen d. Ptol.* 1908 iv.
Sydenham, E. A., *Coins of R. Rep.* 1952.
Syme, R. (1) *The R. Revolution* 1939 (2) *Historia* cii 1958 172–88 (3) CQ xxxi 1937 39 ff. (4) JRS 1948 124 f. (5) 1938 113 ff. (Labienus) (6) 1933 14 ff. (Aug. legions) (7) CQ 1938 39 ff. (Gallus).

Tarn, W. W. (1) CAH x 1934 35–111 (2) with Charlesworth, *Oct., Ant. and Cleo.* 1965 (3) JRS 1931 (4) xxi 1931 173–99 (5) xxviii 1938 165–8 (6) 1932 135–60 (7) CQ xxvi 1932 75 (8) *Mél. Glotz* 1932 831 (9) JRS xxvi 1936 187–9 (10) JHS xlviii 1928 206–9 (11) with Griffith, *Hellenistic Civil.* 1952 (12) *Antigonos Gonatas* (13) JEA 1926 11.
Taylor, L. R. (1) *Div. of R. Emp.* 1931 (2) JHS I 1930 294–7 (3) TAPA lx 1929 (3) CP xxii 1927 162–9 (5) xxv 1930 375–8 (6) AJP lv 1934 101–20 (6) CP 1934 221 ff. (7) JRS 1936 161 ff.
Tcherikower, V., *Hellenistic Civil. and the Jews.*
Thiersch, T., *Der Pharos* 1909.
Tibiletti, G., *Athen.* xxviii 1950 234 ff.
Tondriau, J. (1) *Rev. Phil.* xxiii 1949 41–52 (2) *Mel. Grégoire* 1953 iv (3) CE xli 1946 149–71 (4) *BSA Alex.* xxxvii 1948 1–11 (5) *Et. de Pap.* vii 1948 1–15 (6) see Cerfaux (7) CE 1948 127–46.
Toynbee, J. M. C. (1) *Ara Pacis Reconsidered* (Brit. Ac.) 1953 (2) JRS 1961 153–6.
Treves, P. (1) *Il mito di Alex. e la Roma di Aug.* 1953 (2) *Riv. fil. Class.* xxxiii 1955 250–75.
Turcan, R. (1) *Lat.* xxiv 1965 101–19 (2) 1964 42–53 (3) *Trésor de Guelma* 1963 (4) *Homm. à J. Bayet* 1964 697–704.
Tyrell and Purser, *Corr. of M. Tull. Cicero.*

Vandebeek, *De Interpret. Graeca van de Isisfiguur* 1946.
Vanderlinden, E., *Et. Class.* xxxiv 1966 35–8.

Bibliography

Vandersleyen, C., *Et. Class.* (1) xxxi 1963 265–74 (2) xxxiv 1966 35–8.

Verdière, R., *Maia* xx 1968 7–9.

Vessberg, O. (1) *Studien zur Kunstgesch. d. röm. Rep.* 1941 (2) *Acta Inst. Suec.* viii.

Veyne, P., *Lat.* xxi 1962 49–98.

Visscher, F. de (1) *Muséon (Mél. Lefort)* 1946 (2) AC xxx 1961 67–129.

Visser, E., *Symb. von Osten.* 1946 116–22.

Vittinghoff, F. *Röm. Kolonisation u. Bürgerrechtspolitik unter Caesar u. Aug.* 1952.

Vogt, J. (1) *Stud. pres. to D. M. Robinson* ii (2) *Novus Homo* 1926.

Volkmann, H. (1) *Cleopatra,* transl. Cadoux (2) *Gnomon* xxxi 178 f. (3) Munich ed. of (1) 1953 (4) *Zur Rechtsprechung im Princ. d. Aug.* 1935.

Vollenweider, H. (1) *Schweizer. Num. Rundschau* xxxix 1958–9 (2) *Mus. Helv.* xv 1958.

Wace, A. J. B. (1) *Farouk I Univ. Bull., Fac. Arts,* ii 1944 1–16.

Wagenvoort, H., *Virgils vierte Ekloge u. das Sidus Jul.* 1929.

Wahl, R., *Kleopatra* 1956.

Walle, B. van de CE (1) xxiv 1949 19–32 (2) 1950 31–5.

Waltz, R., *Les Et. Class.* xxvi 1958 3–20.

Ward-Perkins, J. B., *Procs. Brit. Acad.* li 175–99.

Watson, G. R., *Historia* vii 1958 113 ff.

Weber, W., *Der Prophet u. sein Gott* 1925.

Wegehaupt, H., *Die Bedeutung u. Anwendung von dignitas* 1932.

Wegener, E. P., *Mnemos.* xiii 1947 302–6.

Weichert, *Comment. II de Cassio Parm.* Poeta 1834.

Weigall, A. E. P., *Life and Times of Cleo.* 1914.

Weinstock, S. (1) JRS 1960 44–58 (2) 1957 144–54 (3) *Papers Br. School Rome* xviii 1950 44–9 (4) RE viii A1 577 ff.

Weische, A. (1) *Stud. z. polit. Sprache d. röm. Rep.* 1966 (2) *Lat.* 1967 540 ff.

Wenger, L., *Z. Savigny-Stift., Röm. Abt.* xlix 1929.

Wertheimer, O. von (1) *Kleopatra* 1930 (2) *Cleopatra* (English) 1931 (3) *Die genilaste Frau der Weltgesch.*

Wickert, L., NJ iv 1941 14–7.

Wilcken, U. (1) *Urk. d. Ptol.* 1922, etc. (2) *Chrestomathie* (3) JRS 1937 138–44 (4) *Archiv* viii 1927 213 n. 1 (5) *Hermes* xl 1905 (6) *Z. Sav.-Stift.* xxx 1909 504 (7) RE i 1894 1441–2.

Wilhelm, A. (1) *Mél. Bidez* 1934 1007 (2) *Sitz. Ak. Wiss. in Wien* ccxxiv 1946 32 (3) *Wien. Stud.* lxi–ii 1943–7 170 f.

Windisch, H., *Die Orakel v. Hystaspes* 1929.

Wirszubski, C. (1) JRA 1961 12–22 (2) xliv 1954 1 ff. (3) *Libertas as a Political Idea* 1960.

Wistrand, E., *Horace's 9th Epode and its Hist. Background* 1958.

Witter, K., *Horaz u. Virgil* 1922.

Woodman, A. J., *Lat.* xxv 1966 564–6.

Wurzel, F., *Die Krieg gegen Ant. u. Kleo. in d. Darstellung d. Aug. Dichter* 1942.

Yoyotte, J., in *Religions en Eg. hellén. et rom.* (Coll. de Strasbourg 1967) 1969 129 ff.

Zancan, *Atene e Roma* vii 1939 213 ff. and n. 20.

Zangemeister, K., *Eph. Epig.* vi 1885 52–78.

Zogheb (1) *Et. sur l'anc. Alex.* (2) *Le Tombeau de Cléo.*

Zwaenepoel, A., *Et. Class.* xviii 1950 3–15.

Index

Index

Index

Index

Index

Index

Polemon of Laodicea, 193, 243, 254, 257, 261, 287, 341, 443, 445
Polemon, Marcus Antonius, 443
Pollio, 136, 177, 203, 205, 218–19, 222–5, 227–8, 231, 253, 478, 479
Pollio, C. Asinus, 178, 220, 221, 454
Pollio, Salonius, 200
Polybius, xii, 16, 299, 480
Pompeia, wife of Caesar, 114
Pompeii, 217, 234
Pompey, importance of, 5; and Caesar, 5, 10, 31, 35, 39, 41, 47, 88, 91–2, 99, 341, 423; and Ptolemy XII 6–8, 9, 10–12, 15, 39; and Clodius, 10–11; Cleopatra's aid to, 35; murder of, 37, 40; defeated at Pharsalos, 39, 408; as a soldier, 42; land-holdings of, 82; and Cicero, 83; property taken by Antony, 88, 140; and Parthia, 199, 408, 409; and augery, 303; conquest of Syria by, 357; use of barbarians by, 407–9; abuse of power by, 448
Pompey, Sextus see Sextus Pompey
Pons Aemilius, 77
Pontos, 9, 57, 155, 257, 287, 409, 445
Porcia, 85, 131
Porphyrogenitos, Constantinos, 480
Poseidon, 27, 444
Poseidonios, 99, 179
Postumius, 302, 389
Potheinos, 16, 37, 41, 44, 45, 46, 47, 64, 351
Potter's Oracle, 247, 251
Praeneste, 387
Priene, 344
Priscus, Tarquitius, 214, 370
Proculeius, 421, 422, 423
Pronuba, 453
Propertius, 170, 229, 283, 405, 433, 435, 453, 478
Prosperine, 463
Prusias, 443
Psenemon, 485
Ptolemaia, 319
Ptolemaios, 23–4, 163, 323
Ptolemaios of Mauretania, 470
Ptolemaios Philadelphos (son of Antony), 241, 290–1, 442
Ptolemais, xii, 13, 300
Ptolemies, x, xi, 1, 126, 160, 248, 313, 316, 317, 319–20, 414, 425, 434, 441, 444, 447, 450
Ptolemy I, x, xi, 19, 163, 290, 319, 320, 444

Ptolemy II, xi, 19, 242, 290, 293, 319, 412, 444
Ptolemy III, 126, 249, 251
Ptolemy IV, xi, 18, 19, 61, 250, 317–18, 319
Ptolemy V, xi–xii, 16, 21, 317
Ptolemy VI, xii, 61
Ptolemy VII, 23
Ptolemy VIII, xii, xiii, 240
Ptolemy IX, 2, 14, 61
Ptolemy X, 61
Ptolemy XII, 1, 2–4, 6–10, 12–15, 18–22, 30–6, 39, 40–2, 59, 64, 68, 155, 245, 317, 448
Ptolemy XIII, 15–17, 29, 35, 36–7, 38–40, 42–3, 47, 49–51, 52–4, 57
Ptolemy XV see Caesarion
Publicola, 401
Puteoli, 9, 13, 104, 110, 174, 183
Pyrrhos, 444
Pythagoras, 215, 252
Pythodoris, daughter of Antonia, 287

Quinctilianus, 211
Quintilius, P., 458
Quirinal, 89, 90
Quirinus, temple of, 89, 90, 92

Rabirius, Gauis, 8, 13, 14, 16
Raphia, battle of, 248, 317, 318
Re, 60, 248, 251, 252, 433, 434
Rebilius, Caninius, 84
Red Sea, 412
Remus, 97
Rentutet, 433
Res Gestae (Augustus), 71, 477
Revelation (St John), 359–60, 365, 366
Rhamnos, 267
Rhine, River, 189
Rhodes, 7, 25, 27, 48, 152, 158, 175, 179, 318, 320, 405, 440
Rhodon, 428
Rhoimetalkes of Thrace, 388, 445
Rhoitaion, 338
Roma, cult of, 97–8
Roman Games, 235
Rome, expansion of, xiii, 5, 73; and Egypt, xiii, 4–10, 12–15, 32–3, 38, 349, 351, 433–5; social and political development of, 5–6, 73–7, 80–7; cults in, 18, 68, 90–2, 97–101, 293, 297, 434, 436; Cleopatra in, 59, 62–4, 67–8, 71, 87–8, 103–5; army of, 74–5, 77–9; and the triumvirate, 122, 129–30, 133–5; and client-kingdoms, 154–5; and Sextus Pompey, 170–1, 182, 273, 285; disorders

Index

Index